The Special Educator's
ALMANAC

Ready-to-Use Activities for a Resource Room or a Self-Contained Classroom

NATALIE MADORSKY ELMAN
illustrations by BESS C. FORSHAW

Cover art based on a concept by Catherine Bebbington

The Center for Applied Research in Education, Inc.
West Nyack, New York 10995

To Stanley and Freda . . .

with love

Library of Congress Cataloging in Publication Data

Elman, Natalie Madorsky.
      The special educator's almanac.

      1. Resource programs (Education)—Handbooks,
manuals, etc.   2. Creative activities and seat
work—Handbooks, manuals, etc.   3. Activity programs
in education—Handbooks, manuals, etc.   I. Center
for Applied Research in Education.   II. Title.
LB1028.8.E44   1985   371.9   84-21401
ISBN 0-87628-769-0

Printed in the United States of America

ABOUT THE AUTHOR

Natalie Madorsky Elman has had many years' experience as a special educator in Warren Township, New Jersey, having taught children with communication handicaps, perceptual impairments, neurological disorders, emotional disturbances, and hearing impairments.

She is the author of *The Resource Room Primer* (Prentice-Hall, 1981) and has shared her ideas and expertise with other educators as a facilitator at many professional workshops.

As a special education consultant, Mrs. Elman has helped develop special education programs for both schools and individuals. She has appeared as a guest on many radio and television programs to discuss special education issues.

In her community Mrs. Elman has served as president and trustee of the Board of Directors of Our House, Inc., an organization that runs group homes for mentally disabled children and adults. Her professional affiliations include membership in The Association for Children with Learning Disabilities, The Council for Exceptional Children, and The National Education Association.

Mrs. Elman holds a Master of Arts degree from Kean College (Union, New Jersey) and is currently a doctoral candidate at Rutgers University (New Brunswick, New Jersey), where she is also an adjunct instructor of special education.

ABOUT THE ILLUSTRATOR

Bess Forshaw's multi-faceted life includes an eclectic background. Raised in Charlotte, North Carolina and educated as a teacher at the University of North Carolina, she began art studies after moving to New Jersey in 1971. Her interests in studies of creativity and human potential have led to further studies in post-baccalaureate major and graduate studies in art at Kean College (Union, New Jersey).

Ms. Forshaw is the mother of three—two teenagers and a nursery schooler. Her favorite pastimes include teaching art to children and producing her own watercolors.

ABOUT THE *ALMANAC*

The Special Educator's Almanac: Ready-to-Use Activities for a Resource Room or a Self-Contained Classroom is designed for you. Whether setting up a new program or supplementing an established one, you will find new ideas, useful tips, and solutions to aid in program planning. From the first day the resource room, learning center, or self-contained classroom is opened in September to the last day in June when the room's contents are packed away, exciting lessons, learning center ideas, materials lists, and reproducible worksheets are yours to use.

Each month of the school year is focused upon and features:

- a famous person who overcame learning problems
- bulletin board ideas
- a teaching unit
- learning center activities
- lists of free materials and good buys
- professional responsibilities
- professional resource books
- ideas for mainstreaming
- tips to make the job easier and more exciting
- discussions about pertinent school issues

Since a special program's population is varied and requires individualization, a cross section of levels and learning styles is presented in sample lessons and worksheets. You can choose a worksheet independently or in conjunction with a suggested lesson to supplement an ongoing course of study that has been designed for each student.

Each month focuses on a particular discipline, such as math, reading, or social studies. However, you may pick and choose the appropriate lessons as they are needed throughout the school year.

Each month of the *Almanac* is divided into the following sections:

- **Birthographies.** Davida Shipkowitz of Northridge, California, has put together a calendar of famous birthdays or events and suggested activities for every day of the month. Planned to teach a variety of skills, the birthographies are a great way for students to research and identify with a "birthmate."

- **Spotlight of the Month.** Each month features a famous person who has made a notable contribution to society. This person also has had learning problems (or disabilities). The "Spotlight" is included for two reasons: (1) to remind you that human potential is often disguised and must be nurtured, and (2) to encourage the students to look beyond their current problems.

Upon learning about the achievements of people like Thomas Edison, Helen Keller, Woodrow Wilson, Winston Churchill, Albert Einstein, and Hans Christian Andersen, your students can only be awestruck. To learn that they also had learning problems is surprising indeed!

It is suggested that you take the time to talk about each personality each month. Childhood anecdotes are included wherever possible to be read to the students. Experience has shown that many children are encouraged and inspired by learning about these famous people who also struggled with learning problems.

An easy-to-reproduce bulletin board has also been designed for each "Spotlight" personality. The bulletin board can be displayed for the entire month.

• **Bulletin Board Ideas.** Each month offers two bulletin board ideas. Some bulletin boards are accompanied with activities and others are to be decorative or deliver a message.

The bulletin boards have been designed to be projected on an overhead or opaque projector onto a backed bulletin board and colored in with markers. If an overhead projector is used, the bulletin board illustration must first be transferred onto an acetate transparency with an acetate marker. You may choose the colors or use the suggested colors in the bulletin board directions.

• **Teaching Unit.** Each month of activities has an academic theme. These are school orientation, organization skills, reading skills, social skills, reading comprehension, social studies, writing skills, math skills, health and science, and carryover activities.

Each teaching unit has a series of six lesson plans with a list of materials needed for each one, preparation steps, and accompanying reproducible worksheets. They are designed to be a sampling of lessons on a variety of levels, for a variety of deficits for selected areas of skill development. It is suggested that you carefully choose those lessons that are appropriate for individual student needs. Each lesson also recommends a learning center for reinforcement.

• **Learning Centers.** The learning center activities are designed to reinforce each lesson in the teaching unit, and are designated after each unit lesson. The center's activities are labeled primary, intermediate, or advanced depending upon their difficulty. Directions for each learning center are provided for copying onto index cards, and suggestions and illustrations are given on how to set up selected learning centers. Reproducible worksheets and occasional awards are also provided for each learning center activity.

• **Materials of the Month.** Each month offers a discussion of creative ways to acquire useful materials. Sample letters to be copied and sent to parents and merchants are also included.

In addition, free materials as well as good buys to purchase are recommended. The materials are chosen to coordinate with the monthly themes. Suppliers' names, addresses, and ordering directions are also included with each listed item.

Keep in mind that the information given in this section is of a timely nature and, although correct at the time of writing the *Almanac*, may be changed at any given date. It is suggested that you check with the manufacturer before ordering any material.

• **Professional Responsibilities.** From an orientation tea in September to a student reunion in June, professional responsibilities are discussed. Ideas for publicity, public relations, and good staff rapport are emphasized in this section.

• **Professional Resource Books.** Each month includes a list of reference books for both you and the regular teaching staff. If a professional lending library is not already established, it is a good idea to begin one for the staff. Although the books suggested in the *Almanac* deal mainly with special education, many others are suggested to enhance general classroom programming.

• **Modes for Mainstreaming.** Suggestions are given to aid the classroom teacher and the special student in the mainstreaming process. Included are discussions about many problems that may arise and suggestions for their solution.

• **Tip of the Month.** Tried-and-true "tricks of the trade" are given each month. Tips like calling parents in September to reassure them and saying good-bye to students in June are some of the suggestions given.

• **A Final Word.** General issues pertaining to classroom management and school interaction are covered in this section. Frank discussions about teacher attitudes toward mainstreamed students as well as ways to avoid teacher burnout are brought to light.

We all know that no book can be endless; nor can it be all things for all people. To make the best use of this *Almanac*, you must add your own individual creativity and judgment. Teaching is a dynamic activity and, therefore, changeable and unique. By using the activities and suggestions in this book as a catalyst and supplement to your own individualized program, your special education program can become a reflection of your very best creative effort.

Natalie M. Elman

ACKNOWLEDGMENTS

This book could not have been completed without the help and encouragement of many people:

Bess Forshaw, who illustrated this book, was a never-ending source of new ideas and inspiration.

Davida Shipkowitz, a resource room teacher in Northridge, California and editor of the *California Association of Resource Specialists Journal*, researched and wrote the birthographies for each month. In addition, she was a ready fund of suggestions and new ideas.

Diane Turso added her editing expertise above and beyond the expected.

As usual, Arnold Gundersen gave me his full support and for that I am grateful. Barbara Zarret was most helpful with her librarian's expertise, and Jean Rappaport was a whiz at indexing! Susan McDonald transformed my disorganization into organization and Penny Drake did the same.

For all my dear and close friends who were always there to listen, encourage, and support me, I am so very thankful.

Appreciation was not expressed nearly enough to my family—Stan, Susan, Michael, and Elisabeth—whose patience and understanding seemed endless.

TABLE OF CONTENTS

James Lawrence • Mohandas Gandhi • Gertrude Berg • Edward Stratemeyer • Robert Goddard • Ray Kroc • Thor Heyerdahl • Alice Dalgliesh • Edward Rickenbacker • Otto Young Schnering • Giuseppe Verdi • Henry Heinz • Elmer Sperry • Mary Hays McCauley • Dwight D. Eisenhower • William Menninger • Noah Webster • Jupiter Hammon • Richard Nash • John Adams • Mickey Mantle • Alfred Nobel • Franz Liszt • Edson de Nascimento • Sarah Hale • Pablo Picasso • Phillis Wheatley • Mahalia Jackson • Theodore Roosevelt • Jonas Salk • Othneil Marsh • Irma Rombauer • Juliette Low

Crawford Long • Daniel Boone • John Montagu • Walter Cronkite • Paul Sabatier • James Naismith • Marie Curie • Hermann Rorschach • Benjamin Banneker • Sam Howe • Maude Adams • Elizabeth Cady Stanton • Robert Louis Stevenson • Robert Fulton • William Herschel • Burgess Meredith • Francois Appert • George Gallup • Ferdinand de Lesseps • Peregrine White • William Beaumont • Charles Berlitz • Harpo Marx • Henri de Toulouse-Lautrec • Andrew Carnegie • Will Shuster • Charles Schultz • Chaim Weitzman • John Wesley Hyatt • Louisa May Alcott • Samuel Clemens

Social Skills

Lane Bryant • George Seurat • Rowland Hill • Chester Greenwood • Walt Disney • Richard Henry Pratt • Marie Tussaud • Eli Whitney • Clarence Birdseye • Thomas Gallaudet • Melvil Dewey • Robert Koch • Cathy Rigby Mason • Tracy Austin • Alvin York • James Doolittle • Ludwik Zamenhof • Margaret Mead • Ludwig van Beethoven • Tyrus Cobb • Cicely Tyson • Richard Leaky • Richard Atwater • Henrietta Szold • Grote Reber • William Rogers • Kit Carson • Clara

Barton • Robert Ripley • Anwar Sadat • Charles Babbage • Louis Pasteur • Queen Elizabeth Petrovna I • Charles Goodyear • Sandy Koufax • Andreas Vesalius

Langston Hughes • Fritz Kreisler • Jascha Heifetz • Elizabeth Blackwell • Rosa Parks • Henry Aaron • Babe Ruth • Laura Ingalls Wilder • Jules Verne • Lydia Pinkham • Mark Spitz • William Talbot • Abraham Lincoln • William Shockley • Edward Yaeger • Christopher Sholes • George Ferris • John Sutter • John McEnroe • Rene-Theophile-Hyacinthe Laennec • John Travolta • Nicholas Copernicus • Bobby Unser • Presidents Day • George Washington • Robert Baden-Powell • Emma Willard • Wilhelm Grimm • Enrico Caruso • Jim Backus • William Cody • Henry Wadsworth Longfellow • John Tenniel • Gioacchino Rossini

Glenn Miller • Theodore Geisel • George Pullman • Garrett A. Morgan • William Oughtred • Michelangelo Buonarroti • Valentine Tereshkova • Joseph Niepce • Kenneth Grahame • Franz Gall • Lillian Wald • Ezra Jack Keats • John Miller • Joseph Priestley • Margaret de Angeli • Andrew Jackson • James Madison • Norbert Rillieux • Edgar Cayce • David Livingstone • Bobby Orr • Penny Dean • Marlies Gohr • Randolph Caldecott • Roger Bannister • John Wesley Powell • Gutzon Borglum • Leonard Nimoy • Wilhelm Roentgen • Henry Schoolcraft • Jacqueline Smith • Vincent Van Gogh • Cesar Chavez

Math Skills

   William Harvey • Frederic Auguste Bartholdi • Henry Luce • Jane Goodall Van Lawick • Dorothea Dix • Spencer Tracy • Melvyn Douglas • Bette Davis • Gregory Peck • Erich Weiss • Walter Camp • Donald Vesco • Eadweard Muybridge • Matthew C. Perry • Percy Julian • Frederic Melcher • Hardie Gramatky • Thomas Jefferson • James L. Plimpton • Leonardo Da Vinci • Charlie Chaplin • Alexander Joy Cartwright • Clarence Darrow • Jean Lee Latham • Daniel French • John Muir • Vladimir Illyich Lenin • Shirley Temple Black • Robert Bailey Thomas • Guglielmo Marconi • John James Audubon • Samuel Morse • Lionel Barrymore • Edward Ellington • Carl Friedrich Gauss

Health and Safety

Mary Harris • Theodore Hertzl • Bing Crosby • Jacob Riis • Golda Meir • Frederic Church • Elizabeth Cochran • Sigmund Freud • Edwin Land • Henry William Vanderbilt • Howard Carter • Thomas Lipton • Irving Berlin • Lawrence

Berra • Joe Louis • Stevie Wonder • Gabriel Fahrenheit • Ilya Ilich Metchnikoff • William Seward • Edward Jenner • Thomas Midgley • Carl Akeley • Emile Berliner • Mary Anning • Frances Densmore • Arthur Conan Doyle • Margaret Fuller • William Gilbert • Igor Sikorsky • John Wayne • James Arness • Rachel Carson • Louis Agassiz • Bob Hope • John F. Kennedy • Mel Blanc • Aleksei Leonov • Ronald Laird

September

1 Englebert Humperdinck (1854) The stage is set for Humperdinck's fairytale opera! Stepmother sends Hansel and Gretel to fetch berries, but the children fall asleep! Dawn finds them nibbling on the witch's house when she hungrily grabs Hansel! But Gretel steals a magic wand and the two push the witch into the oven! Close curtain. Applause please!

2 Eugene Field (1850) "Wynken and Blynken are two little eyes./And Nod is a little head." So begins a Dutch lullaby by Eugene Field. Listen to feel the cradle rock in the misty sea of twinkling stars and waves of dew. Draw this dreamy scene with water crayons and "wash" for a filmy fanta-sea!

3 Prudence Crandall (1803) Crandall couldn't do much. Angry folks of Windham, CT closed shops when she called, set fire to her cottage, and closed her school for black girls. But no one kept Prudence from teaching young black women. As a teacher, it was Crandall's *civil right* to teach, for her students had their *civil rights* — to learn.

4 Lewis Latimer (1848) We all know of Thomas Edison and Alexander Graham Bell, but few know about Lewis Latimer. He invented lamp sockets so Edison's bulbs might be easily replaced. And, Latimer drew pictures of Bell's telephone parts so many could be made at once. Take apart a phone. Take a part and draw it!

5 Jesse James (1847) Jesse Woodsen James was the hero of more than 400 books! But was he really a hero? For 16 years, Jesse and his brother Frank led outlaws who robbed trains, banks, and stagecoaches. They gave money to the poor but they murdered, too. A $10,000 reward was posted. Would a *hero* be WANTED — DEAD OR ALIVE?

6 Jane Addams (1869) For 20 years, Jane Addams opened the old Chicago Hull House door to new Americans who needed help. She taught English and worked to get laws made to change the things that caused poverty and illness. She helped new immigrants begin a new life in America and open their doors to help others, as well.

7 Anna Moses (1860) The story of Grandma Moses is a story problem! Born in 1860, she died in 1961 at age ___. Anna Moses began to paint wonderful scenes of America in 1937 at age ___. Over 1000 pictures were painted from 1937 to 1961. About how many were painted each year? Find prints of her paintings. Count the people!

8 Sir Thomas Fleet (1685) Mother Goose was Mom to many./ Her children and their children, then./ But always had she time to sing/ Her verses, o'er and o'er again./ One young Miss Goose Tom Fleet did marry,/ And when SO TIRED of song said, "Please!/ I'll print them all and will not tarry/ as MOTHER GOOSE'S MELODIES."/ Then could they READ Tom Fleet's first book/ Of Mother Goose's nursery rhyme/ And thanks to Tom we shall recite/ Her verses, till the end of time.

9 George W. Eastman (1815) We know that George Eastman put film on rolls in Kodak cameras, but who knows Grandpa George Washington Eastman? He gave handwriting lessons when he was a boy. This handwriting expert opened the first business and banking school in America! Write numerals expertly today. Would G.W.E. give you a grade A?

10 Thomas Sydenham (1624) Who has had measles? Or scarlet fever? All of you may remember a sore throat, fever, chills and a rosy rash. But not all of you had the same disease! Thanks to Dr. Sydenham, doctors know the difference between measles and scarlet fever. The clue? Say ahhh! Was that a ROSY RED TONGUE you "stuck-out"?

11 Erastus Beadle (1821) To make labels for bags of grain, Erastus Beadle carved wooden letters to hand print the tags. So began the printer who printed millions of orange-covered 10¢ novels so that everyone could buy books that told tales of life in America. It's "Read a New Book Month" . . . Pick a paperback to honor the printer.

12 Jesse Owens (1913) Too bad Hitler didn't learn the lesson Jesse Owens taught. Jesse won 4 gold medals in 1936 for running and broadjump, but Hitler, who thought only blue-eyed people with blond hair were strong and good, would not shake Jesse's strong, black hand for a job well done. But we'll jump for joy for Jesse!

13 Milton Hershey (1857) and Roald Dahl (1916) Thank goodness Milton Hershey and Roald Dahl were born on September 13, or Charlie might not have had a chocolate factory after all! It's a good day to find out how chocolate bars and cocoa are made in Hershey, PA or to read a chapter from *Charlie and the Chocolate Factory*, and . . . crunch!

14 Ivan Pavlov (1849) A cold mouthful of milk, and — you swallow. You don't think about how, you just do! That's a reflex. Ivan Pavlov taught new reflexes to animals. He fed dogs and, at the same time, rang a bell. Soon the dogs salivated whenever they heard the sound. Can you teach a dog to run to his bowl at the sound of a bell?

15 Carlo Rambaldi (1925) At a birthday party are E.T., King Kong, inter-planetary beings which "closely encountered" our world, White Buffalo, and Alien. In the shadows, the words of birthday greetings are chanted to Carlo Rambaldi. The designer of these wonderful creatures blows out his candles and makes a birthday wish.

> No one knows what he . . . (or she) . . . can do until he . . . (or she) . . . tries.
>
> Pubilius Syrus

✶⊀✶⊀✶⊀✶⊀✶⊀✶⊀✶⊀✶⊀✶⊀✶⊀✶⊀✶⊀✶⊀✶⊀✶⊀✶⊀✶

16 Albert Szent-Gyorgyi (1893) Pick a pepper and share it to celebrate the birthday of Albert Szent-Gyorgyi (Saint George). The vitamin that keeps bones hard, gums healthy, and teeth firmly in place was found by this Hungarian in green bell peppers. Think about how vitamin C helps you to chew as you bite and munch and chomp.

17 Konstantin Tsiolkovsky (1857) A knowledge chain on rockets and space travel began with Konstantin Tsiolkovsky. The information he wrote was used by Goddard to lift rockets, to send Glenn into space, and to set Armstrong on the moon. On each link of a paper chain put the name and date of a person who has improved an idea in time.

18 Jean Foucault (1819) From the ceiling of a Paris building hung a huge pointed ball. It swung the same way each time. Pendulums do that. But, *each line* dug by the point into sand below was different. The lines made a design. It proved the earth, under the ball, turned clockwise. Draw the design that made Foucault famous!

19 Al Oerter (1936) Turn one paper dinner plate on another, rims together. You now have the shape of a DISCUS. Thrown as the thrower whirls around, the 9-inch disk has been thrown around since the Greek Olympics! Mark 194 feet on your playing field to find 4-time Olympic winner Al Oerter's record discus throw.

20 Sir James Dewar (1842) "Don't forget your Dewar flask," Mom calls as you run out the door. "My what?" A Dewar flask is a thermos. Filled with cold lemonade or juice, it will be cold for many hours of refreshing drinks. Sir James Dewar invented the vacuum flask to keep liquids cold. Have a drink from a thermos jug and toast Sir D.

21 Louis Joliet (1645) After Louis Joliet explored Lake Michigan, the Wisconsin River and the Mississippi, he began the trip back to Canada. The canoe overturned and his new maps floated downstream. Joliet had to draw them once more, this time from memory! Like Joliet, draw or cut the outline map of your state from memory!

22 Michael Faraday (1791) Can you see what Michael Faraday saw? You can see and draw the lines of force by sprinkling iron bits around a magnet. Faraday moved wires across those lines of force. The force of those lines pushed tiny electrons in the wires. A current of electrons, or ELECTRICITY, moved through the wires.

23 William McGuffey (1800) Take dictation! Write *dog, the,* and *ran.* Now *cat, mat, is,* and *on.* Add to the list *man, pen, hen, rat,* and *box.* How many sentences can you write with those words? You have just done the exercise that 122,000,000 students have done from 1836 on! Did McGuffey's six readers teach your great-grandma and great-grandpa?

24 James Henson (1936) National Child Care Week is the correct time to count candles on Jim Henson's birthday cake. His Muppets have most carefully cared for millions and millions of kids for countless numbers of hours. Even the Count couldn't count them all! There isn't a kid who can't count on Kermit to constantly care!

25 Benjamin Harris' Newspaper (1690) It's American Indian Day! Undoubtedly, Benjamin Harris put news about Indians in the first newspaper in America. But the English king stopped the press after only one edition! Happy Birthday to the newspaper and to its editor (date unknown) today! Be colonial journalists. Print one edition of NATIVE AMERICAN NEWS!

26 John Chapman (1774 or -75) Write a poem about John Chapman who, with a pot for a hat and a flowing beard, walked barefoot through the Eastern hills giving apple seeds to farmers. He helped to plant the trees that brought sweet, hot cider to chilly fall evenings. Like the trees, Johnny Appleseed always gave, taking little in return.

27 Thomas Nast (1840) It was easier to look at cartoons than to read the news. Cartoons helped people know about world events. Thomas Nast drew Civil War battles, portraits and cartoons. You know what he drew—a Democrat donkey, a Republican elephant, and Santa Claus who looks a bit like Nast with his wide mustache and twinkling eyes!

28 Oscar Tschirky (1866) What can you do with apples, nuts, celery and mayonnaise? Make a Waldorf Salad! Make it for a birthday party for Oscar Tschirky, known as "Oscar of Waldorf." The Waldorf, the block-square hotel in New York City, has a wonderful restaurant where Oscar made the very first Waldorf Salad. Enjoy, enjoy!

29 Enrico Fermi (1901) An experiment under the football stadium had one goal. Below Stagg Field (University of Chicago, 1942) Fermi kicked-off a CHAIN REACTION that drove the world to use atomic energy. But that world changes when mushroom clouds touch down. Take time-out to point out the good or bad of the BIG BANG!

30 William Wrigley, Jr. (1861) Try a jump rope jingle to remember William Wrigley, Jr. He began a gum factory in Chicago in 1891. A package of gum to the winner, of course! . . . Born in 1861,/ William Wrigley made some gum,/ Juicy fruit and spearmint, too./ How many packages can I chew?/ (One, two, three . . .)

These birthographies were prepared by Davida Shipkowitz of Northridge, California.

SPOTLIGHT ON

THOMAS ALVA EDISON (1847–1931)

Edison created his first invention, an electric vote recorder, when he was 21. Not long after, he invented an improved stock ticker. He later invented the phonograph. His most important invention, however, was a practical incandescent light bulb in 1879.

Although Edison was not the first to invent an electrical lighting system, his bulb—together with the system of distributing electric power—made electric lighting practical for home use.

Edison contributed enormously to the development of motion pictures and cameras. He made important improvements in the telephone, in the telegraph and in the typewriter. Among his other inventions were a dictating machine, a mimeograph machine and a storage battery. All totaled, Edison patented more than a thousand separate inventions!

Edison not only was a brilliant inventor but also engaged in manufacturing, as well as organizing several industrial companies. The most impressive of these is the General Electric Company.

The following description of Thomas Edison was printed in *Cradles of Eminence* by Victor and Mildred Goertzel.

> "Boy age six; large head at birth. Thought to have brain fever. Three siblings died before his birth. Mother does not agree with relatives and neighbors that child is probably abnormal. Child sent to school—diagnosed as mentally ill by teacher. Mother is angry—withdraws child from school, says she will teach him herself." (p. XIII).

Lloyd J. Thompson in *Language Disabilities in Men of Eminence* quotes M. Josephson, another biographer, as follows: "Edison was born in 1847 and was considered defective at birth. His head was so abnormally large that the village doctor thought he might have brain fever. After three months in school the boy overheard his teacher say that the boy's mind was 'addled.' He refused to return to school and his mother took over as his teacher."

Josephson's biography further reports that Edison wrote in his diary: "I remember I used never to be able to get along in school. I was always at the foot of the class." A letter Edison wrote to his mother at age 19 after years of individual tutoring is quoted:

> Dear Mother - Started the Store several weeks. I have growed considerably I don't look much like a Boy now - Hows all the folk did you receive a Box of Books from Memphis that he promised to send them - languages.
> Your son Al

Edison also dealt with a severe hearing deficit which was discovered at age 12.

In spite of early school problems, being declared unteachable by his teachers, and having a severe loss of hearing, Thomas Edison probably contributed more to mankind than any other known person of the 20th century. The following quote by Edison gives us excellent insight into how that success came about:

> "Genius is one percent inspiration and ninety-nine percent perspiration."

SPOTLIGHT BULLETIN BOARD

This is designed to be a permanent bulletin board or poster where the featured person is changed each month. If bulletin board space is not available, posterboard affixed to a door or wall can be used. NOTE: Stringing a clothesline and hanging posters or other visual effects with colorful clothespins is another way to expand bulletin space.

Materials:

white background paper

yellow and orange markers for cast light

black marker for can light

overhead projector

acetate transparency

transparency marker

Preparation:

1. Cover the bulletin board with the white background paper.

2. Trace the Spotlight Bulletin Board on page 6 onto clear acetate using a transparency marker.

3. Project the transparency onto the bulletin board.

4. Trace the outline onto the white background paper. Color in with the markers.

The paper used for the personality and figures each month can be removed and replaced while the basic bulletin board remains. NOTE: If large sheets of construction paper are used for bulletin boards, they can be removed and stored for future use. Make a large envelope out of two large sheets of oaktag and staple them together. Slip the boards into the construction paper and label. These can then be stored flat against a closet wall or on a closet floor.

BULLETIN BOARD IDEAS

All the bulletin boards in the *Almanac* are designed to be projected onto the board with an overhead projector and copied. If you prefer, colored construction paper or other materials can be used instead of markers.

WELCOME

This bulletin board is very effective if done in stark white and bold black. However, other colors may be substituted. This board should be placed in a prominent spot to welcome the students upon their return to school.

Materials:

white background paper

acetate transparency

transparency markers

overhead projector

black marker or black paint

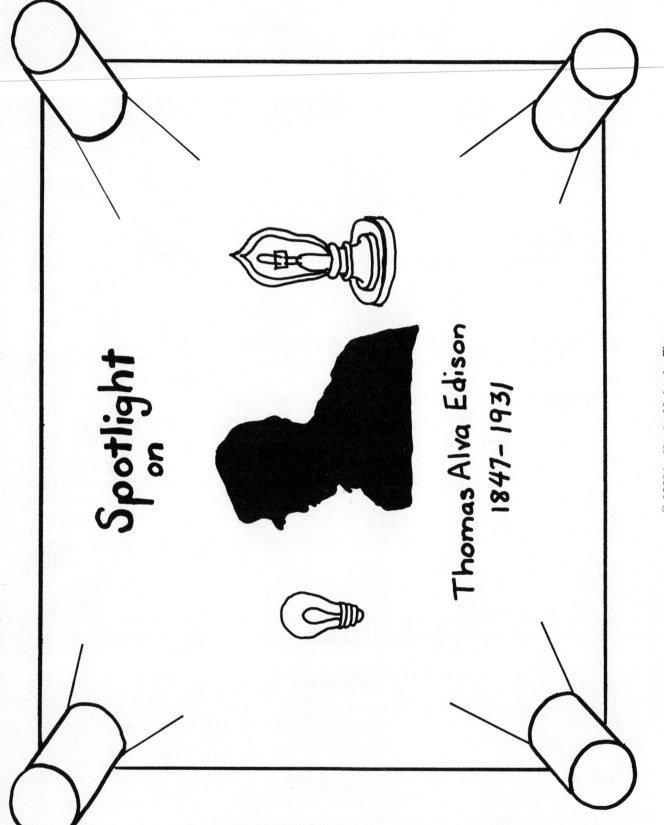

Spotlight on

Thomas Alva Edison
1847 – 1931

Preparation:

1. Back the bulletin board with large sheets of white construction paper.

2. Trace the bulletin board illustration on page 7 onto an acetate transparency with a transparency marker.

3. Project the transparency from the overhead projector onto the bulletin board.

4. Trace the outline of the letters and footprints with a black marker.

5. Fill in the outlines with black paint or marker. (NOTE: Paint spreads much more quickly, although broad markers are available.)

6. Watch for smiling faces as the children enter the room.

NOTE: Another suggestion is to have the bulletin board set up with everything *except* the footprints. On opening day, have each student draw outlines of their own feet on black construction paper, cut out, and place on the prepared bulletin board.

DON'T BE A ROBOT: THINK FOR YOURSELF

This bulletin board reinforces the idea of the student assuming responsibility for his or her own schedule, homework, lunch, etc., that is stressed during the orientation lessons.

Materials:

white background paper

black construction paper or black marker

markers of various colors

acetate transparency and marker

overhead projector

Preparation:

1. Attach the background paper to the bulletin board.

2. Trace "Don't Be a Robot" onto the acetate transparency.

3. Project the transparency onto the bulletin board.

4. Trace the outline with marker onto the construction paper. (If you prefer cut-out construction paper to drawing with markers, put the construction paper in the appropriate spot and copy the design. Then remove it and cut out.)

5. Fill in the outline with markers, using colors of your choice.

TEACHING UNIT

ORIENTATION

The first week or two of school is generally spent orienting the younger or newer children to the locations, routines, and schedules of their classrooms, resource room, or other special programming. For those older students who are already familiar with both the

Don't be a Robot....Think for Yourself !

school floor plan and routines, more time can be spent on organization skills that can be applied toward increased homework loads and heavier classroom demands.

Objectives:

At the conclusion of this unit, students will be able to:

- Find their way independently to and around the classroom and/or resource room.
- Know (independent of teacher reminders) what time they are to be where.
- Know how to use the audio-visual machinery on their own.
- Become familiar with other children in the school.

How to Use the Room

Materials:

clipboard or folders for each child

weekly assignment sheet for each child

overhead acetate with weekly assignment sheet printed on it

chalk

chalkboard

overhead projector

Preparation:

1. Print each child's name on a weekly assignment sheet (see page 11) and attach it to a clipboard.

2. Draw or copy a replica of the weekly assignment sheet on an overhead acetate. Have clean space on the chalkboard large enough to project the weekly plan.

Directions:

1. It is a good idea to pick up the younger children at their classrooms the first day or two of school. Even those children who have attended your program the previous year may be in a new classroom location and a bit disoriented.

2. Note landmarks along the way, such as, "There is the principal's office," and "The water fountain is on our right."

3. Once in the room, give each child his or her own personal clipboard or folder with a weekly assignment sheet. Show the students where the clipboards will be kept, such as on

Assignment Sheet

Name _____

Week of: _____

	Monday	Tuesday	Wednesday	Thursday	Friday
Station: _____					

Comments:
Be sure to use your very neatest writing!

Evaluation:
☺ I really like the way you followed directions today.

a pegboard or in file cabinet. Colorful Con-Tact paper cut in a familiar shape (an apple) with the child's name written in with a bold color marker makes a quick, easy and fun way to label a clipboard or locker door.

4. Walk with the students from station to station as they correspond to the markings on the weekly assignment sheet.

5. With children seated at the group table, project the assignment sheet acetate onto the board using the overhead projector. Use chalk to write in a sample assignment on the assignment sheet.

6. Give each child a chance to read a designated station on the board and then walk to that station. Play this game until each child understands the weekly plan and the layout of the room.

Reinforcement Activities:

Refer to September's "Learning Centers" and have your students do assignments 1 and 2.

Let's Be on Time

Materials:

large toy clock
filled-in worksheet for each child
blank worksheet for each child
pencils
chalk

Preparation:

1. Copy at least two time schedule worksheets per child. (See page 13.)
2. Fill in a schedule for each child on one of the worksheets.

Directions:

1. Using the large toy clock, place the hands of the clock at the beginning of the school day.

2. Begin reviewing events of the school day. "At 8:45 what are we doing?" Encourage the students to fill in the information.

3. Explain to the children that getting to the resource room or other programs on time will be their responsibility. The excuses of "I forgot" or "My teacher forgot to tell me" will be unacceptable. Try to impress upon them the importance of assuming responsibility for their own program.

4. Distribute the filled-in schedule forms. Instruct the children to raise their hands when their program time is called. Start the toy clock at 8:45 a.m. and again review the daily events. (For example, "The bus arrives at this time.") As the children raise their hands for their program time, be sure to give strong positive reinforcement when they raise their hands at the correct time. Sometimes it helps to reinforce again what will be happening in the classroom at the time the child leaves to go to other programs. Have them tell *you* when they will be leaving to be sure they understand.

Resource Room

Time Schedule

Name _____

I arrive

I leave

	I arrive	I leave
Monday	◯	◯
Tuesday	◯	◯
Wednesday	◯	◯
Thursday	◯	◯
Friday	◯	◯

5. Distribute blank schedule forms and have the children fill them out. They can keep these at their classroom desks. NOTE: Some teachers prefer to have the children put their schedule on index cards and tape them to their classroom desks as reminders. Generally, older children prefer not to do this.

6. With older children, review their schedules without the toy clock, if possible. Discuss with them what they will be leaving in the classroom when they go to other programs. This is also a good time to discuss how and when they will make up missed classroom work if they are indeed responsible for it. (See September's "A Final Word.")

Reinforcement Activities:

Refer to September's "Learning Centers" and have your students do assignments 3 and 4.

How Does It Work?

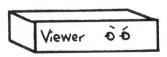

Materials:

tape recorder and cassette tape
filmstrip viewer
film and cassette projector
overhead projector
signs

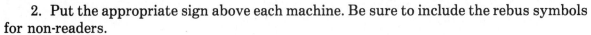

Preparation:

1. Place all equipment on one large table.

2. Put the appropriate sign above each machine. Be sure to include the rebus symbols for non-readers.

3. Test each machine and make sure it is ready to work.

4. Place colored tape on buttons for non-readers, such as green for "on" (start) and red for "off" (stop).

Directions:

1. Seat the children around the table.

2. Demonstrate one piece of machinery at a time.

3. First discuss the name, the sign that will be on the machine and the rebus which will be used.

4. For non-readers, explain that the red button means STOP (when they want to stop the machine) and the green button means GO (when they want to start the machine).

5. Allow each child to use the machine. This can be put in a game format like a radio interview or a talent show.

6. Explain that any problems in working the machines must be brought to the attention of the teacher or the aide. Students are not allowed to "fix" machinery.

7. Instruct the students that all machinery must be rewound and ready for the next person to use before they leave each station.

8. Use additional time for supervised practice by the students on each machine until you and the children feel comfortable with their ability to handle the machinery.

Reinforcement Activities:

Refer to September's "Learning Centers" and have your students do assignments 5 and 6.

LEARNING CENTERS

The learning centers are designed for independent student activities to reinforce the teaching units for each month. They are designed for a variety of ability levels that will be labeled "primary," "intermediate" or "advanced." It will be left to your judgment as to which ability-appropriate activities are to be assigned each student. The use of the assignment sheet on page 11 is an excellent vehicle for individualizing each child's program.

(1) HERE'S CENTRAL!
(PRIMARY)

Materials:

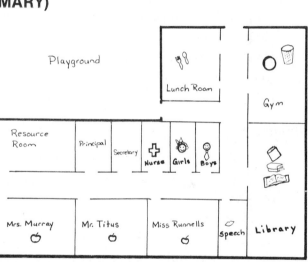

5″ × 8″ index card
school map for each student
marker
pencils
crayons
cassette recorder and earphones
pre-taped cassette

Preparation:

1. Record the dialogue on tape.
2. Copy a map for each primary student. (See the sample map here.)
3. Write the directions on a 5″ × 8″ index card with a colorful marker.

Directions Card:

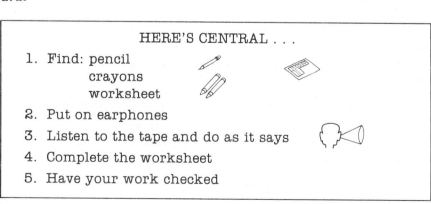

HERE'S CENTRAL . . .
1. Find: pencil
        crayons
        worksheet
2. Put on earphones
3. Listen to the tape and do as it says
4. Complete the worksheet
5. Have your work checked

Cassette Dialogue:

Teacher records the following:

1. Hi, welcome to _____. Be sure you have a pencil, crayons, and your worksheet ready. If not, press "STOP" and get the things you need.

2. You are to do exactly as I say. If you need more time than the tape gives you to finish a task, press "STOP" until you are finished. Press "START" when you are ready to continue.

3. First, find the resource room on your map worksheet. (pause) Have you found it? Good! Write your name in the appropriate square. If there is not enough space, you may write outside the square. (pause)

4. Next, find the boys' room. (pause) Put a blue X in the box. (pause)

5. Find the library. (pause) Put a happy face in the square. (pause)

6. Next, find the girls' room. (pause) Color it green. (pause)

7. Find the speech room. (pause) Put a red S in the square. (pause)

8. Using your finger, trace a path from the resource room to the cafeteria. (pause) Now, with your red crayon trace the path from the resource room to the cafeteria. (pause)

9. Put your name at the top of your worksheet. (pause)

10. After you press "STOP" you may give your worksheet to the teacher. Please turn off the machine.

(2) GETTING TO KNOW THE ROOM
(INTERMEDIATE)

Materials:

resource room/classroom map or picture for each student

small toys or colored construction paper tokens

directions card

pencils

Preparation:

1. Copy the resource room worksheet (see the sample on page 17) for all intermediate students. (NOTE: This can be substituted with a simple sketch of your classroom.)

2. Write the directions on the index card.

3. Place a box of toys or tokens at one of the centers.

Directions Card:

FIND THE SURPRISE!

1. Starting with Center 1, go to each learning center and pick up a token from each one.

2. Put an X on your map to show each center you visited.

3. At one of the learning centers you will find a surprise. Color this X red.

4. You will need to show this surprise to your teacher.

5. Good luck and happy visiting.

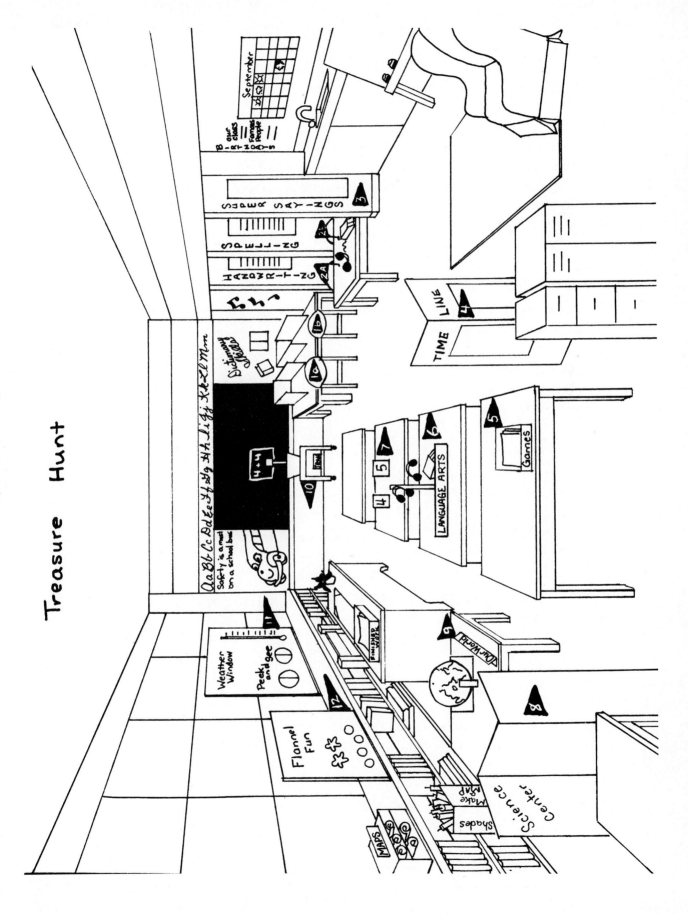

Treasure Hunt

(3) TIME SCHEDULE
(INTERMEDIATE)

Materials:

file box
index cards
alphabet tab cards
clock stamp (see DLM under September's "Materials of the Month")
stamp pad
Time Schedule A for each student
pencils

Preparation:

1. Write the time schedule (see page 19) for each child on an index card.
2. Write each child's name at the top of a different schedule.
3. File the cards in alphabetical order.
4. Prepare the directions card.

Directions Card:

```
            TIME SCHEDULE
  1. Find the index card with your name on it.
  2. On your worksheet, stamp each circle with tne rubber
stamp.
  3. Fill in the clock with the correct resource room time
for arriving and leaving each day.
  4. Have your work checked by the teacher.
  5. Bring your schedule worksheet home.
```

(4) TIME SCHEDULE
(ADVANCED)

Materials:

index cards   alphabet tab cards
file box   Time Schedule B for each student

Preparation:

1. Write the resource room schedule (see page 20) on an index card for each child.
2. Write each student's name at the top of a different card.
3. File the cards alphabetically.
4. Prepare the directions card.

Resource Room
Time Schedule A

Name _____

I arrive

I leave

	I arrive	I leave
Monday	◯	◯
Tuesday	◯	◯
Wednesday	◯	◯
Thursday	◯	◯
Friday	◯	◯

Resource Room
Time Schedule B

Name _____

I arrive

I leave

		Total
Monday	○	○
Tuesday	○	○
Wednesday	○	○
Thursday	○	○
Friday	○	○
Total time per week		

Directions Card:

```
                      TIME SCHEDULE
  1.  Locate your schedule card in the file box.
  2.  Copy your scheduled times on the worksheet.
  3.  Add the number of minutes you will be in the resource
room each day.
  4.  Replace your card in alphabetical order.
  5.  Have your work checked by the teacher.
  6.  The worksheet is to be taken home.
```

(5) WHO'S WHO?
(INTERMEDIATE)

Materials:

tape recorder, microphone and earphones
blank cassette
interview worksheet for each child
directions card

Preparation:

1. Copy the interivew worksheets (see page 22) for all intermediate-level students.
2. Prepare the directions card.
3. Discuss the interviewing techniques as a group lesson.

Directions Card:

```
                      WHO'S WHO?
  1.  Read your interview questions several times.
  2.  Prepare the person you are interviewing:
      a.  Ask the person politely.
      b.  Help the person to be seated.
      c.  Put the person at ease.
      d.  Show the person where the microphone is.
  3.  Turn the recorder to "record."
  4.  Ask your questions into the microphone clearly.
  5.  Wait for a complete answer before you continue.
  6.  Thank the person when you are finished.
  7.  Do not rewind the tape!
```

Name: _____

"WHO'S WHO?" INTERVIEW QUESTIONS

1. What is your full name?

2. Where were you born?

3. How old are you?

4. Do you have brothers and sisters? How many?

5. What do you like about school?

6. What don't you like about school?

7. What do you do for fun outside of school?

8. Who's your favorite person?

9. What's your favorite place?

10. Do you have a pet? If so, what is it?

11. Thank you for your time!

12. I completed this interview at _____ o'clock.

(6a) OUR ROOM RULES
(PRIMARY)

Materials:

blank cassette   pencil
tape recorder   crayons
earphones   drawing paper

Preparation:

1. Pre-record the directions' dialogue.
2. Prepare the rebus directions card.

Directions Card:

OUR ROOM RULES

1. Listen
2. Do

Tape Recorder Dialogue:

Choose one of the rules that we have discussed. On a piece of drawing paper, draw a picture of yourself in this room obeying that rule. Be sure to put your name on the drawing.

(6b) OUR ROOM RULES
(INTERMEDIATE)

Materials:

posterboard   rules worksheet for each student
markers   pencils
reminders worksheet for each student

Preparation:

1. Make a list of reminders on a large sheet of posterboard. (See page 24.)
2. Copy a "Rules Worksheet" for each student. (See page 25.)
3. Use the posterboard from Step 1 as a backdrop for the learning center.
4. Prepare the directions card.

Directions Card:

OUR ROOM RULES

1. Read the list of rules.
2. Fill in the correct answers on the worksheet.
3. Have your work checked by the teacher.

Room Reminders

I will:

___ raise my hand to talk

___ stay in my seat

___ "check out" before I leave the room

___ get my clipboard as soon as I enter the room

___ raise my hand if I need help at a learning center

___ return my clipboard (or folder) when I am finished for the day

___ put my _name_ on my worksheets

Name: _____

RULES WORKSHEET

These are the things I must remember to do.

1. I will _____ when I want to talk.

2. I will _____ in my seat.

3. I will _____ before I leave the room.

4. I will get my _____ as soon as I enter the room.

5. I will _____ when I need help at a center.

6. I will _____ my clipboard when I am ready to leave for the day.

7. I will put my _____ on my paper.

Signed: _____

MATERIALS OF THE MONTH

Deciding what materials are necessary to carry out a quality program and, therefore, worthy for purchase is always difficult. Usually the closest look we get at potential materials is in a catalog. Many of us have had the experience of being disappointed when the materials arrive because of this limitation. Returning materials with all the red tape that this requires in a school system often forces teachers to keep unwanted material or equipment.

Webster McGraw-Hill has an excellent checklist (see page 27) for evaluating materials. If used properly before a decision to purchase is made, it can help to eliminate some painful mistakes.

Another suggestion is to seek out resource libraries in your state. These are generally state or federally funded resource centers for teachers and are an excellent vehicle to not only look at, but take out and use many of the materials in question. Check with your state special education agency to find out if and where they exist near you. The following addresses should help:

STATE SPECIAL EDUCATION DEPARTMENTS

ALABAMA
Exceptional Children and Youth
State Department of Education
868 State Office Building
Montgomery, AL 36130
(205) 832-3316

ALASKA
State of Alaska, Department of Education
Office for Exceptional Children
Special Education Programs
Pouch F 0500
Juneau, AK 99811
(907) 465-2970

ARIZONA
Division of Special Education
Arizona Department of Education
1535 W. Jefferson
Phoenix, AZ 85007
(602) 271-3183

ARKANSAS
Special Education Section
Department of Education
Arch Ford Building, Capitol Mall
Little Rock, AR 72201
(501) 371-2161

CALIFORNIA
California State Department
of Education
Office of Special Education
721 Capitol Mall
Rm. 614
Sacramento, CA 95814
(916) 445-4036

COLORADO
Colorado Department of
Education
State Office Building
201 East Colfax
Denver, CO 80203
(303) 839-2727
ATTN: Special Education

CONNECTICUT
Bureau of Pupil Personnel and
Special Educational Services
State Department of Education
P.O. Box 2219
Hartford, CT 06115
(203) 566-3561

A CHECKLIST FOR EVALUATING MATERIALS
FOR AN INDIVIDUALIZED EDUCATION PROGRAM

Title _____

Author _____ Publisher _____

Evaluation _____ Evaluator _____

Evaluated for use by _____ Type of learning problem _____

		YES	NO
Flexibility			
1.	Can this material be used:		
	a. only as a complete program?	____	____
	b. in small units or modules?	____	____
2.	Can the material be used for:		
	a. group instruction?	____	____
	b. individualized instruction?	____	____
	c. both?	____	____
3.	Are supplementary materials (A-V, manipulatives, etc.) provided or suggested?	____	____
4.	Are supplementary activities (classroom, individualized, field trips, etc.) provided or suggested?	____	____
5.	Is this material useful for:		
	a. a variety of learning problems?	____	____
	b. a specific learning problem?	____	____
	(list (a) or (b) areas if desired)		
Content			
1.	Is the content appropriate to the:		
	a. chronological age of the student?	____	____
	b. mental age of the student?	____	____
2.	Is the content appropriate for the cultural and social background of the student?	____	____
3.	Will the content provide real-life, self-help skills?	____	____
4.	Is the material appropriately paced?	____	____
5.	Is there adequate reinforcement?	____	____
6.	Does the material provide motivation?	____	____
7.	Is there provision for assessment?	____	____
Practicality			
1.	Does the Teacher's Manual provide:		
	a. background information?	____	____
	b. suggestions for reinforcement or extension?	____	____
	c. classroom management help?	____	____
2.	Is the Teacher's Manual well-organized, with clear instructions and/or suggestions?	____	____
3.	Is the student's material:		
	a. durable?	____	____
	b. easy to store?	____	____
	c. safe?	____	____

Comments, if desired _____

_____

_____

(Webster McGraw-Hill has designed this checklist for your use and it may be reproduced for educational material evaluation.)

DELAWARE
Exceptional Children/
Special Programs Division
State Department of Public Instruction
John G. Townsend Building
P.O. Box 1402
Dover, DE 19901
(302) 678-4667

DISTRICT OF COLUMBIA
Special Education
Division of Special Education
     Programs
Presidential Building
Room 602
415 12th Street, N.W.
Washington, D.C. 20004
(202) 724-4018

FLORIDA
Bureau of Education for Exceptional
     Students
Florida Department of Education
204 Knott Building
Tallahassee, FL 32304
(904) 488-1570

GEORGIA
Program for Exceptional Children
Georgia Department of Education
State Office Building
Atlanta, GA 30334
(404) 656-2425

HAWAII
State Department of Education
Special Education Department
45-955 Kam Highway
Kaneohe, HI 96744
(808) 235-2443

IDAHO
Department of Education
Special Education Division
650 West State Street
Boise, ID 83720
(208) 384-2203

ILLINOIS
Department of Specialized
     Education Services
Illinois Office of Education
100 North First Street
Springfield, IL 62777
(217) 782-6601

INDIANA
Division of Special Education
Department of Public Instruction
229 State House
Indianapolis, IN 46204
(317) 927-0216

IOWA
State of Iowa
Department of Public Instruction
Special Education Division
Grimes State Office Building
Des Moines, IA 50319
(515) 281-3176

KANSAS
Special Education Administration
     Section
Kansas State Department of
     Education
120 E. Tenth
Topeka, KS 66612
(913) 296-3866

KENTUCKY
Bureau for Education of Exceptional
     Children
Capital Plaza Tower
8th Floor
Frankfort, KY 40601
(502) 564-4970

LOUISIANA
Division of Special Educational Services
State Department of Education
Capital Station
P.O. Box 44064
Baton Rouge, LA 70804
(504) 342-3631

MAINE
Division of Special Education
State Department of Educational &
    Cultural Services
State House
Augusta, ME 04333
(207) 289-3451

MARYLAND
Division of Special Education
State Department of Education
P.O. Box 8717
Balt-Wash International Airport
Baltimore, MD 21240
(301) 796-8300 Ext. 245

MASSACHUSETTS
Division of Special Education
State Department of Education
Park Square Building
31 St. James Avenue
Boston, MA 02116
(617) 727-5700

MICHIGAN
Special Education Services
State Department of Education
P.O. Box 30008
Lansing, MI 48909
(517) 373-0923

MINNESOTA
Special Education Section
State Department of Education
Capitol Square Bldg.
550 Cedar Avenue
St. Paul, MN 55101
(612) 296-4163

MISSISSIPPI
Special Education Section
State Department of Education
P.O. Box 771
Jackson, MS 39205
(601) 354-6950

MISSOURI
Director of Special Education
P.O. Box 480
Jefferson City, MO 65101
(314) 751-3502

MONTANA
Special Education Unit
Office of Public Instruction
State Capitol
Room 106
Helena, MT 59601
(406) 449-5660

NEBRASKA
State Department of Education
Special Education Branch
301 Centennial Mall South
Lincoln, NE 68509
(402) 471-2295

NEVADA
Nevada Department of Education
Special Education Division
Capital Complex
400 West King Street
Carson City, NV 89710
(702) 885-5700 Ext. 214

NEW HAMPSHIRE
New Hampshire Department
    of Education
Division of Vocational Rehabilitation
Special Education Section
105 Loudon Rd.
Concord, NH 03301
(603) 271-3741

NEW JERSEY
Division of Special Education
New Jersey Department of Education
Division of School Programs
Branch of Special Operations and
    Pupil Personnel Services
Room 232
225 West State Street
Trenton, NJ 08625
(609) 292-4692

NEW MEXICO
Division of Special Education
State Department of Education
Education Building
300 Don Gaspar Avenue
Santa Fe, NM 87503
(505) 827-2793

NEW YORK
Office for the Education of Children
    with Handicapping Conditions
State Education Department
55 Elk Street
Albany, NY 12234
(518) 474-5548

NORTH CAROLINA
Division for Exceptional Children
State Department of Public Instruction
Room 352, Educational Building
Raleigh, NC 27611
(919) 733-4258

NORTH DAKOTA
Division of Special Education
Department of Public Instruction
State Capitol
Bismarck, ND 58505
(701) 224-2277

OHIO
Division of Special Education
State Department of Education
933 High Street
Worthington, OH 43085
(614) 466-2650

OKLAHOMA
State Department of Education
Special Education Section
2500 N. Lincoln Blvd.
Room 263
Oliver Hodge Building
Oklahoma City, OK 73105
(405) 521-3351

OREGON
Special Education
Oregon Department of Education
942 Lancaster Drive, N.E.
Salem, OR 97310
(503) 378-3598

PENNSYLVANIA
Pennsylvania Department of Education
Bureau of Special and Compensatory
    Education
P.O. Box 911
Harrisburg, PA 17126
(717) 783-1264

RHODE ISLAND
Rhode Island Department
    of Education
Special Education Unit
234 Promenade Street
Providence, RI 02098
(401) 277-3505

SOUTH CAROLINA
Office of Programs for the
    Handicapped
State Department of Education
Room 309, Rutledge Building
1429 Senate Street
Columbia, SC 29201
(803) 758-7432

SOUTH DAKOTA
Section for Special Education
Richard F. Kneipe Bldg.
Pierre, SD 57501
(605) 773-3678

TENNESSEE
Division for the Education of the
    Handicapped
State Department of Education
103 Cordell Hull Building
Nashville, TN 37219
(615) 741-2851

TEXAS
Department of Special Education
Texas Education Agency
201 East 11th Street
Austin, TX 78701
(512) 475-3501

UTAH
Division of Staff Development
Utah State Board of Education
250 East Fifth South
Salt Lake City, UT 84111
(801) 533-5982

VERMONT
Special Educational and Pupil
    Personnel Services
State Department of Education
Montpelier, VT 05602
(802) 828-3141

VIRGINIA
Division of Special Education
State Department of Education
1322-28 E. Grace
P.O. Box 6Q
Richmond, VA 23216
(804) 786-2673

WASHINGTON
Division of Special Services
Mail Stop FG11
Old Capitol Bldg.
Olympia, WA 98504
(206) 753-6733

WEST VIRGINIA
Division of Special Education and
    Student Support Systems
West Virginia Department
    of Education
Capitol Complex
Room B-315
Charleston, WV 25305
(304) 348-8830

WISCONSIN
State Department of Public Instruction
Bureau for Crippled Children
126 Langdon Street
Madison, WI 53702
(608) 266-3726

WYOMING
Office of Exceptional Children
State Department of Education
Hathaway Bldg.
Cheyenne, WY 82002
(307) 777-7411

There is also an organization called National Information Center for Special Education Materials (NICSEM). This computer-based organization has catalogs that list every available special education material and where to purchase it. For information write to: National Center on Educational Media and Materials for the Handicapped, USC University Park (RAN), 2nd floor, Los Angeles, CA 90007.

FREE FOR THE ASKING

Search for Solutions Teaching Notes

"Search for Solutions Teaching Notes" is distributed free, three times a year. It demonstrates ways to show students how to solve problems in math, science, or any other subject. This program also provides on a free loan-basis nine 18-minute films on searching for solutions. Teachers from all over the country also share favorite problem-solving techniques. Send a postcard to:

> Search for Solution Teaching Notes
> Playback Associates
> 708 Third Avenue
> New York, NY 10017

The Learning Works Catalog

This free catalog lists over 75 activity books for the primary and intermediate grade levels. The subjects range from the basics of math, science, art and reading to ones that target specific skills and special interests. Send a postcard to:

The Learning Works
Post Office Box 6187
Santa Barbara, CA 93111

Freebies

Many of the free items suggested in the *Almanac* were found by reading an excellent newsletter called "Freebies." This newsprint publication comes out six times a year and is full of very inexpensive or free materials. A year's subscription is under $10 and can yield at least that amount in free materials. It also makes very interesting reading. It is definitely a good buy for teachers. Write to:

Freebies Magazine
Post Office Box 20283
Santa Barbara, CA 93120

GOOD BUYS

The following items are suggested as good buys and can be used with September's teaching unit. Addresses of each publisher are included so you can send for free catalogs and ordering information.

Educational Clock Dial (No. 8062)

This is a heavy-duty square cardboard clock with movable metal hands. It has easy-to-read numbers, with useful teaching information on the back. Under $5. Write to:

Milton Bradley Company
Springfield, MA 01100

Clock Rubber Stamps

These rubber stamps outline a clock so that children can draw in hands and numbers. They are a good reinforcement to teaching time. Under $10. Write to:

Developmental Learning Materials (DLM)
440 Natchez Avenue
Niles, IL 60648

The Big Book Series

This collection of ready-to-use activities comes in easy-to-assemble form. It teaches math and language arts for grades 3–6. Write to:

Goodyear Publishing Co., Inc.
Santa Monica, CA 90401

Tutorgram

This is a compact electrovisual teaching aid that is easily portable and lightweight. It operates on two D-cell batteries and a standard flashlight bulb. Many ungraded programs (54 cards in each) are available. Unit sells for approximately $10 and the programs for approximately $15. Contact:

> ERCA
> Iron Ridge, WI 53035

Where I Am

This 32-page workbook offers independent map and orientation activities. Ungraded, you'll receive a set of 15 for around $25. Write to:

> Developmental Learning Materials (DLM)
> 440 Natchez Avenue
> Niles, IL 60648

Instructo Learning Centers

These Kits come in strong plastic packaging for easy storage, and include 3-dimensional visuals (easy to assemble), games, and worksheets. Kits are available on a variety of subjects and levels for grades K–6. Sells for about $15. Write to:

> Instructo Corporation
> 11 Cedar Hollow Road
> Paoli, PA 19301

PROFESSIONAL RESPONSIBILITIES

ORIENTATION TEA

Getting off to a good start with the staff at the beginning of the school year is very important. A good way to begin is to have an orientation tea either before school officially opens or during the first week or two of school.

Although refreshments are not essential, it certainly does add a warm and gracious touch. Serving something simple like tea and plain cookies goes a long way in setting the atmosphere. Often a school's petty cash fund can be used for the purchase of these refreshments either through the principal's office or the special services department. If a classroom parent system is used, parents may agree to donate baked goods. Use your judgment and follow school policy as to which route to pursue.

Invitations sent to each staff member rather than a notice on the bulletin board makes a friendlier impression. Be sure to set the date with the agreement of the school principal and any other administrator who may be involved in the program.

If your classroom is large enough, try to have the meeting there. This gives each teacher a chance to see where his or her mainstreamed students might be going and what they will be doing. Try to have many bulletin boards and learning centers set up for their perusal. This is also an excellent time to display professional books and materials that will be available for them to borrow. If the room is too small, the teachers' lounge or media center can be used.

A decision has to be made as to who will address the group. The principal or director of special services does seem to make things more official. This must be decided jointly, however, well before the meeting begins.

The following items should be discussed during the formal part of the meeting after refreshments have been served and the staff has had a chance to look over the room and materials.

1. Review the rationale for the special program. Stress the compliance with PL. 94-142 and other state requirements.

2. Explain dual-responsibilitiy of the special program and classroom teachers for each mainstreamed child's program.

3. Explain the Individual Educational Plan (I.E.P.) process and how each child's annual program has been decided in advance with the parent, teacher, special services professional and the child (when it is appropriate).

4. Acknowledge the concerns that teachers have about classroom disruptions when the child leaves and returns; missed classroom instruction; scheduling mix-ups, etc. Deal with each problem in an open and cooperative manner. You may want to point out that it is unfortunate when a student has to miss *anything*, but priorities must be set for each child. Hopefully, the concentration on remediating areas of weakness will help the student to succeed in regular classroom subjects.

5. Many unforeseen problems will arise. You will need information and cooperation from the other teachers in order to succeed with the children.

6. Announce a time each day when the teachers may drop in for an impromptu conference or to borrow available professional books or materials.

7. Discuss teacher conference times, how teachers will be notified, and what information they should have available at these conferences.

8. Let the teachers know that you want to be their "resource" in helping the special children in their classes.

PROFESSIONAL RESOURCE BOOKS

The following books should be available for both you and other staff members. They can be purchased through the school library (which is often open to suggestions for possible professional book purchases) or budgeted as part of the materials needed for the resource room.

Elman, Natalie. *The Resource Room Primer.* (Englewood Cliffs, NJ: Prentice-Hall, Inc., 1981)

Kaplan, Sandra N. *Change for Children.* (Pacific Palisades, CA: Goodyear Publishers, 1973)

Karlin, Muriel Schoenbrun. *Individualizing Instruction: A Complete Guide for Diagnosis, Planning, Teaching and Evaluation.* (West Nyack, NY: Parker Publishing Company, Inc., 1974)

Kephart, Newell C. *The Slow Learner in the Classroom.* (Columbus, OH: Charles E. Merrill, 1960)

Lloyd, Dorothy. *Seventy Activities for Classroom Learning Centers.* (Dansville, NY: Instructor Publications, 1974)

Ryan, Kevin, and James Cooper. *Those Who Can, Teach.* (Boston: Houghton Mifflin, 1975)

Siegel, Ernest. *Special Education in the Regular Classroom.* (New York: John Day Publishers, 1969)

Special Learning Corporation. *Mainstreaming Library.* (Guilford, CT: 1980–1982, updated every two years). Relevant series titles:
    "Special Education"
    "Learning Disabilities"
    "Mental Retardation"
    "Behavior Modification"
    "Emotional and Behavior Problems"
    "Deplexia"
    "Mainstreaming"
    "Psychology of Exceptional Children"

Swift, Marshall and George Spivak. *Alternative Teaching Strategies.* (Champaign, IL: Research Press, 1977)

Turnbull, Ann B., and James Shulz. *Mainstreaming Handicapped Students.* (Boston: Allyn and Bacon, 1978)

MODES FOR MAINSTREAMING

GETTING OFF TO A GOOD START

September is a difficult month for teachers. There are many new faces and personalities to know. Reading and math groups must be formed, and new programs learned and implemented. Often, the knowledge that children with special needs are included in the class roster is not met with great enthusiasm by the regular classroom teacher.

Any pressure you can take away from the classroom teacher at this time will pay back many dividends later. You might:

a. Pick the children up from their classrooms the first week or so. This eliminates the classroom teachers' responsibilities for reminding them about coming.

b. Teach the children their mainstreamed schedules (see "Teaching Units") and impress upon them the need for assuming responsibility for their own schedule. Let the teacher know either in person or via a note that this will be your procedure.

c. Do not observe in the classroom except for emergency situations the first month. Teachers need time to feel comfortable with their new class and program.

The following mainstreaming suggestions should be sent via a memo the first month of school. Later, school conferences and I.E.P. meetings can be scheduled.

1. Place children with attention or sight problems close to the teacher.

2. Write directions on the chalkboard for children with auditory problems.

3. Use visual clues while teaching children with auditory problems.

4. Make allowances for handwriting quality for children with visual-motor problems.

5. Use special materials (which you can lend out) for children with any special problems.

6. Remind particular students to wear their glasses or hearing aids.

7. Suggest reading a file immediately on a particularly difficult child.

It is wise to delay reporting special problems that can wait until next month. It is your responsibility, however, to be sure the classroom teacher is advised about any special problems for which he or she is held accountable and may have forgotten in the hustle and bustle of the first days of school. (See the following sample.)

Sample Memo

Dear Ms Lafky,

I know this is a particularly busy time for you! I just wanted to alert you to the fact that John Smith, a mainstreamed student, is reported to have a very short attention span and needs to be seated as close to you as possible. We'll discuss other approaches to John's problems when you have more time. I hope the opening of school goes smoothly for you.

Sincerely,

Liz Rose

P.S.
2:00–3:00 each day has been set aside for teacher consultations in the resource room. Come visit!

Let the teacher know when you will be calling parents that first week or so of school (see "Tip of the Month") so you can add any comments about the child's classroom performance on the teacher's behalf.

TIP OF THE MONTH

PHONE HOME

One of the responsibilities of a good special education teacher is to establish good rapport with the parents of the children involved in the program. One technique that starts out the school year on the right foot is to call each child's home during the first week of school. For this call you have one purpose in mind—*to say something positive.* Let the parents know that you have seen their child, you are aware of his or her needs, and you are developing an individual program. Explain that you are spending much of the time during the first weeks of school orienting the child to the new school year and their special program. Stress the fact that remediation of their child's deficits will be done in a variety of ways. Inform them that their child seems to be making a good adjustment to school and, most of all, you are aware of their child's existence! Let them know that conferences will be scheduled soon to go over the child's program in detail. Invite the parents to call you at school if they have any questions or comments about their child. Leave them with a positive feeling; unfortunately, many parents of special children have not received many positive phone calls about their child. Yours may be the first!

A FINAL WORD

MAKING UP WORK

It often becomes apparent early in the school year that teachers feel uncomfortable about children missing work in the classroom. A conscientious teacher feels responsible for covering the school curriculum, so when a mainstreamed child leaves the classroom to go to a special program, he or she is "missing" some of that curriculum. The question then arises, "How does the child make it up?"

Depending upon what the student has missed, decisions have to be made. To begin with, careful scheduling should avoid conflicts with subjects like reading or math. These are basic subjects and should not be missed. However, if the student is so far behind his or her classmates that he or she cannot fit in an existing reading or math group, the special program time can be scheduled to take over the teaching of that subject. The classroom teacher then knows that you are totally responsible for the child's program in that subject. It can be made clear that the grade for that subject will be given by you and so designated on the report card.

The best approach is when students can receive their basic math and reading instruction in the classroom and receive remediation and support in a special program. Whenever possible, a student should be able to stay in the mainstream.

A dilemma arises when a student comes to a special program while other subjects, such as social studies, language arts or science, are being taught in the classroom. What should be made up and what should be ignored? Depending upon the extent of a child's disabilities, priorities must be set. Not only must they be set with the agreement of the classroom teacher, but the parents must also understand for which subjects their child will not be held responsible.

A handicapped child who goes home with additional work to "make up" because he or she was receiving remediation becomes resentful. Not only does the child's attitude become a poor one, but often the added burden of more work leads to feelings of defeat and ultimate failure. This is certainly the antithesis of what a special program promises to provide.

Hopefully through in-service programs (see "Professional Responsibilities" for December), teachers and parents have an understanding of learning disabilities. Arguments such as, "Time spent on remediation now will allow Johnny to be able to learn social studies more productively later" are helpful. Trying to teach grade-level subjects to a child who is reading two years below grade level is not really productive. Teachers need to understand this. Writing busy work to a child who has difficulty with handwriting is torture for that child. It places added emphasis on his or her weakness and feelings of frustration.

You must help the classroom teacher to understand a child's deficits and modify the programs accordingly. Try to include as many of these classroom modifications as you can in a child's I.E.P. at the beginning of the year. This helps the classroom teacher to plan in advance and know that an official plan is being followed.

SEPTEMBER REFERENCES

Bartlett, John. *Bartlett's Familiar Quotations.* (Boston: Little Brown and Co., 1955)

Goertzel, Mildred and Victor. *Cradles of Eminence.* (Boston: Little Brown and Co., 1962)

Hart, Michael H. *The 100, A Ranking of the Most Influential Persons in History.* (New York: Hart Publishing Co., Inc., 1978)

Josephson, M. *Edison, a Biography.* (New York: McGraw-Hill, 1959)

Kenin, Richard, and Justin Wintte. *The Dictionary of Biographical Quotations.* (New York: Alfred A. Knopf, 1978)

The Oxford Dictionary of Quotations. (New York: London Oxford University Press, 1953)

Runes, D.D. *The Diary and Sundry Observations of Thomas Alva Edison.* (New York: Philosophical Library, 1948)

Thompson, Lloyd, J., M.D., "Language Disabilities in Men of Eminence." *Journal of Learning Disabilities*, January 1971.

October

****

Happy birthday to . . .

1 Captain James Lawrence (1781) "Don't give up the ship," he said as he was carried off the *Chesapeake.* Wounded by a musket ball in 1813, Captain Lawrence knew his crew could go on fighting without his leadership. Celebrate the birthday of this wise captain by doing one day's classwork completely on your own. Don't give up the ship!

2 Mohandas Gandhi (1869) 1930: Gandhi walked to the sea. It was against the law, then, to use salt not bought from England. But people of India wanted to make salt from their own sea water and were proud to make it themselves! Hundreds walked with Gandhi to the sea to make salt and to prove that the law should be changed. IT WAS!

3 Gertrude Berg (1899) "Yoo hoo, Mrs. Bloom!" began a show called *The Goldbergs.* Gertrude Berg, star of the show, began her career writing and starring in America's second most popular radio show. With warmth and humor she helped her family and neighbors solve their problems, so do the same and help a classroom neighbor solve his or hers!

4 Edward Stratemeyer (1862) What is an alias? Some authors have aliases or pen names. Edward Stratemeyer had many. When he wrote the series about the Bobbsey Twins, he called himself "Laura Lee Hope." He was "Carolyn Keene" for the Nancy Drew Mysteries and "Franklin Dixon" for The Hardy Boys. Pen a story series and sign it with your secret name!

5 Robert Goddard (1882) and Ray Kroc (1902) Sales sky-rocketed when Ray Kroc's "golden arches" lit the sky. Millions of people have eaten McDonald's hamburgers. Rocket scientist Goddard would have loved one! He knew rockets could reach the moon, but people laughed and called him "moon man." Still, he imagined rockets soaring upon the great arches of the sky.

6 Thor Heyerdahl (1914) "Weeks passed. We saw no sign (of) people in the world. The whole sea was ours." Thor Heyerdahl and his crew bravely survived 100 lonely days of strange beasts and ocean currents to prove they, as did ancient people, could safely raft from Peru to Polynesian Puka Puka. Measure those long, lonely nautical miles.

7 Alice Dalgliesh (1893) The cloak kept her warm as she would have been when her mother's arms quieted her fears. Sarah's cloak comforted her when she felt afraid, as most of us do when we are left alone. Alice might have had fears like Sarah's in *The Courage of Sarah Noble*, too! Read her story and wear her cloak of courage!

8 Edward ("Eddie") Rickenbacker (1890) Honor "Eddie" with paper plane races, for speed was his game. At 16 he won the racing car record of 134 m.p.h. A daring pilot of a soaring, rickety biplane, he spun and side-slipped in dogfights over France while 26 German pilots lost to his machine gun. His name? Rickenbacker, air ace of WWI.

9 Otto Young Schnering (1891) For just 5¢ you could have bought a Baby Ruth or a Butterfinger candy bar. Nearly 70 years ago, Otto Young Schnering made the first wrapped candy bars and you can still buy them—but no longer for 5¢. To celebrate Otto's birthday, cut 35¢ candy bars into 5¢ slices. How many 5¢ slices could Otto have cut?

10 Giuseppe Verdi (1813) An opera is a sad or funny play in which the words are sung to orchestra music. Young Giuseppe wanted to write opera but music school would not let him study there. His first opera failed, but HE TRIED AGAIN! This time he was successful. Tell the story of the greatest Italian composer in a famous saying!

11 Henry Heinz (1844) There's a catchy number on a catsup bottle. Does it catch your ears? Henry Heinz thought it would. It did! He wanted everyone to buy foods with 57 on the label, though it did not mean there were 57 varieties of foods! Think of a catchy ad for a brand new brand of catsup that everyone will catch on to!

12 Elmer Sperry (1860) Surging billows tossed the crew of the Santa Maria who saw flaming eyes of monstrous serpents in the boiling waves. Sperry, born 400 years after Columbus' first voyage, invented a GYRO-STABILIZER which would have kept the battered ship upright in angry waters and its crew calmly on course in 1492.

13 Mary Hays McCauley (1754) Mary was carrying cool water to the men, tired from the heat of battle in the blazing sun. She heard John Hays cry out! He fell, wounded. Quickly she took his place! Mary was a Revolutionary War heroine that day at the Battle of Monmouth, June 28, 1778. Write an "emblematic poem" about Mary. Shape it like her nickname!

14 President Dwight D. Eisenhower (1890) President Eisenhower was Commander-in-Chief of the U.S. forces and Commander of Allied Forces in Europe in World War II. When he was young, his mom, who didn't believe in battle, wouldn't let him read about it! But we read books that tell about battles he commanded to end an unbelievable war.

15 Dr. William Menninger (1858) It's National Grouch Day! It's O.K. to grumble today but not every day! Doctors William and Karl Menninger knew that people who worried too much grumbled, so they helped them to worry less and to grumble less, too. Let the last hour of school be "grouch hour." Swap grins for grumbles as you leave from home.

16 Noah Webster (1758) A hundred years have scarcely passed,/Since Noah Webster wrote his speller./When everybody bought one/It became that year's best seller (1783)./To find the perfect spelling/Of a word now, do not tarry,/You'll still learn how to spell it/From a Webster's dictionary!

> Order and simplification are the first steps toward mastery of a subject—The actual enemy is the unknown.
>
> Thomas Mann

17 Jupiter Hammon (1711 or -12) A slave poet? A note on his book told its readers that the poetry was good—so good they might doubt it had been written by a slave. But so it was, and today, on Black Poetry Day, we remember Jupiter Hammon, America's first black poet. Write a verse to tell of your feelings "Upon Slavery."

18 Richard Nash (1674) Beau Nash set the fashions! What he wore, everybody wore. Six horses drew his chariot. With a huge white hat, embroidered coat, shoes and socks (he didn't like boots) and blaring French horns, Nash announced his new clothes. Blue French jeans could have been the rage in Bath, England, 1700 if Nash had only known!

19 President John Adams (1735) Just because John Adams became president doesn't mean he wanted to go to school every day! In fact, he invented "ditching." When he didn't want to study, his father suggested ditching! So he dug and dug. After 2 days, and big blisters, John said he really DUG learning Latin over digging ditches!

20 Mickey Mantle (1931) Who, in spite of painful, diseased legs, was baseball's American League home run leader for 4 years, 1956 Triple Crown winner and holder of the 19___ World Series home run record? Mickey Mantle learned switch-hitting from his dad, Mudd. You might switch his baseball card for another—carefully! His 1952 bubblegum card is worth thousands!

21 Alfred Nobel (1833) Might the same person who invented explosives give prizes for peace? Inventor Nobel gave great sums of money to those who worked nobly to bring peace among nations. And publisher Joseph Pulitzer, too, awarded prizes for excellence. Almanacs print lists of people who have earned PRIZES with pride!

22 Franz Liszt (1811) Many composers were excellent pianists when they were very young. At 9, Liszt left home to study piano. The best of pianists, he was named "King." But unlike most kings, he gave his money to others who needed help. Help your library buy a tape chosen from a list of Liszt's compositions.

23 Edson do Nascimento (Pelé) (1940) His dad taught him to kick a soccer ball of rags in a dusty street in Brazil. Now Edson do Nascimento is the extraordinary Pelé! Even a war in Africa was cancelled for the day of his soccer game. Pelé can tell where his opponent will run. Do the same in checkers. Think. Where will your opponent move?

24 Sarah Hale (1788) To think of thanks, to thank for thoughts/Of turkey brown and smelling fine,/To slowly chew a thousand chews/And think of forest thick with pine,/To know that first Americans/To give thanks did they just the same./To thank, next month, our Sarah Hale/Who got for thee that day we call, THANKSGIVING!

25 Pablo Picasso (1881) War is cruel. Pablo Picasso painted a mural called GUERNICA to show us that. With no words, the huge painting tells us how war feels. His famous work of art hangs in a New York museum, for Picasso wished that it hang only in peaceful countries. Place red dots on war zones to find where in the world "Guernica" cannot go!

26 Phillis Wheatley (1753) and Mahalia Jackson (1911) They both told the world of freedom; Wheatley in poetry and Jackson in gospel song. Phillis Wheatley was the first woman slave to publish a book of poetry in America. Mahalia Jackson sang gospel music, shouting, rocking, swaying and clapping to bring the hope of civil rights to all people in our land.

27 President Theodore Roosevelt (1858) Swirling water, man-eating fish, poisonous insects, rotting foods, sickness and terrible jungle heat nearly killed all 20 men who rowed Brazil's 600-mile River of Doubt. This last hunting trip was Teddy Roosevelt's most difficult. The river gave Teddy a dangerous adventure but he gave it HIS NAME.

28 Dr. Jonas Salk (1914) Eleanor Roosevelt (born on October 11) was President Roosevelt's "legs." She walked where he could not for he had had polio. Years later, Jonas Salk, in 19___, found the vaccine which stopped the terrible disease. If he had discovered it ___ years earlier, Roosevelt might not have spent ___ years in a wheelchair!

29 Othneil Marsh (1831) Marsh went to Kansas and old bones did find,/Small bodied creatures of SAURIAN kind./With high crested skull and neck craned for stooping,/Four long fingered claws, huge 27-foot bat wings for swooping./A toothless curved beak with wide snapping bite!/Hang PTERANADON to terrorize Halloween night.

30 Irma Rombauer (1877) Can't say "no-thanks" now! October is apple, popcorn, pizza and salty pretzel month. It's World Food and School Lunch Days and "restaurant eating" time, too! Taste a treat for Rombauer who joyfully wrote *The Joy of Cooking* cookbook. Say "yes, please" to terrific recipes of trick-or-treat tasties!

31 Juliette Low (1860) She always sent a message to scouts on her Halloween birthday. Juliette Low began scouting for girls after meeting Baden-Powell (2/22). With his idea and her unending energy, troops were joined everywhere! "Day is done" when Low had to convince parents scouting was good for girls. Now, "All is well."

These birthographies were prepared by Davida Shipkowitz of Northridge, California.

SPOTLIGHT ON

WOODROW WILSON (1856–1924)

Woodrow Wilson certainly meets all the criteria to be featured as Spotlight personality for this month. He was a great achiever who had early handicaps to overcome. All historical indications of Wilson's early life are that he was a bright child who had a difficult time learning how to read. His contributions to society as president of both Princeton University and the United States of America were enormous. Learning about his early difficulties certainly reinforces the concept that learning disabled persons can overcome their problems and make great achievements.

Wilson was the 28th president of the United States. He was credited with making the United States a nation of power and an influence in world affairs.

He is recorded to have been a scholar, a teacher, president of Princeton University, and governor of New Jersey. He was a statesman who was recorded in history as believing in the dignity of people and democracy the world over.

While president of Princeton University, he started reforms which included the honor system and replaced large lecture classes with small study groups. This brought him much national attention.

As governor of the state of New Jersey, Wilson took his programs to the people and broke the control of strong political machines.

Wilson's term of office as President was 1913–1921. In that time, history recorded the following events:

Passage of direct election of senators

Income tax

Federal Trade Commission

Clayton Act

Panama Canal opened

U.S. enters war in Europe

Federal farm loan act

Russian Revolution

Prohibition

League of Nations introduced

Woman suffrage

As Lloyd J. Thompson in his article, "Language Disabilities in Men of Eminence," says,

"It may seem almost absurd to suggest that a brilliant man who became president of Princeton University and President of the United States could have any kind of language disability. And yet the Goertzels reported as follows:

'Woodrow Wilson did not learn his letters until he was nine, or learn to read until he was eleven, because his father read to him. He could hardly wait for Woodrow to learn to read the books he himself enjoyed and wanted his son to enjoy. The brilliant and verbal minister kept the boy home, read to him, explained the meaning of what he read, then asked Woodrow's reaction to the ideas in the book. . . . There are letters from relatives who thought it odd that young Woodrow was so dull and backward and expressed sorrow for the parents.' '' (p. 5)

In his biography of Wilson, Lawrence wrote that at eighteen Wilson attended Davison College in North Carolina for a year, but returned home broken in health. As a young student Wilson was not a star. Out of a class of 122 he graduated 41st. His record in the literary and debating societies, however, was conspicuous.

In his 19th year he entered Princeton University and graduated in 4 years. Henry W. Bragdon (1967) in his biography reported that Woodrow's grades at Princeton were little better than mediocre, but he also noted that Wilson was recognized as an excellent orator and debater.

> "Considering the general brilliance of this man, his IQ must have been 130 and his mental age two or three years beyond his chronological age. Conservatively stated then, he had the mentality of an 11 year old when he was "taught his letters" and the general intelligence of a 13 or 14 year old boy before he learned to read. Surely this marked delay in learning his letters and in learning to read cannot be attributed to "being read to" or to poverty of stimulation. Many moderately bright children learn to read on their own initiative before entering the first grade at age of six." (Thompson, 1971)

Sigmund Freud and William C. Bullitt published a psychoanalytic interpretation of Wilson's life. In this fascinating account it clearly leads the reader to believe that Woodrow Wilson had an abnormally close relationship with his father and lived out his life fulfilling his father's expectations of him. As was his father, Wilson became an outstanding orator. Thompson states in his article,

> "dyslexics frequently become fluent speakers, perhaps, in part, as a compensation for poor facility in reading and writing."

Nevertheless, Woodrow Wilson, whatever his early learning problems, overcame them. He became an accomplished writer, speaker and most of all, a leader. A staunch believer in democracy he is credited with the following:

> "Sometimes people call me an idealist. Well, that is the way I know I am an American. America is the only idealistic nation in the world."

SPOTLIGHT BULLETIN BOARD

This is designed to be a permanent bulletin board or poster where the featured person is changed each month. If bulletin board space is not available, posterboard affixed to a door or wall can be used.

Materials:

white background paper
black marker
overhead projector
acetate transparency
transparency marker

Preparation:

1. Cover the bulletin board with white construction paper.

Spotlight on
Woodrow Wilson 1913-1921
28th President of the USA

2. Trace the "Spotlight" bulletin board (see page 44) onto clear acetate using a transparency marker.

3. Project the transparency onto the bulletin board.

4. Trace the outline onto the white construction paper and color in with the marker.

NOTE: An American flag on a stand placed next to the bulletin board can be used instead of the one drawn on the board. This not only saves time, but adds a three-dimensional quality.

Also, for a more colorful and patriotic bulletin board, you might use red, white and blue.

BULLETIN BOARD IDEAS

FALL

This bulletin board is at its best in vivid fall or Halloween colors. The choice is up to you, so feel free to improvise in any way you want. You can use either markers or construction paper to fill in the colors.

Materials:

worksheets

white background paper

markers: black for the outline, title, the witch, the ghost, the bat, and owl

orange for the pumpkin with black outline

red for the apples and spider

brown for the tree

green for the bush

orange and green alternating for the house trim

silver for the spider web

acetate transparency

transparency marker

overhead projector

stapler

17″ × 24″ piece of orange construction paper (for worksheet envelope)

Preparation:

1. Cover the bulletin board with large sheets of white construction paper.

2. Trace the bulletin board illustration onto an acetate transparency with a transparency marker. (NOTE: If an opaque projector is used, this step can be eliminated.)

3. Project the transparency from the overhead projector onto the bulletin board.

4. Trace the outline of the picture with a black marker.

5. Fill in the outlines with either markers or construction paper using the colors listed under "Materials" or of your own choice.

6. Place the construction paper envelope on the board with staples.

a. Fold a 17″ × 24″ piece of orange construction paper in half.

b. Place this on the bulletin board (see the illustration) in the lower right hand corner.

c. Staple along the sides directly onto the board. Be sure to leave the top open to slip in the worksheets.

FALL WORKSHEET (PRIMARY*)

Objective:

Children will pick out hidden pictures on the fall worksheet to improve visual closure skills.

Directions:

1. Instruct the children that there is a bonus "Find the Fall Words" worksheet this month for those who finish their work early.

2. Point out the worksheets in the envelope on the Fall bulletin board.

3. First the students circle the hidden words.

4. Then, they may color the picture and bring it home.

SUCCESS

Reinforcing organization skills is the purpose of the Success Bulletin Board. It is an excellent motivational device for eliciting a discussion on what goes into successful learning for students. The idea of a recipe for success appeals to young and old alike.

Materials:

white background paper

large clothespin or colorful plastic paper clip

red construction paper for apples

green construction paper for leaves

white construction paper for recipe card

aluminum foil for cake pan and mixing bowl

beige construction paper for pie crust

black marker

acetate transparency

overhead projector

transparency marker

Preparation:

1. Cover the bulletin board with the white construction paper.

2. Trace the bulletin board illustration onto an acetate transparency with a transparency marker.

3. Project the illustration onto the bulletin board.

---

*Although this is designed to be a primary-level activity, all ages seem to enjoy this fun worksheet.

Find the Fall Words

Name: _____

Search the picture. Find the Halloween words.
Color the picture.

bat	ghost	broom	tree
hat	boo	witch	apple
cat	owl	pumpkin	leaves

4. Pin up a piece of red construction paper underneath projection of an apple and use to trace the outline of the apple.

5. Cut out the apple and leaves, and use as the stencil to cut out remaining apples and leaves.

6. Follow the above procedure with the aluminum foil for the bowl and pie tin and the beige construction paper for the pie crust.

7. Write out the success recipe with black marker on the piece of white construction paper.

8. Outline the detailing on the pie, spoon and bowl with the black marker.

9. Attach the clothespin or paper clip at the lower right hand corner with double-faced tape, staple or thumbtack (whichever holds best). Place the recipe on the board using the pin or clip.

10. Write out the study tips on the apples with black marker and place on the board with staple or doublefaced tape.

11. Adjust arrangement of objects to make a pleasing display.

NOTE: For smaller or large bulletin boards, decrease number of items or make them smaller or larger by moving the overhead projector closer or further away when making the stencils.

TEACHING UNIT

ORGANIZATION SKILLS

All special students require programs based on their individual needs. Depending on the goals and objectives set forth in each IEP, plans for instruction must be made.

Regardless of the remedial and academic needs of the students, certain basic study skills must be acquired by all students who are attempting mainstreamed placement in the regular classroom. Good organization, basic study skills, and a way to ask for help are necessary for classroom success. These lessons on organization skills are meant to supplement rather than replace individual program designs.

October is the time to make sure students have gotten off to a good start and are keeping up with their work. Review of last year's work is just over by this time and new material, assignments and homework are being presented. Children with learning problems often begin to have difficulties now, so helping them to organize their work both in school and at home is essential.

Objectives:

At the conclusion of this unit students will be able to:

- Keep a record of their daily work.
- Know when homework assignments are due.
- Have an organized and useful notebook system.
- Be able to evaluate their own progress.
- Be more aware of when they need help with their work and know a system to alert their teacher.

Organizing a Notebook (intermediate-advanced)

Materials (for each student):

3-ring looseleaf notebook
3-hole lined notebook paper
3-hole subject dividers
hole puncher
pencil
scissors

Preparation:

If the above materials are not part of the regular supplies for each student in your school, you might want to send a note home to the parents a week in advance of this unit asking that each child bring in the supplies.

Directions:

1. Have each student practice opening and closing the notebook rings.

2. Working on one index divider at a time, have the student copy the subject headings from the chalkboard onto the dividers.

3. Have each student divide the lined paper into equal sections according to the number of subjects in the notebook plus one (for assignments).

4. Ask the student to put each divider and the alloted paper in place in the notebook.

5. Have each student cut the remaining paper vertically down the center. (See the illustration.)

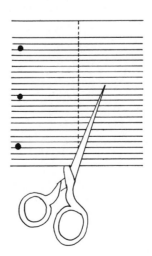

6. Using the hole puncher, help each child to add the 3 holes in the appropriate spots on the unholed side of the cut paper.

7. Place these "skinny" sheets at the back of the notebook to be used for assignments.

Reinforcement Activities:

Refer to "Learning Centers" and have your students do assignments 1 and 2.

Using the Assignment Sheet (intermediate-advanced)

Materials:

    prepared notebook for each child (from previous session)
    pencils
    acetate transparency
    transparency marker
    overhead projector
    chalkboard or screen

Preparation:

Place the overhead projector so that it will project on a clean chalkboard or screen.

Directions:

1. Have each child turn to the assignment section at the back of the notebook.

2. Instruct each student to label the first sheet: ASSIGNMENTS. Write this word at the top of the acetate transparency for students to copy.

3. Give the next directions in a role-playing fashion. For example:

I am Ms. Schmidt and I am giving you your math homework. Get your pencils ready!

First: The date. (Write the date under Assignments on the acetate. Allow students time to copy.)

Next: The subject. (Write MATH on the acetate. Allow copying time.)

Next: The assignment. (Write it on the acetate and allow copying time.)

Continue in this fashion, giving page numbers, problems and new subjects. For the first exercise, allow the students to copy the information from the overhead. Give them as much time as needed.

4. Check each of the students' assignment sheets for accuracy and following directions.

5. Repeat the procedure in Step 3 as often as needed for the students to understand.

6. Turn off the overhead projector.

7. Now repeat Step 3 *without* using the overhead, having students write from oral presentation only.

8. Write the assignments you have just given orally on the chalkboard.

9. Help the students to check their written assignments against the board assignments and fill in left out material or change mistakes.

10. Repeat steps 7-9, changing the assignments until the level of proficiency is acceptable.

11. Explain to the students that this method must be used daily in the classroom. Each child must find the best way for him or her to be sure he or she is getting the assignments written down properly.

12. Some students will have to be on a monitoring system whereby their classroom teacher initials the assignment sheet before the students go home each day. (See "Modes for Mainstreaming.")

Reinforcement Activities:

Refer to "Learning Centers" and have your students do assignments 3 and 4.

<u>*Long-Term Assignments (intermediate-advanced)*</u>

Materials:

2-month worksheets for each child

large calendar from which to copy

hole puncher

pencils

chalk

chalkboard

acetate transparency

transparency marker

overhead projector

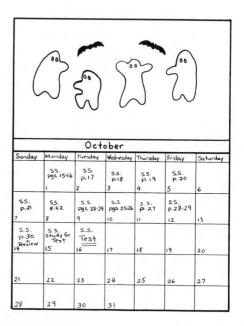

Preparation:

1. Copy two calendar worksheets (see page 56) for each child. (Be sure to fill in the dates for the current year.)

2. Set up a large calendar of October on the chalkboard ledge (or attach with tape).

3. Write a sample of a long-term assignment on the chalkboard. For example:

October 1 – <u>Social Studies</u>

Read pages 15–30.

Take test on October 16.

4. Draw or copy a replica of the calendar worksheet on the acetate transparency. Fill in the dates for appropriate days. (See the sample here.)

Directions:

1. Distribute one calendar worksheet to each student.

2. Using the master calendar, have students copy in the dates for the day of the month starting in the appropriate box.

3. Instruct students to:

    a. Write the numbers in the lower left-hand corner (leaving room for the assignments).

    b. Write in the name of the month.

    c. Draw an appropriate month design in the designated box, such as ghosts for October.

    d. Use a hole puncher to make holes to fit the size of their notebook.

NOTE: Teachers may prefer to fill out each month in advance and copy these worksheets for each student. Although this saves time, filling out each day in the proper sequence according to a fixed calendar helps reinforce calendar comprehension skills *for many students*. (This can be done independently. See Learning Center 5.)

4. When the calendar is complete, draw the students' attention to the assignment on the chalkboard.

5. Show them how to divide up the assignment into small units. For instance: pages 15–30 = 16 pages and October 1–16 = 16 days. That means one page per day.

6. Remind students that they need time for review and study. Write on the board:

$$
\begin{array}{r}
16 \text{ days} \\
- \underline{1} \text{ day for review} \\
15 \text{ days} \\
- \underline{1} \text{ day for test study} \\
14 \text{ days left for reading}
\end{array}
$$

7. Explain that depending on how much homework they have on a given night, students may change their reading assignments accordingly. The important thing is not to leave all the reading, reviewing and studying to the last night before the test or assignment is due.

8. Allow students to work out their own schedule on the monthly worksheet they just finished. Then put a new assignment on the board for them to work out on the second worksheet.

9. Check the students' worksheets to be sure they understand.

10. Let the students erase and work out more assignments if they need the reinforcement.

Reinforcement Activity:

Refer to "Learning Centers" and have your students do assignment 5.

Keeping Track of Work
and Getting Help (primary-advanced)

Materials:

"Staying Afloat" worksheet

pencils

assignment pad from notebook

paper for primary-level students

Preparation:

1. Copy the "Staying Afloat" worksheet for each child.

2. Alert students a day in advance to bring in their notebooks.

3. Confer with the classroom teachers. (See "Modes for Mainstreaming.")

October

Sunday	Monday	Tuesday	Wednesday	Thursday	Friday	Saturday

4. Set up a permanent place in the room to keep the worksheets for the students to take daily.

Directions:

1. Distribute the worksheets. Allow time for the students to look them over.

2. Explain that S.O.S. are the letters used internationally, particularly by ships and aircraft, as a distress signal.

3. Point out the flag on the sinking ship, which is the international flag used at times of trouble when help is needed.

4. Encourage discussion about asking for help. You may want to highlight with the following questions:

    a. When is it time to ask for help and when is it appropriate to keep trying on your own?

    b. Who do you ask for help?

    c. How do you ask for help?

    d. How do you think you might use the "Staying Afloat" worksheet to help you do this?

5. Tell the students:

    a. The left part of the worksheet is used to check off the work they have done at home. (Practice doing this.)

    b. The right half of the worksheet can be cut off and handed to the teacher. This will be done when a student doesn't understand the work or is taking an inordinate amount of time to finish.

    c. It is a good idea to clip the homework ditto or work paper to the SOS form. In this way the teacher knows exactly with what the student is having problems.

    d. The SOS part of the sheet can also be used for classroom work with which the student needs help. It can be given to the classroom teacher or the special program teacher (depending on what has been decided by both teachers in advance).

6. Show students where the "Staying Afloat" worksheets will be kept. When possible, arrange for a place within each classroom for "Staying Afloat" worksheets to be kept for the special students. This avoids some of the "I forgot" excuses. Explain that they must take one each day that they have homework. These forms will be handed into their classroom teacher each day with their homework papers.

7. Give the students time to work out a "practice" worksheet, using yesterday's assignments from their assignment pad.

> NOTE: For primary students, modify the lesson to show them how to use the SOS check-list when they need help.

Reinforcement Activity:

Refer to "Learning Centers" and have your students do assignment 6.

Staying Afloat

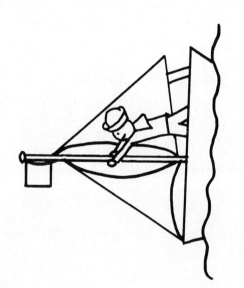

Please, help me with:

☐ Math
☐ Reading
☐ Spelling
☐ Social Studies
☐ Other
☐ Long Term Assignments

Signed _____

S.O.S.

Please, help me with:

☐ Math
☐ Reading
☐ Spelling
☐ Social Studies
☐ Other
☐ Long Term Assignments

Signed _____

LEARNING CENTERS

(1) PUTTING THINGS IN ORDER
(PRIMARY-INTERMEDIATE)

Materials:

worksheet

markers

3 small boxes or jars

1 large box

5″ × 8″ index card

crayon, pencil, pen, scissors, glue, tape, chalk, ruler, small book, paper, barrette, comb, brush, lipstick case, small mirror, nail file, package seeds, small hoe, small shovel, watering can, and small package of gardening dirt

Preparation:

1. Place all items in the large box.
2. Label 3 smaller boxes or jars: HOME, SCHOOL, and GARDEN.
3. Label the larger box: THINGS.
4. Write the directions on the index card.
5. Copy the worksheet (see page 60) for each student.

Directions Card:

PUTTING THINGS IN ORDER

1. Take each item out of the THINGS box.

2. Place each item in one of the three boxes where it belongs.

3. Before you return each item to the THINGS box, draw it in the proper box on your worksheet.

4. Have your worksheet checked by the teacher.

---

(2) FOLLOWING DIRECTIONS
(INTERMEDIATE)

Materials:

5″ × 8″ index card   cassette tape

marker   cassette player

worksheet   earphones

Name _____

Draw the objects in the correct box.

School

Home

Garden

Preparation:

1. Write the directions on the index card.
2. Copy the worksheet for each student. (See the sample on page 62.)
3. Record dialogue on the cassette tape. (Sample dialogue is given.)

Directions Card:

```
┌─────────────────────────────────────────────────────────────┐
│                    FOLLOWING DIRECTIONS                       │
│  1. Put on the earphones and listen to the directions.       │
│  2. Complete the worksheet.                                   │
│  3. Give your completed worksheet to the teacher.            │
│  4. Wait for further directions.                             │
└─────────────────────────────────────────────────────────────┘
```

Cassette Dialogue:

Teacher records the following:

1. Following directions is an important skill to have and will help you to be more organized.

2. Be sure you have your worksheet and a pencil in front of you. If not, press STOP and get the things you need.

3. Find a spot in the room. Decide how you would give someone directions to that spot without telling that person where it is in advance.

4. For instance, take three steps to the right, turn left, walk straight ahead. You will be at the pencil sharpener.

5. You may write your directions on your worksheet. Start your directions from the place you are now sitting.

6. On the back of your paper, write the spot you have chosen.

7. Your directions will be tried by someone else. Be as accurate as you can. Turn your paper in when you finish.

8. Turn off the recorder and begin.

NOTE: As the worksheets are handed in, they can be exchanged by the teacher with other students and the directions tried.

(3) ASSIGNMENT WRITING
(ADVANCED)

Materials:

5″ × 8″ index card	earphones
cassette tape	"skinny" assignment paper
tape recorder	pencils

Following Directions

Name _____

Put an X on the spot where you are now sitting.

Directions to a mystery spot:

First, _____

_____

_____

_____

_____

Preparation:

1. Write the directions on the index card.
2. Record dialogue on the cassette tape. (Sample dialogue is given.)

Directions Card:

ASSIGNMENTS

1. Put on the earphones and listen to the tape.
2. On the "skinny" paper, write the assignments as you hear them.
3. Rewind the tape when you finish and listen to the tape again to check your work.
4. Give your assignment sheet to the teacher.

Cassette Dialogue:

Teacher records the following:

1. You will write out the assignments I give you. Be sure you have "skinny" paper in front of you and a pencil. If not, press STOP.

2. Today is Tuesday, October 3. Your reading assignment is: Read pages 6–10. Answer questions 1–5 on page 10.

3. Your math assignment is: Practice your 5 times table.

4. Review Chapter 1 in Social Studies for a test on Friday.

5. There is no Science homework tonight. That's it!

6. Rewind the tape and listen to the assignments again while you check what you have written.

7. Give your assignment sheet to the teacher.

(4) COPYING ASSIGNMENTS FROM THE BOARD
(INTERMEDIATE-ADVANCED)

Materials:

5″ × 8″ index card
"skinny" assignment paper
chalkboard
chalk

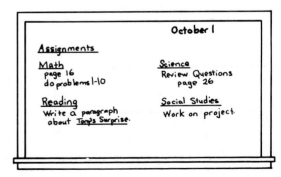

Preparation:

1. Write the directions on the index card.
2. Write the assignments on the chalkboard for copying. (A sample is shown here.)
3. Cut notebook paper in half vertically for "skinny" paper.

Directions Card:

```
┌─────────────────────────────────────────────────────┐
│              COPYING ASSIGNMENTS                     │
│  1. On assignment paper copy assignments from the board. │
│  2. Check your work for mistakes.                   │
│  3. Hand in finished assignment sheet to the teacher. │
└─────────────────────────────────────────────────────┘
```

(5) MAKE-A-MONTH WORKSHEETS
(INTERMEDIATE-ADVANCED)
2-Day Station

Materials:

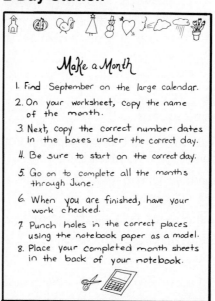

month worksheet

September–June calendar

pencil

crayons or markers

oaktag

hole puncher

3-hole paper

Preparation:

1. Copy 9 month worksheets for each student. (Refer to "Long-Term Assignments" under "Teaching Unit.")

2. Place the commercial calendar in the middle of the learning center.

3. Write the directions on an oaktag poster. (See the illustration.)

(6) S.O.S.
(INTERMEDIATE-ADVANCED)

Materials:

5" × 8" index card

"Help" worksheets

pencil

Preparation:

1. Write the directions on an index card.

2. Copy a "Help" worksheet (see page 65) for each student.

Help!

Name _____

1. List 5 examples of when a person might need help.

_____

_____

_____

_____

_____

2. Write a paragraph telling when you needed help at one time.

_____

_____

_____

_____

_____

3. List 5 examples of when you <u>should</u> ask for help from your teacher.

_____

_____

_____

_____

_____

Directions Card:

```
                        S.O.S.
  1. Read the directions on the worksheet carefully.
  2. Complete the worksheet.
  3. Have your work checked by the teacher.
```

MATERIALS OF THE MONTH

An excellent source for materials for your special program that you might not have thought about is your very own school storage room. Often overlooked, school storage rooms contain many previously used textbooks that can be excellent supplements to helping students with current work. Unused workbooks are especially useful since lower-level editions can be used without the students being so acutely aware that they are from a lower grade.

Many times, discarded room dividers (perhaps needing minor repairs), bookcases and other much-needed paraphernalia for your room can be found hiding in this untapped resource called a storage room.

Occasionally, principals or custodians (whoever has control of the keys) are somewhat resistant to allow teachers free rein in the storage room. Having a list of needed materials handy (like the textbooks or workbooks mentioned above) and a frank discussion with them about budget constraints might bring success. It's certainly worth the try.

There are several books now available devoted to listing free or inexpensive materials. One excellent book is *1001 Valuable Things You Can Get Free* by Thelma Weisinger (New York: Bantam Books, 1982), which sells for under $5. A must for bargain-hunting teachers, it is full of free items from manufacturers and the government. Another inexpensive paperback is *Freebies Book: Hundreds of Things You Can Get Free (Or Almost Free)* by ASAE (New York: Holt, Rinehart & Winston, 1981). This paperback sells for under $10. Check with your school or public library to see if a copy is available.

For those interested in catalogs of every variety to buy wholesale goods, look through *The New Wholesale by Mail Catalogue* by The Print Project, published by St. Martins Press Inc., New York, NY, 1982. This 8½" × 11" paperback sells for under $10. It lists over 300 companies from which you can buy almost anything at 30%–90% off retail prices —by mail. Not only are the bargains excellent, but the free catalogs are an interesting supplement to many subjects being taught. They make excellent reference books for teaching survival skills.

FREE FOR THE ASKING

Kodak's Teaching Tips From Teachers

This is a free 52-page book compiled by Eastman Kodak Company which gives over 250 ways to use photography in the classroom. Send a postcard to:

The Eastman Kodak Company
343 State Street
Dept. 841
Rochester, NY 14650

Free Date Book

Pocket sized, this Hallmark date book has an excellent format for keeping track of assignments (featured this month). It contains a place to file dates and events of importance plus many other useful features. Free copies are available in most card and stationery stores. (A kind request of the store manager usually yields enough date books for 20–30 students.)

Official Birds, Mammals, Trees, Flowers, Insects and Fish

You'll find over 300 choices of all the 50 states in an informative chart. This is an excellent resource to discover the official bird, mammal, tree, flower, insect and fish of each state! An informative and fun chart, it can be displayed and discussed in your classroom. Send a postcard to:

National Wildlife Federation
Dept. 001
1412 16th Street, NW
Washington, D.C. 20036

GOOD BUYS

The following materials are suggested as good buys and are chosen to be used with October's "Teaching Units" and "Learning Centers."

Strategies in Study Skills

Tapes, worksheets, and response sheets are included in these resources. They are available on dictionary skills, reference skills, information, sentence composition and paragraph composition. The worksheets and tapes can be used independently at a learning center. Sells for about $100. Write to:

Milton Bradley Company
Springfield, MA 01100

Successful Learning Kit

Hundreds of items to individualize instruction are included in the *Kit*. These are good resource materials for a wide variety of learning centers, primary–intermediate. Costs approximately $150. Contact:

Love Publishing Co.
6635 East Villanova Place
Denver, CO 80222

Charlie Brown Dictionary by Charles M. Schulz

Written in the "Peanuts" format, it is an excellent introduction to the dictionary for primary–intermediate students. It is a good resource book for independent dictionary skill learning centers. Costs about $20. Write to:

Prentice-Hall, Inc.
Englewood Cliffs, NJ 07632

Organization Skills Workbook

This is a soft cover workbook that covers sequencing, outlining, organizing paragraphs, and organizing story sequences. It is excellent for intermediate- to advanced-level students. Ten workbooks and a teacher's guide sell for about $25. Write to:

> Curriculum Associates
> 8 Henshaw Street
> Woburn, MA 01801

Flying High with Discovery for Intermediate Grades
by Virginia Hamilton and Charlotte Fisher

Learning center ideas are included with reproducible worksheets for all subject areas. It is an inexpensive tool to supply a wealth of ideas to use in your special program. Costs about $25. Contact:

> Discovery Learning
> P.O. Box 1114
> Burlingame, CA 94010

MCP Skill Booster Series

Using a colorful work-a-text format for levels A–E (primary-advanced), the series' titles are *Building Word Power, Increasing Comprehension, Working With Facts and Details, Organizing Information,* and *Using References.* Costs about $3 per workbook. Write to:

> Modern Curriculum Press
> 13900 Prospect Road
> Cleveland, OH 44136

PROFESSIONAL RESPONSIBILITIES

TIME FOR TEACHERS

It is essential to keep in close communication with the classroom teacher. In order for a special program to be successful, the classroom teacher must be kept fully informed about the child's progress and be able to confer with you when questions arise in the classroom.

There are two successful ways of doing this: (1) regularly scheduled private conferences with the classroom teacher; and (2) a set time each day or each week when you are available for materials or impromptu conferences.

Having a set time with the classroom teacher on a regular basis either daily or several times each week has many benefits because problems do arise in between regularly scheduled conferences. Catching you on the "run" or at lunch time does not provide the privacy or forum for openness that is needed.

Remember that materials to supplement those being used in the classroom for the mainstreamed child need to be accessible. Having professional reference books on hand to help a classroom teacher is certainly encouraged.

All in all, from a public relations point of view as well as one that is educationally sound, regularly opening your room to teachers is a good idea.

At the beginning of the school year, when scheduling children, block out a time each day or as many times a week as your schedule allows. Having the same time each day, such as 2:30–3:00 p.m., allows teachers who have planning periods at varying times throughout the week to get to your room eventually. Of course, you will never find a time that is perfect for everyone; inevitably, there will be at least one teacher who has a conflicting schedule. For those teachers, make every effort to plan a special time either before or after school or during one of your free planning periods. *Never* discourage communication with teachers! Good staff interaction is essential to a successful program and cannot be stressed enough. Be sure to send a notice to the teachers informing them about these scheduled times.

Next, have an area set up before the teachers arrive which is conducive to:

1. private communication
2. easy perusal of materials
3. easy check-out system
4. professional growth

This means, have adult chairs set up with a table, if possible, for the classroom teacher and you to be able to talk comfortably. In case other teachers happen to arrive at the same time and a private conference is going on, have a chair or two outside your room for them to wait. Avoid turning anyone away. Having a notepad or small chalkboard for messages near your door for teachers who prefer not to wait is a good idea. Have paper and pencils at the conference area as well.

A bookcase which is solely for the purpose of lending materials and professional books is perfect. Cabinets, closets and even portable cardboard cases can be successfully used, stored and re-used each day.

An index card file with each book or material listed in alphabetical order is an easy and useful way for teachers to check out materials or books. They can use the back of the card to write their name and date and refile it. In this way, the materials can be located quickly if needed. (Ask a parent volunteer to catalog the lending material on the index cards.)

NOTE: Be sure all books and materials are stamped or labeled in some way. Unfortunately, things have a way of disappearing if they're not labeled.

Hopefully there will be a budget to buy professional books. (See each month's "Professional Resource Books.") If there is no budget, perhaps the school library or media center can purchase some of them. If all else fails, you can borrow professional books from local college libraries, city libraries, state learning resource centers, and even hospital libraries. Sometimes these libraries have a lending service from library to library and will lend books directly to your school.

If possible, set aside a place in the teacher's corner of your room to post interesting articles about special education or notices of classes or meetings being held. If your room is large enough to have a permanent teacher's corner, you can place a cardboard screen in front of it when not in use.

Finally, be sure the environment you provide is one of openness. The physical arrangement described here sets the stage, but your attitude is far more important. Every communication you have with the classroom teacher, whether in the halls, the lunchroom or the parking lot, will have a bearing on your professional relationship. Keep it as positive and supportive as possible. As trite as it sounds, behind every successful special education program is a dynamite teacher!

PROFESSIONAL RESOURCE BOOKS

Collins, Myrtle and Dwayne Collins. *Survival Kit for Teachers (and Parents).* (Glenview, IL: Scott, Foresman, 1975)

Lucas, Virginia and Walter Barbe. *Resource Book for the Special Education Teacher.* (Columbus, OH: Zaner Bloser, 1982)

Newman, Thelma. *Change Over—Breakthrough to Individualism.* (State of New Jersey: Department of Education, 1964)

Smith, Sally L. *No Easy Answers—The Learning Disabled Child.* (U.S. Department of Health, Education and Welfare, Publication No. ADM 80-526, 1980)

Vitale, Barbara Meister. *Unicorns Are Real.* (Rolling Hills Estates, CA: Jalmar Press, 1982)

MODES FOR MAINSTREAMING

CLASSROOM TEACHER CONFERENCES

Regularly scheduled conferences with the classroom teacher are the best method for an ongoing information exchange about the special program students. Many states require them in their special education codes, but whether required by law or not, a procedure for holding these conferences should be built into your program.

Four to six weeks is a good time period between conferences as long as the classroom teachers have the opportunity to informally discuss problems in the interim.

There sometimes is a problem about "when" to schedule these conferences. Depending upon the attitude of the staff, you might schedule conferences during a teacher's planning period. The special program children can be excused from your program on conference day and by scheduling teachers according to their planning periods, most can be seen in one day. Those who are unavailable on conference day can be scheduled either before or after school or during another free period the two of you have in common on another day.

Choosing the conference day is best facilitated by checking the roster of planning periods for the day when the largest number of teachers are involved. There is no point in choosing a day when several teachers are not free and need to be rescheduled.

If the classroom teachers are unhappy about giving up planning time for the conference, there are other possible alternatives.

1. A "floating" substitute can be hired to go from class to class depending upon when the teachers are scheduled for their conference. This, of course, is solely determined by whether funding is available to pay for these monthly substitutes and if the administration is willing to pay for them. This must be negotiated.

2. Conferences can be scheduled only before and after school. This sometimes is less preferable than using planning time.

3. If none of the above arrangements are acceptable, meet with the staff and brainstorm a conference time solution. Having resentful teachers at a conference yields very little in the way of positive interaction.

Once the conference is in session, make the most productive use of time. Have on hand:

1. Prewritten notes on items that need to be discussed.

2. Two conference forms (see page 72) for each student with a carbon in between. One is kept in the student's special program file and the other given to the classroom teacher.

3. Any of the student's test scores or actual test booklets that the teacher should see.

4. Special program work the student has done that would be relevant to the conference.

5. Notes from parents that would be appropriate for the teacher to see.

As the conference proceeds write in any facts, suggestions or modifications of the child's program on the conference form. Giving the teacher a copy at the end of the conference is not only a good way of keeping track of changes in the student's program, but is a written reminder of what was discussed for the classroom teacher. NOTE: Proposed changes in a student's program can be reported to administrators by sending them a copy of the conference form.

If you have decided to use the "Staying Afloat" worksheet (see this month's "Teaching Unit"), use the conference to explain the worksheet, which encourages the special student to keep track of his or her own progress. Encourage the teacher to have these worksheets stored in the classroom for the students in the class. Decide at this time whether the classroom teacher or you will be the one to accept these forms from the student. Explain that although the worksheet should be handed in with the daily homework, you will collect them from the teacher if necessary. (Be sure to have a supply of these worksheets to give to the teacher at the conference.)

TIP OF THE MONTH

DISCRETION

As a special education teacher, you are privy to a great deal of confidential information. You hear and see many "war stories" from being in the classroom, reading files, and talking to parents. It is imperative that teachers and parents feel confident that these stories will not be repeated. Be very aware of any references you make about what takes place in other classrooms. Your credibility as a trusted colleague and professional can be destroyed by the knowledge that you repeat classroom business to other teachers or parents. Make every effort to keep information received and observations confidential.

Going into the classroom and getting honest input from the teacher is important to the success of your program. Sharing some idle gossip is clearly not worth the price of jeopardizing others' confidence and trust in you.

Conference Form

Student's Name _____

Teacher's Name _____

Date _____

Areas of Concern _____

_____

_____

_____

_____

Suggestions _____

_____

_____

_____

_____

Modifications to try _____

_____

_____

_____

_____

_____

_____

_____

_____

A FINAL WORD

CLASSROOM OBSERVATIONS

Classroom observations are a necessary part of a special educator's job. Students must be seen in a classroom milieu in order to know what areas need correction. The child whose reading ability seems to be way above his or her functioning level in the classroom may have a distractability problem, which can only be discovered by observing that behavior. In addition, the suggestion of simple classroom modifications can alleviate many problems. These suggestions can only be made after an observation visit. Sometimes just letting the student know that you have seen him or her functioning in the classroom reinforces the idea that his or her progress is a joint interest.

In order to make this observation a positive experience for you and the teacher, here are some techniques you can use:

1. Try to keep your eye contact on the students, *not* the teacher. This will reinforce the fact that you are evaluating the students, not the teacher!

2. Leave a note with the teacher that reflects the student's behavior. For instance, "John seemed to enjoy the story today" or "Gladys sure has trouble sitting still!" This is another way to reinforce your emphasis on the student's performance rather than the teacher's.

3. Be sure you make a note of the visit in the student's file. At the classroom teacher's conference, you can make mention of it.

4. Suggestions of possible classroom modifications should be done in a positive way. *Never* criticize an approach the teacher has used in the classroom. Only suggest positive supplements to what the teacher is already doing. For instance:

> "It might be helpful to Michael if you write the assignment on the chalkboard in addition to telling him. A multi-sensory approach seems to be a good way for him to get information."

Just keep in mind that the approach must always be a positive one.

OCTOBER REFERENCES

Baker, Ray Stannard. *Woodrow Wilson, Life and Letters.* (New York: Doubleday, Page and Co., 1927)

Bartlett, John. *Bartlett's Familiar Quotations.* (Boston: Little Brown and Co., 1955)

Bragdon, H.W. *Woodrow Wilson: The Academic Years.* (Cambridge: Harvard University Press, 1967)

Britannica Junior Encyclopedia. (Chicago: Encyclopedia Britannica Inc., 1971)

Freud, Sigmund, and William C. Bullitt. *Thomas Woodrow Wilson.* (Boston: Houghton Mifflin Co., 1967)

Goertzel, Victor, and Mildred Goertzel. *Cradles of Eminence.* (Boston: Houghton Mifflin Co., 1962)

Lawrence, David. *True Story of Woodrow Wilson.* (New York: George H. Doran Co., 1924)

Thompson, Lloyd J. "Language Disabilities in Men of Eminence." *Journal of Learning Disabilities*, January 1971.

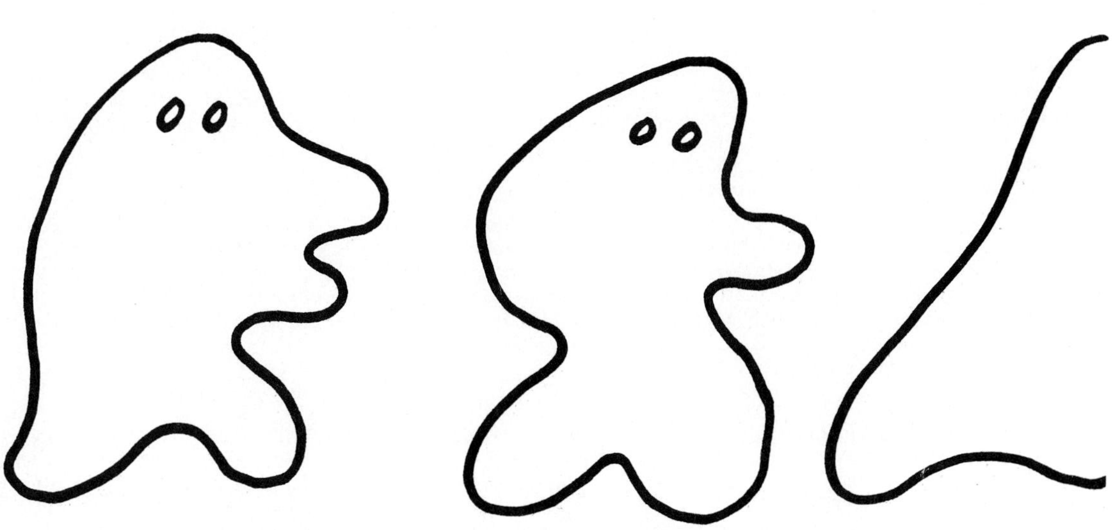

November

Happy birthday to:

1   Dr. Crawford Long (1815)   1844: Dentist Horace Wells said that breathing ether might make pulling teeth painless. 1846: William Morton tried it. As predicted, his patient felt no pain. But we proudly present first prize to Crawford Long whose three patient patients felt perfect during surgery two years prior. Put dates in proper order, please!

2   Daniel Boone (1734)   When captured by the Indians/Boone heard a woeful plan./The tribe would soon attack his town/So he escaped and ran./Four days the Indians gave chase/Four days he kept the lead./He beat the bunch to Boonesboro,/The townsfolk all gave heed! Retell the beginning middle, and end of the poem in pictures.

3   John Montagu (1718)   It's John Montagu's birthday party. The menu? A sandwich! Food between 2 slices of bread is credited to Montagu, the Earl of SANDWICH (a tiny English town). And, please wear a cardigan sweater. Though it is NOT the birthday of John Brudnell, he was the Earl of Cardigan and designed the button-up!

4   Walter Cronkite (1916)   To get the news, Walter Cronkite had to go where the news began. Since 1937, he has covered nearly every important world event. People said they never believed any news till Walter said it! Celebrate Cronkite's birthday. Cover a campus story and report what really happened on "Cronkite's Classroom News."

5   Paul Sabatier (1854)   Butter! Margarine. Butter? It's Sabatier's magic that keeps taste from telling the difference. Sabatier churned an important page in food history when he found the trick of turning plant oil (cotton, corn, safflower) into fake butter! Compare margarine from various plants.

6   James Naismith (1861)   No better time than "Creative Adult Month" to nominate Naismith for a #1 contribution to American sports. When? 1891. Where? Springfield, Massachusetts. Why? To keep troublesome students out of trouble, this P.E. teacher was asked to invent a game. It was basketball and the game won their interest! Win class interest — create a game!

7   Madame Marie Curie (1867)   Madame Curie could not be cured. She had a kind of cancer called LEUKEMIA. Marie worked long years to prove that radium could be taken out of pitchblend and could help cure cancer. But too much radium gives cancer, too, and Marie became ill. Sadly, Curie could not be cured, but through her work, others could.

8   Hermann Rorschach (1884)   Fold a sheet of paper, open it, drip a drop of ink on the fold, and crease! Display the designs! With secret ballots, name each. Rorschach asked people to name 10 ink blots. That was his way of helping people talk about their troubles. Only psychologists can give that test but you can be a namedropper!

9   Benjamin Banneker (1731)   We remember, in this almanac, a writer of almanacs, Benjamin Banneker. A genius of mathematics, he learned astronomy to forecast the weather or tell farmers when shadows would darken the sun. His fondest fun/Was writing some/Story math in rhyme./To honor Ben/Write some and then/Solve each, one at a time!

10   Sam Howe (1801)   Learn how type was used in Boston to teach blind children to read. Dr. Howe's raised letters were read by touch. Louis Braille touched upon another idea. His patterns of dots meant letters that were more easily read. Get an insight into touch type. "Write" words in both and read with feeling!

11   Maude Adams (1872)   Dreams don't always come true, even for Peter Pan! Maude Adams, who played Peter Pan in James Barrie's play, wished for a color-film of the tale. She helped a company build lights for night scenes. Her dreams faded but the play, which you may read, will never lose its colorful story!

12   Elizabeth Cady Stanton (1815)   Women gathered at the first Women's Rights Convention in the United States. Stanton knew that laws were not the same for women as they were for men. Women couldn't vote, own property, or go to college. Stanton knew women should have those rights. Did Susan B. Anthony think those rights were right or wrong?

13   Robert Louis Stevenson (1859)   Practice makes perfect! Stevenson practiced day-in-and-day-out to be the perfect teller of tales. Perfect are the pirates of TREASURE ISLAND and perfectly frightening are DR. JEKYLL AND MR. HYDE. For Children's Book Week, present a verse picked from his perfect GARDEN OF VERSES!

14   Robert Fulton (1765)   It wasn't yellow but Fulton designed one! Dive down this SUB (under) MARINE (sea) history to see when the sub comes up: Leonardo Da Vinci 1500, William Bourne 1578, Cornelius Van Drebbel 1624, David Bushnell 1776, Robert Fulton 1796, Robert Whitehead 1864, Simon Lake 1894, J.P. Holland 1898. . .

15   Sir William Herschel (1738)   T'was a wondrous sight and he named it King George! William Herschel saw the planet, now called Uranus, for the first time through a 7-foot telescope he alone had built. Telescope building was his hobby. Happily, his hobby became his whole life's work. Honor astronomer Herschel. Have a "Hobby Holiday"!

> Reading is to the mind what exercise is to the body.
>
> Sir Richard Steele

16 Burgess Meredith (1909) He really has fans! Actors always do. But HOLY ADVERSARY! He does have one enemy — Adam West. Well, maybe not in real life, but on TV when West plays Bruce Wayne (sh! BATMAN!). Not so secret are Batman's enemies: the Penguin (Meredith), and Catwoman, Joker, and Riddler. Who are they, really?

17 François Appert (1749 or -50) Bonaparte fed an army. But food rotted fast in the heat of the battle. Napoleon offered a prize to the cook who conquered the task of preserving food. Appert, who heated food and sealed it tightly from air, gets credit for canning! Giving a can to a holiday food collection can say thanks to François!

18 George Gallup (1901) Ask 100 people (about the same age) one question. How many say YES? How many NO? Gallup polls, like yours, ask a question. In June, 1971, Gallup asked, "Is there life on another planet?" 53% (or 53) people said YES. 47% (or 47) said NO. "Gallop" around campus. Operate your own poll. Publish opinionated opinions!

19 Ferdinand de Lesseps (1805) A man, a plan, a canal: Panama! That PALINDROME is about Ferdinand de Lesseps who planned the Panama Canal! Like a palindrome which can be read L to R or R to L, ships could go from W to E or E to W through the canal instead of going all around South America. When asked if he planned it, he said, "I ___ ___ ___"!

20 Peregrine White (1620) The first new baby in the new colonies of New England was Peregrine White. The parents left England so Peregrine could grow up with the RIGHT to worship as the child pleased. On that day, 339 years later, the U.N. declared that all children have that right, and more! Read THE RIGHTS OF THE CHILD!

21 William Beaumont (1785) An unlucky Canadian was shot. His stomach could be seen and William Beaumont, army surgeon, could learn how food is digested. Lucky for doctors, for they now could help people who were sick because they did not digest food properly. And lucky for you! You can learn the steps of digestion from a book!

22 Charles Berlitz (1913) At Berlitz's schools you learn languages! Listen: Hungarian (<u>Bol</u>-dog <u>Su</u>/le/tesh/nah/pot), Hebrew (<u>Yom</u> <u>Ho</u>/led/et <u>Sah</u>/mã/ach), Russian (<u>Shas</u>/tin/e/vay <u>Poz</u>/d nã/ah), French (<u>An</u>-i-ver-sar <u>Yu</u>-ro), Italian (<u>Fe</u>/les <u>Coom</u>/ple/ah/ nos), and . . . Happy Birthday Berlitz! Bring other language greetings to learn, too!

23 Harpo Marx (1893) You bet your life! You said the secret word, FAMILY! It's National Family Week — a marvelous time to remember Momma Minnie and The Marx Brothers in their mad musical comedies. Chico, Groucho, Gummo, Harpo and Zippo always managed to impress Momma, especially Harpo. It's no secret. Why did Harpo have a harp?

24 Henri de Toulouse-Lautrec (1864) and Scott Joplin (1868) Lautrec was to art as Joplin was to music. Lautrec painted pictures of faces. "A Picture of Her Face" was a Joplin song. Lautrec drew rushing rhythms of dancing feet and Joplin wrote ragtime rhythms for tapping toes. STOP! LOOK at Lautrec's ladies and LISTEN TO "Maple Rag." Can you "see" can-can dancers dance?

25 Andrew Carnegie (1835) Believing that a rich man's money, not needed by his family, should be given to others, Andrew Carnegie's millions bought books for thousands and helped universities teach hundreds of students. In Civil War days, Carnegie built telegraph lines. Dot and dash off a note to say, "Andrew, thanks a million!"

26 Will Shuster (1893) and Charles Schulz (1922) There's a Charles Schulz TV special for Thanksgiving, Halloween, Arbor Day — and lots more! The characters are special, too: Charlie Brown, Linus, Lucy, Pig Pen and Snoopy. Will Shuster created another special character. Who, wearing a forest ranger's hat, asks us all to be especially watchful for SMOKE?

27 Chaim Weitzman (1874) Mother knows best! Chaim Weitzman's mother "knew" that her 6-year-old would someday be president. When the U.N. delegates voted to call Israel a country, everyone wanted Weitzman to be the first president. In his speech he remembered his dear mother's dream. Ask your mom what she dreams you will be!

28 John Wesley Hyatt (1837) Practically everything is, or can be, made of plastic. Place "P's on stickies and a stickie on everything plastic in the class. That would certainly please John Hyatt. He probably didn't predict that the plastic he produced would be as popular. Predict — then precisely count plastic parts at home.

29 Louisa May Alcott (1832) LITTLE WOMEN made her famous. She was Jo — the others were her sisters. She took care of her family. Her father could not. Alcott's books taught that women must work very hard. Louisa did just that. This little woman with a big heart nursed the wounded and nearly lost her life on the battlefield of the ___ War.

30 Samuel Clemens (Mark Twain) (1835) He read sitting up but he wrote lying down! Mark Twain was in the habit of writing in bed! Robert L. Stevenson did the same. George M. Cohan (July 4) wrote only while riding on a train and some writers gave their clothes away until their work was done! Try Twain's writing habit. Write a tall-tale on your tummy!

These birthographies were prepared by Davida Shipkowitz of Northridge, California.

SPOTLIGHT ON

HELEN KELLER (1880–1968)

Reading skills are highlighted this month. Learning to read can be a laborious and sometimes overwhelming task, and for children with learning problems it is even more so.

Helen Keller was chosen this month's Spotlight personality because she represents someone who overcame almost insurmountable obstacles in order to learn. Her life story and that of her teacher can serve as an inspiration to student and teacher alike.

Although Helen's multiple handicaps seem overwhelming to most of us, her achievements are outstanding. Before reaching the age of two, an illness, which was diagnosed as "brain fever," destroyed her sight and hearing. The loss of her hearing so young did not allow her to develop enough language or memory of the spoken word to speak. For the next five years she grew up totally shut off from the rest of the world. Her early years were, as she herself reports in *The Story of My Life*:

> "wild and unruly, giggling and chuckling to express pleasure, kicking, scratching, uttering the choked screams of the deaf-mute to indicate the opposite."

Shortly before Helen's seventh year, Anne Sullivan came to live with the Keller family and teach Helen. This dedicated teacher changed Helen's life. Through persistent and patient teaching, using the senses Helen had, Anne Sullivan miraculously taught Helen Keller how to talk, read and write! By age 16 she was able to go on to preparatory school and then to Radcliffe College. She graduated with honors in 1904. Anne Sullivan, except for a two-year respite, spent the rest of her life with Helen.

The story of Helen Keller is a story of a woman who rose above her disabilities to become an author and lecturer of international fame. She was responsible for helping handicapped people around the world live fuller lives.

She is credited with the following:

Author of: *The Story of My Life* (1903)
The World I Live In (1908)
Out of the Dark (1913)
My Religion (1929)
Midstream: My Later Life (1930)
The Song of the Stone Wall (1950)
Teacher (1955)

(All translated into 50 languages)

Received: Chevalier's Ribbon of the French Legion of Honor
The Alumni Achievement Award of Radcliffe College
Decorations from governments all over the world
Honorary degrees from Temple University

Active in: Massachusetts Commission for the Blind
National Commission of the Blind
American Foundation for the Blind

Visiting the sick and wounded in military hospitals.

Going on goodwill tours all over the world.

Starting The Helen Keller Endowment Fund of $2,000,000.

Working with blinded soldiers in World War II.

Breaking the code of language changed Helen's entire life. Learning how to read opened up a new world for her, as she so aptly wrote in *The Story of My Life*:

"Literature is my Utopia. Here I am not disenfranchised. No barrier of the senses shuts me out from the sweet, gracious discourse of my book-friends. They talk to me without embarrassment or awkwardness."

Her life epitomized that of a caring altruistic human being who did so much for mankind. Her enthusiasm and love for helping others is expressed in the following quote:

"Science may have found a cure for most evils, but it has found no remedy for the worst of them all—the apathy of human beings."

NOTE: See "Materials of the Month" for a free chart on signing for the deaf.

SPOTLIGHT BULLETIN BOARD

Materials:

white background paper
black marker
overhead projector
acetate transparency
transparency marker

Preparation:

1. Place the background paper on the bulletin board. (See "Tip of the Month.")

2. Trace the "Spotlight" bulletin board onto clear acetate using a transparency marker.

3. Project the transparency onto the bulletin board.

4. Trace the outline onto the white background paper. Color in with a black marker.

NOTE: Although color can be used, the use of black and white is a very effective backdrop for Braille.

BULLETIN BOARD IDEAS

HELP HARVEST A WELL-READ APPLE

This bulletin board not only emphasizes the crisp apples of fall and the Thanksgiving bounty, but is in keeping with this month's theme—reading skills.

Spotlight on

I left the well-house

eager to learn. Everything

had a name, and each

Helen Keller
1880—1968

This is a student participation bulletin board which involves the students in reading new books and reporting them on the apple tree. They can also keep a file of the books they have read on the worksheet on page 83.

Objective:

The children will read books for pleasure.

Materials:

calico design fabric, wrapping paper or self-adhesive paper

brown construction paper for the tree

beige construction paper for the basket

green construction paper for the cart and the leaves

red construction paper for the apples

large envelope or manila folder

black marker for title and outlining the details

tacks

opaque projector

scissors

copy of bulletin board

stapler

Preparation:

1. Cover the bulletin board with the calico design.
2. Project the design onto the board.
3. Place the appropriate colored paper in front of the projected design. Tack it up and draw the outline of the design.
4. Cut out the designs.
5. Outline with a marker and write the directions on the basket and cart.
6. Write the book titles on a few of the apples and place them on the tree as an example.
7. Staple a large envelope or manila folder to hold the worksheets.
8. Make copies of the worksheet on page 82 and place them in the envelope on the bulletin board.

WE GIVE THANKS

This bulletin board is designed to incorporate the spirit of Thanksgiving with the values of learning and knowledge. Counting one's blessings at this time of year should include all those vehicles which bring truth and knowledge to the student. Since reading skills are featured in November, a bounty of books cascading from a horn of plenty has been chosen.

Help Harvest a Well Read Apple

Big Red

The Judge

Big City Tom

Little Women

Lentil

Donna

When you have finished your book harvest your apple.

Worksheets

Write your name on an apple. Place it next to the book you have chosen to read.

NAME

Books I Have Read.....

Name _____

Draw in the apples.
Write the name of a book on an apple.
Color.

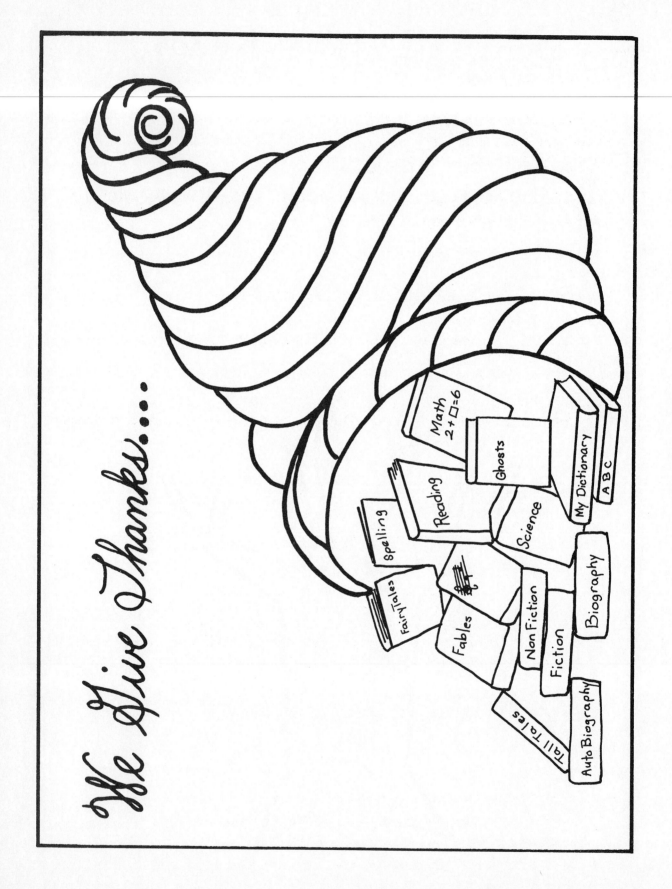

We Give Thanks...

Math 2 + □ = 6
Ghosts
Reading
My Dictionary
ABC
Spelling
Science
FairyTales
Non Fiction
Biography
Fables
Fiction
Tall Tales
Auto Biography

Materials:

gold construction paper

brown construction paper for the horn of plenty

black or brown marker for outlining details and writing the title

a variety of construction paper for books or actual book jackets (NOTE: school libraries usually keep book jackets on file and can be borrowed)

tacks

opaque projector (if an overhead projector is used, a copy of the bulletin board must first be transferred onto an acetate transparency)

scissors

Preparation:

1. Back the bulletin board with the gold construction paper.

2. Project the design of the bulletin board onto the board.

3. Tack the brown construction paper in front of the projected design of the horn of plenty. Draw the outline.

4. Cut out the design.

5. Outline the horn of plenty and the title with a marker.

6. Either construct, draw in with a marker or use book jackets to show the books coming out of the horn of plenty.

TEACHING UNIT

READING SKILLS

The teaching of reading must be very individualized. Depending upon the learning strengths and weaknesses of a student as well as his or her ability level, a specialized reading approach must be found. For example, if the child has a severe auditory discrimination problem, a sight reading approach is best. A phonetic approach, of course, would be considered for a child who is stronger in the auditory skills and weaker in visual memory. The approach to teaching reading must be geared to maximize the use of the strongest learning channels of each student. This promotes the quickest success and the least amount of frustration.

The following teaching unit gives examples of some ways to supplement a basic individualized reading program.

Objectives:

At the conclusion of this unit, students will:

• Be more aware of the position of the letters in the alphabet.

• Be more aware of the uses of a dictionary.

• Be able to relate beginning word sounds to letters.

- Be able to place letters and words in alphabetical order.
- Be able to copy sound patterns.
- Be able to pick out inappropriate words in a story.
- Be able to skim for basic facts in a story.

Now I Know My ABC's! (primary)

Materials:

magazine, coloring ABC book or catalog pictures to go with each letter in the alphabet (examples: A, apple; B, ball; C, cat; D, drum; E, egg; F, fish; G, gun; H, hat; I, igloo; J, jack-o-lantern; K, kite; L, lemon; M, Mother; N, nut; O, octopus; P, pie; Q, question mark; R, rain; S, sign; T, toy; U, umbrella; V, violin; W, witch; X, xylophone; Y, yo-yo; Z, zebra)

NOTE: A very effective lesson is to use small plastic toys instead of pictures. This takes considerably more effort to find and additional expense, but is a one-time purchase and can be used many times.

worksheets for each student

pencils

crayons

primary dictionaries for each child

regulation wall-mounted alphabet cards

Preparation:

1. Cut out pictures and mount on oaktag or construction paper. Laminate, if possible.

2. Label each picture.

3. Copy the ABC Worksheets on pages 87–89.

4. Place the pictures—not in alphabetical order—around the room, such as on the chalkboard ledge, on the windowsills, etc.

5. If not already there, place letter wall cards in alphabetical order on a wall or above the chalkboard.

Directions:

1. Introduce the alphabet. Ask if anyone has ever heard the ABC song. Allow a volunteer to sing it for the group. (You may have to sing it for the group.)

2. Ask, "Are the ABC's always in the same order?"

3. Point out by using the alphabet letter cards in the room that the letters have a special order. They are always the same.

4. Ask, "Why do you think having an alphabet in a special order is important?" (filing, dictionaries, encyclopedias, lists of children in the plan book, etc.)

5. Distribute the classroom dictionaries to the group. Let the students see the order and compare to the order of the letter cards.

6. Talk about which words would go with a few sample letters, that is, A—apple, etc.

ABC Worksheet

Name_____

Write in the name of each item that begins with
the alphabet letter below. Draw the picture.

Aa apple _____

Bb _____

Cc _____

Dd _____

Ee _____

Ff _____

Gg _____

Hh _____

Ii _____

Name_____

Jj _____

Kk _____

Ll _____

Mm _____

Nn _____

Oo _____

Pp _____

Qq _____

Rr _____

Ss _____

Name _____

Tt _____

Uu _____

Vv _____

Ww _____

Xx _____

Yy _____

Zz _____

7. Distribute the ABC Worksheets.

8. Point to the picture cards around the room.

9. Explain that the students are to write in or draw a picture of the correct item to go with each letter.

10. Collect the worksheets when completed.

Reinforcement Activities:

Refer to "Learning Centers" and have your students do assignments 1 and 1A.

Alphabetical Order (intermediate)

Materials:

worksheets for each child

alphabet letter cards in alphabetical order

pencils

crayons

paste

scissors

Preparation:

1. Copy both worksheets (see pages 91 and 92) for each child.

2. Be sure the alphabet letter cards are in the proper order along the ledge of the chalkboard.

Directions:

1. Point to the alphabet cards on the chalkboard ledge.

2. Have a group member read the alphabet.

3. Ask if someone else would like to recite the alphabet without looking.

4. Ask a volunteer to give a word to go with each letter of the alphabet.

5. Distribute the worksheets to each student.

6. Explain:

a. Students are to find an object in the picture to go with each letter of the alphabet on ABC Scramble on page 91.

b. Students are to first write the letters in alphabetical order.

c. Students are to cut out the object and paste it onto the second worksheet (page 92) in alphabetical order next to the proper letter.

Reinforcement Activity:

Refer to "Learning Centers" and have your students do assignment 2.

Can You Copy Me? (primary)

Material:

buzzer board, bell, or small hammer

A B C SCRAMBLE

Find a picture below to go with each letter of the alphabet. Cut out each one.

ABC SCRAMBLE

Paste the cut out pictures here in alphabetical order next to the proper letter.

Name _____

© 1985 by Natalie Madorsky Elman

Preparation:

Place the noise maker on a table where the lesson will be held.

Directions:

1. Show the children how you will make the sound by giving them an example.

2. Explain that they are to copy your pattern exactly by tapping on the table (or clapping) when you call on them.

3. Sound out a short pattern, such as, tap tap.

4. Call on a student to repeat this pattern on the table by tapping.

5. If he or she were not correct, give the pattern again and let the student try again to repeat the sound.

6. Give each student in the group a chance at this level.

7. Once each student is able to replicate the sound at this level, try a more complicated sound, such as, tap—tap tap.

8. Repeat steps 3–7, increasing the complexity or length of the pattern only when students have achieved success at the current level. Give each student several chances on each level.

Reinforcement Activities:

Refer to "Learning Centers" and have your students do assignments 3 and 4.

Let's Listen (primary)

Materials:

enlargement of the award
short story (from students' reader if possible)
bell or buzzer for each child (*optional*)

Preparation:

1. Choose a popular story on the group's level.

2. Pre-read the story to yourself and decide when to put in silly words.

3. If necessary, copy the story and write in the words you plan to substitute.

4. Copy the award on construction paper.

Directions:

1. Explain to the children that you will be reading them a story. You will be making many mistakes while you read. They must listen very carefully and raise their hand or buzz a buzzer or ring a bell if they hear a mistake. For each mistake they find correctly (and are called on), they will receive a point. The student who has the most points at the end of the game receives a ribbon.

2. Read slowly and with exaggerated expression. The following is an example of what you might read:

> Once upon a time there were three <u>chickens</u> (bears). They lived happily with Mama and <u>Brother</u> (Papa) Bear. One day they all decided to go on a <u>skiing trip</u> (walk). While they were gone, they had a visitor. Her name was <u>Silverlocks</u> (Goldilocks).

3. Slow down slightly when you are coming to silly substitutes.

4. Call on students as they raise their hands. Try to give everyone a turn.

5. Let each student keep track of his or her own score.

6. At the end of the story have each student total their points.

7. Give the ribbon award to the winner.

Reinforcement Activity:

Refer to "Learning Centers" and have your students do assignment 5.

<u>Let's Go Skimming (advanced)</u>

Materials:

overhead acetate and marker
overhead projector
story
pencils
marker

Preparation:

1. Copy with marker or by machine onto an acetate the following story.

CHANGES IN WORK*

In the 1790's farming was done mainly by the power of muscle. Men worked their fields. They used horses or oxen to help them.

In the 1890's, there was more help from machines. Factories were using steam and waterpower. But much of the farm work was still done by men and their animals.

In the 1970's machines are taking over more of the farm and factory work. The machines use coal, gas, oil and electricity. Soon machines using atomic power will take over some of the work.

2. Align the overhead so that the full page can be seen by all students.

*Taken from *The Social Sciences/Concepts and Values*, by Paul F. Brandwein et al., © 1970 by Harcourt Brace Jovanovich, Inc. Reprinted by permission of the publisher.

Directions:

1. Explain that skimming is an essential reading skill to acquire. To answer specific questions, it saves much work and time to skim rather than read word for word. Examples are questions at the end of a chapter; studying for tests; and writing reports.

2. Project the prepared acetate onto the screen.

3. Ask a student to read the entire page.

4. Follow this procedure:

a. Ask, "In what year was farming done mostly by muscle?" Explain that we must look for key words. Ask, "What are some key words?" Write them on the board (muscle, a date which is a number).

b. Ask, "How do you know if you are looking for word answers or numbers?"

c. Have students look for the key words one by one by running their fingers across the words, line by line.

d. When students find the word, suggest they now look for the answer (read the original question again). Call on a student to answer the question.

e. Ask, "What happened in 1890?" Point out that looking for a date in a text is easy because numbers stand out from the printed word. Let them find 1890. Call on a student to tell where he or she found it.

f. Ask if anyone remembers the question. If not, read the question again. Call on a student to answer.

g. Go over the above steps with other questions following the same procedure.

h. This skill can be reinforced independently at Learning Center 6 (see the Skimming Skills worksheet on page 107) or the worksheet may be used as part of the group lesson.

Reinforcement Activity:

Refer to "Learning Centers" and have your students do assignment 6.

LEARNING CENTERS

(1) ABC's
(PRIMARY)

Materials:

index card

several popular magazines for cutting

scissors

construction paper (13 sheets per student)

stapler

glue

crayons

Preparation:

1. Prepare the directions card on an index card.
2. Cut 8½" × 11" construction paper in half (26 per student).

Directions Card:

ABC's Booklet

1. On each piece of construction paper write a letter of the alphabet.
2. Find pictures in the magazine to go with each letter.
3. Cut out the pictures and paste them on the correct page.
4. Put your pages in alphabetical order.
5. Staple your booklet together.
6. You may make a cover for your booklet.

(1A) HIDDEN ALPHABET LETTERS
(PRIMARY-ADVANCED)

Materials:

index card
worksheet for each student
pencil
crayons

Preparation:

1. Copy a worksheet (see page 97) for each student.
2. Write the directions on an index card.

Directions Card:

HIDDEN ALPHABET LETTERS

1. Look at your worksheet carefully.
2. Find 26 hidden alphabet letters.
3. Good Luck!

Name _____

Circle the hidden alphabet letters.
Color the picture.

(2) ALPHABETICAL ORDER
(INTERMEDIATE-ADVANCED)

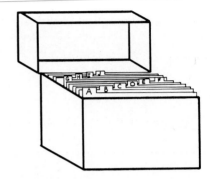

Materials:

    50 index cards
    1 large index card
    card file box with alphabet tab cards
    worksheet for each student
    list of the 50 states

Preparation:

1. Write the name of a different state on the top of each index card.
2. Copy a worksheet (page 99) for each student.
3. Write the directions on a large index card.

Directions Card:

> ALPHABETICAL ORDER
> 1. Put the cards in alphabetical order into the file box.
> 2. Use the letter cards to help you.
> 3. Copy the states in alphabetical order onto your worksheet.
> 4. Have your work checked by the teacher.

(3) COPY CAT

Materials:

    index card
    cassette tape
    tape recorder
    earphones
    worksheet for each student
    buzzer board or sound maker

Preparation:

1. Record the cassette dialogue.
2. Copy a worksheet (see page 101) for each student.
3. Write the directions on an index card.

Alphabetical Order

Name _____   Date _____

List the states in alphabetical order.

1. _____	26. _____
2. _____	27. _____
3. _____	28. _____
4. _____	29. _____
5. _____	30. _____
6. _____	31. _____
7. _____	32. _____
8. _____	33. _____
9. _____	34. _____
10. _____	35. _____
11. _____	36. _____
12. _____	37. _____
13. _____	38. _____
14. _____	39. _____
15. _____	40. _____
16. _____	41. _____
17. _____	42. _____
18. _____	43. _____
19. _____	44. _____
20. _____	45. _____
21. _____	46. _____
22. _____	47. _____
23. _____	48. _____
24. _____	49. _____
25. _____	50. _____

Directions Card:

COPY CAT

1. Put on earphones.
2. Listen to the tape.
3. Do what the tape tells you.
4. Have your work checked by the teacher.

Cassette Dialogue:

Teacher records the following:

1. You will need your worksheet and a pencil. If you don't have them, stop the tape and get them.

2. Look at your worksheet. On the top there is a sample. I will make a sound in a pattern. Listen! (Buzz) pause (Buzz Buzz). On your worksheet I put dots in to show that pattern. Look again while I give the pattern again. (Buzz) pause (Buzz Buzz). The first column has one buzz and the second column has two. If you don't understand, stop the tape and raise your hand. Your teacher will help you.

3. Number one, put in dots for this sound pattern: (buzz buzz) pause (buzz) repeat.

4. Number two, put in dots for this sound pattern: (buzz) pause (buzz) repeat.

5. Number three, put in dots for this pattern: (buzz) pause (buzz) pause (buzz) repeat.

6. Number four, put in dots for this sound pattern: (buzz) pause (buzz) pause (buzz buzz) repeat.

7. Number five, put in dots for this sound pattern: (buzz buzz buzz) repeat,

8. Number six, put in dots for this sound pattern: (buzz buzz) pause (buzz) pause (buzz buzz) repeat.

9. Number seven, this is the last one: (buzz buzz) pause (buzz buzz) pause (buzz buzz) repeat.

10. You have finished your worksheet. Show your work to your teacher.

(4) AMAZING SOUNDS

Materials:

index card
worksheet for each student
pencils
crayons

Copy Mr. Copy Cat

SAMPLE: Tap   Tap Tap
             .   .   .

1.			
2.			
3.			
4.			
5.			
6.			
7.			

Name _____

AMAZING SOUNDS

Name _____

Circle the sounds of home as you work your way to the middle.

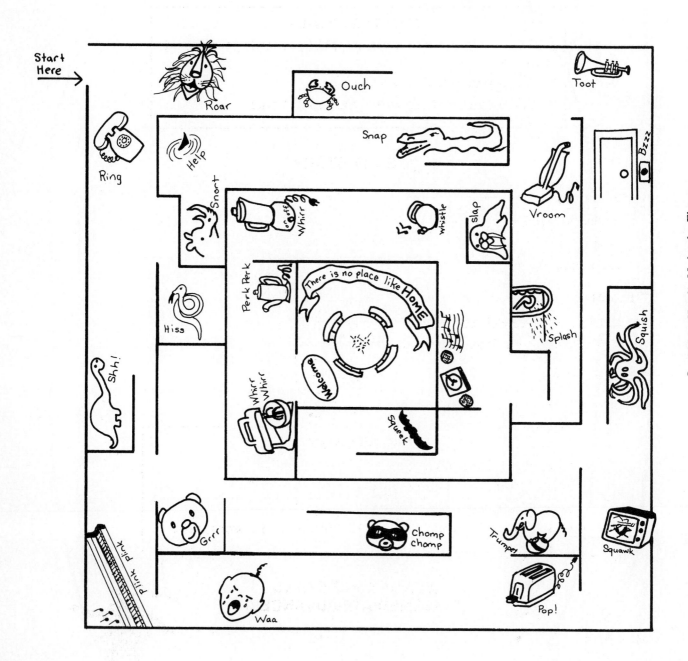

Preparation:

1. Copy a worksheet (see page 102) for each student.
2. Write the directions on an index card.

Directions Card:

```
                    AMAZING SOUNDS
1.  Find your way out of the jungle by listening for sounds
of home.
2.  Use a pencil to show your path.
3.  Color your picture when you reach home.
```

(5) SILLY STORY

Materials:

worksheet for each student
pencil
index card

Preparation:

1. Copy a worksheet (see page 104) for each child.
2. Write the directions on an index card.

Directions Card:

```
                      SILLY STORY
1.  Read the story.
2.  Cross out the silly words.
3.  Put in the correct word.
4.  List your new words at the bottom of the worksheet.
```

(6) SKIMMING SKILLS (INTERMEDIATE-ADVANCED)

Materials:

worksheets for each student
index card
pencils

Name _____

Find the wrong words. Cross them out and write the new word above it. List the new words at the bottom of the worksheet.

SILLY SUSAN

Susan was eight years old. She told her mother that she wanted to kick her goodbye. Off she went to college. Mother waxed goodbye as Susan left.

When Susan arrived at school, her waitress told her to sit down and do her work. Susan began doing her footwork. Soon she was finished. Miss Gray told her she could do the dishes for free time.

Susan arrived home from school at midnight. Mother was sad to see her.

NEW WORDS

1. _____

2. _____

3. _____

4. _____

5. _____

6. _____

7. _____

8. _____

Preparation:

1. Copy the worksheets (see pages 106 and 107) for each student.
2. Write the directions on an index card.

Directions Card:

LET'S GO SKIMMING

1. Read the story "Changes in Work."
2. Answer the questions on the worksheet.
3. Be sure to find the key words first!
4. Have your paper checked by the teacher.

MATERIALS OF THE MONTH

Because of the many demands on your time, the suggestion to "make your own materials" is often rejected. There are some excellent variations on this theme, however, so the idea should not be totally overlooked.

Many books are available to suggest easy, but effective ways to make or copy useful materials.

For instance, *The Kids' Stuff* series by Incentive Publications, Inc., Nashville, Tennessee, offers excellent, inexpensive, large-format books that have easy-to-copy pages and instructions. They are categorized by subject area, which makes it easy to locate lessons quickly. The following titles are especially useful for your program:

Center Stuff for Nooks, Crannies & Corners by Imogene Forte, et al., 1973

Cornering Creative Writing by Imogene Forte, et al., 1974

Creative Math Experiences for the Young Child by Imogene Forte and Jay MacKenzie, 1983

Kids Stuff: Kindergarten & Nursery School by Collier, et al., 1982

Kids Stuff: Reading & Language Experiences—Primary Level by Imogene Forte and Joy MacKenzie, 1975

Kids Stuff: Reading & Language Experiences—Intermediate and Junior High Levels by Imogene Forte, et al., 1973

Nooks, Crannies and Corners—Learning Centers for Creative Classrooms, rev. ed., by Imogene Forte, 1978

These books represent a wealth of information for your special program and are well worth exploring.

Classroom aides or volunteers offer excellent assistance in the preparation of materials. Also, don't overlook local service organizations who are often looking for worthy projects for their volunteers. Senior citizen groups and college clubs, for example, can offer excellent service in the making of materials as well as being a pipeline to volunteer help in the classroom. An additional benefit of this is the cooperation between school and community.

CHANGES IN WORK*

In the 1790's farming was done mainly by the power of muscle. Men worked their fields. They used horses or oxen to help them.

In the 1890's, there was more help from machines. Factories were using steam and waterpower. But much of the farm work was still done by men and their animals.

In the 1970's machines are taking over more of the farm and factory work. The machines use coal, gas, oil and electricity. Soon machines using atomic power will take over some of the work.

*Taken from *The Social Sciences/Concepts and Values*, by Paul F. Brandwein et al., © by Harcourt Brace and Jovanovich, Inc. Reprinted by permission of the publisher.

Name _____

SKIMMING SKILLS

Directions: By skimming for the key words, answer the following questions:

1. How was farming done in the 1790's? Key words to look for: _____

Answer: _____

_____

_____

2. When were horses and oxen used? Key words to look for: _____

_____

Answer: _____

_____

_____

_____

3. What did factories use for power in the 1890's? Key words to look for: _____

Answer: _____

_____

_____

4. What are coal, gas and oil used for in this article? Key words to look for: _____

Answer: _____

_____

_____

_____

_____

Don't forget the older or more artistic students right in your own school who would be delighted to make materials upon request.

For those lessons that require very special materials or experience in requesting things by mail, there is an excellent resource: *The International Catalogue of Catalogues* by Maria Elena de La Iglesia and published by Harper Colophon Books (New York) for $10.95. This book tells how to buy practically everything by mail in the U.S.A. and around the world, listing over 1500 shops and manufacturers. It makes an excellent resource book to use at a learning center on letter writing and catalog reading or to enhance a social studies lesson about a foreign country.

FREE FOR THE ASKING

One Hand Manual Alphabet Used by Deaf People

This is an 11″ × 17″ poster that features actual photographs of Helen Keller's hand spelling out the letters. The flip side lists what to do when you meet a deaf-blind person.

Since Helen Keller is the spotlight personality for November, this free chart would make an excellent supplement to the bulletin board or lesson. Send a postcard to:

> American Foundation for the Blind
> 15 West 16th Street
> New York, NY 10011

Speak to Me!

This is a catalog of 1500 titles ranging from contemporary science fiction to biblical classics—on cassette tapes for rental or purchase. These cassettes feature the well-known voices of Kurt Vonnegut, Jr., and Tammy Grimes reading classics like *The Hobbit* and *Black Beauty*. This is excellent for slow readers who would benefit from following along a text auditorally. Tapes rent for a small fee. Send a postcard to:

> Speak to Me! Cassette Catalogue
> 524 Bryont Street
> Palo Alto, CA 94301

When You Have A Visually Handicapped Child In Your Classroom

This free booklet has been written primarily for teachers. Pointers, however, are given for students as well. These include techniques for being an effective sighted guide; and what to expect when a visually handicapped child works with printed materials. The back of the booklet features a glossary of visual impairments, and a list of common misconceptions about vision.

This would make an excellent supplement to the discussion of blindness when Helen Keller's handicaps are discussed. Send a postcard to:

> American Foundation for the Blind
> 15 West 16th Street
> New York, NY 10011

Move Over Michelangelo

This free booklet shows children how to fashion jewelry, toys, decorations, vases, candlesticks, and pendant necklaces. It also has an excellent recipe for play clay. Send a long self-addressed envelope to:

> Church & Dwight Co.
> Dept. PC, 2
> Pennsylvania Plaza
> New York, NY 10001

GOOD BUYS

Although the following materials have been chosen to use with November's unit on reading skills, they can also be used to supplement your other reading programs.

Mini-Workbooks

These 5½" × 8½" workbooks (pamphlets) come in a 16-page format on a wide variety of skills. They are compact, easy to use and cost only 35 cents each when 10 or more are ordered. Grade levels vary according to intended use as developmental or remedial. They are available for reading, language arts, vocabulary, study skills and mathematics. They are an excellent buy! Contact:

> Learning Systems Corp.
> 60 Connally Parkway
> Hamden, CT 06514
> (203) 288-8807

Auditory Stimulator Teachers Kit

This kit contains one workbook and one teacher's guide for $6.00. The workbook is divided into two parts. Part I asks the child to recall simple facts in a non-sequential fashion; Part II, in a sequential order. Units are organized progressively so that the child must recall an additional fact per unit. A variety of tasks are asked of the student. The kit (available from EPA, address below) helps train auditory memory by having the intermediate-level student concentrate on remembering various directions throughout.

Experiences in Reading Readiness

The program includes flannelboard materials, games, colorful illustrations, manuscript letters, puzzles, and coordinated group work material. It emphasizes verbal, visual and auditory associative skills and ability to discern sequential and logical relationships. The entire kit sells for under $100. Write to:

> Educational Performance Associates Inc.
> 600 Broad Avenue
> Ridgefield, NJ 07657

Auditory Familiar Sounds

Fifty recorded familiar environmental sounds, such as a man's voice, a woman's voice, a dog barking, and a bell ringing, serve as the basis for this valuable teaching aid. Students must match picture cards to the sounds they hear. This aid costs $8 and is available from DLM.

Dual Panel Buzzer/Light Message Unit

This is excellent for exercises involving auditory-visual-motor development skills! The buzzer device is tuned to provide maximum vibrations that can be felt and heard at the same time. The unit costs $30 and is available from DLM.

Alphabet Motor Activities, Book and Tape

A 27-page spiral-bound alphabet book, cassette tape, and teacher script are included in this kit for under $20. It is available from DLM.

Sound Symbol Puzzles

Students match lower and upper case letters to illustrations of common objects. Two durable 12″ × 12″ puzzles sell for under $15. Contact:

> Developmental Learning Materials
> P.O. Box 4000
> One DLM Park
> Allen, TX 75002

Modality-Specific Alphabet Cards

There is a separate set of 26 cards for each modality—visual, auditory, or kinesthetic— for a total of 78 cards. Each 4¾″ × 5¾″ card provides a model of upper and lower case manuscript form, a modality-specific word built on that letter, and a full-color illustration showing a use of the word. The 78-card set and a teacher's manual sell for $25. Write to:

> Zaner Bloser
> 2500 W. Fifth Avenue
> P.O. Box 16764
> Columbus, OH 43216

PROFESSIONAL RESPONSIBILITIES

INVOLVING PARENTS

Communication between the parents and special educator often sets the tone for the students' attitudes. Since involving the parents early in the school year is a good idea, have a parents meeting either before school begins or shortly after the first day of classes. Parental anxieties have a way of multiplying if not dealt with, so allay these fears as soon as possible.

Having a meeting with all the parents, the head of special services, and the principal is a good way to initiate this communication. Although this may be a more formal meeting with everyone present, it is good to have everyone who is sharing the responsibility of the child's program in attendance to give their input.

As with the first staff meeting, try to hold the meeting in your room so that the parents can see where their children go each day and what they are doing. Have the room set up with the appropriate learning centers and display some of the materials the children will use. Also have reference books available for parents to read. (The professional books listed for each month also include books written especially for parents.) The Council for Exceptional Children, 1920 Association Drive, Reston, Virginia 22091 and The Association for Children with Learning Disabilities, 4156 Library Road, Pittsburgh, PA 15234 publish inexpensive pamphlets for parents. Both organizations will furnish a catalog upon request.

Having visual aids as part of the presentation usually helps to clarify points trying to be made. One idea is to put an example of a typical daily program of a special child on an overhead acetate which can be shown during the presentation on an overhead projector. Parents are usually enlightened by seeing just how full their child's day can be. Demonstrate some of the materials that are designed to remediate deficit areas as well as the audio-visual equipment used with the children.

During the discussion part of the meeting, consider bringing up the following points:

- how the children will be evaluated (tests, homework, room assignments, etc.)
- how the parents will receive the information on these evaluations (conferences, report cards, weekly notes, phone calls, etc.)
- how the child's goals and objectives from his or her Individual Educational Plan are translated into the special program's goals and objectives
- when schoolwide tests such as the Iowa Achievement Tests or California Achievement Tests will be given and if the child will be included in this testing
- how the child will be expected to make up or be excused from work he or she has missed in the classroom while attending the special program (this, of course, must be decided with the staff and administration long before this meeting)

As with most school meetings, there will always be the parent who insists on discussing particulars of his or her child. Since this is a general meeting, try to discourage this by explaining that you would like to be able to discuss his or her child in depth when there is more time. Offer to schedule a conference as soon as the meeting is over. Another possibility is to circulate a conference sign-up sheet and suggest that parents sign up for a meeting as soon as possible.

If parent volunteers are a part of your program, this meeting is a good opportunity to solicit their participation. Involved parents are often the most supportive parents and using parent volunteers as classroom helpers or aides is an excellent way to involve them. The following duties should be cited as examples of possible ways for them to help:

- working with individual children under the teacher's direction
- doing clerical work such as filing and running off dittos
- creating or making new learning center materials
- creating bulletin boards or other art work
- sharing special talents or hobbies with the children (rock collecting, glass blowing, art, pottery, etc.)
- checking out materials to other staff members and keeping track of the professional and reference library located in the special education room
- doing any other responsibilities that would be useful to the program and could be done by a para-professional

During the course of the meeting, let the parents know that you are available to them. Suggest that they phone the office and leave a message for you if they have any concerns or information to share in between conference time to better help their child. Parents need to know how important it is to have their support in order for their child to have optimum success. Their attitude is sensed by their child even if it is not expressed verbally. Their support is essential for the success of the program and ultimately in the very best interest of the child.

Allow time after the business part of the meeting for light refreshments, socializing, and browsing.

PROFESSIONAL RESOURCE BOOKS

Cook, Myra, Joseph Caldwell, and Lena Christiansen. *The Come-Alive Classroom.* (West Nyack, NY: Parker Publishing Company, Inc., 1967)

Cruickshank, William M. *Learning Disabilities in Home, School and Community.* (New York: Syracuse University Press, 1977)

Goldstein, Herbert, ed. *Exceptional Children: A Reference Book.* (Guilford, CT: Special Learning Corporation, 1978)

Huff, Darrell. *Score: The Strategy of Taking Tests.* (E. Norwalk, CT: Appleton, Century and Crofts, Inc., 1961)

Liechti, Alice, and Jack Chappell. *Making and Using Charts.* (Belmont, CT: Fearon Publishers, Inc., 1981)

Simpson, Eileen. *Reversals.* (New York: Washington Square Press, 1981)

MODES FOR MAINSTREAMING

MODIFYING CLASSROOM ASSIGNMENTS

Modifying assignments and classroom work expectations of the special child are often necessary.

The student must leave the classroom to attend a special program. A child with learning problems often has other developmental problems that must be helped, so speech and language therapy, physical therapy, or supplemental math or reading are a few other reasons that the child might have to leave the classroom during the day. Each time the student leaves for other instruction, he or she is missing instruction going on in the classroom. This can become a real dilemma. If the classroom work expectations are not modified, the student is being penalized and put under even more pressure for having a learning problem.

From the classroom teacher's point of view, the child must get the work done in order to cover the school curriculum for that year. The teacher feels the pressure of teaching the curriculum to his or her class. Having a student leave while teaching is in progress is a threat to the accomplishment of that goal. Obviously, there must be some goal modifications on the part of the teacher and ultimately the student in order to promote the best possible learning environment.

The best time to set up these modifications is at the child's Individual Educational Plan (I.E.P.) meeting where the teacher, parent, child, and special educator are all present with a member of the multi-disciplinary team who has tested the student. Unfortunately, many I.E.P. meetings are held at the end of the school year, with goals and objectives set for the coming school year. This means that next year's teacher is often not even known. Consequently, the classroom teacher is assigned a child at the beginning of the school year when things are the most hectic and he or she has the least amount of time to learn about a child's record. Aside from the preliminary suggestions you make at the start of the school year, the classroom routine is established and the special program child is often expected to "make-up" missed work. Needless to say, in addition to the regular assignments which often need assistance, the child feels swamped with even more work to do to keep up!

Early classroom teacher conferences must be held to discuss this issue. It is the belief of many special educators that a child can get alternate instruction on his or her own level in the special classroom for whatever is missed in the regular classroom. The child can be excused from those subjects such as health, science, etc., which the child must miss on a regular basis and will not be covered in the special program.

A grade of "M" and an explanation at the bottom of the report card that this means "modified program" usually solves the problem of the classroom teacher feeling as though he or she is shirking responsibility to the child.

These modifications, of course, must be agreed upon in advance by the parents, classroom teacher, special educator, and student.

TIP OF THE MONTH

BULLETIN BOARDS

Throughout this *Almanac*, great emphasis is made on the use of bulletin boards as a learning tool. They are used to spotlight famous people and to teach various skills. The use of construction paper is suggested as a way of backing the bulletin boards. There is an easier way. Use a semi-gloss latex paint and a roller and paint the bulletin boards in bright colors! This is a one-time effort and the bulletin boards are permanently backed in color.

The drawbacks, however, are the cost of the paint (sometimes reimbursable), the initial work, and getting the building administrator's approval. In some buildings, the administrator will not allow the cork to be painted because it is permanent. So be sure to check first with your principal. If you get the approval, paint those boards in your favorite colors and enjoy!

A FINAL WORD

INCLUDING THE STUDENT

In our quest to help and teach children, it seems as though we have sometimes forgotten the most important part of that process . . . the student!

We set goals and objectives for the student, evaluate the student's strengths and weaknesses, have parent conferences *about* the student's progress—and usually don't invite the student to any of the above.

PL 94-142 states that the child should attend I.E.P. meetings when he or she can. Since it is not mandated, often the student is left out. There seems to be great precedence for planning *for* a child rather than *with* the child.

Including students in goal setting is very important. They, after all, are the only ones who can affect change. The teachers and parents can plan and teach endlessly, but without the cooperation and effort of the students, not much will take place. Having the students complete a goals checklist (see page 115) or at least having them discuss it with the teacher is far more effective. When students are included in the goal setting process and know clearly where they are directing their efforts, much change can take place.

Being in attendance at parent/teacher conferences is another way of including students. Certainly the "stars" of the conference should be present. They should hear about their own progress as well as those areas that need improvement. This knowledge should be shared with the ones who can make the growth firsthand and agree to ways of continuing to learn.

Sharing with students their learning strengths and weaknesses is essential. Many of us have learned about our own learning strengths long after we might have benefitted. Through sophisticated testing (which most learning disabled students have had) students can be told the best modality through which they can learn. They must live with their unique characteristics for a life time and can only be strengthened by this knowledge. When students are told about their strong and weak learning channels, be sure to do it positively by stressing examples of ways to learn that will be most successful for them. For example:

> "John, you learn best when you are able to see a word rather than just hear it. This means that you should always ask for visual clues when things are not clear to you."

Certainly there are times when a confidential meeting with the parents is appropriate. As a general rule, however, including the students in their own program planning and evaluation seems to work very positively.

NOVEMBER REFERENCES

Bartlett, John. *Bartlett's Familiar Quotations.* (Boston: Little Brown and Co., 1955)

Keller, Helen. *The Story of My Life.* (Garden City, NY: Doubleday and Co., 1955)

Keller, Helen. *The World I Live In.* (Garden City, NY: Doubleday and Co., 1908)

Lash, Joseph P. *Helen and Teacher.* (New York: Delacorte Press, 1980)

World Book Encyclopedia (Book JK-LL). (Chicago: World Book–Childcraft, International, Inc., 1981)

Name _____ Date _____

GOALS CHECKLIST

This year I would like to:

☐ Improve my reading skills.

This is how: _____

_____

☐ Improve my spelling skills.

This is how: _____

_____

☐ Improve my handwriting skills.

This is how: _____

_____

☐ Improve my math skills.

This is how: _____

_____

☐ Improve my motor skills (sports, exercises, etc.).

This is how: _____

_____

☐ Improve my ability to get along with classmates.

This is how: _____

_____

☐ Improve my ability to get along with my teachers.

This is how: _____

_____

☐ Improve my _____

This is how: _____

_____

Signed: _____

December

1 Lane Bryant (1879) It's comforting to know someone worried about you before you were born. And you'll be comforted to know someone cared about your mom's comfort, too. Seamstress Lane Bryant sold the first MATERNITY clothes, which got bigger and bigger as unborn babies grew! Bigger stores grew from a comfortable idea!

2 George Seurat (1859) Try to get the point! Seurat painted big paintings of tiny, colored dots. If he wanted to paint a green leaf, the dots of color would be blue and yellow. From a distance, the leaf would be green. An orange coat would be dotted ___ and ___, a purple rose ___ and ___. Call his painting POINTILISM. Got the point? Try it!

3 Sir Rowland Hill (1795) Lick and stick a sticky stamp,/Send a letter far away./Stamp May 1 on your memory,/First stamps were used that day./'Twas Rowland Hill, in England,/1840, he perceived/That sticking stamps on envelopes/Could send mail to be received. (U.S. stamps were first used July 1, 1848.)

4 Chester Greenwood (1858) Kids from California don't know much about them. The dictionary says these things, invented by Chester Greenwood, are round coverings, connected by a flexible band, worn to protect the ears! These brightly colored fuzzies do muffle the sound and keep ears from being bitten by frost. What are they? Earmuffs, of course.

5 Walt Disney (1901) We've kept track of Mickey Mouse ever since 1928 when STEAMBOAT WILLIE was the first animated cartoon with a soundtrack. Disney dazzled us with Donald, Daffy, Dumbo and the Dwarves. More dazzling are the dozens of drawings designed to make Mickey move a muscle. Honor Walt! Animate an animal!

6 Colonel Richard Henry Pratt (1840) Jim Thorpe ran two touchdowns against Army! His team? Carlisle Indians of Colonel Pratt's first Indian college! In Pennsylvania, his students learned working skills. And, they played football! Pratt was proud of Jim Thorpe who made 25 touchdowns that 1912 season—two against cadet Dwight D. Eisenhower!

7 Madame Marie Tussaud (1760) Out of the dark, the softly lit sculptures of the world's heroes, true to every detail, appear. Marie learned the fine art of wax sculpture from a friend. Now, her portrait greets visitors to Tussaud's Museum, her London home of wax queens, kings, Mickey Mouse, Lincoln, the Beatles, Princess Diana . . .

8 Eli Whitney (1765) After cotton was picked, the seeds had to be taken from the fuzzy stuff and that, for one pound of cotton, took one day! Whitney's new gin cleaned 50 pounds a day. Take cotton out of your ears and listen to story problems! If there were ___ pounds of cotton, how many days would it take to de-seed it?

9 Clarence Birdseye (1886) Until the ship entered the icy port in Labrador, explorer Birdseye ate only meat and fish. The cargo of fruit and vegetables was kept fresh in barrels of freezing water. Back home, inventor Birdseye opened a frozen foods company. List a "birds-eye view" of frozen foods in your local market.

10 Thomas Gallaudet (1787) and Melvil Dewey (1851) Thomas Gallaudet opened the first FREE school for the deaf in America. Son Tom began the first church for the deaf in New York. And Melvil Dewey's decimal system organized books so that students, deaf or hearing, could quietly find any book by a number code. Find a Dewey number for AMSLAN!

11 Robert Koch (1843) Robert Koch caught on to the causes of disease! A German country doctor, he discovered that germs caused tuberculosis, cholera and cattle disease. Koch also dyed germs with eye-catching color to be clearly seen through a microscope. Koch's germs come in three basic shapes. You can catch on to them, 1, 2, 3!

12 Cathy Rigby Mason (1952) and Tracy Austin (1962) Tracy held the shining cup awarded her. At 16, in 1979, she was the youngest woman ever to win the U.S. Open Tennis Championship. And Cathy, in 1971, was the winner of every women's event at the World Cup Gymnastics Championship! Take time to have a warming cup of soup to celebrate these super-champs!

13 Sergeant Alvin York (1887) "The Sergeant" was a mountain boy,/Born strong in Tennessee,/'Twas World War I in France, one day/A hero, then, was he./He saw his buddies fall and then/In anger fired his gun./Of twenty-five shots twenty men/Did fall where they had run./So quickly were those Germans lost,/'Twas an army, they believed,/But one man took them prisoner,/By York, they'd been deceived.

14 General James Doolittle (1896) Certainly Jimmy Doolittle didn't do little. He was first to fly across the U.S. in less than a day; first to pilot by instruments alone; and, in April of 1942, first to plan and lead the first U.S. bombing raid over Tokyo (WWII). The Congressional Medal of Honor said THANK YOU to Doolittle for doing so much!

15 Ludwik Zamenhof (1859) Hopeful that his new language, ESPERANTO, would be an international language spoken in all countries, Zamenhof signed his book Dr. Esperanto. The word "esperanto" in the language Esperanto means HOPE. Simple and easy to learn, Zamenhof hoped his language would join all people in thought, word, and peace.

16 Margaret Mead (1901) Would you be the very same "you" if you were born somewhere else? Margaret Mead left home to study and learn about other peoples. After years of watching how island children grew up, she answered the question. Since parents are so different in other places, you would be a very different "you" if born elsewhere!

God loves to help (them) who (strive) to help (themselves).

Aeschylus

17 (16?) Ludwig van Beethoven (1770)   Remember the first 8 notes of his 5th symphony and you will note his genius. When totally deaf, Beethoven composed classical music we will hear forever. Although he couldn't even hear the thunderous applause of his listeners, his inner ear heard marvelous melodies as he wrote them for others to play.

18 Tyrus Cobb (1886)   Cobb could clobber with more clout than any other baseball club member could. He led the American League in batting 12 times and hit more than, or as many as, any other player. In fact, Ty hit 5 home runs in 2 days! In 2 days of recess baseball, count how many home runs your classmates can clobber.

19 Cicely Tyson (1933) and Richard Leaky (1944)   He followed his family's footsteps to find man's roots—our first family. Digging in Kenya, Leaky found three humanlike skeletons, one perhaps a relative of earliest man. And America watched Cicely as Binta in Alex Haley's search for family ROOTS. Search for names for a family tree to find your own roots!

20 Richard Atwater (1892)   The great ship moved down the river. Mr. Popper waved goodbye and the penguins, too, raised their flippers in farewell. The dreams Mr. Popper had daydreamed as he painted kitchens and papered walls had indeed come true. He and his penguins sailed poleward! Add tales of arctic antics to MR. POPPER'S PENGUINS!

21 Henrietta Szold (1860)   Beginning with 13 young women, Henrietta Szold founded the Hadassah Society dedicated to teaching, healing, and medical research. As a social worker she knew the troubles of war-torn families. Caring for refugees and asking others to care, Hadassah is now the largest women's organization in the world.

22 Grote Reber (1911)   With sound could he really HEAR stars too far away to be seen? The idea of finding stars by sound hit him! Ham operator Reber built the first radio-telescope. The world's only radio-astronomer from 1939 to 1945, he heard sound waves bounce off distant stars! Thus, radio astronomy had its bright beginning!

23 William Rodgers (1948)   President Carter invited him to a White House dinner! Winning a marathon worked up quite an appetite. The winner of 8 Marathons (Boston, 1975, 1978, 1979, 1980; New York, 1976, 1977, 1978, 1979), special ed teacher, Rodgers, passed all the tests of endurance. Run for Rodgers! Reward the longest run!

24 Kit Carson (1809)   Remember Beadle's 10¢ books? Well, Kit Carson, who couldn't write, told tales of buffalo hunts, Fremont's travels, Indian ambush, and Civil war days to Lieutenant Colonel Peters, who wrote them down, more exciting than they were, and gave them to Beadle to print. Kit's tales were novel for a dime!

25 Clara Barton (1821) and Robert Ripley (1893) and Anwar Sadat (1918)   In a spirit of Peace on Earth, we honor Clara Barton and Anwar Sadat who risked their lives for mercy on the battlefields. With loving care she calmed all wounded. With love, he calmed two warring nations of the Middle East. Both were called angels. She of the battlefield. He of peace. Believe it, or not!

26 Charles Babbage (1792)   Mistakes in math are made by people. Charles Babbage knew that his arithmetic machines made no errors. But English scientists made a huge mistake. They did not believe, in 1827, that this machine would help them solve problems. 124 years later a computer was built. Make no mistake! Tell the year.

27 Louis Pasteur (1822)   "Mad dog!" The shout brought chilling fears and slamming doors! Rabid dogs brought rabies, rabies brought fear, drooling and paralysis. Paralysis brought death. But Frenchman Louis Pasteur brought the cure. After 1885, people bit by mad dogs were no longer maddened. In seven days, Pasteur's cure cured rabies!

28 Queen Elizabeth Petrovna I (1709)   Russian Queen Elizabeth died quietly at age 53. But not quiet were questions curious about the 15,000 quality dresses found in the queen's closet. She was unquestionably a quick change artist! Quibbling about which to wear, three a day were her quota. Count a quantity of days required to wear them all!

29 Charles Goodyear (1800)   Pedal as you may, melting tires wouldn't travel far! In the summer sun, bike tires would be mushy if they weren't vulcanized. Goodyear and Nathaniel Hayward found that heating rubber and mixing it with sulphur kept it hard, strong and stretchy. Goodyear gave your bike a good year on good tires!

30 Sandy Koufax (1935)   Koufax kept a mental card file on every hitter in the league, but he played for more than breaking strike-out records. His greatest thrill was helping the team to win! The youngest ever elected to the Hall of Fame, arthritis pitched him a no-hitter. Painfully he had to strike-out of the game for good.

31 Andreas Vesalius (1514)   A flickering candle in the belly of a CADAVER lit Michelangelo's drawings, muscle by muscle. Da Vinci drew 1000 drawings of 300 CADAVERS in detail. But Vesalius drew the most famous book in the history of medicine (1543): the first complete HUMAN ANATOMY. He brought the whole inside story of a person to light.

These birthographies were prepared by Davida Shipkowitz of Northridge, California.

SPOTLIGHT ON

WINSTON CHURCHILL (1874–1965)

Winston Churchill, a person of great charm and charisma who started out with obvious learning problems, is this month's Spotlight personality. Since social skills will be discussed in December, Winston Churchill certainly is an appropriate example of a person who used social skills and leadership abilities to achieve much in society. Winston's early years gave no indication that he would be a leader of great fame.

A discussion of his accomplishments and ultimate ability to lead people is one way to initiate the unit on social skills.

Winston Churchill is heralded as perhaps the greatest British statesman, historian and orator of all time. He was national leader of Great Britain during World War II. Relman Morin in *Churchill: Portrait of Greatness* states the following:

> "A statesman, a leader without equal in all history . . . , whose first biography was written when he was barely 30 years old . . . who served six sovereigns . . . who was recipient of well over 100 decorations, university degrees and other honors . . . possessed of such an ability to arouse emotion, to inspire and encourage that he transformed his nation's time of trial into its finest hour, Winston Churchill became, indeed, a legend in his own lifetime."

Winston is credited with the following:

* Served in English army as second lieutenant
* Won election to House of Commons
* Conservative member of Parliament
* Under Secretary of State for Colonies
* President Board of Trade
* Secretary for Home Affairs
* First Lord of Admiralty
* Chancellor of the Ducy of Lancaster
* Minister of Munitions
* Secretary of State for War and Air
* Chancellor of Exchequer
* Sentry against Hitlerism
* Member of War Cabinet—mobilized Britain for war
* Helped build the "grand alliance" of Great Britain, United States and USSR
* Prime Minister and Minister of Defense for Great Britain
* Promoted acquisition of allies
* Prime Minister of Great Britain (1940)
* Participated in Casablanca Conference
* Wrote: six-volume history called *The Second World War* and four-volume *A History of the English-Speaking Peoples*
* Nobel Prize recipient for published books and speeches

As a boy there were early indications that not only was he *not* equipped for politics, but that he was also thought to be backward! His Grandmother Jerome is quoted in *Cradles of Eminence* as saying the following about Winston:

> "He rather resembles a naughty little sandy haired bulldog and seems backward except for complicated games with toy soldiers."

His schoolmates called him "Carrots" because of his reddish hair and he never outgrew a lisp in his speech.

In *My Early Life*, Winston himself wrote about a private school called Harrow,

> "How I hated this school, and what a life of anxiety I lived there for more than two years. My teachers saw me at once backward and precocious, reading books beyond my years and yet at the bottom of the form."

Churchill reported that he found himself shy and tongue-tied in the presence of his father. He recalled how greatly he envied one of his classmates who conversed easily with Lord Randolph. This great orator recalled thinking

> "I was only a backward boy and my incursions into the conversation were nearly always awkward or foolish."

The Goertzels report in *Cradles of Eminence* that while at Harrow, Winston's only prizes were for fencing and reciting martial poetry. He refused to study mathematics, Greek or Latin and was placed in the lowest form—in what would today be termed remedial reading class (or a resource room) where slow boys were taught English. His English, however, was not poor and he had an extraordinary knowledge of Shakespeare which was self-motivated. He had no intimate friends and was "cheeky" at school.

It seems quite incredible that from such an uncertain beginning, Winston Churchill became a legend in his own time. His speeches and writings are quoted liberally as the essence of great wisdom and leadership. In a tribute to Neville Chamberlain at the House of Commons on November 12, 1940 Winston said:

> "The only guide to a man is his conscience; the only shield to his memory is the rectitude and sincerity of his actions."

Certainly, Winston Churchill will be remembered for exactly that.

SPOTLIGHT BULLETIN BOARD

Materials:

white background cover paper	overhead projector
yellow or orange markers for cast light	acetate transparency
black marker for can lights	transparency marker

Preparation:

1. Cover the bulletin board with white construction paper.

2. Trace the "Spotlight" bulletin board onto clear acetate using a transparency marker.

3. Project the transparency onto the white-covered bulletin board.

4. Trace the outline onto the white paper. Color in with markers.

Spotlight
on

Sir Winston Churchill
1874—1965

BULLETIN BOARD IDEAS

GIVE A GIFT OF FRIENDSHIP

This bulletin board combines the celebration of the holiday season with social skills. At a time of year when material gifts tend to be the focus, this is a reminder that the giving of friendship is also a special gift to give. The bulletin board is an excellent reinforcement for the lessons on social skills presented later in this monthly chapter.

Objective:

To extend social skills into the everyday life of the student.

Materials:

striped wrapping paper or wallpaper for background (a red and white candy stripe is very effective for the holidays)

7 cardboard boxes in a variety of sizes and shapes, large enough to hold folded notes

clipboard (wrapped in coordinating paper with the bulletin board)

1 hook screw (to hold clipboard)

scissors

Friend-o-Gram worksheets

double-faced tape

wrapping paper and ribbon for boxes

stapler

white construction paper for bow signs

white shelving paper for scroll

marker to make signs

Preparation:

1. Wrap the cardboard boxes with holiday wrapping paper and ribbon.
2. Cut a slit in the top of each box large enough to place notes.
3. Cover the bulletin board with striped wrapping paper.
4. Attach the boxes to the bulletin board with strong double-faced tape.
5. Write the bulletin board sign on the shelving paper. Leave a sufficient amount on either end to roll in scroll fashion.
6. Affix the scroll with staples.
7. Write the seven gifts of friendship on white ribbon-shaped construction paper and staple onto the bulletin board next to each box.
8. Wrap the clipboard with holiday wrapping paper.
9. Screw the hook screw into the bulletin board and place the clipboard on it.
10. Write the directions on a sheet of construction paper and place it next to the bulletin board.

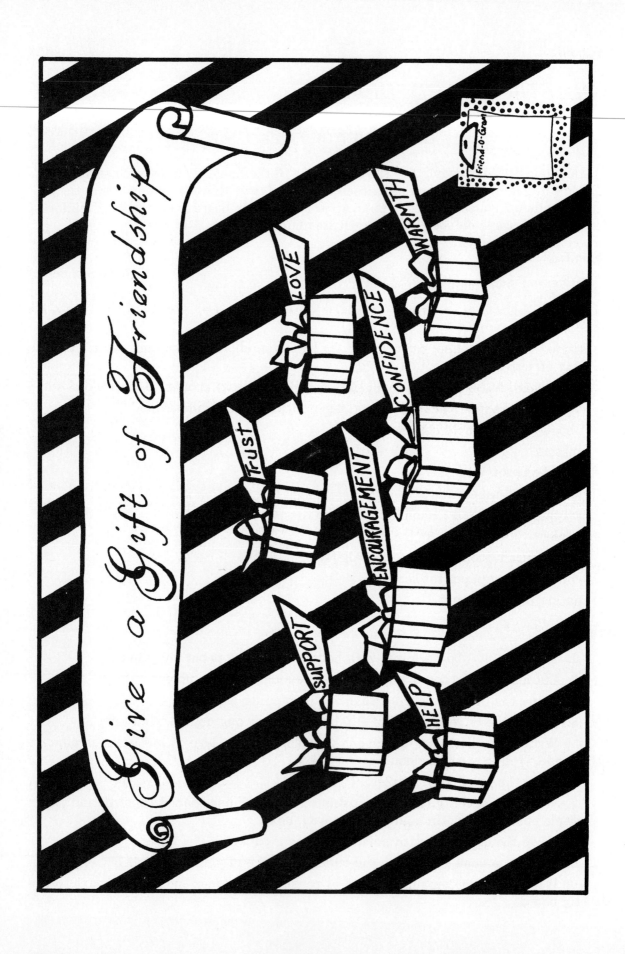

Procedure:

Using the bulletin board as a motivating focal point, introduce the concept of friendship. Talk about all the components that go into making a good friend. This is also a good time to tie in the holidays and good will toward others, no matter what your beliefs are. The concept of friendship lends itself nicely to the entire holiday season.

Directions:

1. Each student will take a Friend-o-Gram worksheet (see page 124) for each gift box. She then decides to whom she will give this gift of friendship and fills out the form accordingly. Each student should fill out seven different worksheets, one for each box. The student then places the forms in the appropriate box. (NOTE: You should consider sending a Friend-o-Gram to each student in your program. This insures that everyone will receive at least one. A Friend-o-Gram from you also adds a special flair to the project. Try to involve others on the staff as well.)

2. On the day of the party or any other designated day, each student delivers the Friend-o-Grams to friends.

3. As a follow up to this activity, it is a good idea to have a time when each student in the room can tell how he or she performed his or her acts of friendship.

IT'S A SMALL WORLD

The bulletin board of children linking hands around the globe reinforces the idea of good will toward others during the holiday season.

Materials:

overhead projector
overhead acetate
overhead marker
white background paper
red marker for people
green marker for globe
red and green markers for lettering

Preparation:

1. Copy the bulletin board illustration (see page 125) onto acetate (either by machine or with an acetate marker).

2. Cover the bulletin board with white construction paper. NOTE: Alternate colors or wrapping paper can also be used.

3. Project the bulletin board design onto the background paper.

4. Outline the design onto the board using the designated colors.

5. The letters for the title and greeting can be done in green and red alternately or the top line in green and the bottom in red. NOTE: Use any color pattern that makes the bulletin board appear festive.

FRIEND-O-GRAM

From: _____

To: _____

My gift of friendship is: _____

_____

This is how I will show it: _____

_____

_____

_____

_____

_____

_____

_____

_____

_____

_____

_____

_____

_____

Happy Holidays!

Signed: _____

It's a Small World After All ....

Happy Holidays!

TEACHING UNIT

SOCIAL SKILLS

All too often, the absence of social skills makes life that much more difficult for a learning disabled student. Skills for everyday social living are often taken for granted by the person who is not learning disabled. It is important for teachers to be aware of this and teach many things that seem "obvious." Frequently, a teacher must say obvious things like "children won't like you if you call them names." Some children don't connect their actions to the fact that others may react towards them. They must be told.

The following lessons on social skills are meant to supplement the *ongoing* lessons on social awareness that must go on continuously in a classroom for students with learning problems.

The month of holiday parties and family gatherings is an excellent time to emphasize family awareness, social skills, manners, and good grooming.

Objectives:

At the conclusion of this unit students will:

- Have an awareness of their special place in their family.
- Have an awareness of their place in a classroom society.
- Have a better awareness of their strengths and weaknesses.
- Have a better awareness of their likes and dislikes.
- Recognize feelings of others through facial and body gestures.
- Be able to relate others' feelings to their actions.
- Be aware of more positive ways of handling social situations.
- Be aware of personal grooming.
- Have an awareness of good manners and when to use them.

<u>Who Am I? (primary-advanced)</u>

Materials:

baby photos of each student
variety of construction paper for booklet cover
stapler
1 set of worksheets from Learning Center 1

Preparation:

1. One week before, send a note home to parents requesting baby photos of each child.

2. Remind students when the photos are due. (A note on the chalkboard is a good idea.)

NOTE: Some teachers prefer to take their own pictures right in the classroom so they are sure to have them. There are many instant cameras that are very inexpensive and useful for a variety of activities. (See "Materials of the Month.")

3. Copy the worksheets from Learning Center 1.

Directions:

1. Ask each student to show his or her baby photos to the group.

2. Talk about how each child has grown.

3. Write a list on the chalkboard of a baby's progression of development, such as:
   a. lifts head
   b. turns over
   c. begins to crawl
   d. says simple words
   e. begins to stand by holding on
   f. lets go
   g. takes first step

4. Emphasize how far the children have come. "Look at how much all of you have grown and *learned.*" Compare them now to what they were as infants. Make students aware of how much they have developed and progressed.

5. Discuss how, although we develop in a similar manner, we are all very different. Talk about how much each of us looks different, talks differently, and has different things we are good at and like.

6. Talk about what strong areas and weak areas are. Write some on the board:

Strengths	*Weaknesses*
sympathy for others	
math	math
reading	reading
handwriting	handwriting
babysitting	map skills
finding things	cutting
building things	

7. Ask individuals what are some of their strengths and weaknesses. Underline these on the chalkboard as they talk.

8. Explain that they will have an opportunity to list all of their strengths and weaknesses when they make their booklets at Learning Center 1.

9. Show the worksheets that will be used at Learning Center 1 to make their "Meet Me" booklets.

10. Distribute construction paper for students to use to make the covers.

11. Explain that a baby picture of each one will be glued to the cover. (See the sample "Meet Me" cover on page 139.)

12. Ask students to decorate their covers with crayons or markers.

13. When they have finished, collect the covers to be used when Learning Center 1 is complete.

Date _____

FAMILY QUESTIONNAIRE

Dear Parents,

We are doing a lesson on family heritage and are trying to develop a family tree for each student. It would be helpful if you could give us the following information.

Family name _____

Mother's maiden name _____

Family's place of birth: Mother _____

Father _____

Siblings; Father's side (please list) _____

_____

Siblings; Mother's side (please list) _____

_____

Maternal grandparents' names _____

_____

Paternal grandparents' names _____

Occupations of grandparents _____

_____

Occupations of parents _____

_____

Thanks for your cooperation. Please return with your child.

Sincerely,

_____
Special Program Teacher

Reinforcement Activities:

Refer to "Learning Centers" and have your students do assignments 1 and 2. (NOTE: These booklets can be part of the students' holiday gifts to bring home.)

Family Tree (primary-advanced)

Materials:

copy of "My Family Tree" worksheet for each student
completed family questionnaires

Preparation:

1. One week before, send home the family questionnaire to parents. (See page 128.)

2. Remind the students to bring in their family tree information. (A note on the chalkboard is helpful.)

Directions:

1. Using a sample questionnaire, talk about the answers to the family heritage questions.

2. Draw a picture of a family tree on the chalkboard. (NOTE: Cousins and other family relations can be added.)

3. Talk about the meaning of the word "generation." Use the family tree as an example.

4. Explain that the top line is the student and the other lines are for family members. Use the board drawing as the example.

5. Show students the "Family Tree" worksheet. (See page 130.) Explain that they will fill in their own family trees. Help them fill them out according to the information their parents sent in. (This can be added to the "All About Me" booklet.)

Reinforcement Activity:

Refer to "Learning Centers" and have your students do assignment 3.

Classroom Family Tree (primary-advanced)

This lesson expands the child's concept of family to include his or her role in the classroom. The finished tree provides a meaningful holiday decoration.

Materials:

large sturdy tree branches   wooden curtain rings (1 per student)
white spray paint (for tree branches)   glue
utility bucket   ribbon
plaster of paris   red, white or green poster paint for frames
Optional: felt (red, white or green for backing)

> NOTE: Alternative frames can be made using one of the following: Play-doh, cardboard, pipe cleaners, construction paper, macaroni, braided yarn, popsicle sticks, or tooth picks (see "Materials of the Month" for December).

My Family Tree

Name _____

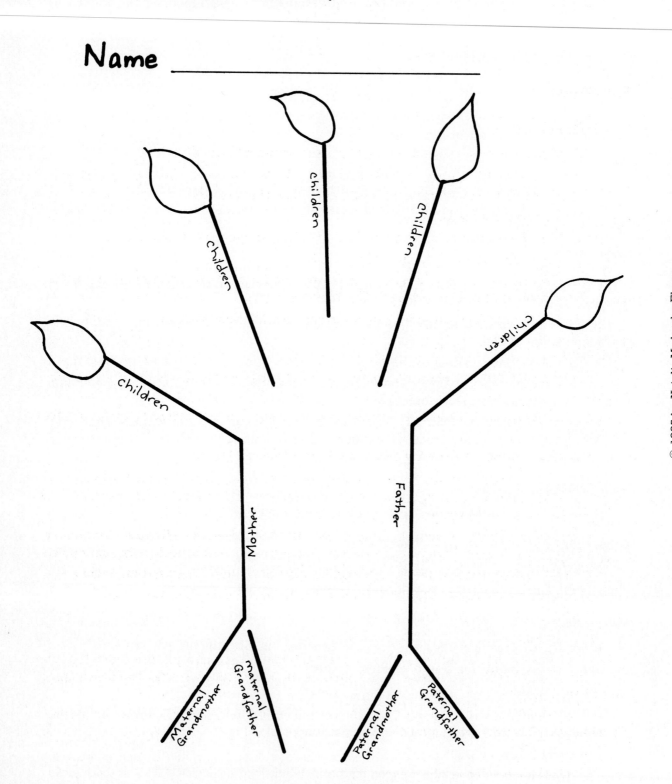

Preparation:

One week before

1. Send home a note requesting a photo of the student's family.

2. Remind students to bring in their photos. (A note on the chalkboard is helpful.)

3. Spray paint the tree branches white and allow them to dry.

4. When branches are dry:

   a. Mix the plaster of paris according to the package's directions.

   b. Pour the mixture into the utility bucket.

   c. Place the painted tree branches in the middle, arrange artistically, allow the plaster to dry. You may have to hold the branches in place.

5. Purchase unfinished wooden curtain rings (one for each student).

Directions:

1. Have each student show the picture of his or her family and explain who each person is.

2. Encourage each student to chronologically place him- or herself in the family according to age.

3. Define "family": A mother and father and their children.

NOTE: Other family patterns must also be discussed. For example, a father and children or a mother and children or grandparents and children. These family arrangements should come from the children first and be expanded upon.

4. Explain: "There is another kind of family. *The American Heritage Dictionary* says a family can be: A group of like things, like a class." Ask students for examples.

5. Ask, "Do you think we are a particular kind of family?" Expand upon this.

6. Explain: "We are a classroom family. We have our own classroom tree."

7. Show the classroom family tree.

8. Explain:

   a. We will paint each curtain ring (red) and it will become a picture frame for our family picture. NOTE: If photos are not possible for some students, they can draw a picture of their family.

   b. We will lay the dry, painted ring on our picture and carefully draw the outline we will cut. (Be sure students outline the outside of the ring.)

   c. Cut out the photo.

   d. Glue one side of the ring and place it carefully on the cut picture.

e. Allow the picture to dry on the frame.
Optional: Glue felt on the back to finish the curtain ring.

f. When dry, place a 3″ piece of ribbon through the metal loop on the top of the ring. Tie a bow.

g. Hang each framed picture on a branch of the tree.

9. Have the students tie a large ribbon or crepe paper around the pail.

10. Enjoy a beautiful holiday tree!

11. Students may take their pictures home on the last day before holiday vacation to give to their parents as a holiday gift.

Reinforcement Activity:

Refer to "Learning Centers" and have your students do assignment 4.

How Are You Feeling?

Materials:

magazine pictures of facial expressions (commercial pictures are available which depict feelings, see "Materials of the Month," for December)
10 index cards
chalkboard
chalk
clear Con-Tact
marker

Preparation:

1. If you are using magazine pictures, either laminate or put clear Con-tact on them for protection.

2. Choose those pictures that will elicit feeling words, such as, happy, angry, hurt, lonely, sad, mad.

3. Write one feeling on each index card.

Directions:

1. Ask, "What are feelings?" Write the responses on the chalkboard.

2. Ask, "How can we tell what another person is feeling?" (Answers include facial expressions, hands, eyes, body position.)

3. Have students show examples of the different ways people express how they feel.

4. Show a feeling picture. Ask for someone to tell you:

   a. How does this person feel?

   b. How do you know?

   c. Why do you think he or she feels this way?

   d. How would you talk to this person if you were with him or her?

5. As you show each picture, have a discussion about sensitive ways of dealing with people who are feeling a particular way.

6. Give each child a feeling card.

7. Have them draw their own picture of how they look when they feel that way.

8. Discuss each picture with the group when they are finished.

9. Have each student role play his or her feeling while another student responds to him or her.

10. Give feedback on their responses. Ask the observing students for feedback and other suggestions.

11. Put the feeling pictures on display.

Reinforcement Activity:

Refer to "Learning Centers" and have your students do assignment 5.

Good Grooming

Materials:

large piece of oaktag for poster
Mr. Clod worksheet for each student
chalkboard
chalk
pencils

Preparation:

1. Copy the "Brush Up" poster on page 134 onto oaktag.

2. Copy the two clown worksheets (see pages 135 and 136) for each student.

Directions:

1. Show the poster on good grooming.

2. Ask if someone knows what "grooming" means.

3. Explain that grooming is the way someone makes him- or herself clean, neat, trim and polished.

Brush Up for Good Grooming

Clean Hair
Clean Teeth
Clean Nails
Clean Hands
Neat and Clean Clothes
Clean Shoes
Daily Bath

Mr. Clean Clown's Checklist

Name _____

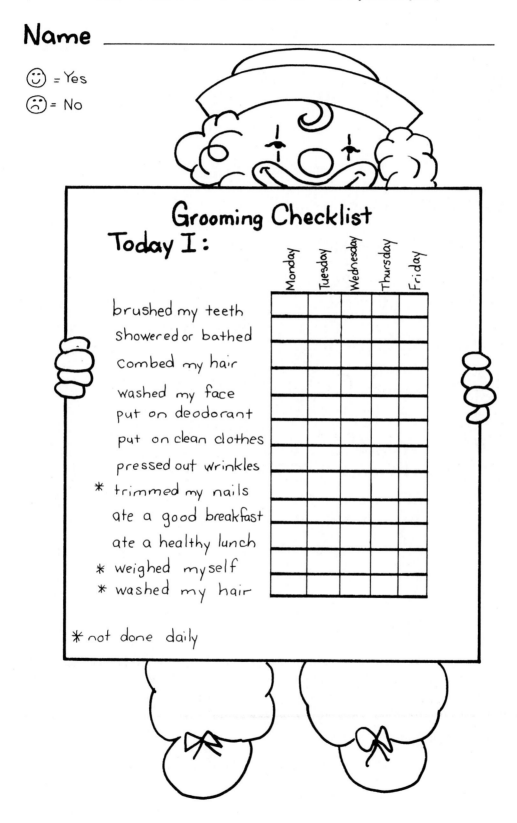

☺ = Yes

☹ = No

Grooming Checklist

Today I:

	Monday	Tuesday	Wednesday	Thursday	Friday
brushed my teeth					
showered or bathed					
combed my hair					
washed my face					
put on deodorant					
put on clean clothes					
pressed out wrinkles					
* trimmed my nails					
ate a good breakfast					
ate a healthy lunch					
* weighed myself					
* washed my hair					

* not done daily

Name _____

Meet Mr. Clod Clown

List the ways Mr. Clod Clown
could be better groomed.

_____
_____
_____
_____
_____
_____
_____
_____
_____
_____

4. Ask for examples of how a person can do this. (Refer to the poster.)

5. Discuss each aspect of the poster with the students.

6. Ask if they all followed the rules of good grooming.

7. Ask, "What are the basic rules of good grooming that we can all follow?"

8. Write these rules on the chalkboard. (Examples are brush teeth, take a bath, comb hair, clean clothes, clean nails, wash hair.)

9. Distribute the "Mr. Clean Clown's Checklist" worksheets.

10. Go over the Mr. Clod Clown worksheet together. Discuss what areas of grooming are good and what areas need to be improved.

11. Allow children time to write in the proper labels (copied from lists on the chalkboard).

12. Show the checklist from Learning Center 6 that they will be filling out for themselves. NOTE: These checklists can be kept on a bulletin board and checked off daily by each student or may be stored in their personal notebooks and kept privately (preferred by older students).

Reinforcement Activity:

Refer to "Learning Centers" and have your students do assignment 6.

Manners

Materials:

paper plates and cups for each student
a plastic spoon, knife and fork for each student
napkins for each student

Preparation:

Set the table for each student at the group.

Directions:

1. Invite the group to join you at the table. NOTE: They will all notice the settings and be anticipating food.

2. Explain: "There will be no food today. We are going to talk about how we use the things in front of you and what makes 'good manners.'"

3. Ask: "Who knows what manners are?" (Write responses on the chalkboard.) Make the following observations:

   a. "Actually good manners mean acting well behaved and polite."

   b. "Manners are any behaviors which respond to others thoughtfully. They are designed not to make things more difficult for people, but to make everyday living easier to be with people."

4. Ask the students to give examples of the above statements. Write their responses on the chalkboard, such as:

    a. Covering your mouth when you cough or yawn.

    b. Saying hello, good-bye, thank you, you're welcome. (These make others feel good.)

    c. Excusing yourself before you leave the table. (So others know where you are.)

    d. Not interrupting or talking when others are talking.

    e. Offering food to others when you are eating.

    f. Waiting until others are served before eating.

    g. Keeping mouth closed while chewing.

5. Let's practice table manners with the place settings.

    a. Put your napkin on your lap.

    b. Take elbows off the table.

    c. Sit up straight.

    d. Keep feet on the floor.

(Pretend you are serving.)

    e. Everyone wait to start until each person has been served.

    f. Take fork and begin.

    g. Replace fork when drinking.

    h. Hold knife and fork properly for eating and cutting.

    i. Use appropriate table conversation and tone of voice.

    j. Eat slowly with mouth closed.

    k. Cut meat as you eat it, not all at once.

    l. Do not overeat with helpings that are too large or taken too often.

    m. Replace fork and knife across place when finished.

Optional:

6. Explain that they will be having a holiday party where others will be invited and will have a chance to practice their manners with company. (See "Professional Responsibilities" for December. This will be planned at another lesson.)

7. Have each student clear his or her own place.

Reinforcement Activity:

Refer to "Learning Centers" and have your students do assignment 7.

LEARNING CENTERS

The independent activities at the learning centers for social skills are not only meant to reinforce the lessons, but to also inspire each student to think about him- or herself. It is only through personal awareness and sensitivity of others that a person can become skilled in social situations.

Often, children with learning problems are oblivious to social cues and the impact that their behavior has on others. By beginning a program of self-awareness, hopefully an ongoing analysis of behavior (both their own and others) will begin.

(1) ME
(PRIMARY-ADVANCED)

Materials:

> copy of each worksheet for each student
>
> index card
>
> crayons or markers
>
> pre-prepared "Meet Me" booklet for sample
>
> stapler or brads

Preparation:

1. Copy the seven worksheets for each student. (See page 140–146.)
2. Prepare a "Meet Me" booklet of your own data as a sample.
3. Write the directions on an index card.
4. Put the sample booklet on display at the Center for students to peruse.
5. Collate the students' worksheets into booklets.

Directions Card:

> ME
> 1. Look at Ms. Jones' booklet.
> 2. Complete each page of your booklet.
> 3. Use crayons to color your pictures.
> 4. Think carefully about your answers.
> 5. Use the cover you made.
> 6. Staple your booklet together when you are finished.

ME

Name _____

Age _____

Birthday _____

Where I Live _____

My House (Draw a picture of your house.)

ME

My mother's name is _____

My father's name is _____

I have:

_____ sisters

Their names are _____

_____

_____

_____

_____ brothers

Their names are _____

_____

_____

_____

Here is a picture of my family. (If a photo is not available, draw a picture.)

ME

Things I like to do:

_____

_____

_____

_____

_____

_____

_____

_____

Select one and draw a picture of it here:

Things I don't like to do:

_____

_____

_____

_____

_____

_____

_____

_____

Select one and draw a picture of it here:

ME

Things I do best:

_____

_____

_____

_____

_____

_____

_____

_____

_____

Select one and draw a picture of it here:

Things I need to improve in:

_____

_____

_____

_____

_____

_____

_____

_____

_____

Select one and draw a picture of it here:

ME

"THESE ARE A FEW OF MY FAVORITE THINGS" . . .

FOOD _____

COLOR _____

HOBBY _____

_____

FRIEND _____

CITY _____

_____

SCHOOL SUBJECT _____

_____

TEACHER _____

_____

SPORT _____

_____

TV PROGRAM _____

_____

BOOK _____

_____

SONG _____

_____

MUSICAL GROUP _____

_____

ME

WISHES

I WISH I COULD . . .

_____

_____

_____

_____

I WISH I HAD . . .

_____

_____

_____

_____

I WISH I KNEW . . .

_____

_____

_____

_____

ME

FEELINGS

I feel good when _____

_____

_____

I feel bad when _____

_____

_____

I feel happy when _____

_____

_____

I feel sad when _____

_____

_____

I feel angry when _____

_____

_____

I feel jealous when _____

_____

_____

When I feel okay I _____

_____

_____

(2) OH, WHAT A BEAUTIFUL BABY

Materials:

a "Then and Now" worksheet for each student

hand mirror

pencils

baby pictures of each student

index card

Preparation:

1. Copy the directions on an index card.

2. Copy a "Then and Now" worksheet for each student.

3. Place the hand mirror at the Center.

4. Be sure each student has a baby photo. (NOTE: If none are available, students can draw their own picture of when they were babies.)

Directions Card:

```
        OH WHAT A BEAUTIFUL BABY
1.  Look into the mirror
2.  Look at your baby picture
3.  Complete the worksheet
4.  Have your work checked by the teacher.
```

(3) CLASSROOM TREE
(PRIMARY-ADVANCED)

Materials:

list of each student's name

a "This Is Our Resource Room" worksheet for each student

pencil

index card

Preparation:

1. Prepare a list of each student (either on a worksheet or the chalkboard).

2. Copy a "This Is Our Resource Room" worksheet for each student. (See page 149.)

3. Write the directions on an index card.

Name _____ Age _____

THEN AND NOW

When I was a baby I could not:

_____

_____

_____

_____

_____

Now, I can:

_____

_____

_____

_____

_____

This is how I have changed:

_____

_____

_____

_____

_____

Next year I will be able to:

_____

_____

_____

_____

_____

This Is Our Resource Room

Name _____

On each branch write the name of a student in the Resource Room.

On each flower write the name of a person in your group.
Add more branches or flowers if necessary.

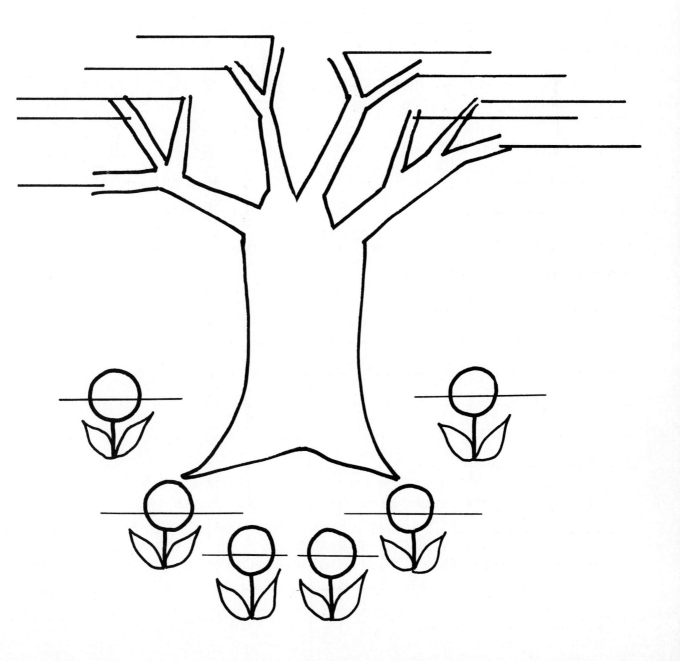

Directions Card:

```
┌─────────────────────────────────────────────────────┐
│                    CLASSROOM TREE                     │
│  1. Using the class list, fill in the resource room   │
│     tree.                                             │
│  2. Be sure to spell each person's name correctly.    │
│  3. Do you know everyone's name in the resource room  │
│     with you?                                         │
│  4. If not, find out!                                 │
│  5. Have your work checked by the teacher.            │
└─────────────────────────────────────────────────────┘
```

(4) MY LIFE STORY
(INTERMEDIATE-ADVANCED)

Materials:

an "And Here's" worksheet for each student
completed family tree questionnaire from home
index card
pencils

Preparation:

1. Be sure the completed family questionnaires have been returned. (See page 128.)
2. Instruct students ahead of time about how to use the "And Here's" worksheet.
3. Copy a worksheet for each student.
4. Write the directions on an index card.

Directions Card:

```
┌─────────────────────────────────────────────────────┐
│                    MY LIFE STORY                      │
│  1. Be sure you have your Family Tree Questionnaire.  │
│  2. Answer the questions on the worksheet. Find the   │
│     answers on your questionnaire.                    │
│  3. Write your life story. This is called an          │
│     autobiography.                                    │
│  4. Have your work checked by the teacher.            │
└─────────────────────────────────────────────────────┘
```

AND HERE'S . . .

Name _____

Birthday _____

I was born at _____

Address _____

Telephone number _____

My mother's name is _____

My mother was born in _____

My father's name is _____

My father was born in _____

My grandparents' names are _____

_____

_____

_____

They were born in _____

_____

_____

_____

This is my life story _____

_____

_____

_____

_____

_____

_____

_____

(5) NAME THAT FEELING

Materials:

copy the silhouettes   pencils
worksheets for each student   index card
clear Con-Tact paper

Preparation:

1. Copy the worksheets (see pages 154–157) for each student.
2. Copy the silhouettes and cover with clear Con-Tact paper.
3. Write the directions on an index card.

Directions Card:

```
                    NAME THAT FEELING
     1. Look at the pictures.
     2. Decide how the person must be feeling.
     3. Decide how you would respond in each scene if you were
     the person with the arrow.
     4. Complete the worksheet.
     5. Have your work checked by the teacher.
```

(6) LOOK AT ME

Materials:

"Mr. Clean Clown's Checklist" for each student
pencils or markers (NOTE: small stickers might be used instead to mark the boxes)
index card

Preparation:

1. Copy a "Mr. Clean Clown's Checklist" (see page 135) for each student.
2. Decide where the checklists will be displayed.

NOTE: Older students may prefer to keep their checklists privately rather than at the Center.

3. Write the directions on an index card.

Directions Card:

```
                    LOOK AT ME
1.  Read Mr. Clean Clown's Checklist carefully.
2.  Draw a   ☺   in the box if the answer is "yes."
3.  Draw a   ☹   in the box if the answer is "no."
4.  Be sure you put your answer in the correct box.
5.  Tack your checklist onto the Good Grooming board.
6.  Be sure to fill it in daily before you leave.
```

(7) MANNERS MEAN MORE
(PRIMARY-INTERMEDIATE)

Materials:

magazine or catalog picture of a place setting
a place setting worksheet for each student
pencils
index card

construction paper
clear Con-Tact paper
glue
scissors

Preparation:

1. Find and cut out magazine or catalog picture of a place setting. Cover the picture with clear Con-Tact paper.

2. Copy the directions onto an index card.

3. Copy a place setting worksheet (see page 158) for each student.

Directions Card:

```
                MANNERS MEAN MORE
1.  Cut out the utensils on the worksheet.
2.  Place them in the proper order on the construction
paper. Do not use glue yet.
3.  Check your work first.
4.  Glue on the pieces in the proper places.
5.  Have your work checked by the teacher.
```

Mom

Jane

Jane's View

1. This is what is happening _____
_____
_____
_____

2. This is how Jane is feeling _____
_____
_____
_____

3. This is what Jane should say or do _____
_____
_____
_____

Mom's View

1. This is what is happening _____
_____
_____
_____

2. This is how Mom is feeling _____
_____
_____
_____

3. This is what Mom should say or do _____
_____
_____
_____

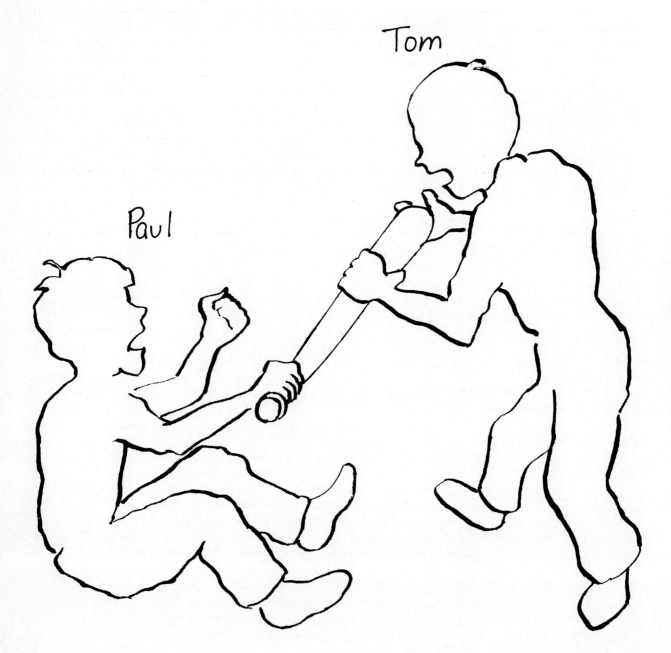

Name _____   **Name That Feeling**

Paul's View

1. This is what is happening _____

_____

_____

_____

2. This is how Paul is feeling _____

_____

_____

_____

3. This is what Paul should say or do _____

_____

_____

_____

Tom's View

1. This is what is happening _____

_____

_____

_____

2. This is how Tom is feeling _____

_____

_____

_____

3. This is what Tom should say or do _____

_____

_____

_____

Name _____

Directions: Cut out and glue the pictures in proper order on to another piece of paper. Be sure you set the table properly!

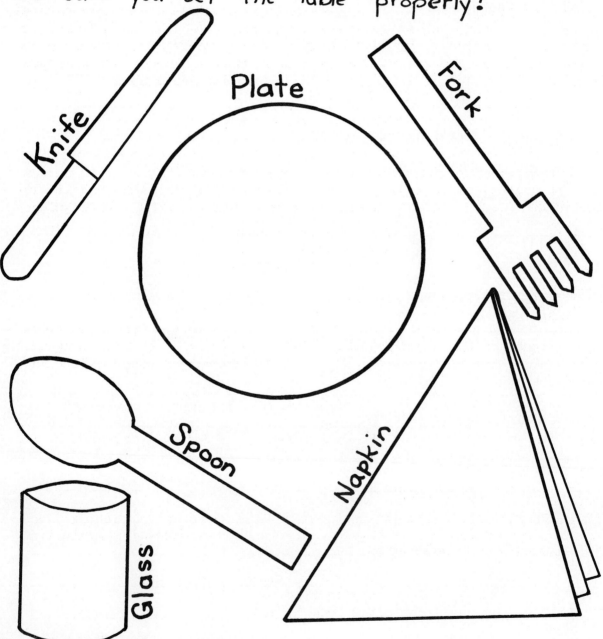

Knife

Plate

Fork

Spoon

Napkin

Glass

MATERIALS OF THE MONTH

There is an excellent source of free or inexpensive materials that is often overlooked. An inquiry at your local shopping area often yields interesting surplus materials very appropriate to use for craft activities.

Things like milk crates (local dairy) for book shelves; carpet samples for sit-upons or collages (carpet store); orange crates for classroom furniture (fruit and produce market); refrigerator boxes to make semi-enclosed learning centers or study carrels (appliance store); polyfoam shapes used for packing to make collages or other items (any store where items are shipped); and surplus computer run paper for fingerpainting, cutting, or other activities (computer store or large office building) are often available just for the asking. Usually, an explanation of the type of class you are teaching and why you need the materials gets a cooperative and enthusiastic response. Use your imagination and keep your eyes open. Many materials that are thrown away can be very useful to your program.

FREE FOR THE ASKING

Skin Care and You

This is an excellent supplement to the lesson on grooming! This booklet explains the skin's three basic parts and offers guidelines on skin care. It also discusses nutrition, exercise, water and sleep and their influence on a person's complexion. Send a postcard to:

> Dove Skin Care Booklet
> P.O. Box 1254
> Maple Plain, MN 55348

Guide to Consumer Product Information

This 192-page guide offers advice on how to buy and use 50 types of common household, personal and health care products. It also includes a chapter on adverse drug reactions. This is an excellent resource to use with grooming and good manners lessons. Send a postcard to:

> Bristol-Myers Co.
> Dept. NC
> 345 Park Avenue
> New York, NY 10154

Quick and Easy Guide to Beautiful Nails

Hints on proper nutrition, the tools you need and how to repair split, chips and tears in your nails are offered in this 6-page booklet. It offers interesting reading for those concerned with good nail grooming. Send a postcard to:

> Kristy Wells Inc.
> 53 West 23 Street
> New York, NY 10010

Play Clay Play

This big instruction sheet shows how to make "play clay" out of corn starch, water and baking soda. It also includes recipes for sand clay, salt clay, and pastry tube clay. This is an excellent way to make inexpensive clay, particularly for the classroom family tree picture frames mentioned this month! Send a postcard to:

> Play Clay Play
> Dept PC-FR
> Box 307
> Coventry, CT 06238

GOOD BUYS

The following items are considered good buys and are commercially available. Although they have been chosen to supplement this month's lessons on social skills, they can be used with a variety of other lessons and subjects.

Polaroid Swinger

This is an instant-picture camera. The advantage is that it requires very little focusing and gives the finished product immediately. It sells for under $50 and can be bought on sale for much less.

Personal Care Kit

A Teaching Strategy manual, 13 teacher's handbooks, accompanying sound cassette and 15 certificates of success for each skill are offered in this kit. The entire kit sells for $100.

Toward Affective Development (TAD) Discussion Pictures

These are 19" × 15" sturdy pictures of faces, gestures and situations with different feelings expressed as well as body expressions. They are excellent for use with social skills development. A set of 93 pictures sells for under $40 and are part of a larger set. Contact:

> American Guidance Service
> Publishers Building
> Circle Pines, MN 55014

Consequences

Thought-provoking problems are discussed on 71 cleverly illustrated, durable 12" × 6" cards. These are good for class discussion on social situations and alternative decisions. The kit, available from DLM, includes cards, teacher's manual and a classroom storage box for under $15.

Sensitivity

Included are humorously illustrated cards depicting problems and situations faced by many young people. The 46 9" × 12" cards are good for discussing feelings in others. Also included are a teacher's manual and classroom storage box for under $15. These are available from DLM.

Self Care Sequential Cards

These 3" × 4" cards are cleverly illustrated. There are four sequences of six cards each. Topics covered are brushing teeth, washing face and hands, showering and dressing. The cards sell for under $5 and are available from DLM.

Developing Understanding of Self and Others (DUSO) K-4

This is a complete kit of materials for an entire program of social skills. It includes a teacher's guide, story books, audio cassettes, activity cards, puppets, blackline master activity sheets, and letters to parents. The complete kit sells for under $200. Contact:

> Developmental Learning Materials
> P.O. Box 4000
> One DLM Park
> Allen, TX 75002

PROFESSIONAL RESPONSIBILITIES

HOLIDAY PARTY

A very good way to reinforce social skills and especially good manners is to have a party as a culminating activity where all the newly learned skills can be practiced. Since December is the month of holidays, the reasons for having a celebration are many.

One way to insure the students' use of company manners is to invite company: You might invite parents, other faculty or another class. Sometimes if the type of party and the menu are decided upon first, the guest list becomes obvious.

Having a "pot luck" meal is a good choice when parents are invited. By dividing the meal into "appetizers," "main course" and "dessert," parents can choose what they would like to bring. An invitation with a returnable slip at the bottom allowing a choice of food to be checked off is a good idea. An example is shown on page 162.

Having a "tea" with punch and cookies is also an excellent way to celebrate the holidays and practice good manners. Since the refreshments are simple, more people can be invited. Therefore, the possibility of inviting children from another classroom, the staff and the aides can be considered.

If your school has facilities for baking or cooking, the cookies or other simple refreshments can be made by the children in advance. If you do choose to bake or cook the refreshments with the students, both language arts and math skills can be incorporated into a baking lesson. This also encourages the students to feel more involved in the party and to take more pride in making every detail perfect.

The following invitation can be copied by the children and delivered to their teachers.

Dear Ms. Bensen,

We cordially invite you to attend our Holiday Tea on December 12 at 2:00 p.m. in the resource room. RSVP.

Sincerely,

Laura Lafky

Dear Parents,

    The children of the Central School Resource Room and I cordially invite you to our holiday pot luck supper.

    It will be held on December 10 at 5:30 p.m. in the resource room (room 119).

    Since this will be a pot luck supper, we are asking everyone to bring their favorite dish. (Prepare enough for approximately 5 people.) Please return the slip below no later than December 3 by sending it to school with your son or daughter.

    We look forward to seeing you at our party and know you will be very impressed with our use of good manners and social skills which we have been practicing.

                             Sincerely,

                             Ms. Post

                             Resource Room Teacher

☐ Sorry. I am unable to attend.

☐ I will bring (circle one)   appetizer   main dish   dessert.

This will be _____

Signed _____

Discuss the following questions with your students and make final decisions.

1. What food will be served?
2. How and when will the food be made?
3. Where will the food be placed?
4. What tables or other provisions will be used? How will they be gotten?
5. What eating utensils will be needed? How will they be gotten?
6. Will tablecloths be necessary? NOTE: Paper tablecloths can be decorated in advance. If placemats are preferred, there are several attractive ways to make them. Here are six suggestions.

Placemat Idea 1 (woven paper)

Cut strips of construction paper into 1″ × 24″ lengths. Lay five strips horizontally on your desk. Weave a sixth strip vertically under and over all five strips. Staple both ends when each strip is woven. Continue in this manner. Choose creative color combinations or monochromatic schemes.

Placemat Idea 2 (lacey edge)

Color or paint large sheets of construction paper. Glue a lacey border onto the edges of the paper. You can use paper lace doilies or fabric lace remnants.

Placement Idea 3 (holiday cards)

Cut up holiday cards and glue them onto construction paper in various designs. For a more permanent placement, cover the finished design with clear Con-Tact paper, which can be wiped clean with a damp cloth.

Placemat Idea 4 (wrapping paper)

Glue holiday wrapping paper onto a stiff backing, such as cardboard or oaktag. Cover the finished placemat with clear Con-Tact paper for durability.

Placemat Idea 5 (relief design)

Place a large sheet of construction paper on a prominently textured surface, such as a radiator grating, rough cement, or a basket weave. Use the side of a crayon (with the wrapper removed) to rub over the paper. The design of the surface will come through in the crayon's color. As a finishing touch, you might want to fringe the paper's edges by cutting them with scissors.

Placemat Idea 6 (shapes)

Using stencils, cut out a holiday shape (bell, dreidle, menorah or snowman, for example) and use it as a placemat.

As you make the supplies list on the chalkboard, be sure you have a "party secretary" recording everything on a piece of paper so there is a permanent record. With each decision about who will bring each item, be sure the specified volunteer writes him- or herself a note to bring home. It is a good idea to have the parent or guardian sign the note and return it to school. Another precaution is to have the non-perishables brought in advance. The more things on hand before the party, the less will be forgotten on the day of the party.

Be sure to clear the date with the administration ahead of time. Consider inviting principals and special education administrators to involve them in the program.

Plan a committee to help set up before the party, a committee to serve at the party and a committee to clean up afterwards.

Discuss party protocol, actual party manners, appropriate clothing and party dialogue *before* the party. No mention of these things should be made after the party begins. The children should be allowed to use the skills that they have learned and enjoy the party.

PROFESSIONAL RESOURCE BOOKS

Becker, Wesley. *Parents Are Teachers.* (Champaign, IL: Research Press, 1971)

Canfula, Jack, and Harold C. Wells. *100 Ways to Enhance Self Concept in the Classroom.* (Englewood Cliffs, NJ: Prentice-Hall, Inc., 1976)

Fugitt, Eva D. *He Hit Me Back First!: Creative Visualization Activities for Parenting and Teaching.* (Rolling Hills Estates, CA: Jalmar Press, 1982)

Lupin, Mimi. *Place, Harmony, Awareness.* (Hingham, MA: Teaching Resources, Corp., 1977)

Osman, Betty. *Learning Disabilities a Family Affair.* (New York: Random House, 1979)

Osman, Betty. *No One to Play With, the Social Side of Learning Disabilities.* (New York: Random House, 1982)

Simon, Sidney. *Caring, Feelings, Touching.* (Niles, IL: Argus Communications, 1976)

Vitale, Barbara. *Unicorns Are Real.* (Rolling Hills Estates, CA: Jalmar Press, 1982)

MODES FOR MAINSTREAMING

WHEN TO EXCUSE STUDENTS

Every special educator is faced almost daily with requests from the regular classroom teacher to allow mainstreamed students to stay in the regular classroom for one reason or another when they are scheduled to be in your room. Certainly, classroom work is not to be discounted, as it is important and necessary. It is indeed unfortunate when a student has to "miss" a lesson or a movie or a multitude of other things.

The child's program, which includes time in the special program, should be prioritized according to his or her needs. The Individualized Educational Plan (I.E.P.) puts in writing those services that are necessary for the development of a learning disabled child. Therefore, the services the child is prescribed to receive in the special program are a necessary part of his or her educational program. The trick is, however, to find a balance between setting the tone of the importance of attending the special program and being flexible.

There will be times when it is appropriate for the child to stay in the classroom and *not* come to your room. Unfortunately, there is no hard and fast rule for when this should be the case. Some instances will be obvious, such as, classroom plays or concerts and practicing for them, specially scheduled sports contest, a party in the classroom, a class trip, and classroom presentations of which they are a part. These are only a few examples of times it would be wise for you to either reschedule the student for another time during the day or excuse him or her until the next visit. When the child's absence from an event will penalize him or her either academically or emotionally, it is a good idea to consider yielding the child's special program time.

There will also be times when the classroom teacher needs to re-evaluate his or her schedule. For instance, the student's special program time is not an appropriate spot in the day for the rest of the class to have recess on a regular basis. Although this avoids the special student from missing academics, the child is likely to feel as though he or she is "missing all the fun" because of the special program. This makes the child feel resentful about coming to the program, and not very motivated to learn. Usually, a frank discussion with the classroom teacher will eliminate this problem.

Keep in mind that not all children will discuss why they are upset. Sometimes it takes a little detective work to find out what the problem is. Do not always assume that the student is "just in a bad mood." Classroom teachers have many children with which to deal and are not always tuned in to slights like the one mentioned above.

Good judgment is really the only way to decide which reasons are appropriate to excuse a child. It is important for you to understand your vital role in the remediation of children with learning problems. Missing time from the students' prescribed program is serious and should be conveyed to the school staff. As long as there is an atmosphere of cooperation, with everyone joining in for the good of the student, most problems can be worked out.

TIP OF THE MONTH

EARLY HOLIDAY PARTIES

During holiday time when there is a lot of activity going on in the school, it is a good idea to schedule your room's events to take place earlier than the other mainstreamed activities.

Commonly, events like holiday pageants, concerts, classroom parties, caroling, etc., take place the last two weeks before the holiday break. Even though it may take early planning and organizing by you, it is very important to schedule your events to happen before the others. Resource room parties, plays, parent teas, etc., should be scheduled during the first or second week in December. This avoids conflicts with other school activities and assures the participation of everyone. Nothing is more disappointing to a student than to anticipate and prepare for an activity and then not be able to attend.

Early scheduling also avoids over-stimulation of the students by too much happening at once. It is clearly worth the extra effort of early planning to be able to include everyone and have your galas unobstructed by conflicts.

A FINAL WORD

"With visions of sugar plums dancing in their heads," very few children avoid feeling the holiday excitement. This has its positive and negative effects. Certainly, learning disabled children tend to be more distractible than other children. Combine this tendency with the excitement all around them and a change in the regular routine to make room for parties and special events, and you have the potential for problems.

It is unrealistic to expect the learning disabled child to go about business as usual in the midst of all the holiday excitement. Consequently, modifications and allowances must be made. Here are some suggestions:

1. Try to avoid more changes in a student's program than are absolutely necessary.

2. Try to keep activities as low keyed as possible.

3. Allow the student time to unwind, such as time in the gymnasium to get rid of pent up energy.

4. Schedule periods just for physical exercise instead of academics as a safety valve for the student during this holiday time.

5. Build in more time in the schedule for listening to relaxing music and craft activities, like clay modeling or fingerpainting.

6. Change the nature of the work away from academics, which need more concentra-

tion, to less stressful activities, such as the lessons on social skills discussed earlier. These lessons focus on needed life skills and avoid concentration on areas of difficulty for the student. This is a time to take pressure *away* if possible.

7. Be alert to the fact that the learning disabled youngster is having a stressful time now. It is easy to forget in the midst of the holiday spirit.

8. Inform the regular classroom teachers about the above suggestions. They, too, need to be reminded that this may be a difficult time for the mainstreamed child. It is unfortunate when through no fault of the student, he or she is penalized because of his or her behavior.

These precautions may help to make the holidays pleasant rather than a disaster for the learning disabled child.

Happy Holidays!

DECEMBER REFERENCES

Albjerg, Victor L. *Winston Churchill.* (New York: Twayne Publishers, Inc., 1973)

Bartlett, John. *Bartlett's Familiar Quotations.* (Boston: Little Brown and Co., 1955)

Britannica Junior Encyclopedia, Volume 4. (Chicago: William Benton Publisher, 1971)

Churchill, Randolph. *Winston S. Churchill.* (Boston: Houghton Mifflin Co., 1966)

Goertzel, Victor and Mildred. *Cradles of Eminence.* (Boston: Little Brown and Co., 1962)

Goldstein, Herbert. *Exceptional Children: A Reference Book.* (Guilford, CT: Special Learning Corporation, 1978)

Morin, Relman. *Churchill: Portrait of Greatness.* (Englewood Cliffs, NJ: Prentice-Hall, Inc., 1965)

Watney, John. *The Churchills, Portrait of a Great Family.* (London and New York: Gordon & Cremonise Publishers, 1977)

January

1 Betsy Ross (1752) Resolve! Don't brag! Betsy's grandson bragged a bit too much. He bragged that she had sewn the first Stars & Stripes. It isn't so. But she may well have pointed out to General Washington how 6- and 8-pointed stars were a bit too hard. 5 points could be cut from a circle with one snip. Try it! Make Betsy a star!

2 Flora Jean Little (1932) Students in special education will be especially happy to celebrate Jean Little's birthday. Her specialty is writing books for special kids with special problems, in a very special way! Make a special effort to find one of Jean Little's books which just may tell about someone just like very special you!

3 Lucretia Coffin Mott (1793) She helped Harriet Tubman lead slaves on journeys to the North by the Underground Railroad. Her home was a REFUGE for runaways. And she spoke out for SUFFRAGE. Mott sheltered those with NO RIGHTS to freedom and spoke for women who had NO RIGHTS to vote freely. America was not yet a "land of the free."

4 Benjamin Rush (1745) Benjamin Rush did enough for 3. He was a PATRIOT: signed the Declaration, fought for absolution, and was treasurer of the U.S. Mint; TEACHER: wrote the first text of chemistry and taught 100s of doctors; DOCTOR: tried to cure insanity and yellow fever, and opened the first free clinic. His story is a TRILOGY!

5 King Camp Gillette (1855) Before razors, sharp sea shells scraped whiskers. Egyptians pulled them out, hair by hair. Gillette didn't think either idea too sharp. Tired of sharpening his straight razor, a sharp idea took the edge off the tiresome task. With his "throw away" safety blades, he could look and be sharp at every shave.

6 Carl Sandburg (1878) The sounds of the city and folk sayings of farm folk are found in his prize-winning poetry. Sandburg, a reporter for the *Chicago Sun*, also shone as the great biographer of Lincoln. He read his poems and sang folk songs to his guitar. It's "Guitar Month." Strum along to Sandburg's poem, *BIOGRAPHY!*

7 Millard Fillmore (1800) Our most forgotten president, they say, is Millard Fillmore (perhaps it's his number 13). Our country fathers should shower him with gratitude! Fortunately, few forget to bathe now for Fillmore was the first to affix a tub to the White House floor. Don't slip! Fill more tubs for Fillmore, tonight!

8 Elvis Presley (1935) The moving star of music put together the rhythm of blues, rock and country music! 600,000 records of his music were sold for hundreds of millions of dollars. The whole world of kids still moves to Elvis' rhythms which now are moving memories of Elvis Presley, the king of ROCK 'N ROLL!

9 Carrie Catt (1859) Susan B. Anthony, Elizabeth Stanton, Lucretia Mott, Carrie Catt: 4 names tell a story of suffrage. Carrie Catt was a teacher. Later, as leader of suffragettes, Catt caught the attention of thousands of women. Congressmen heard the clamor and the 19th Amendment became constitutional!

10 John Pitcairn (1841) John got him there! A plot to assassinate Lincoln was uncovered by Alan Pinkerton, private detective, out to catch railroad thieves. This time he caught a rumor: murder! Pinkerton put a young telegraph operator, Pitcairn, in charge of the train which brought Lincoln, secretly, to his inauguration in 1861.

11 Alexander Hamilton (1755) Washington appointed Hamilton treasurer. His job was to keep records of government money. Hamilton did an excellent job of SETTLING THE ACCOUNTS for the first President after the Revolutionary War. But one issue was not settled well! He was killed by ___ in a duel to settle an old FEUD.

12 Johann H. Pestalozzi (1746) and David Wechsler (1896) A ruler would smack you if you didn't sit straight! But thanks to Pestalozzi, rules changed. Kids could be comfortable. Fear changed to fun. And Wechsler's test made classrooms even more comfortable. His test told each teacher what to teach and how to teach it best to each student tested with the WISC.

13 Michael Bond (1926) There are over 20 PADDINGTON books — enough, undoubtedly, for a Bear-Fair to celebrate Bond's birthday! Each one read one book (or hear one) and prepare a Paddington project! Judge Bear-Fair entries fairly! Paddington Prizes: party plates, poetry, puppets, puzzles, plays, postage stamps, etc., etc.

14 Albert Schweitzer (1875) Share this day with Schweitzer. As a child, he got so many gifts he said "I must share them." And he promised then to share his life with others. He and his wife brought medical help to Africans who had none. He lived to share his days with patients. At night he wrote, to share his ideas in books.

15 Dr. Rev. Martin Luther King (1929) "I have a dream that this nation will rise up and live out the true meaning of its creed. 'We hold these truths . . . that all men are created equal.'" His dream, as were the dreams of Lincoln, was silenced with a bullet. He dreamt of killing hatred. One who hated killed him.

16 A.J. Foyt (1935) Four-year-old A.J. Foyt got off to a fast start in a miniature car built by his dad! A.J. left high school to concentrate on racing. But the only 4-time winner of the Indianapolis 500 did not drop out of sporting history. Fly a black-and-white flag for this 7-year Auto Club National Champ winner!

> Happy is he (she) who knows the reason for things.
>
> Virgil

★★★★★★★★★★★★★★★★★★★★★★★★★★★★★★★★★★★★★

17 Benjamin Franklin (1706) POOR RICHARD'S ALMANAC wrote he/And printed books of quality./Was first to own a tub so he/Wrote books while soaking comfortably!/Enlightened electricity,/Made bifocals for eyes to see./Began a university,/And a circulating library./Fought for the cause of Liberty,/And wished the end of slavery./And Ben, we truly wish that thee/Had writ thine own biography!

18 Peter Mark Roget (1779) He wrote a THESAURUS. He wrote a VOLUME. He wrote a BOOK. He wrote a TEXT. He wrote a REFERENCE. He wrote a TOME. He wrote a TREASURY of words. His volume or book or text or reference or tome held his treasures, words! His name was Roget. His ___ was Roget. His ___ was Roget. His ___ was Roget!

19 Edgar Allen Poe (1809) Flames warmed a parchment. A code appeared. In Poe's story of the Gold Bug, the code written in invisible ink told a treasure's tale. Like Poe, write mystery clues in an alphabet code. Search the library for names of two inventors born today. (Clues: 1736 and 1813.) Use starch and water ink and heat to read!

20 Harold Gray (1894) There's black-eyed Orphan Annie of Mr. Gray's comics and Little Orphan Annie of James Whitcomb Riley's poem who told tales of goblins 'round a kitchen fire. Leapin' lizards! They both would have been proud to see Annie on film and stage! Don't wait till TOMORROW to sing for Gray's red-dressed Annie!

21 John Fremont (1813) In 1853, Solomon Carvahlo accompanied John Fremont on his fifth and last expedition to the unmapped lands west of the Mississippi. Fremont mapped trails for wagons while Carvahlo proved, with photographs, that the railroad could be routed through the Rockies. Be Fremont! Map the miles of his Oregon Trail.

22 (23?) D.W. Griffith (1875) His memory never faded. He directed the story of "The Birth of a Nation" with no written script! And movie makers still use the methods D.W. Griffith master-minded to make movies better. First to use night LIGHTS, a moving CAMERA and ACTION from afar, he shot the fine art of film making far ahead!

23 John Hancock (1737) Dear Person, I collect autographs! I want your JOHN HANCOCK in my collection! Thank you! Huh? Well, Hancock was first to sign the Declaration. Because his AUTO (by him) GRAPH (write) was so big, his name now MEANS autograph! Start an autograph collection. It may be so famous your John Hancock might become a collectible!

24 Neil Diamond (1941) "I guess . . . I'm still tied to that kid who was not popular in school, not good-looking, not good at sports. I didn't know how to talk to people." But he speaks well now in songs (14 gold records) and in concerts attended by "record" numbers of people. Sing *Song Sung Blue* and a birthday tune to that kid! (See page 130 in Christopher Anderson's *People*, New York: G.P. Putnam's Sons, 1981.)

25 Paul Spaak (1899) Would that war be the last war? A charter, signed in San Francisco, June 26, 1945, might settle worries among nations by warring . . . with words! Belgian Paul Spaak, who spoke out for peace before World War I, would now speak for all nations as first president of the world's UNITED "peace-loving" NATIONS!

26 Roy Chapman Andrews (1884) Most dinosaurs are famous for their fantastic size. Not so for the PROTOCERETOPS ANDREWSI. It is named for Roy Andrews who came upon unborn Protoceretops skeletons in fossilized eggs—the first dinosaur egg ever found. National Egg Month is a fine time to remember the Protoceretops. Eat an edible egg for Andrews!

27 Wolfgang Amadeus Mozart (1756) He was old enough to go on concert tours but young enough to cry if someone disturbed him! How young? Mozart played piano at 3, composed at 4, and gave concerts in castles at 6! At 7 he played violin, at 12 wrote opera! By 35 he had written 789 masterworks! In Mozart's memory, hear an early minuet!

28 Alan Alda (1936) Eleven years of M*A*S*H made Alan Alda almost a member of the family! The TV set is now on view at the Smithsonian Institute in our nation's capital. It will always remind us of Hawkeye, whose humor helped to tell the truth of a tragic war. Ask Radar to send greetings to Alda. He'll track him down!

29 John Horsley (1817) It is late for sending Season's Greetings to greet John Horsley, artist of the first holiday card! Sir Henry Cole printed 1000 copies! (Two are now in the Hallmark Museum!) Some English thought the idea foolish! It certainly isn't foolish to greet someone with greetings today!

30 Franklin Delano Roosevelt (1882) "There is nothing to fear but fear itself!" were Roosevelt's famous words. Little did he know that, on his 51st birthday, Hitler became Germany's ruler. And little did he know that he would have to fight Hitler without fear. Hitler's aim to destroy the world was destroyed by 4-term President F.D.R.!

31 Anna Pavlova (1882) and William Russell (1812) Exactly one month ago, 19___ ended. Is this year different from the last? As years are different, so are people. How is Pavlova, PRIMA BALLERINA, different from rough 'n ready Russell who began the PONY EXPRESS? Each did very special things to change the way things were, from year to year.

These birthographies were prepared by Davida Shipkowitz of Northridge, California.

SPOTLIGHT ON

AUGUSTE RODIN (1840–1917)

Rodin is ranked by many as the greatest sculptor of the 1800s. He dealt almost entirely with the human figure. The emotional intensity with which his sculptures were created is most unique. His pieces express a wide range of human vitality, passion and suffering. Rodin primarily modeled in clay and wax rather than to carve in stone. He left many works incomplete or fragmentary to deliberately create a mood or feeling about the work. Looking at his pieces, however, you do not get the feeling that they are in any way incomplete.

Born in Paris in 1840, Rodin's work did not win instant acclaim. Gradually, however, appreciation for his work spread. By 1880 he was well recognized for his genius in sculpture.

Some of his more famous works are: The Thinker, The Kiss, The Burghers of Calais, Orpheus, and many more.

According to Lloyd J. Thompson in his article "Language Disabilities in Men of Eminence," there is considerable evidence to be found in David Weiss' biography to indicate that Rodin was possibly dyslexic.

The points that Thompson cites are:

1. At the age of five, Rodin showed great fondness for and some talent in drawing, but his father objected and even destroyed the drawing materials. Auguste entered a nearby Jesuit school when he was about six years of age. Auguste had great difficulty memorizing the catechism, understanding math, reading, writing, etc. He did poorly in all subjects because he was supposedly nearsighted. Art in his school was taboo.

2. By 1848, "Auguste's eyes grew worse." He had become the worst pupil in the school. He became a truant and his father is reported to have said in exasperation, "Voilà, I have an idiot for a son." Auguste was then sent to his Uncle Alexander's school at Beauvais.

3. After four years, Uncle Alexander was forced to admit that the Jesuits were correct about Auguste. He informed his brother that "He is ineducable. The sooner you put him out to work, the better." He even doubted that Auguste could make a living.

Although early reports indicate that Rodin couldn't read, later evidence showed that Rodin did learn to read somehow. When in Napoleon's army, he was assigned to a reserve corps and appointed corporal because he could read. Weiss also stated that Rodin did considerable research for his works of art. Reportedly this gifted man found his own way to reading as he became an adult.

Thompson points out that in *Naked Came I*, Weiss attributes Rodin's difficulty with school work and especially reading to poor eyesight. Yet years later, he is reported to have researched until dawn by a flickering light. Not a likely task for someone with poor eyesight!

Evidence from Rodin's early life show clearly that he had great difficulty with reading, writing, and arithmetic in school. Whether this was due to a learning disability, poor motivation or poor eyesight is not clear. What it does indicate, however, is that academic achievement and genius are not necessarily one and the same.

SPOTLIGHT BULLETIN BOARD

The "Spotlight" bulletin board for January is designed to simulate a TV set. Communication vehicles like television, newspaper, radio, etc., are used to present social studies concepts. The TV format can be carried out for other Spotlight bulletin boards as well.

Materials:

white background paper

black marker

overhead or opaque projector

acetate transparency

transparency marker (NOTE: If an opaque projector is used, you will not need the transparency and transparency marker.)

Preparation:

1. Cover the bulletin board with the white background paper.

2. Trace the "Spotlight" bulletin board (see page 172) onto clear acetate with a transparency marker if an overhead projector is used to project the image onto the bulletin board. If an opaque projector is used, the illustration of the bulletin board can be used right from the book or from a black and white copy.

3. Project the bulletin board illustration onto the backed bulletin board.

4. Trace the outline of the television and knobs first and then the material which goes inside.

5. Black and white make an effective bulletin board, especially for the television format. Colors can be used, however, if you prefer.

BULLETIN BOARD IDEAS

HIT THE BULL'S-EYE:
UNDERSTAND WHAT YOU READ

Since comprehension skills are the focus for this month, the January bulletin board lends very nicely to this theme.

A discussion about the skills (Read Carefully; Ask Questions; Take Notes; Find the Main Idea; and Summarize Information) listed on each circle can all be applied to reading for understanding.

Listing on the chalkboard all the components that go into reading carefully, for instance, can be a learning experience not only in comprehension, but in study skills as well. For example:

Read Carefully

A. Look for important facts.

B. Focus in—Don't daydream.

C. Keep asking yourself if you understand what you are reading.

Ask Questions

A. Try to think of questions you could ask on a test about what you are reading.

B. As you read the facts, put them into question form in your head.

Spotlight on........

Auguste Rodin 1840 — 1917

off on
On

Volume

WRR-TV

Color

C. Jot down important questions as you read.

D. Try and answer them when you have finished reading.

Take Notes

A. Jot down important facts, such as, names of people and places, and dates when things happened.

B. These notes should be directly related to the questions you have formulated.

Find the Main Idea

A. Try to put the main idea of each paragraph in your own words.

B. Be sure the main idea covers the whole paragraph or it is not the *main* idea.

Summarize Information

A. Be able to narrow down the information you have read and say it in your own words.

B. Try to express the essence of the reading without relaying every event or detail.

C. Be able to apply the information or concept to a different situation.

Materials:

yellow background paper

red marker for the target lines

black marker for the titles

margarine containers or other small plastic containers

thumbtacks

ping-pong balls (paper wads or other small balls can be substituted)

opaque projector

small basket or mesh bag

copy of the bulletin board

Directions:

1. Cover the bulletin board with the yellow paper.
2. Project the bulletin board illustration (see page 174) onto the yellow paper.
3. Outline the target with a red marker.
4. Write in the titles and board directions with a black marker.
5. Attach the plastic containers with thumbtacks where shown on the illustration.
6. Affix the basket with thumbtacks. Put in the balls and have fun!

NOTE: The footprints are optional. They can be drawn with the original outline of the board, or the pattern from Learning Center 3 can be used.

WINTER WONDERLAND

January is an appropriate time to feature a winter wonderland theme. In states where snow is a rarity, a reminder of the changing seasons and how the results of those changes affect other people is an important lesson about the world around us.

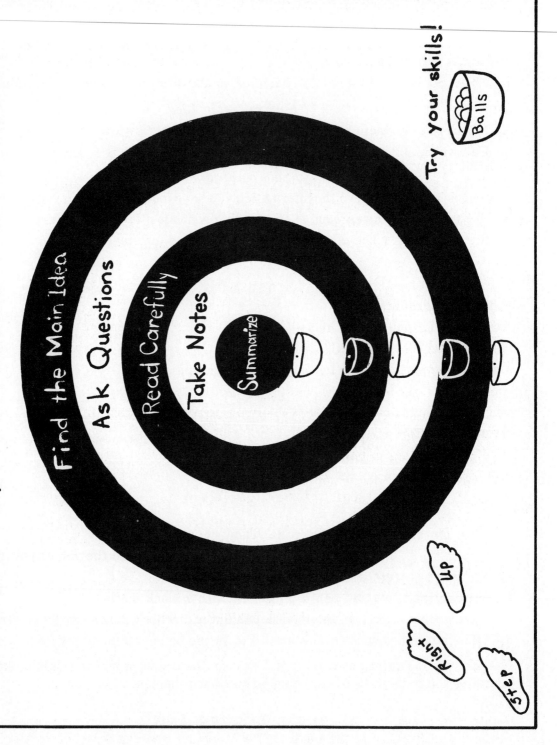

Hit the Bull's Eye....Understand What You Read!

Find the Main Idea
Ask Questions
Read Carefully
Take Notes
Summarize

Try your skills!
Balls

Step
Right
up

Materials:

black or dark blue background paper (NOTE: dark blue calico material or wrapping paper also makes a very effective backdrop.)

white construction paper for buildings and snowflakes

white marker for board title	copy of the bulletin board
scissors	thumbtacks
opaque projector	stapler

Directions:

1. Cover the bulletin board with the dark paper.

2. Project the bulletin board illustration (see page 176) onto the board.

3. Tack the white construction paper onto the board temporarily. Place the paper the height of the projected buildings.

4. Outline the skyline with a marker on the white paper.

5. Remove the white paper and cut out the skyline where drawn.

6. Staple the cut out shapes onto the board.

7. Make the snowflakes.

    a. Take a square sheet of plain white paper.

    b. Fold the paper in eighths.

    c. Round the corners by cutting with scissors.

    d. Cut out notches on the folds in a variety of patterns.

    e. Open up the folds when finished cutting.

    f. Voilà, an original snowflake!

NOTE: Making snowflakes is an excellent activity for the students because everyone is successful.

8. Randomly staple the snowflakes to the board.

9. Write the title with a white marker on the dark construction paper.

TEACHING UNIT

READING COMPREHENSION

Understanding the written word is really the meaning of reading. Being able to decode words is merely an exercise in puzzle solving without comprehension. Care must be taken to be sure students not only decode accurately, but also understand what they have decoded.

In order for a student to make progress in any subject, he or she must first be able to understand the reading assignments. The following are examples of comprehension lessons on a developmental continuum which can be expanded upon.

Since good comprehension can be compared to using clues to solve a mystery, the use of a detective theme makes the lessons more fun. An illustration of a detective's badge

Winter Wonderland

can be enlarged and copied and given to each student as a motivating activity to begin this unit. Further elaborations of this theme will be used in the learning centers.

Objectives:

At the conclusion of this unit students will:

- Be aware that events in a reading happen in a specific sequence.
- Be able to find the main idea of a reading.
- Be able to use context clues to aid in comprehension.
- Be aware of the difference between fact and fantasy in a story.
- Be able to draw conclusions or imply future events from a reading.
- Be aware of the mood or feeling of a reading.

And What Happened Next? (primary)

Materials:

package of flower seeds
bag of potting soil
digging utensils
flowerpot
chalkboard and chalk
worksheet

Preparation:

1. Buy planting materials.
2. Copy a worksheet (see Learning Center 1) for each student.

Directions:

1. Explain: "You are going to plant some seeds."
2. "We are going to keep track of each step we do."
3. "Everything we do has an order to it. Something has to be first."
4. Ask: "In order to plant these seeds what will we do first?"
   (Put the dirt in the pot.)
5. Write down the students' responses numbered on the chalkboard:
   a. Put the dirt in the pot (halfway).
   b. Place seeds in the dirt.
   c. Cover the seeds with more dirt.
   d. Water the plant.
   e. Place in the sunshine (windowsill).
6. As each step is mentioned, actually do it before you write it on the board.
7. When the seeds are planted ask: "What will happen now?" (A flower will grow.)

8. Talk about other things that have a definite sequence. For example: "What we do when we get up in the morning," "How we put on our clothes," "How we do our homework."

9. Distribute copies of the worksheet from Learning Center 1. Explain to the students they must put the pictured events in the correct order by numbering them. (NOTE: For those children for whom it would be appropriate, they can cut and paste the pictures in the correct order onto a piece of construction paper.)

Reinforcement Activity:

Refer to "Learning Centers" and have your students do assignment 1.

Find the Main Idea (primary-intermediate)

Materials:

overhead projector
overhead transparency and marker
worksheet

Preparation:

1. Copy a "Find the Main Idea" worksheet for each student.
2. Copy the paragraph below onto the overhead transparency.

Directions:

1. Ask: "What does 'main idea' mean?" (A main idea is the words expressed to give the general idea of a reading. *It can be an actual sentence from a paragraph which summarizes that paragraph.*)

2. Project or write the following paragraph onto the board.

MR. MICHAEL STEVENS WAS THE MOST IMPORTANT MAN ON MOUNTAIN AVENUE. SOME PEOPLE SAY THAT HE IS THE MOST IMPORTANT PERSON IN SUMMIT CITY. HE WAS A WELL-KNOWN WRITER. WHEN HE WAS NOT WRITING EXCITING STORIES, HE WAS WRITING ARTICLES FOR NEWSPAPERS AND MAGAZINES. PEOPLE FROM ALL OVER THE WORLD WROTE HIM LETTERS ABOUT HIS WRITING. MR. MICHAEL STEVENS WAS AN IMPORTANT PERSON.

> NOTE: Other paragraphs on appropriate reading levels from reading, social studies or science textbooks can be substituted or used in addition to this one. (See "Materials of the Month.")

3. Have a volunteer read the paragraph aloud.

4. Ask if someone can find the one sentence that summarizes the entire paragraph. (The last sentence is the main idea of the paragraph.)

5. If other sentences are suggested as the main idea, test them by asking if that sentence would accurately describe all the other sentences.

6. When the correct sentence has been found, underline it on the board.

7. Ask for a volunteer to put the main idea sentence into his or her own words.

8. Use other examples of paragraphs to reinforce the main idea concept.

Name _____

Underline the correct main idea in each box.

Time to get up.
Time to go to bed.
Time to do homework.

Hooray! It's my birthday.
Oh, no! My ice cream fell.
Isn't it a lovely day?

This is a good parking spot.
This is the wrong place to park.
This is the wrong place for a
    parking sign.

This is a goalie.
This is a batter.
This is a tackler.

9. Distribute the "Find the Main Idea" worksheet on page 179 to each student. Explain that pictures are another way of telling a story. They are going to tell the main idea of each picture by circling the correct answer.

Reinforcement Activity:

Refer to "Learning Centers" and have your students do assignment 2.

Be a Good Detective (intermediate-advanced)

Materials:

worksheets
mystery (detective) story (see "Materials of the Month")

Preparation:

1. Copy the "Use Good Detective Skills" and "Be a Good Detective" worksheets (see pages 182–184) for each student.

2. Find a short detective story in the library.

Directions:

1. Ask if anyone can tell you what a mystery is.
2. Show some examples of mystery story books from the library.
3. Read a short mystery story from a primary book.
4. Ask if anyone knows what the "clues" were in the story. List them on the board.
5. Explain:

> "Clues lead you to the solution of a mystery."
> "Clues can be used in reading much the same way."
> "We call them context clues."

6. "By being good detectives and using the meaning of a sentence to help us with unknown words, we are using *context clues.*"

7. Give the following directions:
"Please listen very carefully. Try and tell which word is incorrect and doesn't fit in with the rest of the sentence.

> Jerome fell off a *lack* and hurt himself.
> (What are the clues?)
>
> The strong winds made the little sailboat rock
> back and *first.* (What are the clues?)
>
> *Hipping* high, the frog landed right on the
> lily. (What are the clues?)
>
> Candy is my favorite *foot* next to ice cream.
> (What are the clues?)

NOTE: More examples can be given to reinforce using context clues.

8. Explain:

"While reading, if something doesn't make sense be sure all the words have been read correctly. Re-read and see if the meaning becomes more clear."

9. Distribute the worksheets. Have the students find the clues to solve the mysteries.

Reinforcement Activity:

Refer to "Learning Centers" and have your students do assignment 3.

Fact or Fantasy (primary-intermediate)

Materials:

worksheet

students' reader

Preparation:

Copy "The Fact or Fantasy" worksheet (see page 185) for each student.

Directions:

1. Discuss the difference between fact and fantasy.

Fact: Something known with certainty. Having real demonstrable existence. (Taken from the *American Heritage Dictionary*)

Fantasy: An event, statement or occurrence that has been invented or feigned rather than having actually taken place. (Taken from the *American Heritage Dictionary*)

2. Ask for an example of a fact. (Columbus discovered America in 1492.) Write it on the board.

3. Ask for an example of fantasy. (Papa Bear said, "Who are you?") Write it on board.

4. Elicit more examples from the students.

5. Go over the table of contents of a book reader they are familiar with.

6. Discuss which stories really could have happened (even though they are made up) and which stories are fantasy and couldn't have happened because they are make-believe.

7. Obtain examples of fact and fantasy statements from the students.

8. Now give examples and have students raise their hands to tell whether they are fact or fantasy. For example:

> Sally took her notebook to school. (Fact)
>
> Superman flew off the Empire State Building
> into the air. (Fantasy)

9. When it appears that everyone understands the concepts of fact and fantasy, distribute the worksheet for further reinforcement.

Reinforcement Activity:

Refer to "Learning Centers" and have your students do assignment 4.

USE GOOD DETECTIVE SKILLS

Name _____

Read the following story. Cross out the *wrong* words. Write the correct words above them. Rewrite your story on the lines at the bottom of the page.

Billy left the school at four o'cat. His brother Jeff was watering for him on the counter. "How come you're so lit? I've been waiting for over an hair," said Jeff. "Aw, the teacher mud me stay asker," wined Billy. "All I did was thaw a little wade of paper."

"Mom is going to be real wart, so let's hairy home. I sure hop you don't get a sparkling," warned Jeff.

Off the boys ran as quack as their lists would carry them.

Rewrite the story the correct way.

_____

_____

_____

_____

_____

_____

_____

_____

_____

_____

_____

Be a Good Detective: Draw in the scenes to complete each case.

Name _____

1

2
Help!

3

4

1

2

3

4

Be a Good Detective: Draw in the scenes to complete each case.

Name _____

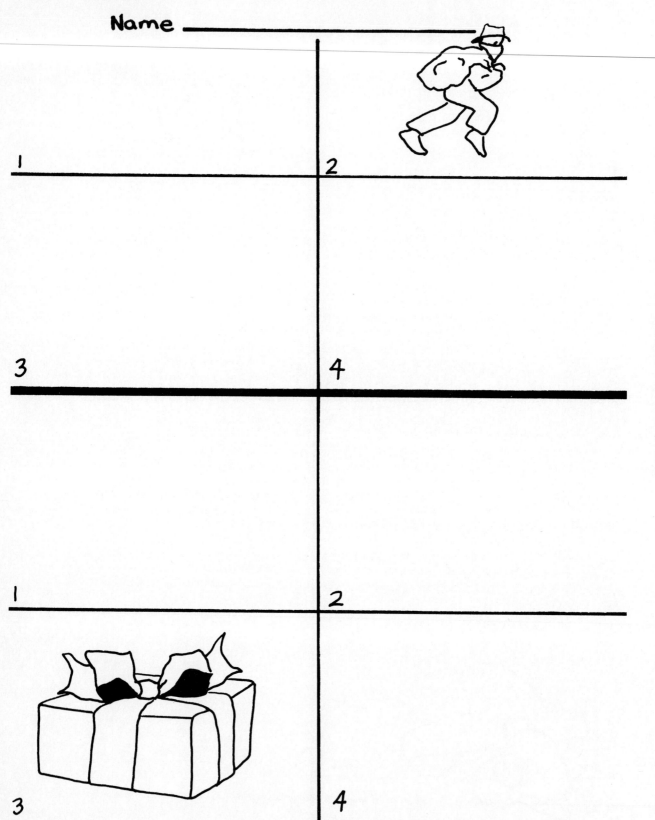

1

2

3

4

1

2

3

4

FACT OR FANTASY

Name _____

Read each sentence below. Write an R (Real) on the line if the sentence is factual and F on the line if it is fantasy.

_____ Charles told Gail to be careful crossing the street.

_____ Casey Cat spoke to the mouse in a quiet whisper.

_____ The airplane made an emergency landing near the airstrip.

_____ Father made dinner and called in the family when it was ready.

_____ The teensy weensy spider went up the water spout.

_____ The cow jumped over the moon.

_____ The Oompa Loompas continued working in the chocolate river.

_____ The giant peach rolled and rolled over the land.

_____ The clouds spoke gently to the sun.

_____ Pencil lead can either be hard or soft.

_____ Every student in this school gets good grades.

_____ It is 25° Fahrenheit on this cold wintry day.

_____ November is the month of the election.

Drawing Conclusions

Materials:

worksheets

Preparation:

Copy the three "Drawing Conclusions" worksheets (see pages 187–189) for each student.

Directions:

1. Explain:

a. Drawing a conclusion means that you make a decision about something based on what you read about it or already know.

b. We make decisions based on the facts around us all the time. For instance, if we are cold, we put on a sweater or coat; if we see it raining we get an umbrella or a rain coat. If someone looks angry (show an angry expression) we act differently than we would if the person looked happy (smile).

2. Get input from the students about when they draw conclusions; how they modify their behavior or thinking based on the facts given.

"When we read, in order to understand the author's intent, we must often draw conclusions or make inferences."

3. Read the following paragraph. Then ask for inferences or drawn conclusions.

David Erwin was a good eater. There was, however, one food he absolutely hated, SPINACH. He managed to avoid eating spinach for years. His mother and father knew how much he hated spinach and provided him with many other vegetables instead. His teacher knew how much he hated spinach and never made him eat it in school. One day, however, David Erwin found himself sitting in front of a spinach souffle! He was invited to dinner at his best friend's house. He forgot to mention how much he hated spinach. Mrs. Smith had gone to great trouble making a special dinner just for David Erwin. Everyone was sitting and waiting for David Erwin to start eating so they could start. . . .

What do you think happened?

4. Encourage logical answers based on the facts presented.
5. Distribute the worksheets for reinforcement.

Reinforcement Activity:

Refer to "Learning Centers" and have your students do assignment 5.

Name _____

DRAWING CONCLUSIONS

Write a paragraph about what you think will happen next.

_____

_____

_____

_____

_____

_____

_____

_____

_____

_____

Name _____

DRAWING CONCLUSIONS

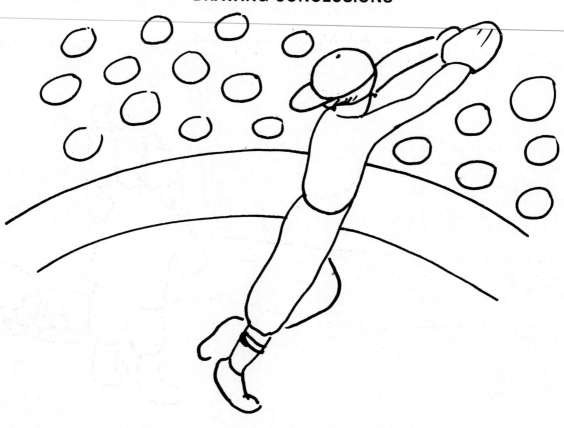

Write a paragraph about what you think will happen next.

_____

_____

_____

_____

_____

_____

_____

_____

_____

_____

Name _____

DRAWING CONCLUSIONS

Write a paragraph about what you think will happen next.

_____

_____

_____

_____

_____

_____

_____

_____

_____

_____

Identifying the Mood (intermediate-advanced)

Materials:

text from Step 2 below

Preparation:

Find readings that create a mood.

Directions:

1. Explain: "The way a story makes you feel as you read it is the mood. Each thing you read makes you feel a certain way. Recognizing the mood of a story helps you understand the story."

2. Read the following paragraph and ask students to be thinking of how the reading makes them feel. (Sections from other books and especially poetry selections are excellent ways to reinforce this concept. See "Materials of the Month" for suggestions.) NOTE: Ask students to sit back, get comfortable, close their eyes, and try to feel the mood of the reading.

> All you could see as far as you could look was sand. The wind was blowing as seagulls flew above flapping their wings. The sun was setting in the distant sky. The waves washed up and died on an empty beach. Summer was over.

"How does this description make you feel?"

3. Elicit responses of how the students feel and what the mood is. Words like "lonely," "sad," "alone," "peaceful" and "empty" should be encouraged.

4. Point out the words that elicit feelings like "wind blowing" and "setting sun." Conjure up mental images.

5. Other passages should be read for further reinforcement. Follow the above procedure.

Reinforcement Activity:

Refer to "Learning Centers" and have your students do assignment 6.

LEARNING CENTERS

The activities at the learning centers for comprehension are meant to reinforce the basic skills needed to read for understanding. Each independent activity involves the student in an analysis of the content designed to encourage comprehension.

Skills like placing events in order, finding the main idea, using context clues, knowing the difference between fact or fantasy, drawing conclusions, and understanding the mood of a story are reinforced in the following learning center activities.

It is suggested that each learning center be labeled Precinct I, Precinct II, etc. (See the illustration of a precinct learning center.) This is in keeping with the detective theme and finding clues to comprehension. See page 177 for a detective's badge that can be copied and given to each child at the beginning of the unit as a motivational device or at the end of the unit as an award.

(1) THIS IS HOW IT ALL HAPPENED
(PRIMARY-INTERMEDIATE)

Materials:

worksheets
index card
pencil
marker

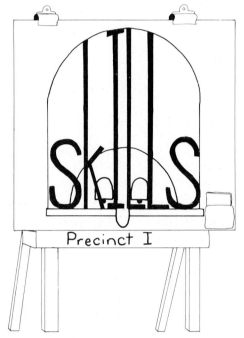

Preparation:

1. Copy the two "This Is How It All Happened" worksheets for each student.

2. Write the directions on an index card.

Directions Card:

THIS IS HOW IT ALL HAPPENED . . .

1. Look over the three pictures in each row on the worksheets.

2. Decide in which order the events in each row happened.

3. Number the pictures in their proper order.

4. Have your work checked by the teacher.

---

(2) WHAT'S THE BIG IDEA?
(PRIMARY-INTERMEDIATE)

Materials:

worksheets
pencil
index card
crayons

Preparation:

1. Copy the two "Main Ideas" worksheets for each student.

2. Write the directions on an index card.

NOTE: The precinct illustration from Learning Center 1 can be copied and used for the learning center backdrop or directions card.

This Is How It All Happened

Name _____

Put the following
pictures in the
correct order.

This Is How It All Happened

Name _____

Put the following
pictures in the
correct order.

_____ _____ _____

_____ _____ _____

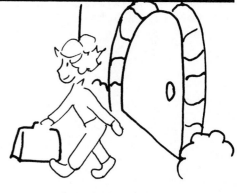

_____ _____ _____

_____ _____ _____

Main Idea

Name _____

1.

Underline the correct main idea in each box.

It's summer.
It's winter.
It's fall.

2.

Let's have a party.
Let's go to the movie.
Let's buy a new car.

3.
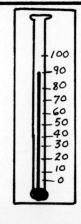

It's time for dinner.
It's time to go to bed.
It's time to go to school.

4.

Let's go swimming.
Let's play ball.
Let's go hiking.

Main Idea

Name _____

5.

It's time for trick or treat.
It's time for baskets and jelly beans.
It's time for giving gifts.

6.

It's time for dinner.
It's time for ice cream.
It's time for breakfast.

7.

Let's go to school.
Let's go to the movies.
Let's go to the zoo.

8.

Let's go to a concert.
Let's go shopping.
Let's go fishing.

Directions Card:

> ### WHAT'S THE BIG IDEA?
> 1. Look carefully at each picture on the worksheets.
> 2. Decide on the sentence which best describes the <u>whole</u> picture.
> 3. Circle the correct answer.
> 4. Have your work checked by the teacher.
> 5. If you have time, you may color the worksheet.

Underline the correct main idea in each box.

(3) SOLVE THE CASE (INTERMEDIATE-ADVANCED)

Materials:

large refrigerator box
footprint stencil
two folders to hold worksheets
worksheets
stapler
index card
large sheet of construction paper for sign
large magnifying glass
heavy string to hang magnifying glass

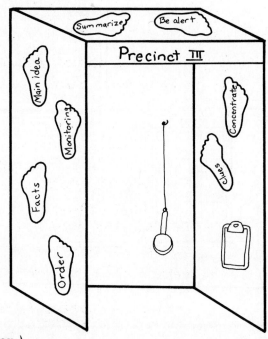

Preparation:

1. Set up learning center. (See the illustration.)
2. Cut out the footprints using the pattern on page 198.
3. Label the footprints with context clues and staple them onto the box.
4. Print the Precinct III sign.
5. Hang up the magnifying glass.
6. Staple the folders to the box to hold each worksheet.
7. Write the directions on an index card.
8. Make copies of the two "Missing" worksheets on pages 199 and 200.

Directions Card:

```
                        THE CASE OF:
    1. This is your case to solve!
    2. Read the clues of the case carefully.
    3. By using context clues, see if you can crack the mystery.
    4. Write and tell what happened.
                        Good Luck!
```

(4) FACT OR FANTASY
(PRIMARY-INTERMEDIATE)

Materials:

> worksheet   marker
> index card   crayons

Preparation:

1. Copy a "Truth Detector" worksheet (see page 201) for each student.
2. Write the directions on an index card.

Directions Card:

```
                    TRUTH DETECTOR TEST
    1. Look at the pictures on the worksheet carefully.
    2. Decide if they are real (R) or fantasy (F).
    3. Place the correct letter in the box next to each picture.
    4. Have your work checked by the teacher.
```

(5) DRAWING CONCLUSIONS
(INTERMEDIATE-ADVANCED)

Materials:

> worksheet   marker
> index card   paper

Preparation:

1. Copy the puzzle worksheet (see page 202) for each student.
2. Write the directions on an index card.

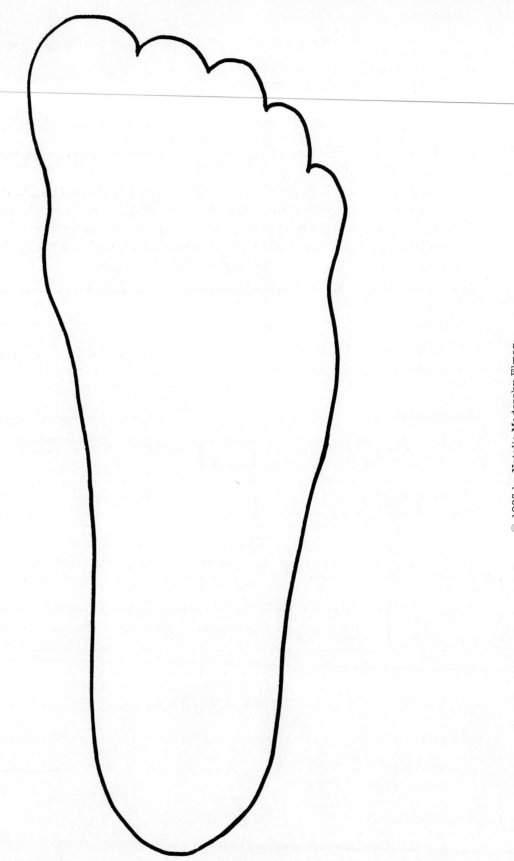

Detective's Name _____

THE CASE OF THE MISSING PROFESSOR

Read the clues carefully. See if you can figure out what
happened to the professor. Write your solution at the
bottom of the page. Good Luck!

    The Professor had been working on a long-term experiment for hours. He was
close to a solution, but hadn't found it yet.

    The phone rang. It was midnight. He spoke briefly on the phone. He reluctant-
ly left his work. He put some papers and a book from the shelf into his briefcase.
The professor put his hand on the door knob to leave.

    By 9:00 a.m. the next morning he still had not arrived home. HE WAS MISSING!!

What do you think happened? _____

_____

_____

_____

_____

_____

_____

_____

_____

_____

_____

_____

_____

_____

_____

_____

Detective's Name _____

THE CASE OF THE MISSING CHERRY PIE

Read the clues carefully. See if you can figure out what
happened to the cherry pie. Write your solution at the
bottom of the page. Good Luck!

Father finished baking the pie at approximately 2:00 p.m. He was humming merrily as he placed the pie in the open window to cool.

Mother came home at 4:00 p.m., gave Father a kiss hello, smelled the pie and went to look at it cooling in the window. She complimented him on his success as a baker and went upstairs to change her clothes.

At 5:15 p.m., Bobby and Larry came home from soccer practice. Smelling the cherry pie they immediately started looking for it.

When the family sat down for dinner at 7:00 p.m., Father came into the dining room looking very angry and excited. He said, "The cherry pie is gone and I want to know who took it!!!" Everyone sat in stunned silence.

What do you think happened? _____

_____

_____

_____

_____

_____

_____

_____

_____

_____

_____

_____

_____

_____

Truth Detector

Name _____

R = Real

F = Fantasy

Drawing the Correct Conclusion

Name _____

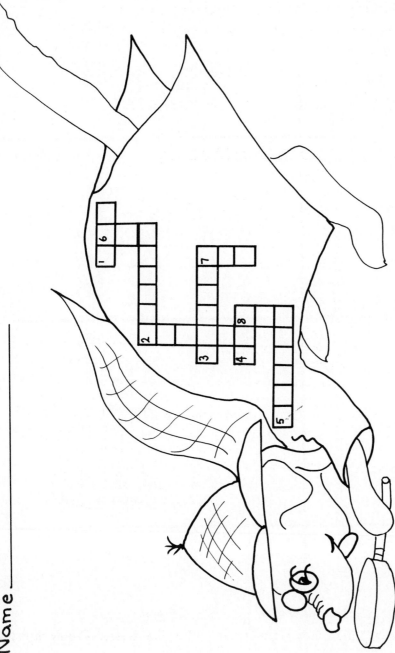

Across

1. When I look I _____.
2. Hot weather means _____.
3. The first day in the school week.
4. He helped the _____ lady across the street.
5. _____ weather means winter is coming.

Down

2. In the Fall _____ begins.
6. What you use for hearing.
7. The boy said, "_____, I want a cookie."
8. Isn't it a nice _____?

Directions Card:

> DRAWING CONCLUSIONS
> 1. Figure out the clues under the crossword puzzle.
> 2. Be a good detective and use all the clues you find.
> 3. Fill in the correct words in the puzzle boxes.
> 4. Have your work checked by the teacher.

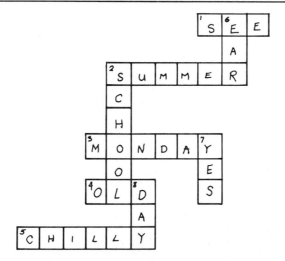

(6) CREATE A MOOD
(PRIMARY-ADVANCED)

Materials:

> record player or cassette player
> index card
> record or tape of different types of music
> marker
> earphones
> worksheet
> large sheets of white construction paper

Preparation:

1. Copy the "Mood Music" worksheet (see page 205) for each student.

2. Locate a tape or record which has 3–5 selections of mood music. (Frank Sinatra's albums are good.)

3. Write the directions on an index card.

4. Locate the activity in a quiet corner of the room with few distractions.

5. Cut out large white clouds using the pattern on page 204. Use them as a backdrop for the station.

Name _____

MOOD MUSIC

Circle the correct mood for each song.

Song 1: _____
        (title)

    This song made me feel: happy   sad   lonely

                                dreamy   angry   determined

                                excited   scared   _____
                                                             (other)

Song 2: _____
        (title)

    This song made me feel: happy   sad   lonely

                                dreamy   angry   determined

                                excited   scared   _____
                                                               (other)

Song 3: _____
        (title)

    This song made me feel: happy   sad   lonely

                                dreamy   angry   determined

                                excited   scared   _____
                                                                (other)

Song 4: _____
        (title)

    This song made me feel: happy   sad   lonely

                                dreamy   angry   determined

                                excited   scared   _____
                                                                (other)

Directions Card:

CREATE A MOOD

1. Music, like literature, creates a mood.
2. Put on the earphones and listen to the music.
3. On your worksheet, circle how each song makes you feel.
4. Have your work checked by the teacher.

MATERIALS OF THE MONTH

An excellent source of hidden materials is often right in the student's home. It is amazing to discover the number of useable classroom items that are thrown out on a daily basis. Things like empty orange juice cans (covered with colorful paper, they make excellent pencil or marker holders at the learning centers or for gifts); styrofoam or plastic meat trays (these make good shadow box frames for collages or other craft projects); extra material scraps or yarn (great for collages, and weaving projects); old lamp shades or window shades (lamp shades when hung from the ceiling can be an extra bulletin board and window shades can be an easy-to-store, permanent, roll-up poster for phonic rules, etc.); broken radios, etc. (a great learning center for the mechanics in the class); un-needed or broken furniture (can be used in a number of ways in the classroom; irrepairable wooden furniture can be broken up and used at a carpentry station). This list can go on and on. With a little imagination, many unused items ready for the trash can be useful to the special education teacher.

At the beginning of the school year, you might send the following note home:

Dear Parents,

Often, unused household items ready for the trash are treasures to the classroom teacher! The recycling of worn out or unwanted items at home is an excellent lesson in conservation for your children as well.

Therefore, the following items would be gratefully accepted if sent with your child:

    empty orange juice cans
    styrofoam or plastic meat trays
    old lamp shades
    old window shades
    material scraps
    yarn scraps
    old or broken radios or small appliances
    small furniture items
    unused games
    old children's books (no longer used)

egg cartons
large empty plastic soda bottles
spools from thread
shirt cardboard
shoeboxes
cigar boxes
corks

Thanks so much for your help. We will try to put your discarded treasures to good use.

Sincerely,

Freda Lafky
Teacher

FREE FOR THE ASKING

Winter Storms Leaflet L-96

This is an excellent leaflet to initiate a discussion on winter weather. It is an informative brochure on tips for winter weather survival. Send a postcard to:

Federal Emergency Management Agency
Office of Public Affairs
Winter Survival Campaign
Washington, D.C. 20472

Children's Fire/General Safety Coloring Book

A 42-page coloring book to the tune of "Mary Had a Little Lamb," this coloring book deals with safety on the street as well as fire safety at home. It is a good wintertime reminder. Send a large 6" × 9" self-addressed, stamped envelope with $.63 postage to:

Children's Fire/General Safety Coloring Book
Public Requests Desk
Corporate Relations Dept. D-5
Kemper Group
Long Grove, IL 60049

The Making of a Car

This is a very exciting reading comprehension exercise for all youngsters interested in cars. It appeals to the elementary school student and gives basic information about auto manufacturing and careers in the automotive industry. The kit includes a teacher's guide folder, bibliography of related books and films, four activity masters and a colorful two-sided wall chart. Send a postcard to:

The Making of a Car
P.O. Box 14312
Dayton, OH 45414

New Games Resource Catalogue

This catalogue is issued by the New Games Foundation, a non-profit group that works to promote new games. Featured in the catalogue are books on "Nine Men," "Morris" and "Kick the Can." The Foundation's belief is that children raised playing cooperatively-based games grow to have better social skills. This catalogue is worth looking at for Spring game ideas. Send a postcard to:

> New Games Resource Catalogue
> Dept. FB
> P.O. Box 7901
> San Francisco, CA 94120

GOOD BUYS

The following materials are chosen to supplement the lessons and learning centers on comprehension featured this month. Of course, they can be used with a variety of other lessons as well.

Increasing Comprehension

This is part of the Skillbooster series of skill booklets. Available on a variety of elementary levels, it comes in a text/workbook format. The cost is approximately $3 per booklet. Write to:

> Modern Curriculum Press
> 13900 Prospect Road
> Cleveland, OH 44136

S.R.A. Skill Series: Comprehension

This series includes 48 lesson plan cards, 10 student magazines, 48 cassette lessons, 96 ditto masters, tests, student folders and a teacher's guide for grades 4–8. It is an extensive set of materials for a large span of levels, costing approximately $300. Contact:

> Scholastic Research Associates
> College Division
> 1540 Page Mill Road
> Palo Alto, CA 94304

Listening Comprehension Skills Programs

Four multi-level kits are available. The reusable cards are color coded and sequentially organized for quick identification of specific skills. Each kit contains 109 selection cards, a teacher's manual, spirit master response sheets, and listening guide and box for grades 1–5. The program costs approximately $70. Contact:

> Curriculum Associates Inc.
> 5 Esquire Road
> North Billerica, MA 01862

Comprehension Through Involvement

Two workbooks comprise the program. The workbooks help develop the basic comprehension skills of main idea, sequence, detail, inference, vocabulary, comparison and cause and effect. The workbooks are sequential in difficulty. Grades 3–5. Approximately $3 per workbook. Write to:

> Developmental Learning Materials
> P.O. Box 4000
> One DLM Park
> Allen, TX 75002

The following books are recommended as good books to read to children to encourage reading comprehension and to help determine the mood created by a reading. NOTE: Descriptions and further ideas in how to use many of the books can be found in *Elementary School Librarian's Almanac* by Ruth Toor and Hilda Weisburg (West Nyack, New York: The Center for Applied Research in Education, Inc., 1979), *Read Aloud Handbook for Parents and Teachers* by Jim Trelease (Middletown, Connecticut: Weekly Reader Books, 1979), and *The Elementary School Library Collection* (Newark, New Jersey: Bro-Dart Foundation, annual publication).

Alexander and the Terrible, Horrible, No Good, Very Bad Day by Judith Viorst (New York: Atheneum, 1972)

Crow Boy by Taro Yashima (New York: Viking Press, 1955)

The Elephant's Child by Rudyard Kipling (New York: Walker & Co., 1970)

Hailstones and Halibut Bones by Mary O'Neil (New York: Doubleday, 1961)

Where the Sidewalk Ends by Shel Silverstein (New York: Harper & Row, 1974)

Winds by James Barkely (New York: Doubleday, 1970)

The following list is recommended to accompany the lessons on comprehension and especially context clues. They are all easy-to-read, short mystery stories.

Case of the Cat's Meow by Crosby Bonsall (New York: Harper & Row, 1966)

Case of the Dumb Bells by Crosby Bonsall (New York: Harper & Row, 1966)

Case of the Hungry Stranger by Crosby Bonsall (New York: Harper & Row, 1963)

Ghost Named Fred by Nathaniel Benchley (New York: Harper & Row, 1968)

Strange Disappearance of Arthur Cluck by Nathaniel Benchley (New York: Harper & Row, 1967)

PROFESSIONAL RESPONSIBILITIES

PARENT CONFERENCES

A necessary part of any school program is the reporting methods used to the parents or guardians. Although report cards will be discussed later in the *Almanac*, the person-to-person meeting or conference is really the most effective way to communicate with parents. Each person at that conference has the advantage of seeing the student in a particular light. The parent brings to the meeting his or her own very special knowledge of the child from infancy, and the teacher brings his or her insight into what that student is like in a school setting. If both of these perspectives are joined in a positive and productive way, a successful conference has taken place.

How to Prepare

1. Have as much background material as possible on each student. This is very important. Knowing recent test scores from the school's testing program as well as any diagnostic test scores recently taken is also needed. An up-to-date copy of the student's I.E.P., instructional guide, etc., help to give parents current information on their child. Parents will want to know (even if told before) where their child is weak, where their child is strong, and how you plan to help the child.

2. Schedule your conferences so they are at least 10–15 minutes apart. This gives leeway for conferences running overtime and still keeps things on schedule.

3. Send conference schedule notices home at least 2 weeks in advance. This allows working parents time to reschedule at a more convenient time. Be sure to mention the time allotted for the conference, such as 1:00–1:30.

4. Take into consideration those parents who have more than one child in the school, especially on all-school conference day. Try to arrange your schedule with the other teachers involved so the parents don't have to return to school several times.

5. Confirm all conference appointments ahead of time.

6. Have a comfortable place for parents to wait if they should arrive early.

7. Be sure the conference area is in a *private* place.

8. If the student is involved in the conference, try to prepare him or her ahead of time. Explain the issues that will be covered and what the student's role will be.

At the Conference

1. Arrange the chairs at the conference in a semi-circle if possible. Having the parents on one side of the desk and the teacher on the other doesn't set as open a tone as you would want.

2. Try to begin the conference with positive remarks.

3. Don't deal in generalities. Give specific examples of the child's behavior.

4. When negative behavior is discussed, it should be done in a productive fashion. Complaining about a child seldom promotes positive returns. It should be done with an attitude of "what can be done to make it better."

5. Find out what the parent is feeling and thinking about the child.

6. *Listen!* Try to promote a feeling of *working together* rather than the teacher having all the answers.

7. Two or three suggestions at one conference is adequate. Overloading a parent with too many things to do can be overwhelming.

8. Encourage parents to take notes. (Have paper and pencil handy.)

9. At the close of the conference, recap what was discussed. This helps everyone at the conference to have the same impressions about what was discussed.

10. Leave the parents with a specific time when you plan to be in touch with them again.

11. Extend a welcome to call or come in again with any concerns.

12. Keep a written record of the conference on file.

13. For those parents who appear hostile or dissatisfied, encourage a future meeting with the program administrator.

14. Be sure *you* act on any suggestions you agreed to at the conference.

In those programs where professional materials and books are able to be loaned to parents, a display at conference time encourages their use. Refer to each month's list of professional resource books for buying suggestions.

PROFESSIONAL RESOURCE BOOKS

Banas, Norma, and I.H. Wills. *Identifying Early Learning Gaps.* (Guilford, CT: Special Learning Corporation, 1976)

Banas, Norma, and I.H. Wills. *New Approaches to Success in the Classroom.* (Guilford, CT: Special Learning Corporation, 1976)

Cathon, Laura E. *Stories to Tell to Children.* (Pittsburgh: Carnegie Library of Pittsburgh, 1974)

D'Antoni, Alice, Darrel Minifie, and Elsie Minifie. *A Parents Guide to Learning Disabilities.* (Elizabethtown, PA: Continental Press Inc., 1978)

Dechant, Emerald. *Improving the Teaching of Reading*, 3rd ed. (Englewood Cliffs, NJ: Prentice-Hall, Inc., 1982)

Goldstein, Herbert, ed. *Exceptional Children: A Reference Book.* (Guilford, CT: Special Learning Corporation, 1978)

Golick, Margaret. *She Thought I Was Dumb But I Told Her I Had a Learning Disability.* (Guilford, CT: Special Learning Corporation, 1976)

Levy, Harold B. *Square Pegs, Round Holes; The Learning Disabled Child in the Classroom and at Home.* (Boston: Little Brown and Co., 1973)

Siegel, Ernest. *Special Education in the Regular Classroom.* (New York: Day Co., 1969)

Spache, George D. *Good Reading for Poor Readers.* (New Canaan, CT: Garrard Publishing Co., 1974)

Thorum, Arden. *Instructional Materials for the Handicapped; Birth Through Early Childhood.* (Salt Lake City: Olympus Publishing Co., 1977)

MODES FOR MAINSTREAMING

IN-SERVICE PROGRAM

By January, many problems have cropped up in the regular classroom with the mainstreamed students. Some teachers deal with these problems in a timely and open fashion, others, unfortunately, let them build up.

The in-service workshop is not meant to take the place of ongoing communication between you and the regular classroom teacher or the early-in-the-year orientation meeting. It does, however, provide a forum for presenting new ideas and a good opportunity for teachers to deal with possible solutions to unaddressed classroom problems.

Children with learning problems are by definition students who need special care. This means that the very busy classroom teacher has additional responsibilities to contend with. Sometimes, classroom teachers have feelings about this that they are reluctant to discuss. Having a meeting where many teachers can give their input sometimes allows a teacher to express negative feelings about handicapped children in a less threatening environment. For some teachers, just hearing others express feelings they may also have is a rewarding experience.

First, a date and time must be set with the building administrator. Many school districts have in-service days already built into the school calendar. If this is the case, permission to use one of these days must be obtained in advance of the proposed workshop. If pre-assigned in-service days are not an option, an after-school or lunch meeting is a possibility, though certainly not preferred by most staff members.

Once a date is set, a format for the meeting must be established. There are many successful ways to implement a professional workshop. Take a look at *Planning, Conducting and Evaluating Workshops* by Larry Davis and Earl McCallon (Austin, Texas: Learning Concepts, 1975). It deals with all aspects of workshop planning and implementing and is an excellent resource to guide decision making about in-service workshops.

A sample agenda is shown here.

AGENDA

Welcome (refreshments)

Introduction (The theme of the workshop is established, with warm-up activities at this time)

Film or Other Activity pertinent to the theme

    Note: Many of the professional associations like Association for Children with Learning Disabilities can provide information on films to loan or rent. Don't forget local, county or state libraries who often have appropriate films available to loan. Just be sure you preview them ahead of time.

Discussion about film or activity

Assignments to small groups for PM session

Lunch

Small groups meet with specific task

Assembly to give feedback and discussions from group

Recap of main points

Materials display

Preparation

1. Have the date set and approved well in advance of the workshop.
2. Send out advance notices to publicize the workshop.
3. Pursue film acquisition and previewing of same.
4. Decide on a format for the day.
5. Invite workshop presenters to participate.
6. Plan refreshments and how to acquire.
7. Decide on room and furniture set up. (Refer to the book *Planning, Conducting, and Evaluating Workshops* previously discussed.)
8. Make up group task cards and problem chart.* For example:

Presented Problem (written on oaktag and posted at the front of the room)

Johnny, a mainstreamed youngster, is in a regular third grade class with twenty-seven other students. He frequently calls out of turn, does not follow verbal directions, wanders around the room, and is generally a nuisance. Ms. Jones feels her frustrations building daily. She feels with twenty-seven other students, she does not have adequate time to spend with Johnny.

Group Tasks (each group receives one)

Task #1   How to change the physical environment of the child in the classroom

Task #2   How to modify the academic environment

Task #3   How to modify inappropriate behavior of the child

Task #4   How to improve teacher-child relationship

Task #5   How to understand the teacher's reaction to the behavior of the child

9. Copy the evaluation form on page 215, making enough copies for all participants.
10. Remind presenters and announce a meeting with participants by a memo.
11. Have an actual rehearsal with workshop participants.
12. Set up the room(s) according to plan.
13. Put out paper, pencils, wall charts, markers, etc.
14. Double check audio-visual equipment on the day of the workshop.
15. Good Luck!

An evaluation form distributed to the workshop participants at the end of the day helps to plan for next year's workshop. Also, keep your ears open for feedback from the staff. Be open to suggestions and understand that one of the goals of the in-service workshop is to provide a forum for discussion. If teachers are discussing it, you have achieved at least one goal.

---

*This material was taken from *The Resource Room Primer* by Natalie Elman, Englewood Cliffs, NJ: Prentice-Hall, Inc., 1981, p. 171.

TIP OF THE MONTH

STUDENT MEMO BOARD

A very effective way of communicating with the students is through the use of a Student Memo Board. This can be a portable kitchen-type bulletin board, a peg board, the back of a door, etc. The important thing is that it be a permanent part of the room.

The memo board is an excellent way to give positive reinforcement. Children love the "grown up" idea of receiving a note just for them. It works not only as a reward system, but is also an excellent way to make suggestions for improvement in a very non-threatening way. The memo board is an excellent vehicle of private communication between you and the student.

Things to remember:

1. Print for primary students and use easy words.

2. Always keep the tone positive. For example: "I liked the way you worked today. Keep it up! Mrs. E."

3. Write legibly.

4. Do not leave anyone out. Each student should get at least one note for something in a given period of time.

5. Make a rule that each person may only read his or her own note.

6. Fold over each note and put the child's name on the outside for privacy.

A FINAL WORD

EXTRA DUTIES

Very few teachers love the idea of lunch duty and bus duty. They are hard work and there is the argument that they are not professional endeavors. The reality, however, is that many schools require teachers to assume some responsibility for monitoring children during lunch, at recess time, and before and after school.

Some districts have aides who assume these duties, which eliminates the problem. For those districts where special education teachers rotate the responsibility of the supervision of large groups of students with other teachers, there are some concomitant benefits.

Watching the students relate socially in a non-structured environment can give a whole different perspective on a student. This also allows you to be included in the "regular" part of the student's life, a benefit when working with the student later.

Also, being seen by and relating to the general school population is important. Often, special educators are seen as "different" by the other students. Having the opportunity to relate positively to the students as another teacher can have an excellent public relations effect. It makes those students currently attending the special program feel a little better about it and those who may be coming in the future much less apprehensive.

In-Service Workshop Assessment Form

Topic: _____ Date: _____

Please answer the questions below. Your honest input will help us prepare future programs.

1. Did you find this in-service workshop responsive to your classroom needs?

_____

_____

    a. content was covered to your satisfaction

_____

_____

    b. assessment of presentation

_____

_____

    c. was there time for your questions to be adequately answered?

_____

_____

2. What part of the in-service workshop was most useful? _____

_____

_____

3. Added comments, questions or suggestions on future workshops. (use back side if necessary)

_____

_____

4. How could this in-service workshop be improved? _____

_____

_____

_____
Name (optional)

There are some districts where the "specialists" (resource room teachers, art teachers, etc.) are excused from extra duties. As tempting as this fringe benefit may seem, it may not be worth the price because other staff members can become very resentful! Working cooperatively with the staff is essential to the progress of your program, so avoiding staff resentment will certainly make that cooperation easier to achieve. Extra duties may just have to be tolerated in exchange for staff acceptance and more student involvement.

JANUARY REFERENCES

Bartlett, John. *Bartlett's Familiar Quotations.* (Boston: Little Brown and Co., 1955)

The Elementary School Library Collection: A Guide to Books and Other Media. (Newark, NJ: The Bro-Dart Foundation, 1977)

Goertzel, Victor and Mildred. *Cradles of Eminence.* (Boston: Little Brown and Co., 1962)

Thompson, Lloyd J. "Language Disabilities in Men of Eminence." *Journal of Learning Disabilities*, January 1971.

Weiss, D. *Naked Came I.* (New York: William Morrow, 1963)

World Book Encyclopedia, Volume R. (Chicago: World Book Inc., 1980)

World Book Encyclopedia, Volume U. (Chicago: World Book Inc., 1980)

February

Happy birthday to . . .

1 Langston Hughes (1902)   Langston Hughes is as famous for his poetry, Broadway shows and books as are the people he writes about. Biographies of black heroes and makers of music and jazz tell stories of Americans whose birthdays are forgotten but whose names are a roll call to be honored. Read his stories of HENSON, DOUGLAS, . . .

2 Fritz Kreisler (1875) and Jascha Heifetz (1901)   Fiddle around with the family of fiddles! First, cut out 4 fiddle forms, ranging their sizes from small to large. Then, fit 4 fine strings for each and fasten. To finish find the name of each fiddle. Find out which ones the fabulous fiddlers, Heifetz and Kreisler, fiddled so famously at age 4!

3 Elizabeth Blackwell (1821)   Why are portraits of people on postage stamps? One purpose is PRIDE! Americans are proud to remember Elizabeth Blackwell, the first woman to graduate from medical school! Other stamps remember Jackie Robinson, Babe Zaharias, Ernie Pyle, and Bobby Jones. You'll feel proud when you find out why!

4 Rosa Parks (1913)   How would you like to sit in the back of a city bus just because you have black hair, or eyes, or skin? Rosa didn't think that was fair. With courage she stood up for her civil rights by sitting down in the "white folks' front." Though Rosa was jailed, that day was the real birthday of black freedom!

5 Henry Aaron (1934)   Could Henry "Hank" Aaron really break Babe Ruth's record — a lifetime record of 714 home runs? 900,000 people sent him letters. He got letters that called him names. He was angry! But Aaron wanted to show kids that success comes if you keep on trying. 9:07 p.m., April 8, 1974. Home run #715! WOW! Let's celebrate — tomorrow . . .

6 Babe Ruth (1895)   He pointed to the center field fence and swat the next pitch right over it, just where he had promised! 714 home runs — a record topped only by ___! Question: Whose record did he break (1927) for home runs in a 154-game season? Now, play ball! Two teams, the Aarons and the Ruths. Will the Aarons keep the lead?

7 Laura Ingalls Wilder (1867)   Little House on the Prairie was not published until Laura Ingalls Wilder was 65. "It can never be a long time ago," she thought as she wrote the 7 books which tell of hard working days on the South Dakota plains. And her tales will not seem a long time ago to you! Take "Little House" to your house to read!

8 Jules Verne (1828)   Submarines, TV, spacecraft — all are part of Verne's novels long before they were actually realized. His stories seemed so real — so real that folks who read From the Earth to the Moon volunteered to go there along with him! You'll meet Nelly Bly in May. She tried to beat Phineas Fogg's trip in Verne's book, ___.

9 Lydia Pinkham (1819)   Before doctors knew that only certain medicines could cure certain aches, syrups and salves that were cooked up in kitchens were sold by mail or carnival wagon to remedy every ill! Vegetable syrup and alcohol cured nothing, but millions praised Lydia Pinkham's powerful pink PATENT MEDICINE pills!

10 Mark Spitz (1950)   Send a singing telegram to swimmer Mark Spitz. It's the birthday of that melodious message and Mark's, too! Sing to say hurray for winning 9 Olympic gold medals (7 in 1972)! Asked why he didn't go to afternoon religious school but practiced instead, his dad said, "Even God likes a winner!" And win, Mark did!

11 William Talbot (1800)   Don't be negative about William Talbot! By coincidence, Talbot began experiments with photography at the same time the Frenchman Daugerre did! But Talbot made positive improvements. The first negative and the first book of photographs were his! Hang negatives on the windows and make positive identification.

12 Abraham Lincoln (1809)   "Abraham Lincoln/His Hand and Pen/He Will be Good/But God Knows When." Young Abe couldn't wait for a little red schoolhouse to be built near his old Kentucky home. He was always reading under shady trees or at an open fire. Again he wrote, "Good boys who to their books apply,/Will all be great men by and by."

13 William Shockley (1910) and Capt. Edward Yaeger (1923)   You didn't hear the big news on a transistor radio in 1947! Shockley hadn't invented the transistor when Capt. Yaeger flew over California at 670 m.p.h., the first flight OVER the speed of sound! Millions might have heard on transistors about Maj. Wright's flight of 4,534 m.p.h. Millions of transistors were around by then!

14 Christopher Sholes (1819) and George Ferris (1859)   Click and clack and hunt and peck/Write forget-me-not and sonnet/Capitalize on Sholes's typewriter/Spell I-LOVE-YOU upon it./And, then find just the tip-top place/To present your Valentine!/Atop George Ferris's giant wheel/Might you ask, "Will you be mine?" ***Type birthday rhymes for Valentines!

All experience is an arch to build upon.

Henry Brooks Adams

15 John Sutter (1803) Sutter tried to keep the secret. It was the afternoon of January 28, 1848, just after Sutter's new sawmill had been built. James Marshall came, carrying in his arms his old white hat filled with flakes of gold. The secret got out! Gold miners rushed in, leaving Sutter with no claim to fame or fortune.

16 John McEnroe (1959) His nickname, "Super Brat," was not really a compliment. Like many young adults, John had something to overcome. It was not easy for McEnroe to control his temper! But it was easy for him to control a tennis ball. With "super skills" he won the Davis Cup and Wimbledon! Try your hand at this "racket."

17 Rene-Theophile-Hyacinthe Laennec (1781) He began with a roll of papers. With one end to his ear and the other to a chest, Laennec heard a soft LUB-DUB, LUB-DUB. Might a wood tube do better? Yes! He clearly heard heart sounds he had never heard before! With a cardboard tube against a classmate's back, hear LUB-DUB, LUB-DUB!

18 John Travolta (1954) Though he dropped out of high school, he went back for a second chance when "school" opened in September 1973 at James Buchanan High School, Brooklyn. His teacher? Gabe Kotter. The class list? Juan Epstein, Arnold Horshack, "Boom Boom" Washington and Vinnie Barbarino. Welcome back to TV school, John Travolta!

19 Nicholas Copernicus (1473) Aristarchus in 300 B.C. said the earth revolved around the sun. In 212 B.C. Archimedes said so, too. No one listened until Copernicus from Poland said it in 1543. He convinced the world that the earth, one of many planets, circled our star, the sun. With a model of the planets, convince your classmates once more.

20 Bobby Unser (1934) "Gentlemen, start your engines!" Roars of power rose as a green flag was waved. Crowds cheered as cars curved, lap by lap, to the finish. That's how races go for brothers Bobby and Al Unser. Both won the Indianapolis 500 and more! Don't lose speed finding a record of their records in car racing and wave a 🏁

21 Presidents Day (when observed, from 1732) It's Presidents Day — and National Pencil Week! Patiently pencil lists of presidents by birthdate, wives' names, age when president, months of presidency, political party, postage pictures, or particular aspects you possibly prefer. After the pledge, proudly praise them with, "Happy Birthday dear Presidents!"

22 George Washington (1732) and Sir Robert Baden-Powell (1857) Resourceful, self-reliant and courageous; Washington and Baden-Powell were all of these. And both men taught these traits to others. Washington to the tattered soldiers of the Revolution and Powell to the first troop of Boy Scouts. Thanks to them, a new nation and a new idea were soon welcomed world over.

23 Emma Willard (1787) The girls carved potatoes into pyramids and cones. Wooden shapes were too costly and Emma Willard wanted her girls to learn more than reading, writing, painting, and singing. She knew they needed a higher education to shape their futures. Do as Willard's college students did. Carve pyramids from potatoes!

24 Wilhelm Grimm (1786) Which old Chinese tale may be told in celebration of the Chinese New Year? CINDERELLA. In 900 A.D., long before Brothers Grimm RETOLD it, CINDERELLA was first written in China. Now, enjoy the best known of all old stories to start the New Year. Hear Grimm's grim tale that ends happily ever after!

25 Enrico Caruso (1873) and Jim Backus (1913) Hear 2 notables known by their voices! Caruso, the world's best known tenor, sang opera to thrill the audiences he so truly loved — loved so well he bought their tickets for them! And the voice of Backus brings to mind clearly seen cartoons of not so clear-sighted Mr. Magoo! Sing out if you've ever heard their first names!

26 William Cody (1846) He successfully killed 4,280 buffalo! Today Cody would learn his nickname by saving them! But they did feed railroad crews who set Union Pacific tracks traveling west to join the Central Pacific with a Golden Spike. And Cody's Wild West show sent Annie Oakley and Sitting Bull traveling with wild success.

27 Henry Wadsworth Longfellow (1807) Find something to write about, tell what it is for, and what is to be done with it! So said a teacher of the gentle poet, Longfellow. Children adored him and you will love his poems forever. Read his THE OLD CLOCK ON THE STAIRS. Now find a clock, tell what it is for and what is to be done with it!

28 John Tenniel (1820) Tenniel drew Alice, kneeling on the mantle. Looking into the cloudy silver mist she stepped THROUGH it into THE LOOKING GLASS room. Things looked a bit backwards, but much better for birthdays! Humpty Dumpty proved that to Alice. Wouldn't 364 unbirthday presents be merrier than just one 365th?

29 Gioacchino Rossini (1792) How did Rossini ever celebrate his birthday? He was born on February 29, which comes only in leap year, once every 4 years! But you can hear Rossini's music all year when Tonto gallops alongside the "Lone Ranger." Listen as he "rides again" to Rossini's William Tell Overture! "Hi-yo, Silver, away!"

These birthographies were prepared by Davida Shipkowitz of Northridge, California.

SPOTLIGHT ON

BROOKS ADAMS (1849–1927)

Grandson of President John Quincy Adams, Brooks Adams was an American historian and a critic of capitalism. He believed that commercial civilizations rise and fall predictably.

In *The Law of Civilization and Decay* (1895) Adams observed that as new population centers emerged in the West, centers of world trade shifted (Constantinople to Venice and Amsterdam to London). He predicted in *America's Economic Supremacy* (1900) that New York City would become the world trade center. He was correct.

Charles A. Beard who wrote the introduction for *The Law of Civilization and Decay* stated the following:

> "It (the book) represents the first extended attempt on the part of an American thinker to reduce universal history or at least Western history to a single formula or body of formulas conceived in the spirit of modern science. . . . Brooks began to wonder whether 'a science of history' was not possible, and if possible, what form it would take. While Henry Adams had studied, taught and written history in a manner somewhat orthodox, Brooks had searched assiduously in the data of history for a clue to the rise and decline of civilization."

Yet, according to the Goertzels in *Cradles of Eminence*, Brooks Adams, born shortly after his five-year-old brother died, was defiant and incomprehensible to his erudite family. His family would isolate him on a hassock in the middle of the room during the family reading circle. While there, he would pull and twist his clothes and the rug while he laughed, ranted, twisted and jumped about inappropriately.

He performed poorly at school and was a poor speller and reader. His parents took him to the family physician to ask whether a blow on the head by a cricket ball could possibly account for his strange behavior and "stupidity." The doctor assured them that the boy had suffered no physical damage from the blow. Neither Mr. or Mrs. Adams expected Brooks to go on to college! He retained his childhood awareness of this rejection as an adult.

This is but another indication of a youngster who seemed to show severe learning problems (and thought of as "stupid") who later contributed much to society. His historical writings are thought brilliant even today.

In *The Law of Civilization and Decay* the following is stated:

> "This is the text which Brooks Adams designed especially for the American audience. It achieved the largest circulation in the United States, was the most widely reviewed in the American press, and stirred up the greatest intellectual ferment."

SPOTLIGHT BULLETIN BOARD

Materials:

white background paper	acetate transparency
black marker	transparency marker
overhead projector	bulletin board illustration

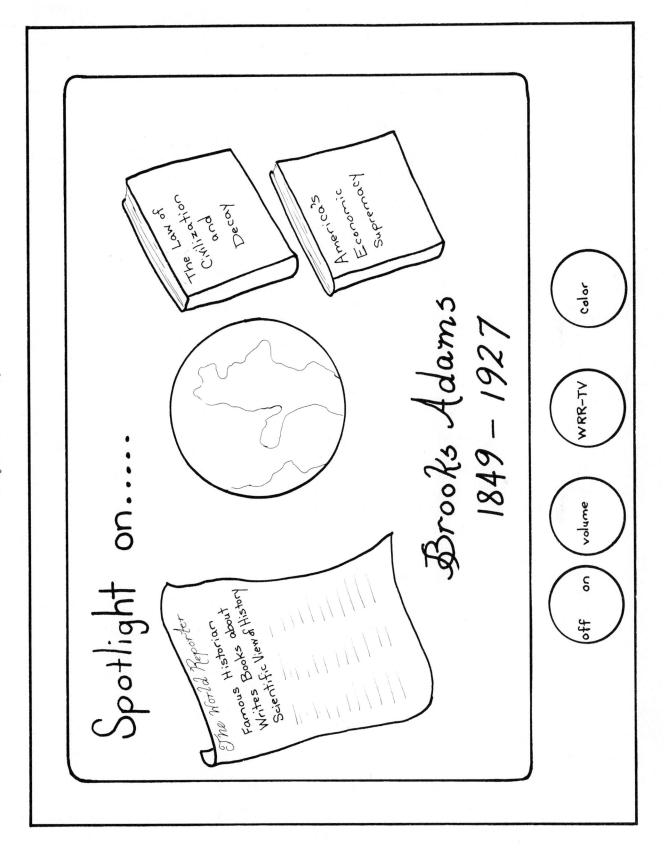

Preparation:

1. Cover the bulletin board with the white background paper.

2. Trace the "Spotlight" bulletin board (see page 221) onto clear acetate using a transparency marker.

3. Project the transparency onto the backed bulletin board.

4. Trace the outline and fill in the titles and words.

BULLETIN BOARD IDEAS

Social studies are emphasized in the "Happy Birthday," "Our Times" and "Blast Off" bulletin boards.

Since social studies is concerned with the world around us, the bulletin boards set the theme with a glimpse of our past (the presidents), of our present (current events) and our future progress (a rocket ship). The teaching units and learning centers follow through with this theme to further reinforce the concepts of past, present, and future.

HAPPY BIRTHDAY

Materials:

opaque projector

a copy of the bulletin board illustration

bright yellow background paper

colored markers (green, orange, etc.) for the lettering

colored construction paper for the balloons

real balloons (*optional*)

brown and white construction paper or markers for the birthday cake

pastel construction paper or markers for the candles

stapler

scissors (*optional*)

yarn or string (*optional*)

double-faced tape (*optional*)

Preparation:

1. Cover the bulletin board with the yellow background paper.

2. Project the illustration of the design (see page 223) onto the bulletin board.

3. Either outline the illustrations with a marker and fill in, or attach appropriately colored construction paper and draw the designs onto it from the projection.

4. Cut out the designs if construction paper is used.

5. Write in the titles, dates and balloon names. (If real balloons are used, write the information directly on the inflated balloons with felt-tipped markers. Affix the balloons to the bulletin board with double-faced tape.)

Happy Birthday

Bill of Rights

FATHER of Our Country

Constitution of USA

1732–1799

1809–1865

Civil War

GETTYSBURG Address

Freed Slaves

OUR TIMES

This is an excellent bulletin board to display on a permanent basis to encourage the students to bring in current events articles. This bulletin board can be used in conjunction with most language arts skills as well as social studies. (For those students whose reading levels prevent them from being able to read news articles, have them bring in newspaper photographs instead.) The bringing in of articles helps to reinforce reading as an ongoing and useable skill outside of school.

Resource people from the community who can reinforce current events make welcome classroom guests. This helps to make the news more alive and relevant to students. In addition, follow-up letters to personalities the students have read about often bring return responses that also make the news of the world very much a part of students' lives.

Objective:

To encourage students to become aware of the world around them by reading the newspaper.

Materials:

opaque projector   white background paper
a copy of the bulletin board illustration   black marker

Preparation:

1. Cover the bulletin board with the white background paper.

2. Project the bulletin board illustration (see page 225) onto the background paper.

3. Outline the design with a black marker. (NOTE: Although colors could be used, the black-and-white format is most appropriate for the newspaper theme.)

4. Fill in the title letters.

BLAST OFF

This bulletin board, emphasizing the possibilities of the future, asks for student participation. Reproducible worksheets are included so that as the students complete them, they can be placed in the sky portion of the bulletin board or in the jet stream.

Objective:

The students will be able to project themselves into a future theme with emphasis on their roles in a progressing world.

Materials:

blue background paper (wrapping paper that has white stars on a blue background can be very effective)

markers or construction paper (red for the rocket and white or gray for the jet stream)

worksheet   large manila envelope to hold worksheets

opaque projector   stapler

a copy of the bulletin board illustration   scissors (*optional*)

OUR TIME

Mrs. E

February

Resource Room News

EXTRA! EXTRA! — Bring in an Article

Preparation:

1. Cover the bulletin board with the background paper.

2. Project the bulletin board illustration (see page 227) on the background paper.

3. Outline the illustration with markers.

4. If construction paper is used instead of the markers for the design, tack the appropriate paper in front of the projection and outline it for cutting.

5. Cut out the designs if construction paper is used instead of markers.

6. Make copies of the worksheet and place them in a manila envelope that has been stapled to the bulletin board.

TEACHING UNIT

SOCIAL STUDIES

Social studies is concerned with the world around us. Our past reflects where we come from, our present represents what we are doing with what we have learned from the past, and our future envisions goals for progress and improvement toward a better world.

The following lessons are designed to supplement other social studies activities to develop the past, present and future concepts.

The news reporting theme has been chosen as the backdrop for presenting these concepts because it allows the students to deal with past, present and future by putting themselves in each time frame.

Objectives:

At the conclusion of this unit, students will:

• Be exposed to the concept of happenings before their birth (past).

• Become aware of what is happening in their world today (current events).

• Be able to understand the concept of future.

• Become aware of the possibilities of their role in building a better world.

The Present

Materials:

chalkboard
chalk
worksheet

Preparation:

Make a copy of the "Sands of Time" worksheet (see page 230) for each student.

Directions:

1. Ask the students if they know what *the present* means.

2. Explain that the present means what is happening right now.

Name

What My
Future Holds...

Cut out the star
on the dotted lines.
Write a paragraph.
Place on the rocket trail.

3. List on the board events that are occurring right now. Ask for students to participate. For example:

Present

1. We are here in this classroom.
2. Johnny is working at a learning center.
3. The sun is shining.
4. The clock is ticking.
5. It is 9:30 in the morning.
6. Elizabeth is wearing a blue shirt.
7. I am wearing a black suit.
8. etc.

4. Tell a story about the present. For example:

Today is Monday, February 2, 19___. Betsy is combing her hair to get ready to catch the bus for school. Mother calls upstairs, "Betsy, your cereal is ready and on the table." "Okay, Mother," yells Betsy.

Betsy eats her breakfast, kisses her Mother goodbye and leaves for school.

5. Ask the students, "What about this story tells you it is happening in the present—right now?"

6. "What changes would make it be happening in the past?" (Take suggestions from the students. It may be necessary to re-read the story sentence by sentence.)

7. Distribute "The Sands of Time" worksheet to each student.

Reinforcement Activity:

Refer to "Learning Centers" and have your students do assignment 1.

Current Events

Materials:

television set
newspaper
worksheet

Preparation:

1. Plan the lesson for a time when a news broadcast is being shown. (Check your local programming guide.)

2. Make a copy of the "TV News Script" worksheet for each student.

3. Set up the TV and focus the picture.

Directions:

1. Ask, "What are current events? What does *current* mean?" (According to the *American Heritage Dictionary*, it means belonging to the time now passing; now in prog-

Name _____

The Present...

Today is _____

The time right now is _____

I am presently in _____

_____

_____

_____

_____

_____

This is what I am doing now:

Here is a picture of the present:

This is what I will be doing next:

The Sands of Time

ress.) "What does *event* mean?" (According to the *American Heritage Dictionary*, it means an occurrence, incident, or experience, especially one of some significance.)

2. "A current event is something that is happening right now in our world."

3. "Where are current events reported?" (newspaper, radio, television, word of mouth)

4. "What is another name for these reports?" (news)

5. "How many of you have ever watched the news on television?"

6. "We are going to watch the news now."

7. Suggest that the students pay attention to what is being said so that you can talk about it later. (NOTE: If possible, video tape a news broadcast in advance of the lesson and play it back later to the students. This will allow for turning the broadcast on and off to discuss and clarify the news.)

8. Alert students to look for the following items in the broadcast. Write these on the chalkboard.

local news   (in our town or nearby)
national news   (what's happening around the country)
the weather
the editorial   (a personal opinion)
the sports

9. Discuss each of the above items when the broadcast is over.

10. Explain that each student is to make up his or her own broadcast of current events in the school.

11. Distribute the "TV News Script" worksheet on page 232 to the students.

Reinforcement Activity:

Refer to "Learning Centers" and have your students do assignment 2.

TV Reporting

Materials:

sharp cutting edge
large refrigerator box
paint
completed script worksheet
chair
tape recorder and blank tape for practice

Preparation:

1. Cut out the refrigerator box to simulate a television set. (See the illustration.) Paint on knobs, etc.

2. Put the chair in place.

3. Do the previous "Current Events" lesson so that a script has been completed by each student.

TV NEWS SCRIPT

Hello, this is _____ your RR-TV Anchorperson.

Today is _____.

(date)

The weather report is _____° and _____

(rainy, sunny, etc.)

Tomorrow's weather prediction is _____

_____

The local news is _____

_____

_____

The district news is _____

_____

_____

The sports report is _____

_____

_____

The editorial for today is _____

_____

_____

The local gossip is _____

_____

_____

This is _____ signing off.

Directions:

    1. Using the "TV News Script" worksheet, have each student write a script.

    2. Write the following parts of the script on the board:

       a. Introduction

       b. Weather report

       c. Local news

       d. Area news

       e. Sports

       f. Editorial

    3. The meaning of each of the above should be defined again.

    4. When scripts are completed, check them.

    5. Each student should practice his or her script several times before presentation. (A tape recorder can be helpful.)

    6. On the scheduled day, allow each student time to present his or her news to the rest of the class.

    NOTE: If possible, video taping the presentations is very effective. The tape can be played back for the students and/or for the parents, staff or other classes at an appropriate time. Also, inviting a reporter or newscaster from a local TV station or newspaper to talk to the students is a very exciting event. It makes the news become much more alive and encourages a more aware eye on the world around them.

Reinforcement Activities:

    Refer to "Learning Centers" and have your students do assignments 2 and 3.

Writing a Short Report for the Time Machine Video Program

Materials:

    filmstrips, tapes, etc., on American history

    history books on appropriate reading levels

    encyclopedias on appropriate reading levels

    paper

    pencils

    worksheet

    filmstrip projectors, tape recorders, etc., as needed

    index cards

Preparation:

    1. Find appropriate level books in the school or public library on American history. (See "Materials of the Month.")

    2. Borrow encyclopedias on the appropriate reading levels to have available.

    3. Find appropriate level filmstrips and tapes on American history.

    4. Set up the films and tapes in the machines for use by the students.

    5. Decide which student will report on each topic.

6. Put each child's name on an index card and place with the books and filmstrips about his or her topic.

Directions:

1. Explain to the students that they will be doing reports and illustrations on an area of American history.

2. List on the board all the historical main events they can remember. (NOTE: By presenting the events on a horizontal line across the board, students are being exposed to the concept of a time line.) For example:

		Revolutionary	Declaration of
Columbus	The Pilgrims	War	Independence

3. Ask for students to tell what they know about each one. Fill in information where necessary.

4. Explain that for each event, they will prepare a report.

5. Show them the research materials you have collected for them.

6. Assign a report topic to each child.

7. Distribute the "My Report" worksheet to each student.

8. Allow time for each student to work independently, reading his or her material and looking at filmstrips, etc. (NOTE: Since this may take several lessons, it is an excellent activity for eliciting the aid of parent volunteers. The students may need help to focus on and understand the independent study.)

9. Show students how they may begin filling in their report worksheets.

10. When the reports are finished, check and correct them.

11. Have students present each report orally to the group.

NOTE: Those students who are at a more advanced level can find their own research materials in the library.

Reinforcement Activity:

Refer to "Learning Centers" and have your students do assignment 4.

Time Machine Video Presentation

Materials:

large roll of white butcher paper

paintbrushes

poster paints

American history books with illustrations for reference

video equipment (NOTE: This presentation may also be given as a play without video equipment being used)

Name _____

MY REPORT

Subject or Event _____

_____

_____

_____

Date it happened _____

Names of the person or people involved _____

_____

_____

_____

Main idea _____

_____

_____

_____

_____

_____

_____

How this person or event changed history _____

_____

_____

_____

_____

_____

_____

_____

Directions:

First Day

1. Ask, "Who knows what a time machine is?"

2. Explain that a time machine is a make-believe vehicle for going backward or forward in time. Many science fiction movies feature time machines as the backdrop for showing life in a different time frame.

3. Explain to the students that they are going to make a time machine presentation on videotape. They will show the history of the United States with pictures on a mural and oral presentations about their picture. (NOTE: Almost any time or place in history can be used.)

4. A discussion of the sequence of events in American history with student input should be reviewed at this point. Discuss how this can be shown in a time machine presentation.

5. As a culminating activity, explain that they will each design a scene on their topic, which they will then draw on a mural to be used as a backdrop to depict a specific time in American history. These will be in sequence. Write out this sequence on the board with the students' input. In this way, they will make their own version of a time machine.

6. The following projects can be assigned:

   a. Christopher Columbus

   b. The Pilgrims' First Thanksgiving

   c. The Colonies and How They Grew

   d. The Revolutionary War

   e. The Declaration of Independence

   f. George Washington

   g. Boats and Trains Unite the Nation

   h. Pioneers Go West

   i. Abraham Lincoln

   j. America—The Melting Pot (The Statue of Liberty)

7. Discuss how students will present their written reports about each scene. This will be presented as part of the time machine on videotape.

8. Discuss which group (parents, other classes, teachers, etc.) should be invited to the presentation.

9. Allow time for students to decide on a scene to use for the mural.

Second Day

1. Help each student with the mural design. It must be drawn on practice paper before attempted on the large mural.

2. When all the scenes have been designed, lay them out on the floor or on the board ledge to see how they all look together.

3. When everyone agrees, decide on the materials needed for the actual mural. (NOTE: Poster paints, markers, iridescent chalk, and crayons are all possibilities.)

Third Day

1. Lay the butcher paper in one long piece. This can be placed on the floor (if there is room) or tacked up on the wall. Wherever it is placed, it must be accessible for children to easily draw on it.

2. In the proper sequence let each student choose his or her section to pencil in the scene. (NOTE: If space or behavior is a problem, the paper can be cut into sections, worked on individually, and taped back together when the drawings are finished. Or drawing paper can be used and taped onto the butcher roll when finished.)

3. Once the pencil drawings have been approved, the color may be added. Don't forget to put in the titles and dates under each picture. (NOTE: Additional time may be needed for this lesson.)

Fourth Day

1. Once the paint has dried, the mural is ready to be posted. NOTE: If the mural is in pieces, it must be taped together in sequence from the back. Two-inch wide masking tape works well for this.

2. When the mural is in place, have the students practice telling about their picture as they stand next to the appropriate drawing on the mural.

> NOTE: When the mural is no longer needed for videotaping, it can be displayed in the classroom or in the hallway for others to see. The videotape can be viewed by each class individually at an assigned time or by several classes at a time depending on the size of the viewing screen.

Fifth Day

Allow each student time to practice the presentation before the videotaping.

Video Presentation of the Time Machine

Materials:

TV monitor	construction paper
video camera	felt-tip markers
blank videotape	costumes for each student

completed time machine mural and scripts

tape recorder and cassette if needed (background music, such as "Star Wars" or "Chariots of Fire," softly played during the presentation is very effective)

Preparation:

1. Send invitations to the audience decided upon.

2. Send notes and make phone calls to prepare costumes for the students. Here are some suggestions:

George Washington

a. knee socks worn over slacks to give effect of knickers

b. white wig or cotton balls made into a wig tied in back with a black ribbon

c. ruffles or jabow made out of white crepe paper streamers

d. black cape made of crepe paper

e. hat fashioned out of construction paper

Christopher Columbus

a. sea captain's hat

b. beard made out of steel wool and glued onto paper

c. a map in his hand with burned edges to show aged parchment

d. a paper sword

Pilgrim (male)

a. knee socks worn over slacks to give effect of knickers

b. dark colored long sleeve shirt

c. white pilgrim collar made from white construction paper

(female)

a. long dark skirt (can be made from crepe paper if necessary)

b. dark blouse or sweater

c. white pilgrim collar made from construction paper

Note: Pilgrim hats can be fashioned out of construction paper. For the females, a nurse's cap works very well.

Abraham Lincoln

a. black slacks and jacket

b. white shirt

c. black bow tie

d. beard made from steel wool and glued onto paper

e. top hat made from black construction paper

Directions:

1. Have students practice their oral reports several times.
2. Double check on costumes to be sure they are all available.
3. Plan a dress rehearsal.

    a. Assign a student who does not have a report to give to be a promptor.

    b. Have the students in costume (the appropriate one for each report) read or give their report as they stand next to their scene on the time machine.

    c. When the time machine presentation is finished, have all the characters in the program come forward and take a bow.

4. Once all the "bugs" have been worked out, you are ready for the final performance.
5. Be sure all the video equipment is on hand and working.
6. Be sure someone is available to operate the video equipment.
7. Roll the camera and have fun!

NOTE: For a more elaborate presentation, simple refreshments can be served. These can be brought in by parents or purchased in advance.

Future Shock

Materials:

magazine pictures of modern machinery, rocket ships, jet airplanes, computers, etc.
occupation pictures (commercial or magazine pictures)
clear Con-Tact paper
worksheets
scissors

Preparation:

1. Cut out magazine pictures of modern machinery and occupations.
2. Laminate pictures with clear Con-Tact paper if possible.
3. See "Materials of the Month" for commercial occupation pictures.
4. Make copies of the worksheets (see pages 241 and 242) for each student.

Directions:

1. Ask: "What does *future* mean? Get feedback from the students. The *American Heritage Dictionary* says: 1. The indefinite period of time yet to be; time that is to come. 2. That which will happen in time to come.

2. Show pictures of modern machinery. Ask: "Do you think these things always existed?" Get feedback from students.

3. Explain the concept that all things at some time were thought up for the future.

4. Discuss inventions that have changed our lives. Examples are:

> telephone
> electric light bulb
> wheel
> automobile
> airplanes
> computers
> rocket ships

5. "What do you think are some times or inventions that may come in the future?" (Space travel for everyone, moon living, computers cleaning houses, shopping, etc.) List the students' suggestions on the board.

6. "Let's look at the different workers and think about how the future may change their jobs."

7. Show the laminated occupation cards one by one. Ask for suggestions on how the future can change these jobs. For instance:

Milkman—people will punch a computer in their homes to have milk delivered either by another computer or a different type of milkman.

Secretary—a computer will replace all of the secretarial chores including answering the phone and taking messages.

Teacher—teaching machines will take over much of the teacher's work.

8. Distribute the two worksheets.

9. Explain to the students that they will look at the occupations and think of some ideas of their own which will change the job functions.

Reinforcement Activities:

Refer to "Learning Centers" and have your students do assignments 5 and 6.

LEARNING CENTERS

The learning centers beginning on page 243 can be used with the teaching units on social studies or as independent activities to complement a variety of subjects. The concepts of past, present and future are important language concepts needed to understand the world around us. They are designated primary, intermediate or advanced depending on the comprehension and reading level of the activity.

Name _____

Tell how future inventions might affect the following jobs.

<table>
<tr><th>PILOT</th><th>DELIVERY MAN</th></tr>
</table>

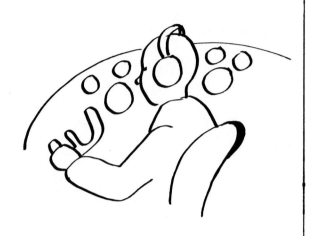

Name _____

Tell how future inventions might affect the following jobs.

DOCTOR	**NURSE**

(1) EXTRA, EXTRA, READ ALL ABOUT IT! (ADVANCED)

Materials:

reporter's visor patterns
construction paper
worksheets
tape
newspapers for backdrop
marker
index card

Preparation:

1. Copy the visor patterns worksheet (see page 244) for each student. Have the students trace the patterns onto construction paper.

2. Copy the "Resource Room News" worksheets for each student. (See pages 245–246.)

3. Display newspapers and headlines to decorate the station.

4. Write the directions on an index card.

Directions Card:

EXTRA, EXTRA

1. You are a newspaper reporter.
2. Cut out and staple your visor.
3. Cut out and pin on your official pass.
4. Write the articles for The Resource Room News.
5. Use good punctuation and spelling.
6. Have your work checked by the teacher.

---

(2) PERSONAL INTERVIEW (INTERMEDIATE-ADVANCED)

Materials:

worksheet
pencil
index card

Preparation:

1. Copy a "Personal Interview" worksheet for each student.

2. Write the directions on an index card.

Expansion Band

Resource Room News
Reporter
PASS
Official

Reporter _____

Write two news articles by answering the questions.

Resource Room News

Todays News

Who? _____
_____
_____
_____
_____

What? _____
_____
_____
_____

Where? _____
_____
_____

When? _____
_____
_____

How? _____
_____
_____
_____

Sports

Who? _____
_____
_____
_____
_____

What? _____
_____
_____
_____

Where? _____
_____
_____

When? _____
_____
_____

How? _____
_____
_____
_____

Reporter _____

Write two news articles by answering the questions.

Resource Room News

Weather Report

Where? _____
_____
_____
_____
_____

When? _____
_____
_____
_____

What? _____
_____
_____

What to expect: _____
_____
_____
_____
_____
_____
_____

Editorial

Should summer vacation be shortened? _____
_____
_____
_____

Why? _____
_____
_____
_____

How? _____
_____
_____

When? _____
_____
_____
_____
_____
_____
_____

Name _____

PERSONAL INTERVIEW

Name of person being interviewed _____

_____

What is the job of person being interviewed? _____

_____

Why did he or she choose this job? _____

_____

_____

_____

Does he or she like the job? _____

_____

_____

What plans does the person have for the future? _____

_____

_____

_____

_____

_____

What else does this person like to do? _____

_____

_____

_____

_____

_____

Directions Card:

PERSONAL INTERVIEW

1. Choose an important person to interview for The Resource Room News.

2. Read over the questions on the worksheet before the interview.

3. Ask each question, slowly and carefully.

4. Write down the person's answers as best you can.

5. Re-write your interview when you return to the resource room.

---

(3) COMMUNITY HELPERS
(PRIMARY)

Materials:

laminated occupation pictures
worksheets
crayons
index card

Preparation:

1. Copy the two "Helpers" worksheets for each student. (See pages 249–250.)
2. Display the occupation pictures.
3. Write the directions on an index card.

Directions Card:

Community Helpers
1. LOOK at the pictures.
2. Do the worksheet.
3. Color the worksheet.

Name _____

Draw a picture of each helper.
Helpers

Nurse	Teacher
Police Officer	Firefighter

Name _____

Draw a picture of each helper.

Helpers

Librarian	Store Clerk
Doctor	**Attorney**

(4) TIME LINE
(INTERMEDIATE-ADVANCED)

Materials:

easy book on American history

worksheet

crayons

pencil

index card

Preparation:

1. Copy a "Time Line" worksheet (see page 252) for each student.
2. Write the directions on an index card.
3. Locate an easy reading book on American history.

Directions Card:

```
┌─────────────────────────────────────────────────────┐
│                    TIME LINE                        │
│  1. Using the American history book, fill in the empty │
│  spaces on the time line worksheet.                  │
│  2. Color the pictures.                              │
│  3. Have your work checked by the teacher.           │
└─────────────────────────────────────────────────────┘
```

(5) FAMOUS INVENTORS
(PRIMARY-INTERMEDIATE)

Materials:

index card

magazine pictures of lightbulb, car, telephone, peanut butter, sandwiches, etc.

worksheets

easy books about inventors

cassette recorder

markers

earphones

scissors

blank cassette tape

clear Con-Tact paper

easy books on inventors (see "Materials of the Month")

posterboard (*optional*)

TimeLine

Name

Fill in the missing information.

1492

1620

First
Newspaper

Declaration
of
Independence

1789

Abraham
Lincoln

Today
High Technology

Preparation:

1. Laminate the magazine pictures with clear Con-Tact paper.

2. Mount the pictures on posterboard or hang on a wall or bulletin board near the learning center.

3. Have easy library books on inventors available at the learning center.

4. Record the dialogue on the tape.

5. Write the directions on an index card.

6. Make copies of the four worksheets on pages 255–258.

Cassette Dialogue:
Teacher records the following:

Good Day! We are going to talk about inventors. Did you know that before electricity was invented it would have been impossible for you to be listening to this tape right now? A person had to think up the idea of how to use energy which could be stored and brought right into your house or school or store or many other places. Benjamin Franklin was instrumental in developing electricity.

The electric light over your head was invented by a person. This person's name was Thomas Alva Edison. After many years of trying and trying to come up with a light, he finally found out how to make a successful light bulb. Because of him we have lighting in our homes. We can send messages across the country using a telegraph and we can take photographs!

Look at your worksheets. Find a big picture of Edison's most famous invention. Draw in the other things that we have today because he discovered the light bulb. Stop the tape until you are finished coloring in your pictures. Then, press START and listen for some more directions.

Another famous inventor was Alexander Graham Bell. He discovered, after many, many tries, the telephone. The telephone has allowed people all over the world to talk to one another. It is even possible to send graphs, charts and pictures over the telephone today. Doctors are able to send complicated reports and charts by the telephone to help people get well. Patients who have heart trouble are able to be checked over the phone! When Alexander Graham Bell first dreamed of the telephone, he probably had no idea of just how far his invention would progress. He also invented the first record player with a very large speaker. As a matter of fact, this very tape recording you are listening to right now would probably not have been possible without Alexander Graham Bell's inventions.

Find the worksheet that looks like a bell and draw in some of the things that Alexander Graham Bell can take credit for. Stop the tape and press START when you are ready to listen again.

If you are having a peanut butter sandwich for lunch today you have two people to thank. George Washington Carver, who invented peanut butter, and The Earl of Sandwich, who invented the idea of putting food between bread and making a sandwich.

As a tribute to George Washington Carver and The Earl of Sandwich, draw a big sandwich on the third worksheet. Stop the tape and start again when you are ready to listen again.

Well, you have heard of the inventions of several people that have made our lives better and easier. Remember, their inventions started with a dream; a dream of how to solve a problem and make something new. Do you have a dream? Do you have an idea for an invention? On the fourth worksheet, you be the inventor. Draw a picture of *your* invention under *your* name. Good Luck!

Directions Card:

(6) FORTUNETELLER

Materials:

round fishbowl   markers
towel or scarf   index card
worksheet

Preparation:

1. Place a round fishbowl upside down with a towel around the bottom to simulate a crystal ball.

2. Copy the worksheet (see page 259) for each student.

3. Write the directions on an index card.

Directions Card:

> Fortuneteller
> 1. Be a fortuneteller.
> 2. Look into the crystal ball and ''tell'' the future.
> 3. Complete the worksheet.
> 4. Have your work checked by the teacher.

MATERIALS OF THE MONTH

Some very effective resources for obtaining social studies materials are through Chambers of Commerce, travel agencies, and gasoline service stations.

Chambers of Commerce for the various cities, states and countries spend great fortunes on preparing literature to advertise their areas' attributes. Sending a postcard with

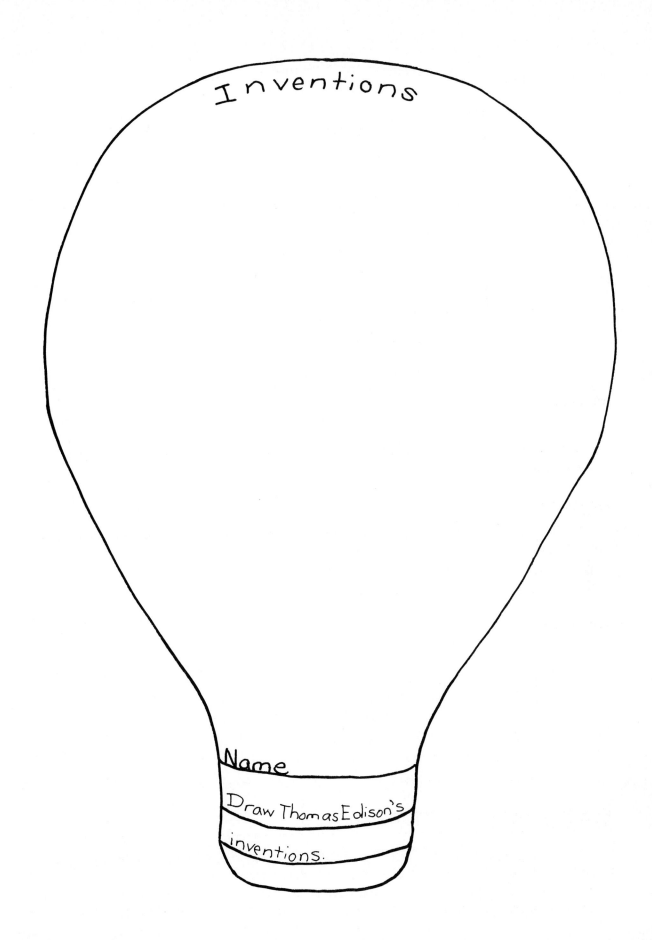

Inventions

Name

Draw Thomas Edison's inventions.

Inventions

Name _____

Draw some of Alexander Graham Bell's inventions.

Draw a picture of your own sandwich as a tribute to the
two inventors of the peanut butter sandwich .....
George Washington Carver and The Earl of Sandwich.

Invented by _____

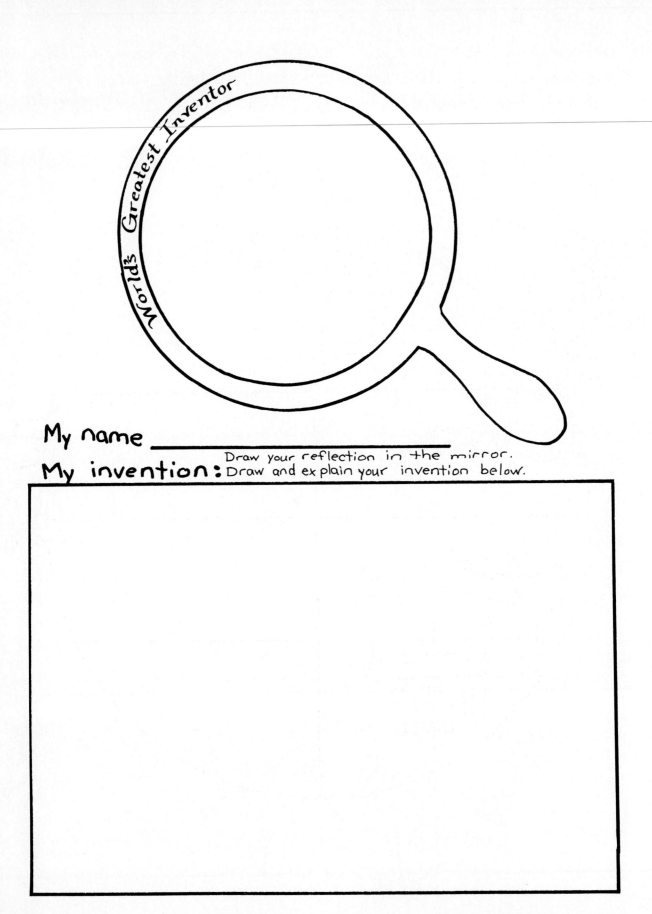

World's Greatest Inventor

My name _____

My invention: Draw your reflection in the mirror.
Draw and explain your invention below.

Name _____

Look into the crystal ball. Draw the items as you
think they will look in the future.

a return name and address requesting information on a particular area generally yields loads of useful brochures and information in return. Not only is this excellent information for the students to use in researching for reports, but colorful posters and pictures, which make great enhancements for bulletin boards, are often included. The following list was compiled by *Freebies* Magazine in the June 1983 issue.

ALABAMA

Bureau of Publicity and Information
532 S. Perry St.
Montgomery, AL 36130

Alabama Chamber of Commerce
P.O. Box 76
Montgomery, AL 36195

ALASKA

Alaska Division of Tourism
Department of Commerce and
  Economic Development
Pouch E
Juneau, AK 99811

Alaska State Chamber of Commerce
310 2nd St.
Juneau, AK 99801

ARIZONA

Arizona Office of Tourism
3507 N. Central Ave.
Phoenix, AZ 85004

Phoenix Metropolitan Chamber of
  Commerce
34 W. Monroe St., Suite 900
Phoenix, AZ 85003

ARKANSAS

Arkansas Department of Parks &
  Tourism
1 Capitol Mall
Little Rock, AR 72201

Greater Little Rock Chamber of
  Commerce
One Spring St.
Little Rock, AK 72201

CALIFORNIA

California Office of Tourism
1120 N St., Room 2125
Sacramento, CA 95814

California State Chamber of Commerce
c/o Dept. of Economic and Business
  Development
1030 13th St., Suite 200
Sacramento, CA 95814

COLORADO

State Division of Commerce and
  Development
1313 Sherman, Room 500
Denver, CO 80203

Colorado Association of Commerce and
  Industry
1390 Logan St., Suite 308
Denver, CO 80203

CONNECTICUT

Department of Commerce
210 Washington St.
Hartford, CT 06106

Greater Hartford Chamber of Commerce
250 Constitution Plaza
Hartford, CT 06103

DELAWARE

Delaware State Travel Service
630 State College Rd.
P.O. Box 1401
Dover, DE 19901

Delaware Chamber of Commerce
1102 West St.
Wilmington, DE 19801

FLORIDA

Division of Tourism
126 Van Buren St.
Tallahassee, FL 32301

The Florida Chamber of Commerce
136 S. Bronough St.
P.O. Box 5497
Tallahassee, FL 32301

GEORGIA

Department of Industry and Trade
P.O. Box 1776
Atlanta, GA 30301

Georgia Chamber of Commerce
1200 Commerce Building
Atlanta, GA 30335

HAWAII

Hawaii Visitors Bureau
3440 Wilshire Blvd., Suite 203
Los Angeles, CA 90010

Japanese Chamber of Commerce and
  Industry of Hawaii
476 Hinano St.
Hilo, HI 96720

IDAHO

Idaho Division of Tourism & Industrial
  Development
Room 108, State Capitol
Boise, ID 83720

Greater Boise Chamber of Commerce
P.O. Box 2368
Boise, ID 83720

ILLINOIS

Illinois Office of Tourism
222 S. College St.
Springfield, IL 62706

Greater Springfield Chamber of
  Commerce
3 W. Old State Capitol Plaza
Springfield, IL 62701

INDIANA

Tourism Division
Indiana Department of Commerce
440 N. Meridan St.
Indianapolis, IN 46204

Indiana State Chamber of Commerce
One No. Capitol, Suite 200
Indianapolis, IN 46204

IOWA

Iowa Development Commission
Tourism and Travel Division
250 Jewett Building
Des Moines, IA 50309

Iowa Development Commission
250 Jewett Building
Des Moines, IA 50309

KANSAS

Travel and Tourism Division
Kansas Department of Economic
  Development
503 Kansas Ave.
Topeka, KS 66603

Kansas Association of Commerce and
  Industry
500 First National Bank Tower
Topeka, KS 66603

KENTUCKY

Kentucky Department of Public
  Information
Capitol Plaza Tower
Frankfort, KY 40601

Kentucky Chamber of Commerce
P.O. Box 817
Frankfort, KY 40602

LOUISIANA

Office of Tourism
Box 44291
Baton Rouge, LA 70804

The Chamber/New Orleans & the River
Region
301 Camp St.
P.O. Box 30240
New Orleans, LA 70190

MAINE

Maine Publicity Bureau
97 Winthrop St.
Hallowell, ME 04347

Maine Chamber of Commerce
One Canal Plaza
P.O. Box 65
Portland, ME 04112

MARYLAND

Office of Tourist Development
1748 Forest Drive
Annapolis, MD 21401

Maryland Chamber of Commerce
60 West St., Suite 405
Annapolis, MD 21401

MASSACHUSETTS

Department of Commerce and
Development
Division of Tourism
100 Cambridge St.
Boston, MA 02202

Greater Boston Chamber of Commerce
125 High St.
Boston, MA 02110

MICHIGAN

Department of Commerce
Box 30226
Lansing, MI 48909

Lansing Regional Chamber of
Commerce
P.O. Box 14030
Lansing, MI 48901

MINNESOTA

Minnesota Department of Economic
Development
Tourist Information Center
480 Cedar St.
St. Paul, MN 55101

Greater Minneapolis Chamber of
Commerce
15 S. Fifth St.
Minneapolis, MN 55402

MISSISSIPPI

Mississippi Department of Economic
Development
Division of Tourism
P.O. Box 22825
Jackson, MS 39205

Jackson Chamber of Commerce
P.O. Box 22548
Jackson, MS 39205

MISSOURI

Missouri Division of Tourism
P.O. Box 1055
Jefferson City, MO 65102

Jefferson City Area Chamber of
Commerce
P.O. Box 776
Jefferson City, MO 65102

MONTANA

Travel Promotion Unit
Montana Department of Commerce
1424 9th Ave.
Helena, MT 59620

Helena Area Chamber of Commerce
201 E. Lyndale
Helena, MT 59601

NEBRASKA

Travel and Tourism
State Department of Economic
  Development
P.O. Box 94666
Lincoln, NE 69509

Greater Omaha Chamber of Commerce
1606 Douglas St.
Omaha, NE 68102

NEVADA

Nevada Department of Economic
  Development
Capitol Complex
Carson City, NV 89710

Carson City Chamber of Commerce
1191 South Carson St.
Carson City, NV 89701

NEW HAMPSHIRE

Office of Vacation Travel
P.O. Box 856
Concord, NH 03301

New Hampshire Office of Industrial
  Development
105 Louden Rd.
P.O. Box 856
Concord, NH 03301

NEW JERSEY

Department of Labor and Industry
State Promotion Office
Trenton, NJ 08625

New Jersey State Chamber of
  Commerce
5 Commerce St.
Newark, NJ 07102

NEW MEXICO

Travel Division
Bataan Memorial Building
Santa Fe, NM 87503

NEW YORK

Division of Tourism
Department of Commerce
99 Washington Ave.
Albany, NY 12245

New York Chamber of Commerce and
  Industry
200 Madison Ave.
New York, NY 10016

NORTH CAROLINA

Travel and Tourism Division
Department of Commerce
430 N. Salisbury St.
Raleigh, NC 27611

Greater Raleigh Chamber of Commerce
P.O. Box 2978
Raleigh, NC 27602

NORTH DAKOTA

Tourism Promotion Division
1050 E. Interstate Ave.
Bismarck, ND 58505

Greater North Dakota Assn.
808 3rd Ave. S.
P.O. Box 2467
Fargo, ND 58108

OHIO

Office of Travel & Tourism
P.O. Box 1001
Columbus, OH 43216

Ohio Chamber of Commerce
17 S. High St., 8th floor
Columbus, OH 43215

OKLAHOMA

Tourism and Recreation Department
500 Will Rogers Memorial Building
Oklahoma City, OK 73105

Oklahoma State Chamber of Commerce
4020 N. Lincoln Blvd.
Oklahoma City, OK 73105

OREGON

Travel Information Section
Room 101, Transportation Building
Salem, OR 97310

Salem Area Chamber of Commerce
220 Cottage St. NE
Salem, OR 97301

PENNSYLVANIA

Travel Development Bureau
Department of Commerce
416 Forum Building
Harrisburg, PA 17120

Pennsylvania Chamber of Commerce
222 N. Third St.
Harrisburg, PA 07101

RHODE ISLAND

Rhode Island Department of Economic
  Development
7 Jackson Walkway
Providence, RI 02903

Greater Providence Chamber of
  Commerce
10 Dorvance St.
Providence, RI 02903

SOUTH CAROLINA

Department of Parks, Recreation and
  Tourism
Inquiry Sections
P.O. Box 71
Columbia, SC 29202

South Carolina Chamber of Commerce
1301 Gervais St.
P.O. Box 11278
Columbia, SC 29211

SOUTH DAKOTA

Division of Tourism
221 S. Central
Pierre, SD 57501

Pierre Chamber of Commerce
P.O. Box 548
Pierre, SD 57501

TENNESSEE

Division of Tourist Development
P.O. Box 23170
Nashville, TN 37202

Nashville Chamber of Commerce
161 4th Ave. North
Nashville, TN 37219

TEXAS

Texas Tourist Development Agency
Box 5064
Austin, TX 78763

Texas State Chamber of Commerce
815 Brazos #801
Austin, TX 78701

UTAH

Travel Council
Council Hall, Capitol Hill
Salt Lake City, UT 84114

Sugar House
1179-C Simpson Ave.
P.O. Box 6022
Salt Lake City, UT 84106

VERMONT

Travel Division
Agency of Development and
  Community Affairs
61 Elm St.
Montpelier, VT 05602

Vermont State Chamber of Commerce
P.O. Box 37
Montpelier, VT 05602

VIRGINIA

State Travel Service
6 North 6th St.
Richmond, VA 23219

Virginia State Chamber of Commerce
611 E. Franklin St.
Richmond, VA 23219

WASHINGTON

Department of Commerce and
  Economic Development
Tourist Development Division
G-3 General Administration Building
Olympia, WA 98504

Olympia Chamber of Commerce
P.O. Box 1427
Olympia, WA 98507

WASHINGTON, D.C.

Washington Convention and Visitors
  Bureau
1575 Eye St. NW, Suite 250
Washington, DC 20005

Chamber of Commerce of the United
  States
1615 H St. NW
Washington, DC 20062

WEST VIRGINIA

Travel Development Division
1900 Washington St.
E. Capitol Building 6, Room B-564
Charleston, WV 25305

West Virginia Chamber of Commerce
P.O. Box 2789
Charleston, WV 25330

WISCONSIN

Wisconsin Division of Tourism
P.O. Box 7606
Madison, WI 53707

Wisconsin Association of
  Manufacturers & Commerce
111 E. Wisconsin Ave. #1600
Milwaukee, WI 53202

WYOMING

Wyoming Travel Commission
Frank Norris Jr. Travel Center
Cheyenne, WY 82002

Greater Cheyenne Chamber of
  Commerce
P.O. Box 1147
Cheyenne, WY 82001

For map skills the local service stations sometimes have free state and local maps available. Recently some stations have begun charging for their maps. Many, however, are still free for the asking.

Travel agencies always have stacks of material available on a variety of vacation spots. Agencies are usually delighted to advertise their wares by giving out these brochures. Travel agents, by the way, make excellent resource people to talk to the students. They are generally trained in speaking to groups and can give good information to the class. Knowing about a country's vacation spots and tourist attractions gives an added dimension to the students' perspective about an area.

There is also a huge volume called *Educators Guide to Free Social Studies Materials* published by Educators Progress Service Inc., Randolph, Wisconsin. An edition is put out annually for about $25 including postage. It lists hundreds of films, filmstrips, slides, printed materials like magazines, maps, posters, etc., and is a wealth of information on a variety of subjects. It is a great value for teachers on a low budget looking for interesting and different materials.

FREE FOR THE ASKING

The Handbook of Trade and Technical Career and Training

This handbook, among other things, lists and describes some types of trade and technical specialties. Each listing is followed by a state-by-state dictionary of NATTS accredited schools offering that particular program. Each school is cross referenced with its name and address. This is an excellent resource for discussing future occupations. Send a postcard to:

> NATTS
> 2021 K Street, NW
> Washington, DC 20006-1077

Topographical Maps from the U.S. Geological Survey

This 28-page booklet explains in detail how the maps are made and how a person goes about reading them. It is recommended by *Freebies* magazine as an excellent blueprint to make a three-dimensional papier-mâché map of your own area as a class project. This could be an excellent "hands on" project where the students learn by doing. Send a postcard to:

> NCIC-E
> U.S. Geological Survey
> 507 National Center
> Reston, VA 22092

Sample Culturegram

Brigham Young University publishes four-page briefings on 81 countries as well as a collection of intercultural books and pamphlets. The university will send a culturegram on request. It is filled with succinctly written information all about the life and times of a country. It covers proper greetings, visiting protocol, eating etiquette, personal appearance, useful words and phrases, gestures, and traveling within a country. Attitudes of the people as well as maps are also covered. Send a self-addressed, stamped envelope to:

> Culturegram
> Brigham Young University
> Box 61-Y FOB
> Provo, Utah 84602

Voter Information Guide

This 64-page guide brings federal officials' addresses and phone numbers to your attention. It gives state listings of current senators' and representatives' Washington addresses with phone numbers. It also lists cabinet members and other important government officials and gives addressing procedures. Included also are Washington Action Line numbers. Send a postcard to:

Public Affairs Department
The Budd Company
3155 W. Big Beaver Road
Troy, MI 48084

GOOD BUYS

The following suggestions are materials to purchase to complement this month's lessons on social studies.

Career Flip Book

This 25-page flip book represents basic aspects of 50 careers. Three sections complete each page and present the name of the occupation, a person on the job, and the tools or implements associated with that occupation. The flip book sells for under $10, and is available through DLM.

Job Puzzles

These 8½" × 11" puzzles depict lifelike portrayals of people on the job. The set includes eight puzzles and sells for under $12. Contact:

Developmental Learning Materials
P.O. Box 4000
One DLM Park
Allen, TX 75002

Controlled Syntax Biography Series

The series includes six individual work-a-text booklets on Annie Oakley, Chief Joseph, Thomas Jefferson, Brigham Young, Mathew Brady, and Stonewall Jackson. All six books sell for under $20. Write to:

Dormac Inc.
P.O. Box 1699
Beaverton, OR 97075

Research Reports

A specialty report booklet and Capsule Report Booklet are available in spirit master format. This structure provides a simple, rational approach emphasizing clear thinking and purposeful organization for the written and oral report. They are excellent for the unit on social studies reporting. The spirit master book sells for under $15. Write to:

Curriculum Associates
5 Esquire Road
North Billerica, MA 01862

MCP Social Studies Work-a-Texts

Geared to middle grade levels, these work-a-texts combine solid instruction with illustrations, maps, charts, and photos. Included are *Learning About the Earth, People Who*

Made Our Country Great, and *Western Hemisphere and Eastern Hemisphere.* Each work-a-text sells for approximately $5. Contact:

Modern Curriculum Press
13900 Prospect Road
Cleveland, OH 44136

The following books are easy books on American History to help with reports suggested in this month's activities.

Brown, F. *When Grandpa Wore Knickers.* (Racine, WI: Whitman, 1966)

Cavahah, Frances. *Our Country's Story.* (New York: Rand McNally and Company, 1945)

Coy, H. *The Americans.* (New York: Franklin Watts, Inc., 1958)

Famous Black Americans. (Pasadena, CA: Audio Visual Enterprises, 1970)

Feurelicht, R.S. *In Search of Peace.* (New York: Messner Co., 1970)

Knight, James E. *The Village.* (Mahwah, NJ: Troll Associates, 1982)

Kohn, Bernie. *Spirit and the Letter: The Struggle for Rights in America.* (New York: Viking Press, 1974)

Payne, Elizabeth. *Meet the Pilgrim Fathers.* (New York: Random House, 1966)

Rich, Louise Dickinson. *The First Book of the Early Settlers.* (New York: Franklin Watts, Inc., 1968)

PROFESSIONAL RESPONSIBILITIES

REPORT CARDS

Report cards are traditionally the most popular reporting method from schools to parents. There are a variety of formats and styles within this tradition, however.

Whenever the responsibility of a child's academic teaching is shared, the question arises as to *who* will grade the student. When there is one report card, generally the classroom teacher is responsible for giving the grades. If there is a subject for which the student receives all or most of the instruction in your special program, then you seem to be the logical person to do the evaluating.

A decision has to be made as to whether a separate special program report card should be issued in addition to the regular classroom report card. It does entail a bit more work on your part, but can solve some important reporting issues. In this way, input can be made about the child's academic progress as well as other areas of development that may not be addressed in the regular classroom.

For instance, a child may be working on visual motor skills in your room only. A separate report card insures that this effort will be recognized and evaluated for the parents. Social skills is another area which may not be addressed in the traditional report card, but can certainly be discussed in the special program report. The example of a special program report on page 269 leaves space for a variety of topics to be discussed. In addition, there is a place for students and parents to respond to the report with their comments.

SPECIAL PROGRAM REPORT

Name _____   Date _____

Teacher _____

READING _____

_____

_____

MATH _____

_____

_____

HANDWRITING _____

_____

_____

SPELLING _____

_____

_____

ORGANIZATION SKILLS _____

_____

_____

SOCIAL SKILLS _____

_____

_____

GENERAL COMMENTS _____

_____

_____

STUDENT'S COMMENTS _____

_____

_____

PARENTS' COMMENTS _____

_____

_____

Signed _____
                    Special Program Teacher

Signed _____
                           Parent

Signed _____
                          Student

PROFESSIONAL RESOURCE BOOKS

Carlson, Bernice. *Listen! and Help Tell the Story.* (Nashville, TN: Abingdon Press, 1965)

Durfee, Maxine. *Teaching for Social Values in Social Studies.* Association for Childhood Educational International, 1974.

Jarolimek, John. *Readings for Social Studies in Elementary Education.* (New York: Macmillan, 1974)

King, David C. *International Education for Spaceship Earth.* Foreign Policy Association, 1971

Levy, Harold. *Square Pegs, Round Holes: The Learning Disabled Child in the Classroom and at Home.* (Boston: Little Brown and Co., 1973)

Metzner, Seymour. *American History in Juvenile Books: A Geographical and Chronological Guide.* (Bronx, NY: H.W. Wilson, 1973)

National Council for Social Studies. *Skill Development in Social Studies.* Department of National Education Association, 1973

Younie, William J. *Instructional Approaches to Slow Learning.* (New York: Teachers College, Columbia University, 1967)

NOTE: Explanations on the contents of these books can be found in *The Elementary School Library* collection published annually by Bro-Dart Foundation.

MODES FOR MAINSTREAMING

DISCIPLINE PROBLEMS

When a mainstreamed student is acting out in the classroom, on the bus, in the lunchroom or on the playground, you are often the first to know. Much like being a parent, when the student is "bad," he or she is "your child." When things go well, the progress is shared by all. Such is life!

Actually, knowing when a mainstreamed student has problems with behavior is important information to have. This gives you the opportunity to handle the situation or to at least have input into discipline decisions.

Sometimes the adults who may be in charge at the time when problems arise may not understand the student's particular case. Playground aides, bus drivers, lunchroom aides, etc., usually haven't had the benefit of I.E.P. meetings and updates to understand the components of a child's behavior. Therefore, their response to this student may not be helpful to the situation and in some cases may even exacerbate things. Consequently, when there are reports of repeated behavior problems outside the classroom, a meeting with adjunct personnel may help.

It is important at this meeting to stick to the facts. Listen to what the complaints are and take notes. Understanding the problems that the aides are dealing with can lead to concrete helpful suggestions. It is important at this meeting not to divulge confidential information about the student.

Constructive ideas are:

"Johnny needs to be isolated when you see he is having difficulty. Don't wait for him to get overstimulated. Move him as soon as you see signs of agitation." (Discuss what those signs are.)

"Susie needs to be sent to the office if she is rude. Don't continue a discussion with her about why she said what she did. Send her either to the resource room or to the office immediately."

Present general rules like:

a. Try to avoid power struggles.
b. Look for signs of trouble and circumvent them by removing the student from the situation.
c. Report incidents immediately so that discipline can be reinforced by one authority. (Chosen in advance.)
d. Be consistent.
e. Avoid using threats.
f. Allow the classroom teacher or resource room teacher to make a plan or procedure with the aides for frequent offenders.

Try to be as supportive to the adjunct staff as possible. Acknowledge the difficulty in dealing with certain youngsters. Convey the idea that much of the acting-out behavior has a cause and that the adjunct staff can be of great value in helping the students to grow. Leave the door open for further formal or informal meetings at their request or yours. Follow up by checking on how things are going. It is helpful if you appear from time to time at the location of the problems. This gives the aide or teacher support and also lets the student know that you are involved with him or her outside of the special program as well.

TIP OF THE MONTH

THE PLAN BOOK

Plan books are viewed by teachers in a variety of ways. For some, they are a necessary evil; for others they are "a bible" without which they could not function. No matter how you feel about your plan book, it can be a goldmine of ideas for future teaching.

With each week's lessons, staple or clip the actual worksheets, ditto masters or art projects to the plans. On a sheet placed at the beginning of the book, jot down special lessons next to the date for an informal table of contents. For instance:

Week	Materials
2/7	Newspaper, community helpers
2/14	Great Future lesson
2/21	Directions for Time Machine

In this way, at the end of the year you not only have an excellent resource book to use again, you have also cataloged your worksheets and best lessons to find again. For more elaborate indexing, self-stick note pads are available commercially which individually can be used as tabs to more easily find things.

Most plan books have sturdy covers for durability and long shelf life. Used in this way, plan books become your own personal wealth of ideas that can be used over and over again to enhance future lessons.

A FINAL WORD

TESTING PROCEDURES

Responsibility for testing students who are recommended for a special program varies from state to state. In many states, multi-disciplinary teams, which include a psychologist, a social worker and a learning consultant, screen and test the students and then make program recommendations by law.

In some districts, however, and especially private schools where funding for this purpose is more limited, the screening and testing responsibility rests mainly with the special education teacher. It is hoped that in all cases the more sophisticated testing which needs prior training, like with a WISC or other IQ test, be done by trained and certified personnel.

Teachers who are put in the position of giving tests for which they have not been trained are operating with a distinct hardship. Certain tests need special training in order to administer and interpret properly. If these tests are administered to students without that training, the results and interpretations can be questioned.

Screening tests and achievement tests that are designed to be given by a teacher are appropriate tests to use when evaluating levels for special programming. The information gained from this type of testing is beneficial to both the teacher and the student. Observing test-taking behavior firsthand is important information for you to have.

Those teachers who are asked to give tests for which they have no training must work very hard to change the testing responsibility. For private schools, make outside referrals to appropriate professionals. For public schools, know your state rules and regulations on testing and take the necessary steps to follow these regulations. If the necessary legislation has not been written, work through your local and state associations to see that it is forthcoming.

FEBRUARY REFERENCES

Adams, Brooks. *America's Economic Supremacy.* (Salem, NY: Ayre Co., 1947)

Adams, Brooks. *The Law of Civilization and Decay.* (New York: The MacMillan Co., 1943)

Banks, James A. *Teaching Strategies for the Social Studies.* (Reading, MA: Addison-Wesley Publishing Co., 1974)

Bartlett, John. *Bartlett's Familiar Quotations.* (Boston: Little Brown and Co., 1955)

Beringhause, Arthur. *Brooks Adams: A Biography.* (New York: Alfred Knopf, 1955)

Cavanah, Frances. *Our Country's Story.* (Skokie, IL: Rand McNally and Co., 1945)

Educators Guide to Free Social Studies Materials. (Randolph, WI: Educators Progress Service, Inc., 1983)

The Elementary School Library Collection: a Guide to Books and Other Media. (Newark, NJ: The Bro-Dart Foundation, 1977)

Goertzel, Victor and Mildred. *Cradles of Eminence.* (Boston: Little Brown and Co., 1962)

Howe, DeWolfe. *Who Lived Here.* (Boston: Little Brown and Co., 1952)

Roy, Mary M. *Spark: A Handbook of Ideas to Motivate the Teaching of Elementary Social Studies.* (Stevensville, MI: Educational Service Inc., 1965)

Weisinger, Thelma. *1001 Valuable Things You Can Get Free.* (New York: Bantam Books, 1982)

World Book Encyclopedia, Volume A. (Chicago, IL: World Book Inc., 1980)

March

1 Glenn Miller (1904) Before the Beatles and Elvis Presley, there was Glenn Miller! Clarinets and saxophones made the mellow tunes of his BIG BAND! Any juke box on a Saturday night played others: Harry James, Benny Goodman, Stan Kenton, Woody Herman, Artie Shaw! Be *In the Mood*! Swing to BIG BANDS for Glenn's birthday!

2 Dr. Theodore Seuss Geisel (1904) CAT IN THE HAT/And FOX IN SOX/GREEN EGGS AND HAM/We liked those lots/And McELLIGOT'S POOL/LORAX as well/And meany ol' GRINCH/We liked 'em swell/Just can't forget/HORTON and WHO/But today we just love/HAPPY BIRTHDAY TO YOU! Celebrate Seuss . . . read the "oldies" to young kids on campus!

3 George Pullman (1831) President of the Palace Car Company, George Pullman patented a perfect train sleeper. A porter pulled the bed from its place in the wall! Pull out your Pullman case, pull down the berth, pull up a pillow and purr till your train pulls into Pullman, Illinois! Now, pull out a pencil. Any more words with pull?

4 Garrett A. Morgan (1877) 32 men were trapped 200 feet below the lake. Were they already dead? Who would risk his life to find out? Garrett would! Wearing his new invention to keep out deadly fumes, the men were carried to safety. Gas masks continue to save lives as do his traffic lights! Go! Light green candles for Garrett!

5 William Oughtred (1575) How many times can you use times in a sentence? Two times two is four and three times . . . Oughtred was the first to use the × sign, so it's a great time to take time to practice troublesome × tables! And take time to remember Henry Briggs who took time to invent the steps of long ÷. Bill would say 6 × 8 and Henry, 48 ÷ 8!

6 Michelangelo Buonarroti (1475) and Valentina Tereshkova (1937) Michelangelo, the sculptor, architect, and painter of the Sistine Chapel, was said to be far above all the others in the universe! And, far above the earth, exploring the architecture of the universe, was Valentina Tereshkova, first woman astronaut who saw the earth as you see a globe. Where on earth were they born?

7 Joseph Niepce (1765) There is Troy's wooden horse and one on the merry-go-round and the hobbyhorse built by Niepce: 2 wooden wheels connected by a bar upon which a rider sat and pushed himself forward by walking. Snakes and horses were carved onto the bar of this "smooth" hobbyhorse. Build a model of this model first bike!

8 Kenneth Grahame (1859) Frog leaped for joy! He was bound to own that magnificent motor car. With that, thoughts of his old boats and new gypsy-cart just didn't seem to move him anymore. "Fickle Frog," thought Rat. "What will he spring for next? What could possibly please Frog at a birthday banquet, in the gentle WIND IN THE WILLOWS?"

9 Dr. Franz Gall (1758) Some ideas seem fine till someone finds them fake! Franz believed bumps on the skull were formed by the brain and so they told something about the one to whom the brains belonged. PHRENOLOGY is an idea believed mostly by Franz. If the idea is MESMERIZING, put your hands on the story of Franz A. Mesmer!

10 Lillian Wald (1867) Horrified by the dirt and neglect in the homes of children she nursed in the hospital, Lillian Wald gathered nurses to visit homes. To help parents keep homes healthier and to reduce contagious disease, her nurses became school nurses! Ask your school nurse to visit your class and tell more about Wald.

11 Ezra Jack Keats (1916) It was a shame to wash them off the kitchen table! Ezra's mom covered them but took the cloth off to show the neighbors! Keats continued to draw, from tabletops to drawing books, telling tales (SNOWY DAY/GOGGLES) with terrific talent. It's Youth Art Month. Let your youthful magic and your markers tell a tale!

12 John Miller (1702) Why did he print a German almanac if he lived in America? John Miller printed an almanac and a Bi (2) LINGUAL (language) newspaper so new immigrants would understand their new land and its language. His paper was first to tell about the Declaration! Be first to tell what bilingual newspaper is still printed!

13 Joseph Priestley (1733) There's 2¢ plain in ice cream sodas, 2¢ plain in yummy egg cremes and 2¢ plain in bottles! The first plain carbonated water, made by Joseph Priestley who discovered oxygen, was just plain no good! T. Speakman added fruit (1807) and became the pop of pop! Have a bubbly, 2¢ plain!

14 Margaret de Angeli (1889) A monk said, "Each of us has his place in the world. If we cannot serve one way . . . a door always opens to something else." Robin was lifted above his handicap by wings of song. De Angeli's friend, lame and bent, was the real Robin. Together her old friend and Robin opened A DOOR IN THE WALL, to all!

15 Andrew Jackson (1767) Making a list of presidents and their birthplaces sounds easy! Almanacs say Andrew Jackson, our 7th President, was born in South Carolina. Or was he? Many historians say he might have been born on a ship from Ireland, at sea on its way to America in 1755! If true, could he have been our 7th President?

16 James Madison (1751) How did the WHITE HOUSE get its name? The hottest fight of the 1812 War left Washington burning. Madison barely escaped! Dolly saved Washington's portrait from flames and fled before the British officers ate the meal set for Madison and set fire to his home. Blackened by flames, it was repainted white!

> The great law of culture is: Let each become all that he (or she) was created capable of being.
>
> Thomas Carlyle

★★★★★★★★★★★★★★★★★★★★★★★★★★★★★★★★

17 Norbert Rillieux (1806) Anyone have a sweet tooth? Norbert really did! Born on a Louisiana plantation, Rillieux invented a way to change sugar cane stalks to pure white sugar. Using steam in a vacuum, he boiled the brown sugar cane syrup until it changed to white crystals. Have a piece of candy to sweetly say thanks to Sugar Daddy!

18 Edgar Cayce (1877) He said he could know what a book said by sleeping on it and he was famous for helping doctors miraculously cure patients they had long given up! Cayce made predictions. Some right, some wrong. One prediction: An earthquake will break California away from the other states in ___ . He gave no date. Right or . . . ?

19 David Livingstone (1813) A single drop of water began the Nile! Drops joined to form rivulets which joined to form brooks which joined to form the rivers which joined to form the mighty Nile! Doctor Livingstone, a missionary, searched Africa to find its beginning. Your search? Find out where H. Stanley joined Livingstone, and why.

20 Bobby Orr (1948) It was Bobby Orr or nobody! For 8 years straight he won the NHL Best Defenseman Trophy, and 5 others as well! Incredible goals! A Minor Squirt at 6, he has played on organizational teams ever since. At 16, with older boys, his career was in the net! Is it magic or hockey when Orr does hat tricks on ice?

21 Penny Dean (1955) and Marlies Gohr (1958) This planet's people are not only living longer and growing taller but moving faster! The fastest woman runner is Marlies Gohr who ran a world speed of 24 m.p.h. in E. Germany on 7/1/77. Penny Dean swam the English Channel (England to France) in a record 7 hrs., 40 min. Betcha' a penny they practiced!

22 Randolph Caldecott (1846) *Cinderella* (Marcia Brown), <u>A Tree Is Nice</u> (Marc Simont), *The Littlest House* (Virginia Burton), <u>Duffy and the Devil</u> (Margot Zemach), *The Egg Tree* (Katherine Milhous), *Chanticleer and the Fox* (Barbara Cooney), *One Fine Day* (Nonny Hogrogian), *The Snowy Day* (Ezra Keats), and *Time of Wonder* (Robert McClosky).

23 Roger Bannister (1929) Watch as the second hand crosses the 4-minute mark! In 1954, Bannister collapsed breaking the world running record of the 4-minute mile in 3 minutes, 8 and .8 seconds. A mile is 5,280 feet. How many feet would he have run in one minute? 30, 15, or 5 seconds? Pace off the 5-second distance and run a Bannister Bolt!

24 John Wesley Powell (1834) The Grand Canyon was known but only Powell explored all of its mighty rivers, dangerous falls and whirling rapids. The Indians called him "KAPURATS," or one-arm. He wrote about the Indians and of the rocky waters in his diary, begun May 24, 1869. In picture symbols, tell the story of one day on the Green River!

25 Gutzon Borglum (1867) Hey, what's the big idea? It's carving the giant faces of 4 presidents, an awesome memorial at Mt. Rushmore! Begun in 1927, Borglum's massive sculptures are a monument to the memories of ___ , ___ , ___ and ___ , great men with grand views! We'll always look up to them, uplifted by their lofty ideals!

26 Leonard Nimoy (1931) His show was really out of this world but his travels are part of our lives on earth! With or without his ears, Leonard Nimoy is always seeking answers to the mysteries of the universe. As science officer of the starship Enterprise and as host of TV's *In Search Of*, he looks for answers no man has found before!

27 Wilhelm Roentgen (1845) Raise your hand if you've had an X ray! Examining your insides were X-rays which passed right through your body and exited onto a film. Developed like a negative, the black and white exposed the exact problem that the doctor could expertly treat. Examine an X ray and express your thanks to Roentgen!

28 Henry Schoolcraft (1793) Need a book about Native Americans? Schoolcraft wrote one in 6 volumes. Title? HISTORY AND STATISTICAL INFORMATION RESPECTING THE HISTORY, CONDITION AND PROSPECTUS OF THE INDIAN TRIBES OF THE U.S. Whew! And this first book of legends took 6 years to write! Look ahead to May 21 for more about Native Americans.

29 Jacqueline Smith (1951) Look out below! Jacqueline Smith looked out below, and jumped! Her parachute swelled white against the blue Yugoslavian sky. At this world championship, Smith held the world record of 10 perfect falls, right into the center of a circle! Women's parachuting is a new sport, but Jackie really fell for it!

30 Vincent Van Gogh (1853) Van Gogh used colors as authors use words to tell stories. In 3000 paintings, he told beautiful stories of people. And, like music, his colors made songs to see, as notes of a violin are heard. Colors of flowers were "electric" as were swirling stars of deep blue night. See his works to see how he saw!

31 Cesar Chavez (1927) Cradled in his grandmother's arms he was soothed by her words, "Good, you didn't hit back!" He knew she was right. But he did fight back with words when farmers paid too little to pickers who moved from one filthy workhouse to another. He led the workers to form a new union! Who else, like him, fought with words?

These birthographies were prepared by Davida Shipkowitz of Northridge, California.

SPOTLIGHT ON

HANS CHRISTIAN ANDERSEN (1805–1875)

Hans Christian Andersen was Denmark's most famous author. His fairy tales are among the most widely read works in world literature. His stories have enchanted generations of youngsters and adults alike. Many of his tales have serious moral meanings intended for adult readers. Andersen first gained attention in 1829 by writing a travel sketch and his first play. He is most famous for his fairy tales, however. He published the first of his 168 fairy tales in 1835 and continued writing until he died. They became popular in the early 1840's.

His famous writings include:

The Tinder Box

Little Claus and Big Claus

The Traveling Companion

She was Good for Nothing

The Wind Tells About Valdemar Daae and His Daughters

Holger Danske

The Emperor's New Clothes

The Rags

The Story of a Mother

The Shadow

Thumbelina

The Naughty Boy

Little Ida's Flowers

The Princess and the Pea

The Improvisatore

Hans was born in Adense, Denmark, on April 2, 1805. He was the son of a poor shoemaker who died when Hans was 8 years old. According to a 1958 article in *The Pageant of Medicine* called "Ugly Duckling Genius," Hans struggled in school.

"Schooling was intermittent: he fled in flight from his first class when the school teacher rapped his knuckles, had to leave another school at the age of eight when his father died. Later he attended the city school for poor boys, but he was no scholar; he preferred to sing in his soprano voice, play with dolls (until he was sixteen), recite his childish poems and plays to anyone who would listen, and dream of when he would be famous."

Hans reportedly feared his grandfather who was mentally ill. A dread of familial insanity haunted him all his life. Many traumatic experiences from childhood stayed with him and obviously affected much of his adulthood. The article continues:

"A backward and unwilling pupil, Hans finally fled to Copenhagen with the memory of the school as 'the darkest dreams of my recollection.' With the aid of private tutoring he passed his student examinations and was at twenty-three, ready to challenge the world as a literary man . . . At fourteen, Hans was an odd combination of shyness and effrontery:

a feminized boy who cried easily and was afraid of the dark, yet with an unshakable faith in his talents as a singer, dancer and actor. 'I shall be famous,' he told his mother and left for Copenhagen with 13 Rigsdoler (about $13) and a determination to seek his fortune in the Royal Theatre.''

The theme of an unhappy, isolated childhood is apparent in Andersen's work. His most famous story, ''The Ugly Duckling,'' could actually be about himself. He was sometimes called the ugliest man alive and a noted Danish sculptor remarked on the strange shape of his head.

One biographer reported that Andersen was a weak, sickly child who had ''fits'' which were thought to be epilepsy.

Although Andersen's biographers paint a picture of a poor student in school, an unhappy child with possible schizophrenic tendencies in adulthood, Andersen was able to reach generations of children (and adults) through his writing. His fairy tales are delightful stories that in many ways reflect his own life.

Wrote Andersen in *The Fairy Tale of My Life*:

''I get hold of an idea and tell a story for young ones, remembering all the time that father and mother are listening and we must give them something to think about, too.''

SPOTLIGHT BULLETIN BOARD

The paper used for the personality and figures each month can be removed and replaced while the basic bulletin board remains. NOTE: If large sheets of construction paper are used for bulletin boards, they can be removed and stored for future use. Make a large envelope out of two large sheets of oaktag and staple them together. Slip in the construction paper and label. These can be stored flat against a closet wall or on a closet floor.

Materials:

white background paper	acetate transparency
black marker for TV, knobs, and lettering	transparency marker
bulletin board illustration	markers
overhead projector	

Preparation:

1. Cover the bulletin board with the white background paper.

2. Trace the ''Spotlight'' bulletin board (see page 278) onto clear acetate using a transparency marker.

3. Project the transparency onto the backed bulletin board.

4. Trace the outline and color in with markers.

BULLETIN BOARD IDEAS

The March bulletin boards hint at spring with a buzzing bee introducing writing skills and a circus big top announcing A Young Authors' Book Fair. Both bulletin boards feature a variety of writing examples that are followed with activities to teach and reinforce them.

Spotlight on....

Hans Christian Andersen
1805-1875

The Tinder Box
The Ugly Duckling
The Emperor's New Clothes
The Princess and the Pea

Color   WRR-TV   volume   on off

BEE IN THE WRITE

Materials:

opaque projector

bulletin board illustration

yellow background paper

black marker for bee and story titles

green marker for title, leaves and grass

variety of colored markers for flowers

NOTE: Three-dimensional flowers can be made by students with bright colored tissue paper instead of markers. Attach these to the board with staples or double-faced tape.

Preparation:

1. Cover the bulletin board with the yellow paper.

2. Project the bulletin board illustration (see page 280) onto the backing.

3. Outline the illustration with the appropriate color markers.

4. Write in the titles, headings, etc.

5. If you prefer, make the artificial paper flowers with the students and affix to the board with hidden staples or double-faced tape.

6. Now, start buzzing!

THE BIG TOP

Materials:

opaque projector

bulletin board illustration

white background paper

red marker for tent outline, scallops and doorway

blue marker for titles

variety of bright colors for flags and Book Fair balloon

black marker for ropes and posts

NOTE: Bright colored construction paper can be used instead of markers.

Preparation:

1. Cover the bulletin board with the white paper.

2. Project the bulletin board design (see page 281) onto the backed board. (NOTE: If construction paper is used instead of markers, tack up the desired color in front of the projected design, outline and cut out. It can be stapled, taped, or glued to the board.)

3. Outline the designs with the appropriate colored markers.

4. Turn off the projector and fill in the outline with the same colors.

5. Join the circus fun!

Bee in the Write....Honey up your writing skills

Mystery
Mood Stories
Picture Books
Poetry
TALL Tales
Cartoons
Letters

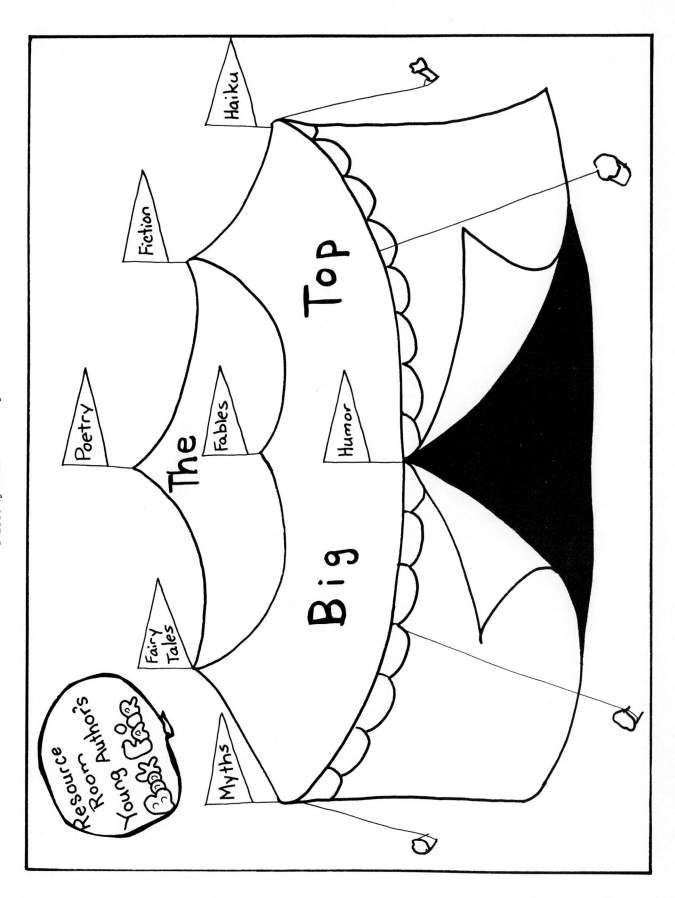

TEACHING UNIT

WRITING SKILLS

A Young Authors' Book Fair

An excellent idea used in many schools is the presentation of a Young Authors' Book Fair. Each participant not only writes and illustrates his or her favorite story, but binds it as well. These books are registered and placed in a book fair to which other students, teachers, parents, administrators, etc., are invited. In California, this is a districtwide event, but it can be made as large or as small as you want. The wonderful thing about this event is the variety of writing skills the student not only learns, but immediately reinforces by using them in a life situation. This unit, along with the learning centers, will present lessons that can lead to a book fair. They can also be used independently as supplemental lessons in writing skills.

Students of all levels are capable of producing a book of some kind, from a picture book (Maurice Sandek) to a mystery (Nancy Drew). They can create a book, bind it (some with help and others more simply) and show it in the Book Fair. This is a project where "everybody wins." Reports are that the enthusiasm for writing and reading grows by leaps and bounds from this activity.

> NOTE: An added dimension to the students' book fair can be to invite published authors of children's books to attend. Each guest can give a short workshop with possibilities for selling the books. Most authors welcome the chance to meet their "public" and do it as a complimentary gesture.

The "learning centers" for March give a framework of lessons to involve the students in the planning, supplying and implementing of a Young Authors' Book Fair. This teaching unit is devoted to introducing the book fair idea and teaching students how to bind their books.

Objectives:

At the conclusion of this unit, students will:

- Know how to bind a book.
- Know how to organize and keep a daily log.
- Have experience with creative story writing, joke writing, mysteries, mood stories, and tall tales.
- Write original poetry.
- Illustrate for a purpose.
- Know how to write an invitation letter and address an envelope.

Introducing the Young Author's Book Fair (Log Keeping)

Materials:

small notebook or composition book
pencil

Preparation:

1. Develop guidelines that the students can follow to prepare for the Young Author's Book Fair.
2. Plan a trip to the library with the students to look at bindings, picture arrangement, and different book types.

Directions:

1. Explain to the students about the idea of having a book fair.
2. List on the chalkboard the items that must be decided on. For example:

   a. A master plan

   b. What kind of books will be written (picture books, stories, poetry)?

   c. Will everyone contribute an original work?

   d. What length will the book be? (Be realistic, sometimes a 2- or 3-page book is very effective and rewarding.)

   e. How will it be illustrated? (for a purpose)

   f. How will it be bound? (Show a bound book)

   g. When will the students have the opportunity to do each step? (an explanation of lesson plans for the next several weeks)

   h. Where will the fair be held? (school gym, library, resource room)

   i. When will it be held? (date)

   j. What will the hours be? (This depends on the complexity of the program because outside authors take additional time and student authors who give presentations take more time than just having books on display. Time must be allotted accordingly.)

   k. Who will be invited? (teachers, staff, other students, parents, administrators, etc.)

   l. How will they be invited? (See the sample letter in Learning Center 8.)

   m. Will there be refreshments? If so, what and who will prepare?

3. Have students begin a daily log in their notebooks. For example, each student must copy the master plan from the board on their first page. (See the illustration.)

4. Each subsequent page should be dated according to the student's program schedule.

5. Have students fill in each page with possible activities, leaving a space to record their progress.

6. Explain that each learning center will give them the opportunity to prepare a finished product for the book fair.

NOTE: Allow time for students to visit the library again if they need more ideas or direction.

Reinforcement Activity:

Refer to "Learning Centers" and have your students do assignment 1.

A Note on Book Binding

The following lesson on book binding may be too difficult for very young or motor-impaired youngsters. For those students for whom small motor tasks are too frustrating, use this modified version.

Their books can be covered in construction paper or cardboard which is either decorated by them or covered with Con-Tact paper (with help). The pages of the book can be stapled rather than sewn directly to the cover. This also makes an attractive and effective cover for a child's book.

Materials:

9" × 12" drawing paper

old book covers or binders board (2 for each book)

Con-Tact paper, wallpaper, burlap, pictures, fabric or graphics for cover

2"-wide vinyl tape

9" × 12" colored construction paper for each book

3"-wide muslin strips

awl, student compass or other sharp point

old magazine for hole-making cushion

large-eyed tapestry needle or darning needle

heavy thread or yarn (learning disabled children will be able to handle yarn and a large needle more easily than thread)

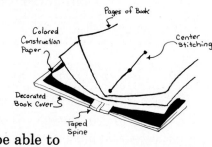

masking tape

scissors

ruler

glue

sharp cutting instrument to cut heavy cardboard (NOTE: use old book covers to eliminate the need for cutting)

Directions:

These directions have been modified from *Young Authors Conference: A Resource and Planning Guide* by Douglas E. Brandt, Consultant, Education Improvement Center—NW, Morris Plains, New Jersey.

FIRST DAY

Preparing Pages

1. Determine the number of pieces of drawing paper needed by dividing the number of pages in the final draft by 4 in order to get the number of sheets needed.

2. Fold the 9" × 12" drawing paper in half to make a 6" × 9" book when each sheet is placed inside the other. (See the illustration.)

3. One folded sheet of construction paper is used as the two end pages of the book. When the book is finished, these pages are glued to the insides of the covers to produce a neat finish. (See the illustration.)

Sewing

1. A 2"- or 3"-wide piece of muslin approximately 8" long for a 9" book should be attached with masking tape to the center of the outer sheet of construction paper along the fold. (See the illustration.) The tape will be removed before the book is completed.

2. Lay the book open flat on top of a magazine or other cushion with the white pages facing you.

3. Carefully poke 3 holes with a sharp object (awl or compass) as shown in the illustration. Begin 2" from the top and bottom, leaving 2½" on either side of center hole.

4. Measure out a length of thread 27" to 36" for 9" book. Double the thread and sew through the holes following the sequence given in Step 5.

5. From the inside fold (see the illustration), begin at center hole 1 and sew through the back piece of muslin. Pull the thread through and up to 2 (second hole), return thread through first hole 1, enter 3 from back and return through 1. Knot the thread securely on the back and trim excess thread.

SECOND DAY

Constructing Covers

1. Covers should be ¼" more than the height of the book.

2. Decorate the covers with Con-Tact paper, fabric, wallpaper, student drawings, illustrations, rubbings, etc.

3. The decorative material should be 1″ larger than the cardboard on three sides. (See the illustration.)

4. The spine edge, which will be finished with tape later, does not need to be finished at this point.

5. Miter cut each corner of decorative material and remove the cut (45 degree angle) section. (See the illustration.)

6. Fold the covering over the edges of the cardboard. Do the top and bottom, then crease end of each corner with your fingernail. (See the illustration.)

7. If pictures are used on the front cover, apply clear Con-Tact paper in the same way described in Step 6.

8. Bind the spine by placing the book covers on the vinyl tape and holding the book covers together. Use a 10″ length of tape for a 9″ book.

THIRD DAY

Assembling Book

1. Remove the masking tape from the muslin.

2. Open the sewn book pages at the center and place onto the open book covers. (See the illustration.) Only ⅛″ of the cover should be showing on all sides.

3. Close the book. The pages should protrude into the taped spine approximately ¼″ or less. (See the illustration.)

4. With the book lying flat, apply white glue on the muslin and construction paper outer sheet. Close the book to affix the glued page to the cover. (See the illustration.) Do both sides.

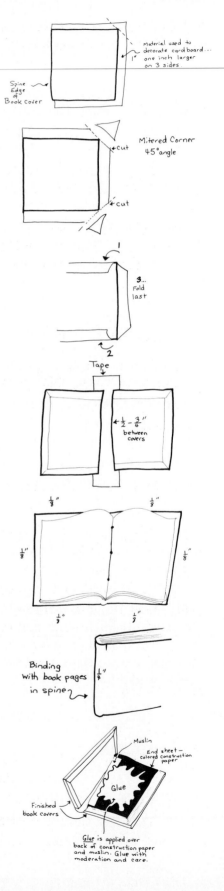

5. Wipe off any excess glue. Dry the book under the weight of several larger books. (The parts of the book are shown in the illustration.)

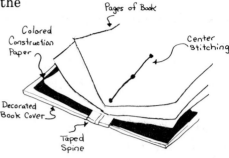

LEARNING CENTERS

The learning centers for March are designed to reinforce writing skills while preparing for a Young Author's Book Fair. It is suggested that the skills needed for each learning center be taught in advance of the learning center activity.

(1) BOOK PLAN

Materials:

student books on a variety of subjects (mysteries, cartoons, autobiographies, biographies, poetry, fiction, etc.)

book jackets (borrow from library)

book shelves

"Book Plan" worksheet

index card

markers

Preparation:

1. Select several books on a variety of levels and styles.

2. Display the books on shelves at the learning center.

3. Attach the book jackets to a bulletin board or folding screen.

4. Instruct the students that this learning center must be the first step toward writing their books.

5. Visit the library where you can point out book jackets, binding, where the illustrations belong on the page, etc.

6. Write the directions on an index card.

7. Make copies of the "Book Plan" worksheet. (See page 288.)

Directions Card:

```
              AUTHOR'S CORNER
1. Look through the books.
2. Read over the "Book Plan" worksheet.
3. Decide what kind of book you would like to write.
4. Complete the worksheet.
```

BOOK PLAN

Young Author's Name _____

Type of book I will write:

☐ Mystery   ☐ Picture book

☐ Story (fiction) ☐ Riddle or Joke book

☐ Story (factual) ☐ Cartoon book

☐ Poem

☐ Other _____

Title of the book I will write: _____

_____

_____

Type of art work I will use:

☐ illustrations of the story   ☐ cartoons

☐ designs   ☐ collage

☐ other _____

Size of final book:

☐ 6″ × 9″

☐ Other _____

Cover design:

☐ Con-Tact paper (easiest to use)

☐ pictures

☐ burlap or other material

☐ other _____

(2) TALL TALES
(INTERMEDIATE-ADVANCED)

NOTE: Primary students can draw a picture of a tall tale or tell the story on a tape recorder.

Materials:

worksheet

pencil

tall tale books (for example, Paul Bunyan)

index card

marker

Preparation:

1. Do a lesson on tall tales.
2. Locate library or reading books of tall tales.
3. Write the directions on an index card.
4. Make copies of the tall hat worksheet. (See page 290.)

Directions Card:

```
              TALL TALES
1.  Look through the books of tall tales.
2.  Take a few minutes to think of a tall tale of your own.
3.  Write your story in the tall hat on the worksheet.
4.  Have your work checked by the teacher.
```

(3) STORY WRITING
(INTERMEDIATE-ADVANCED)

Materials:

"What Is the Mood?" and "Story Writing" worksheets

several easy fiction library books with pictures

index card

marker

Preparation:

1. Discuss the idea of moods before assigning the learning center.
2. Make copies of the two worksheets for each student. (See pages 292-293.)
3. Have library books available for students to peruse.
4. Write the directions on an index card.

Author _____

Write a TALL TALE about what
happened to you when you put on
the TALL TALE hat.

Directions Card:

```
                    STORY WRITING
1. Look at the pictures on the first worksheet carefully.
Decide on the mood of the picture. Write your answer on
the line next to the picture.
2. Write about a mood on the second worksheet. Use any
style you wish.
3. Draw a picture of your mood on that worksheet.
4. Have your work checked by the teacher.
```

(4) MYSTERY
(INTERMEDIATE-ADVANCED)

Materials:

"My Mystery" worksheet
a variety of easy mystery books
index card
pencil

Preparation:

1. Read aloud an easy mystery story and discuss it with the class.
2. Make copies of the worksheet (see page 294) for each student.
3. Write the directions on an index card.
4. Locate easy mystery books to have at the learning center for students to peruse.

Directions Card:

```
                    MYSTERY
1. Read the worksheet carefully.
2. Plan out your mystery story.
3. Fill in the worksheet.
4. Write your story.
```

Name _____

WHAT IS THE MOOD?

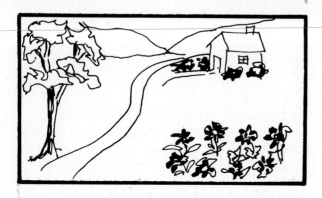

STORY WRITING

Author _____

Moods

    Story writing can take many forms. It can be a paragraph, a sentence or even a word. Use story form or poetry to write about feelings. What is your mood? Use the back of this paper if you need more space to write.

_____

_____

_____

_____

_____

_____

_____

_____

_____

Draw a picture to illustrate the mood of your story.

Author _____

MY MYSTERY

Idea for the story: _____
_____

Title of the story: _____
_____

This is my mystery story:

_____
_____
_____
_____
_____
_____
_____
_____
_____
_____
_____
_____
_____
_____
_____
_____

(5) POETRY
(INTERMEDIATE-ADVANCED)

Materials:

worksheets
markers
easy poetry books for students to read
index card

Preparation:

1. Conduct a lesson on poetry before assigning the learning center. Read different kinds of poetry to the group.

2. Locate easy poetry books (see "Professional Resource Books") for students to peruse.

3. Make copies of the worksheets for each student.

4. Write the directions on an index card.

Directions Card:

```
                    POET TREE (A)
1.  Look at the Poet Tree words.
2.  Fill in the poems with the missing rhyming words.
3.  Color the worksheet.

                    POET TREE (B)
1.  Look at the poetry books.
2.  Decide on the kind of poem you would like to write.
3.  Write your poem on the worksheet.
4.  Have your work checked by the teacher.
```

(6) BOOK OF PICTURES (PRIMARY)

NOTE: This learning center is one possible activity for making a book of pictures. Alternate suggestions are: making a collage using magazine pictures or scraps, etc.; photographs for the budding photographer; graphics or shapes. A picture book can be as varied as the student's imagination.

Name _____

POET TREE (A)

Using the words from the Poet Tree, complete the two poems below.

The bee flew away from the _____.

    As it did, down came a _____.

It landed plop on my _____.

    Oh, boy! Did I get a _____.

The clown stood on his _____.

    As the children watched he _____.

"Come be a _____.

    You'll never _____.

Life will always be _____,

    Each and every _____."

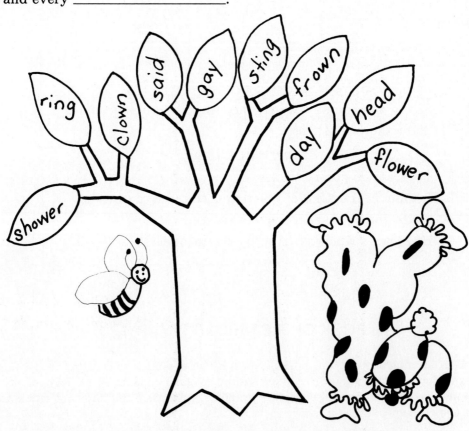

Name _____

POET TREE (B)

Make up your own poems using the
words in the Poet Tree. Add some of
your own, too.

_____

_____

_____

_____

_____

_____

Make up your own poems
using the words in the
Poet Tree. Add some
of your own, too.

Materials:

worksheet
crayons, watercolors, Craypas markers
9″ × 12″ drawing paper
9″ × 12″ construction paper
scissors
old magazines (for cutting)
old photographs
picture books from the library
index card
marker
rubber cement

Preparation:

1. Make several copies of the worksheet (see page 299) for each student.

2. Locate colorful picture books for the students to peruse.

3. Conduct a lesson on the variety of possibilities in making a picture book to express a feeling or tell a story before assigning this learning center.

4. Write the directions on an index card.

Directions Card:

> BOOK OF PICTURES
> 1. Look at the books.
> 2. Think about your book.
> 3. Draw or paint your story on several worksheets.

(7) THE JOKE'S ON YOU!
(INTERMEDIATE-ADVANCED)

Materials:

index card	crayons
"The Joke's on You" worksheet	markers
pencils	easy-to-read joke books

Preparation:

1. Select several easy-to-read joke books from the library for students to peruse.

2. Give a lesson on appropriate jokes and illustrations before assigning the learning center.

Fold

3. Make copies of the worksheet for each student.

4. Write the directions on an index card.

Directions Card:

```
                    THE JOKE'S ON YOU
    1.  Look over the joke books.
    2.  Read the joke on the worksheet.
    3.  Design your own jokes and write them in the boxes.
    4.  HA! HA! HA! HA!
```

(8) WRITING INVITATIONS
(INTERMEDIATE-ADVANCED)

Materials:

"Invitation Worksheet" and "Envelope Worksheet"

envelopes

stationery

stamps

pens and pencils

phone books or other address directories

index cards for names and addresses

Preparation:

1. Locate telephone and address directories for the appropriate areas.

2. Write a sample invitation on the chalkboard for students to copy.

3. Make copies of the worksheets for each student. (See pages 302–303).

4. Instruct the students in advance of this activity on how to write personal letters and invitations and how to address an envelope.

5. Assign each student one or two people to invite to the Book Fair. (Prepare name and address index cards of guests in advance.)

6. Write the directions on index cards.

Directions Card (A):

```
                    INVITATION
    1.  Fill in the invitation worksheet.
    2.  Have your work checked by the teacher.
    3.  Copy your invitation onto the stationery.
```

Name _____

THE JOKE'S ON YOU!

What did one bug say to the other?   Stop peopling me!

Write and illustrate your jokes in the boxes below.

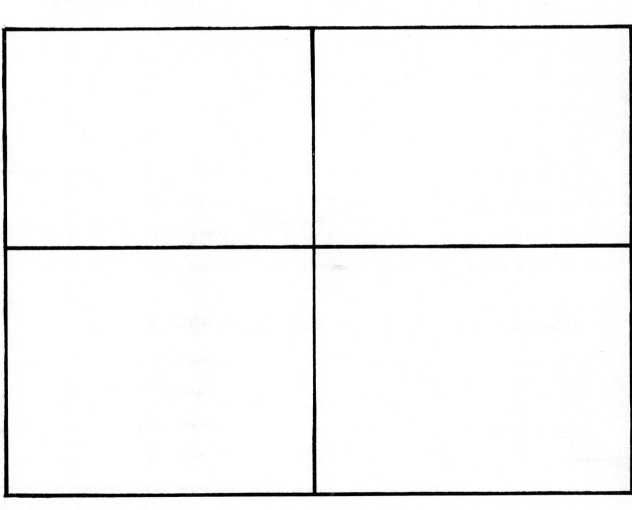

Envelope Worksheet

Stamp

(your name)

(your number and street)

(your city and state) (zip)

name of Guest

number and street

City   State   zip

INVITATION WORKSHEET

Name _____

Directions: Fill in the worksheet. Have your work checked. When your work has been corrected, copy the invitation onto stationery. Work carefully!

Name and Address of Guest:

<u>M</u>___ (and Mrs.) _____ _____

_____   _____ ____
(Number)   (Street Name)

_____   _____ ____
(City)   (State)   (ZIP)

Dear M_____ (and Mrs.) _____,

    Our classroom is having a Young Author's Book Fair on

_____ at _____.
(Date)   (Time)

    We would be honored to have you attend. Please R.S.V.P.

to _____ on or before
(Teacher's Name)

_____.
(Date)

Thanks. Hope to see you there.

                Sincerely,

                _____
                    (Your Signature)

Directions Card (B):

```
              ADDRESSING AN ENVELOPE
1. Fill in the envelope worksheet with the guest's name
and address.
2. Have your work checked by the teacher.
3. Copy the address carefully onto an envelope.
4. Put a stamp on the envelope and mail.
```

MATERIALS OF THE MONTH

Once the room has been set up using learning centers, many materials are suddenly seen through different eyes.

One of the wonderful advantages of using learning centers is their versatility. The more varied the activities, the more effective they are. Consequently, things like old board games, radios, visual aids, electronic games, old children's books, etc., can be put to excellent and effective use.

Garage sales, flea markets, and house sales are often gold mines of inexpensive and useable material for learning centers. Children's games (with all the pieces) can make excellent motivating activities for a learning center. Games like "Candyland" and "Winnie the Pooh," and hand puppets are excellent for primary students. More difficult games, like "Battleship," are excellent for directionality and visual motor skills for the intermediate to advanced level students.

Spending a few hours at sales of used household items can yield excellent results in inexpensive materials that can be put to good use in your classroom.

FREE FOR THE ASKING

Getting Started in Writing

Put out by *Readers Digest*, this handy 18-page booklet outlines some of the necessary mechanics of writing professionally. This is a useful booklet to supplement the Young Author's Book Fair. Send a self-addressed stamped envelope to:

Writers Digest
9933 Alliance Road
Cincinnati, OH 45242

Free Films for 16 mm Projectors

Many films on a variety of subjects are available on loan, with the users usually only paying return postage. Some of these films (though designed for adults) make excellent motivators for young authors. They are available on sports, art, science and social studies including space. To obtain more information, write to:

Association—Sterling Films
600 Grand Avenue
Ridgefield, NJ 07657

Free Stuff for Kids

This is an excellent book for reinforcing letter writing skills. It guarantees a reply and something for nothing at that. This is a 120-page book that lists 250 things that kids can receive just by writing a letter or postcard. (Some offers stipulate a small fee, usually under $1.) This book sells for $2.95 plus $.80 for postage. Order from:

Meadowbrook Press
Dept. DM
18318 Minnetonka Blvd.
Deep Haven, MN 55391

Cassette Catalog

This catalog lists tapes for children, an excellent way to expose students to literature that is above their reading ability. Some tapes tell stories from all over the world, while others are stories from a particular author like Rudyard Kipling. There are song tapes to listen to and sing along with. All the singers, musicians and storytellers are performers, too. A free catalog is available for the asking. Send a postcard to:

Cassette Catalogue
A Gentle Wind
Box 3103
Albany, NY 12203

Will Rogers Biography

This is a biography of a man who touched many people in his lifetime. It is an excellent example of biography writing for students to read. 25 copies per school are available free. Send a postcard to:

Will Rogers Memorial
P.O. Box 157
Claremore, OK 74017

GOOD BUYS

The following items are considered good values for the money and are chosen to supplement the unit on writing skills

The Whole Word Catalogue 2

This is a large soft cover book with advice on everything from Haiku to horror stories, including ways to publish student works. Edited by Bill Zavatsky and Ron Padgett, it sells for about $15. Published by McGraw-Hill Paperbacks, it is available from:

Teachers and Writers
186 West 4 Street
New York, NY 10014

Pacer Junior (Viewer)

This is an easy to operate, individual use filmstrip viewer. The viewer, made of plastic with easy-to-follow directions printed right on it, is excellent for use at a learning center where filmstrip and/or cassette is used. (The cassette can be played on a separate tape player at the same time.) The best part is the price! It sells for under $15. Write to:

> Eye-Gate Media, Inc.
> P.O. Box 303
> Jamaica, NY 11435

Puppetry in Early Childhood Education

This is a 260-page softcover, illustrated "puppet encyclopedia." Part I defines specific puppetry applications (geared for the classroom); Part II is devoted to puppet making both for teachers and children; and Part III describes ways that puppets can be used to teach. An excellent sparker for creative writing, it sells for under $15. Write to:

> Nancy Refro Studios
> 117 W. Ninth Street
> Austin, TX 78703

Creative Writing

This is a liquid duplicating book of 24 lessons for grades 3–5 in a variety of writing skills: autobiographies, keeping diaries, writing poems, writing jokes, tall tales, writing letters, invitations, mysteries and more. The book sells for under $10. Contact:

> E.S.P. Inc.
> P.O. Box 5037
> Jonesboro, AR 72401

PROFESSIONAL RESPONSIBILITIES

STAFF EVALUATION OF THE PROGRAM

Whether a resource room or a special education classroom is a brand new program in the school or a well established one, an annual evaluation meeting can be very helpful.

Eliciting evaluations from the regular staff members whose students are mainstreamed in the program is essential for many reasons. Most resource room programs, no matter how effective, can be improved. Excellent suggestions can come out of a wholesome exchange of ideas. Not only are problems uncovered, but often solutions not immediately obvious to you can be uncovered. Furthermore, the very act of including the staff in an evaluation of the program gives a strong message that their input is important and necessary to its success.

Some teachers who have opinions to share about the program will feel more comfortable expressing them in writing rather than at an open meeting. Therefore, it is a good idea to distribute evaluation forms (see page 307) well in advance of the meeting for the teachers to fill out and return to you. (Sometimes, depending upon the nature of the group involved, you might not require the evaluation forms be signed.)

SPECIAL PROGRAM QUESTIONNAIRE

1. Do you feel the scheduling is efficient? Is the amount of time adequate? If not, how can it be changed?

_____

_____

_____

_____

2. Do you see the carryover of skills learned in the special program to the students' class work? If not, why?

_____

_____

_____

_____

3. How do you think the students feel about attending the special program? What reactions have you observed?

_____

_____

_____

_____

4. Is there enough communication between you and the special education teacher? If not, how could this be changed?

_____

_____

_____

_____

5. How do the children who do not attend the special program feel about the program? What reactions have you observed?

_____

_____

_____

_____

6. Do you have any ideas or suggestions that could be helpful to the program for next year? What are they?

_____

_____

_____

_____

Reviewing the forms before the meeting allows you time to collate the responses and have the results ready to present using visual aids.

At the meeting, you may want to consider projecting the evaluation form with the collated results on an opaque projector for the staff to see. This gives them a familiar format from which to form judgments. Encourage comments or additions to what is being presented. Ask for possible solutions to the problems presented. Listen attentively and seriously consider all possibilities. Try to think openly. Sometimes we can become so "locked in" to the present procedures that we cannot see the possibilities for new ones. Ideas that at first seem to be the least acceptable, with modifications, can sometimes become excellent solutions.

Be generous with your recognition of good ideas. Be sure to tell someone at a later date that you tried an idea and how well it worked. *Everyone* needs to feel important—a little praise can go a long way in eliciting a cooperative attitude. Making your program an integral part of the total school milieu is your goal. Include everyone!

PROFESSIONAL RESOURCE BOOKS

Carlson, Ruth Kearny. *Writing Aids Through the Grades: One Hundred Eighty-Six Developmental Writing Activities.* (New York: Teachers College Press, 1970)

Cianciolo, Patricia. *Illustrations in Children's Books.* (Dubuque, IA: Wm. C. Brown, 1970)

Dill, Barbara E., ed. *Children's Catalog.* (Bronx, NY: H.W. Wilson, 1976)

Hopkins, Lee, and Annette Shapiro. *Creative Activities to Stimulate Children.* (New York: Scholastic Book Services, 1969)

Howland, Virginia. *Children's Literature: A Guide to Reference Sources.* (Washington, D.C.: Library of Congress, 1966)

Livingston, Myra Cohn. *When You Are Alone/It Keeps You Capone; An Approach to Creative Writing with Children.* (New York: Atheneum, 1973)

Spoeke, George D. *Good Reading for Poor Readers.* (Champaign, IL: Garrard Co., 1974)

NOTE: Additional book suggestions as well as explanations of some of the above books can be found in *The Elementary School Library Collection* published annually by Bro-Dart Foundation.

MODES FOR MAINSTREAMING

STAFF MEMOS AND NEWSLETTERS

An excellent way to keep staff members informed of new techniques in special education is by use of a memo. In addition to in-service workshops and regularly scheduled conferences, the memo is an excellent vehicle of communication. It allows the teacher to read it when he or she has the time and is not pressured for a response. The written memo also gives the reader the advantage of re-reading it for better understanding.

The memos can be informal notes attached to a copy of a new study:

Dear _____,

Thought you might like to read this. Please pass on to _____ when you are finished. (A faculty checklist can be used to circulate it to the entire staff.) Thanks.

Natalie

A more ambitious approach can be a newsletter published at regular intervals. This can contain notices of special education meetings of interest to the teachers, announcements of new materials or books available for loan, synopses of interesting articles or studies in special education, anecdotes about the teachers' students, etc. The newsletter can be an excellent way to get information to staff members without taking up more time for meetings or putting yourself in a threatening role.

Parent volunteers or aides might be a possible source of help for producing this newsletter. It can be as simple or as elaborate as you choose. Once initiated, the versatility of this type of communication seems endless.

TIP OF THE MONTH

NO MISTAKES, PLEASE!

Often, it is necessary for notes to be sent home. Teacher conferences, request for materials, notice of trips, invitations to school parties, and I.E.P. meetings are but a few reasons to send notes to parents. Since these notes reflect the teacher who has sent them, it is essential that they be letter perfect!

In the hustle and bustle of a normal school day, it isn't unusual for a teacher to feel rushed when doing written tasks. This rush, unfortunately, can cause careless mistakes. Careful proofreading is a must before notes are sent home. As an extra precaution, have a colleague or school secretary go over it again to be sure there are no mistakes. Good public relations can be quickly dispelled by a note or letter that goes home with spelling or grammatical errors. Try to avoid that from happening . . . double check!

A FINAL WORD

TEACHER EVALUATIONS

There are about as many approaches to administrators evaluating teachers as there are administrators. Sometimes, the procedure is set and not a subject for change! Often, however, administrators welcome suggestions about how to make the evaluation process more useful and acceptable to the teacher.

Since the implementation of resource rooms and special education classes vary so greatly and are so different from traditional classroom teaching, a different evaluation approach seems in order.

An important goal to keep in mind is that you should not only be the subject of, but try to be included in the evaluation process. A checklist of evaluation criteria should be

Resource Room Teacher's Name _____ Date _____

EVALUATION FORM

EVALUATION AREAS	RATING*	SUGGESTIONS

Room Design

    Flow of students
    Materials displayed
    Clear directions available
    Multi-ability materials available

Scheduling

    Adequate time allotted
    Pupil contact time
    Observation time
    Conferencing
    Conflicts with classroom specials
    Pupils' understanding of schedule

Student Programming

    Pretesting
    Progress evaluation
    Lesson plans
    Diagnostic teaching
    Individualized instruction

Teacher Attitude

    Enthusiasm
    Flexibility
    Reliability

*3—Excellent
2—Adequate
1—Needs improvement

shared with you at the *beginning* of the evaluation period if possible. In this way it helps you to organize the program accordingly and know from the beginning what is expected. You should request this criteria if necessary.

An example of a possible evaluation form designed to evaluate a resource room teacher is found on page 310 (Elman, 1981). This form can easily be adapted for the special education classroom as well.

The ideal is for the evaluation form to be filled out in conjunction with the administrator and the resource room teacher. In this way, if there are problems, you are included in the solution. Chances are, you are already aware of the problem and will welcome the opportunity to be helpful and get additional input into its solution.

Change often takes many tries over much time. If the evaluation procedure is currently not ideal, work toward improving this by constructive suggestions presented in a non-defensive way. This may have to be done more than once, but can pay off in a more successful evaluation procedure for you.

MARCH REFERENCES

Andersen, Hans Christian. *The Fairy Tale of My Life.* (New York: British Book Centre, 1974)

Andersen, Hans Christian. *Fairy Tales.* (Bowie, MD: Heritage, 1945)

Ardizzone, Edward. *Fourteen Classic Tales.* (New York: Atheneum, 1979)

Bartlett, John. *Bartlett's Familiar Quotations.* (Boston: Little Brown and Co., 1955)

Marti-Ibanez, Felix (*ed.*) "Ugly Duckling Genius." (New York: *The Pageant of Medicine*, December 1958)

Stirling, Monica. *Andersen, Hans Christian 1805–1875.* (New York: Harcourt Brace and World, 1965)

Toksuig, Signe. *Andersen, Hans Christian 1805–1875.* (New York: Harcourt Brace and World, 1934)

World Book Encyclopedia, Volume I. (Chicago: Field Enterprises Educational Corp., 1977)

April

Happy birthday to . . .

1 William Harvey (1578) Heartfelt thanks to William Harvey who worked with all his heart to learn how blood flows through the heart, arteries and veins. Measure 2 ounces of water. The heart pumps that much blood with every beat. With an average of 70 beats per minute, how many pounds are pumped in each minute, hour, and day? Learn the facts by heart.

2 Frederic Auguste Bartholdi (1834) "Give me your tired, your poor," Liberty says silently to ships entering the New York harbor. A gift from France, this 152-foot copper statue stands on Liberty Island, a monument to freedom. Thank Bartholdi and his mom because he sculpted her face to greet your family's immigrants! First stop! Ellis Island. Second stop? New York to . . .

3 Henry Luce (1898) and Jane Goodall Van Lawick (1934) Monkey see, monkey do! What people do, monkeys do back! Now, Mommy see, Mommy do! Goodall watched chimps to see how monkey mothers mothered and she did the same for her son! Find founder Henry Luce's TIME Magazine issue of 10/30/69 and read how Goodall learned good mothering from monkeys!

4 Dorothea Dix (1802) Peering into the dimly lit dungeon, she could barely see beaten bodies of men, chained to cold, stony walls. But she clearly saw her future goal. She would see to it that mentally ill patients had treatment in clean hospitals. Dorothea Dix looked for a better way to help troubled people. Can you see why?

5 Spencer Tracy (1900), Melvyn Douglas (1901), Bette Davis (1908) and Gregory Peck (1916) Share a *-shaped cake for 4 * * * * ! Light 4 flickering candles for * Bette Davis, * Gregory Peck, * Melvyn Douglas and * Spencer Tracy. And, in the twinkle of an eye with an almanac, find the April *s born on: 4/28/41, 4/3/24, 4/26/36, 4/10/21, 4/23/42, 4/2/08, 4/7/28, 4/11/32, 4/27/22, 4/24/34, 4/3/42, and 4/24/42!

6 Erich (Harry Houdini) Weiss (1874) His mom always wondered where the cookies went! She knew she had turned the lock! But Erich could open locks then as he did when, as Houdini, he opened locks while under water in his famous Chinese Underwater Torture Trick! Most daring of all magicians, the secrets of his escapes are locked away forever!

7 Walter Camp (1859) Though William Ellis invented the game in England, Walter Camp is the father of football. He explained the sport so everyone would play and watch it. Camp's rules and Daily Dozen warm-up exercises still rule the game! Don't pass up knowing about the father of another famous sport this week, next month!

8 Donald Vesco (1939) 308.81 m.p.h. was his average speed! What's an average? To average, + two speeds of 304.64 m.p.h. + 302.97 m.p.h. Then ÷ the sum by 2 because he rode a motorcycle twice. Don Vesco's world speed record, riding a 21-foot cycle: 308.81 m.p.h. He also set a ¼!mile world record! How fast can you find it?

9 Eadweard Muybridge (1830) Leland Stanford made a bet. Muybridge proved him right. To find out if 4 legs left the ground when a horse galloped, Muybridge set 24 cameras in a row. Long strings attached to cameras flipped shutters as a horse shot ahead. What was the photo-finish proof? Make a bet you can make a flip-book gallop!

10 Commodore Matthew C. Perry (1794) The adventure seemed dangerous. With 300 men, Perry went ashore with a question for the Emperor. Would Japan be interested in trade with America? Two small ports soon opened to us. MADE IN JAPAN labels say that important items are still imported. Read labels! List items labeled MADE IN JAPAN!

11 Percy Julian (1899) The townfolk tried to burn his home. They tried because he was black. Would white soldiers not use the foam he invented to save lives from fires? Would white people not use the cortisone he invented to lessen the pain of arthritis? It is painful to know he didn't invent pills for prejudice.

12 Frederic Melcher (1879) and Hardie Gramatky (1907) Gold medals mean splendid tales. Since 1922, Melcher has pinned Newbery medals on fine books of the year. But not all books win medals. Gramatky's LITTLE TOOT won *everyone's* heart. Toot is a train (A WHAT) that acts like a person (A WHO). Find a Newbery winner in which a WHAT acts like a WHO.

13 Thomas Jefferson (1743) President Jefferson SWIVELED to his desk and signed his name to the biggest purchase of land ever: 8,000,000 square miles from France doubled the size of the U.S.! 14 days later, Lewis and Clark set out to pace this Louisiana Territory to the Pacific and see the other "shining sea." Trace their paces!

14 Dr. James L. Plimpton (1828) Joseph Merlin's first wooden spool skates were smashing! They went only in 1 direction—straight into a fine, huge mirror! Then a 5-wheel skate, a 1-wheel skate and a long roll skate came before the 4 wooden wheels of James Plimpton. You would skate for the pleasure of honoring Plimpton, wouldn't you?

15 Leonardo Da Vinci (1452) Most of what Da Vinci began was unfinished. Thousands of pages of untidy notes are lost, but few are needed to note his genius. Drawings of bicycles, flying machines, helicopters, submarines, clocks, cars, tanks . . . inventions all described in MIRROR WRITING centuries before they were "invented" for keeps!

> "When (people) are rightly occupied their amusement grows out of their work, as the colour petals out of a fruitful flower."
>
> John Ruskin

✝✝✝✝✝✝✝✝✝✝✝✝✝✝✝✝✝✝✝✝✝✝✝✝✝✝✝✝

16 Charlie Chaplin (1889) Follow in the footsteps of the great Charlie Chaplin! With a derby, cane and a black square mustache, you could look like Chaplin, the baggy trousered tramp who kept audiences laughing with his pantomime! Mime the starving miner from *The Gold Rush*! Boil your soles, cut your peas, and "chew leather."

17 Alexander Joy Cartwright (1820) 1 old cat, 2 old cat, 3 old cat, you're out at the OLD ball game! It may be a legend that Abner Doubleday invented baseball in 1839, but it is for sure that Alexander Joy Cartwright wrote the rules that brought joy to Mudville—and everywhere else! Run to get 3 basic facts about the first game on record!

18 Clarence Darrow (1857) Darrow defended John Scopes who was being tried for teaching a science class that man's family, back millions of years ago, just may have been monkeys. Because it was different from the Bible story of creation, Scopes was found guilty of teaching EVOLUTION, which was against Tennessee law.

19 Jean Lee Latham (1902) Impossible! Could a 3rd grade drop-out correct 8,000 errors on mathematical tables used by navigators at sea? Yes! Nathaniel Bowditch did just that! His story won the 1956 Newbery Medal. Its author, Jean Latham, wrote many biographies. Choose one and tell about someone else who did something else impossible!

20 Daniel French (1850) Be ready in a minute! 16,000 Boston civilians became Revolutionary War soldiers, ready to fight at a minute's notice! Daniel French spent many minutes sculpting a MINUTEMAN, which stands at Concord to remind us that we must cherish each minute of FREEDOM. Salute French at attention for a minute!

21 John Muir (1838) Blind? Then he and dog Stickeen must see the world before he could see no more. First to the Sierra's unknown glaciers; then to Alaska, Liberia, China, and . . . He lost neither his sight nor his hope for National Parks. Help preserve the world's beauty with an Earth Day project to preserve Muir's memory.

22 Vladimir Illyich Lenin (1870) Because Russians were poor, starving and tired of war (WWI), it was easy for Lenin to call workers and farmers to fight the few rich factory and land owners. The Russian Revolution began in Petrograd (now LENINgrad). Because of the Revolution, all kids learned to read and write for the first time.

23 Shirley Temple Black (1928) Why does Mrs. Black, once the U.S. Ambassador to __, have many curly-haired dolls that look just like her? She was the star of storybook films "Wee Willy __," "Heidi," and "Rebecca of __ __." Wearing 56 curls, tiny 7-year-old Shirley was the youngest to have won an Oscar, the golden doll won by Hollywood's greatest stars.

24 Robert Bailey Thomas (1766) The yellow OLD FARMER'S ALMANAC has forecast weather for 191 years! First published when Washington was president, Robert Thomas's editions have foretold

○ ◑ ● , ✳ ▲▲▲ ▼▲▼ ✑   etc. Predictions are in poetry. "Grey skies, snow flies." Write a weather rhyme!

25 Guglielmo Marconi (1874) By the time he was 22, he had invented the "wireless" which could send a wireless signal over 3 miles. By 27, he received signals across 3,000 miles! Radio waves sent those signals as now radio waves bring planes to smooth landing and smooth music to our ears. Research radio. Who discovered radio waves?

26 John James Audubon (1785) He knew his subjects "from-the-inside-out." Once a taxidermist, Audubon's fame as a bird watcher soared. His brush flew silently over his pages capturing each bird's beauty for bird watchers, forever. Know your bird inside out! Draw a bird skeleton. Then draw a bird. Name your prints and bird watch!

27 Samuel Morse (1791) Good news traveled fast! Morse's dots and dashes carried messages on wires strung high above the lonely countryside. The East now knew quickly what the West already knew and no longer would the mail depend on ponies. Simple tapping of the telegraph took the place of long and tiresome travel. —*.*. ..*. ..*..*-.*.*. ..*

28 Lionel Barrymore (1878) The Barrymores proved that acting can "run in the family"! Lionel's great grandmother, grandmother, parents, uncle and brother John were all wonderful actors! His shy sister Ethel became a leading lady of the American stage! Check the marquee! Did their children and grandchildren follow in the family footsteps?

29 Edward Ellington (1899) He hated to practice piano scales for Mrs. Clinkscale, but he didn't hate to play! Out of school with a cold, Ellington wrote the *Soda Fountain Rag*! He soon left his job at the ice cream counter of the Poodle Dog Cafe! Instead of making sodas, the DUKE mixed melodies with rhythms and made JAZZ!

30 Carl Friedrich Gauss (1777) Ready? Add all the numbers from 1 to 100. $1+2=3+3=6+4$ . . . It just didn't add up that Carl found the answer in seconds and could $+$, $-$, $\times$ and $\div$ better than his class, better than his teacher . . . even better than other famous mathematicians! It all adds up because Carl was a genius. How long did it take you to add it all up?

These birthographies were prepared by Davida Shipkowitz of Northridge, California.

SPOTLIGHT ON

ALBERT EINSTEIN (1879–1955)

Albert Einstein epitomizes the brilliant scientist. He is known most for developing the theory of relativity, but was also a great teacher, scholar and humanitarian. Many records of his early schooling, however, show a youngster who, in spite of his brilliant mind, had difficulty with languages and even failed entrance examinations for college the first time he took them (Thompson, 1971).

Einstein is famous for his ideas about the universe. His ideas were the forerunners of the atomic bomb and many other electronic innovations including television.

Einstein's theory of relativity is one of the greatest scientific contributions to date. The formula $E = MC^2$ (see April's bulletin board) is one of the most famous equations in the scientific world. E stands for energy, M for mass, and C^2 for the speed of light multiplied by itself. This formula proved that matter, when changed to energy, produced a very powerful energy source. With the knowledge of the theory of relativity, the development of the atomic bomb was soon to follow.

Much of Einstein's work is difficult to understand, but some is based on commonly known ideas. For example, direction is relative since it depends on where a person is. He used the same approach in explaining motion. When a person is sitting in a vehicle and another vehicle passes by the window, it is difficult at first to tell which vehicle is moving. To be certain something is moving, one must have something not moving with which to compare, for motion is relative (Britannica Junior Encyclopedia, 1971).

Einstein received the 1921 Nobel Prize for Physics. In 1932 the Institute for Advanced Study at Princeton University in the United States offered him a lifetime professorship. In 1940 Einstein became a United States citizen.

Considering the fact that he was 26 years of age when he submitted his "Special Theory of Relativity" to a physics journal, there appears to be a wide discrepancy between his ability and his functioning level. According to the Goertzels (1962):

"Albert Einstein was considered dull by his teachers and by his parents. His son, Albert, Jr., while a professor of agriculture at the University of California in Berkeley, told Bela Kornetzer who interviewed him while gathering data for his book *American Fathers and Sons*:

'Actually I understand my father was a well-behaved child. He was shy, lonely and withdrawn from the world even then. He was even considered backward by his teachers. He told me that his teachers reported to his father than he was mentally slow, unsociable and adrift forever in his foolish dreams.'

"It was for this reason that the father, when Albert was sixteen, urged him to forget his philosophical nonsense and apply himself to the 'sensible trade' of electrical engineering. A slowness of speech had predisposed his parents to think him dull."

How odd that a youngster of such brilliance is reported to have had no friends and in later years, when approached, his teachers had no recollection of him. According to the Goertzels, tests were a traditional part of schooling that he most disliked. Their elimination, he felt, would do away with painful dulling of the memory, and it would no longer be necessary to take years to hammer soon-to-be-forgotten facts into students' heads. Conceivably such strong feelings could come from painful memories of his own failures.

His thirst for knowledge was always there. In an article called "What I Believe" (Forum, October, 1930) Einstein said the following:

"The most beautiful thing we can experience is the mysterious. It is the source of all true art and science."

SPOTLIGHT BULLETIN BOARD

Materials:

white background paper

black marker or construction paper for lights and figures

overhead projector (NOTE: If an opaque projector is used, the transparency and marker are not necessary. The book page or a dark copy need only be projected from the opaque projector onto the bulletin board.)

acetate transparency

transparency marker

Preparation:

1. Cover the bulletin board with the white construction paper.

2. Trace the Spotlight Bulletin Board on page 316 onto the transparency acetate with the marker.

3. Project the image of the board onto the background paper.

4. Trace the outline of the board and the lights with a black marker.

NOTE: If cut outs of construction paper are preferred to drawing with the marker, place the desired colored construction paper in front of the projected image and trace the outline directly onto it. Cut out the construction paper and staple or tack it onto the board when finished. Either approach makes a very effective bulletin board.

BULLETIN BOARD IDEAS

HAPPY C DAY

This bulletin board is designed to introduce HAPPY C DAY. (C is the Roman numeral for 100.) This is a day devoted to culminate weeks of special activities planned to reinforce the concept of the number 100. The teaching unit and the learning centers for April are samples of some of these activities.

C Day can be celebrated by sending 100 helium-filled balloons into the sky! Therefore, the bulletin board uses actual balloons (helium filled) with fun-filled activities to reinforce the number 100 inside.

The balloons on this bulletin board can each contain a slip of paper with an activity to reinforce the concept of 100. When the student has completed an assignment or at another given time, he or she may "pop" the balloon with a pin to see what the fun activity might be. A "One Free Pop" ticket (see the illustration) can be given for finished assignments.

Spotlight
on

Theory of Relativity

$E = MC^2$

Time
Motion
Space
Gravity
Mass Atoms

Albert EINSTEIN
1879 – 1955

The following activities have been suggested by Beverly Radloff, a second grade teacher from Simi-Valley, California, who is the originator of the C Day idea. These may be written or typed on small slips of paper, folded, and placed into the balloons before they are blown up. NOTE: A variation can be to have the slips folded and picked out of a basket or hat!

1. How many numbers can you write in 100 seconds? Set the egg timer and GO!

2. How many letters of the alphabet can you write in 100 seconds? Set the egg timer and GO!

3. How many times does your heart beat in 100 seconds? Find your heartbeat, set the timer and GO!

4. How many words can you write in 100 seconds? Set the timer and GO!

5. You have $100 of play money to spend in the TOY catalog. Fill out the order form. Remember to stay within $100!

6. Write 100 words. Time yourself. How many minutes did it take you?

7. Write 100 adjectives to describe school. Watch it!

8. Write 100 verbs to describe what you do at school.

9. Can you think of 100 things (nouns) you see around the school? Write them down.

10. Write a story exactly 100 words long.

11. Write a 100-word letter to your pal.

12. Write exactly 100 sentences.

13. Read 100 pages in a library book. Write a 100-word report about the 100 pages.

14. Bring in 100 different stones. Put them on the display table.

15. Bring in 100 food labels. Put them on the display table.

16. List all the things that could weigh 100 pounds.

17. What can you find that is exactly 100 inches long?

18. Cut off 100 inches of string. What things could you do with it?

19. Make 100 dots into a design.

20. Make something out of 100 cotton swabs.

21. Make a picture using 100 lines.

22. Make a collage out of 100 things (magazine pictures, etc.).

23. Make a T-shirt design using the number 100.

24. Design a bumper sticker using the number 100.

25. Design a book cover using the number 100.

26. Bounce a ball 100 times. Time yourself. How long did it take?

27. Jump rope 100 times. Time yourself. How long did it take?

28. Hop on one foot 100 times. Time yourself. How long did it take?

29. Skip 100 times. Time yourself. How long did it take?

30. Line up 100 chocolate chips. Measure the line. How long is it? You and several friends may eat the chips when you know the answer.

31. How many times can you lick a lollipop? If you make it to 100, you may keep the lollipop.

32. Toss a penny 100 times. How many heads? How many tails?

33. Make a design using 100 circles.

34. Make a design using 100 happy faces.

35. Make a design using 100 triangles.

Add as many fun activities as you can think of to reinforce the number 100. Have the students think of additional activities, too. Once you have the activities listed on a sheet of paper, prepare the bulletin board.

Materials:

bulletin board illustration

opaque projector

light blue background paper

white construction paper for the balloon over the basket

yellow, brown, red, and blue markers for the balloon and details

multi-colored helium-filled balloons

stapler or tape

note paper to write the balloon tasks

scissors

large blunt-end knitting needle

bright colored yarn or string for the balloon ties

Preparation:

1. Cover the bulletin board with the light blue background paper.

2. Project the copy of the "Happy C Day" bulletin board (see page 320) onto the backed board.

3. Place the white construction paper in front of the projection of the large balloon and trace around the outline.

4. Remove the balloon outline and cut it out with scissors.

5. Outline the sections of the balloon with yellow marker, and make the sections in alternating colors of white, red, and blue.

6. Fill in the sections with the colors. (NOTE: The sections can be left white and only outlined in the various colors. However, the more intense the colors, the more effective the bulletin board.)

7. Color in the basket with a brown marker or cut it out of brown construction paper.

8. The ribbons trailing from the balloon should be left white, with the words written in red.

9. The helium-filled balloons should be in a wide variety of bright colors. Most toy stores or department stores have helium tanks for filling balloons, or many novelty stores will rent out a helium tank for a small fee. There is a safety factor, however, so discuss this first with the principal. (NOTE: If helium is not available, air inflate the balloons and attach them to the board with double-faced tape. If real balloons are not used, make them out of construction paper and write the tasks on the back of each one.)

10. Write the directions and title in a marker color of your choice.

11. Write the tasks on small slips of paper and place them inside the inflated balloons.

12. A large blunt-end knitting needle is a safe and effective way to have each student pop the balloon. (NOTE: For safety reasons, keep the knitting needle until a child needs it and then let it be used only under your supervision.)

13. Bright colored yarn or string can be tied to the balloons and affixed to the board with a staple or tape. Or, draw the strings directly onto the backing with a marker.

OCTOPUS BULLETIN BOARD

The octopus bulletin board is a cheerful way to present set theory to students. The collections of student favorites make the adding and subtracting of sets quite appealing.

If you prefer, actual toys, small objects, or magazine pictures can be used to construct the sets on the bulletin board. This not only adds dimension to the bulletin board, but after the board is no longer needed, the small objects can be given as rewards or tokens.

Materials:

blue background paper

yellow construction paper for the octopus (NOTE: Markers can be used directly onto the backing or calico print wrapping paper or material can be used)

bulletin board illustration

black marker for details and lettering

opaque projector

10 sets of 10 small toys or party favors or magazine pictures (NOTE: Most novelty stores carry party favors that are inexpensive and the right size for the bulletin board sets)

scissors

stapler, tape, or glue

Directions:

1. Cover the bulletin board with the blue background paper.

2. Project the bulletin board illustration (see page 321) onto the backed bulletin board.

3. Tack the yellow construction paper or calico print onto the board in front of the projected octopus design and trace the outline.

With each earned token
A balloon can be broken!
An activity inside
Is yours to be tried.

It is Happy CDay

up up and away

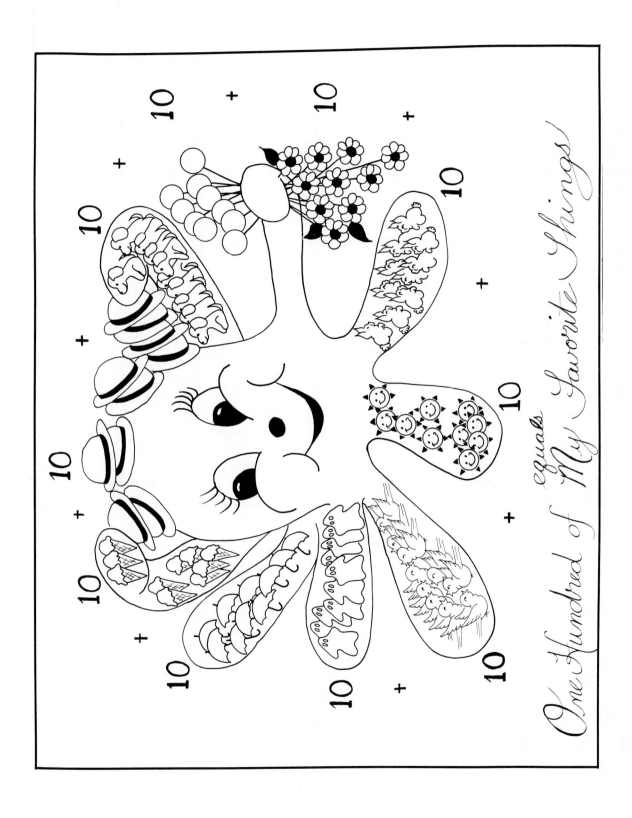

One Hundred of My Favorite Things

4. Cut out the octopus design. Staple, glue, or tape it onto the backed board.

5. Draw in the eye, other details, and title with a black marker.

6. Staple, tape, or glue the objects into each octopus tentacle.

7. Be sure to put in the numbers 10 + 10 + 10, etc.

TEACHING UNIT

MATH SKILLS

Happy C Day

Learning disabled children often have difficulty conceptualizing numbers, especially large numbers. Beverly Radloff, a second grade teacher from Simi-Valley, California, has found an excellent way to help children to develop this skill.

She has developed a series of activities devoted to working with and understanding the number 100. Some of the activities are done in learning centers, some in group activities, and some as part of a bulletin board activity (see the "Happy C Day" bulletin board). The activities are culminated with "C" DAY (C is the Roman numeral for 100) when 100 helium-filled balloons are sent skyward! The date for this can be arbitrarily chosen or done on the *one hundredth day* of school to further reinforce the number concept.

The important thing is the number of party-like activities that lead up to the big day. These activities are all designed to reinforce the conceptualization of the number 100.

The teaching unit can be built around the number 100 if desired. (Smaller or larger numbers can be used depending on the level of the students.)

The "Happy C Day" bulletin board (see page 320) lists dozens of suggestions for fun activities. These can be used as suggested as part of the bulletin board activity or independently as reinforcement at any time. Have fun with this while you are helping students to experience the number 100.

Objectives:

At the conclusion of this unit, students will:

- Be able to discriminate between and name different shapes.
- Be able to know that sets of things can be joined, separated and counted.
- Be able to estimate size and measure items.
- Be able to estimate amounts, count change, and understand money value up to $100.
- Be able to define "census" and have the experience of taking a survey.
- Know how to fill in a graph based on specific information.

Shapes

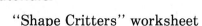

Materials:

"Shape Critters" worksheet

3-dimensional shapes out of wood or plastic (see "Materials of the Month") or flat shapes cut out of coarse sandpaper

shopping bag or canvas tote bag

large shape templates (see "Materials of the Month") or templates made by cutting the shapes out of oaktag

masking tape

Preparation:

1. Copy the "Shape Critters" worksheet on page 324 for each student.

2. Obtain the following shapes: square, rectangle, circle, triangle, octagon, etc. NOTE: The number of shapes presented at one time will depend upon the level of the students to whom you are presenting them. For example, for a primary group, one to three shapes (a square, a circle and a triangle) are enough to concentrate on in one lesson. More shapes can be added as the students are ready.

3. Place the 3-D shapes in a bag.

4. Tape the templates to the chalkboard.

Directions:

1. Take one shape out of the bag (one at a time) and hold it up.

2. Ask for the name of the shape. Pass the shape among the students, encouraging them to feel it carefully as they pass it along.

3. Call upon a student to outline the same shape on a template on the board. Have each student take a turn doing this.

4. If sandpaper shapes are being used, have students feel them as they say the name of the shape.

5. Continue in the same pattern until all the shapes have been presented.

6. Place the shapes back into the bag. Holding the bag above eye-level for each student, let them reach in and feel a shape. (See the illustration.) They must name it before

Shape Critters

Name _____

Make a critter out of the shapes
in each box

△'s ○'s	○'s ▭'s
△'s ○'s ▢'s	▢'s △'s

they pull it out to see. Allow each student several turns until it is evident that he or she can recognize and name the shapes presented.

7. Distribute the animal shapes worksheet (see page 324) for them to draw.

Reinforcement Activity:

Refer to "Learning Centers" and have your students do assignment 1.

Sets

Materials:

several sets of 100 sticks, toothpicks, Popsicle sticks, pencils, noodles, pretzels, etc.
"Set Worksheet"
rubber bands, wire ties or ribbon

Preparation:

1. Copy the "Set Worksheet" (see page 326) for each student.

2. Separate the set items in groups of ten and wrap each one with a rubber band or other tie. NOTE: If possible, have 10 sets for each student.

Directions:

1. Distribute the bundles of sticks, etc.

2. Let each student take apart each set and count the number of items per set.

3. Encourage them to log this on the "Set Worksheet."

4. Do a variety of set combinations together. Write your calculations on the chalkboard. For instance:

"Let's each take 2 bundles or SETS of sticks. Count them. How many are there?"
Write: 20

"Now let's count one more set."
Write: 20
          +10

"Count the total number of 20 + 10. How many do you have?"
Write: 20
          +10
           30

5. Continue using this pattern until a variety of addition and subtraction problems have been tried.

6. Have them use their sticks to complete the "Set Worksheet."

Name _____

SET WORKSHEET

Set ____ has _____ items

Set ____ has _____ items

Set ____ has _____ items

Set ____ has _____ items

Set ____ has _____ items

Set ____ has _____ items

Set ____ has _____ items

Set ____ has _____ items

Set ____ has _____ items

Set ____ has _____ items

TOTAL   (   )

There are _____ sets of _____ .

SET TASKS

1. Add 2 sets to 1 set. How many do you have? _____

2. Add 4 sets and 2 sets. How many do you have? _____

3. Put 5 sets together. Take away 2 sets. How many are left? _____

4. Put 2 sets together. Take away 5 sets. How many are left? _____

5. Add 8 sets and 2 sets. How many do you have? _____

Take away 3 sets from this.   _____

How many are left?   _____

Reinforcement Activity:

Refer to "Learning Centers" and have your students do assignment 2.

Measurement

Materials:

ruler (inch or metric) for each student

yardstick or meter stick for each student

string (enough to go around windows, doors, etc.)

classroom furniture

"Measurement Worksheet"

Preparation:

1. Copy the "Measurement Worksheet" for each student.
2. Arrange the items to be measured so they are unobstructed by other items.

Directions:

1. Hold up a ruler and ask, "How many inches are in a foot? How many of these feet do you think would make 100 inches?" (Take guesses) Line up eight rulers on the floor. (Revise these questions if a metric ruler is used.)

2. "How many of your footprints do you think will make 100 inches or a little over 8 feet?" (Take guesses)

3. Invite the children one by one to walk in heel-to-toe fashion along the eight rulers, counting their steps aloud with the group. Record the numbers on the chalkboard.

4. Ask, "Can you think of other things that might equal 100 inches or a little over 8 feet?" (Take guesses)

5. Distribute the worksheets and explain to the students that they will first be using string to measure around doors, windows, tables, etc. They will then measure the string with their rulers and record the results on the worksheet. (NOTE: A demonstration of how to measure around an object with string and how to cut the string is helpful and saves alot of time.)

6. When all the objects have been measured and the worksheets have been completed, have the students correct their own papers with the group to compare answers.

7. List on the board those objects that measure close to 100.

8. Discuss other things at home students can measure that might be close to 100 inches.

9. Distribute "one free pop" awards (see page 317) when the activity is finished.

Reinforcement Activity:

Refer to "Learning Centers" and have your students do assignment 3.

MEASUREMENT WORKSHEET

Name _____

Directions: Measure the following objects in the room
and write down your results.

Chair _____ inches

Table _____ inches

Desk _____ inches

Doorway _____ inches

Window frame _____ inches

Bookcase _____ inches

Chalkboard _____ inches

The _____ is closest to 100 inches.

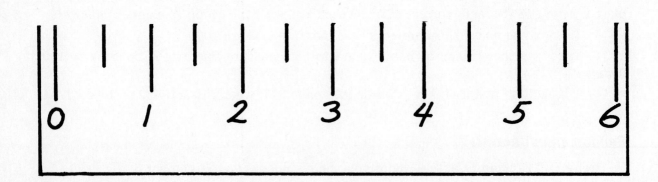

Money Values

Materials:

play money (bills and coins)
purse worksheet
scissors
stapler or glue
shallow box or square lid

Preparation:

1. Copy the purse worksheet (see page 330) for each student.
2. Prepare $10 in toy bills and $1 in toy change for each student.
3. Put the remainder in a shallow box.

Directions:

1. Have the students cut out and either staple or glue the purse together. (Put these aside.)
2. Hold up each bill. Review the number and what it is worth.
3. Distribute $10 worth of bills to each student. Have them place them in their purses.
4. Hold up each coin and discuss the value. Ask someone to come up and count out a dollar in change.
5. Record this on the chalkboard.
6. Ask each student to count out a specific amount from his or her purse. If he or she is correct, the student may keep it. If the student is incorrect, he or she must give the money back to the bank (the teacher). NOTE: Start out small. For example "Please give me 15¢." Expand the numbers according to the ability level of the group.
7. Continue with counting tasks, giving each child several opportunities.
8. At the end of the session, have each student count his or her money and record the amount on the purse. The person who has the most money left is the winner.
9. The winner may get an award or a chance to choose a C Day Activity from the bulletin board.

Reinforcement Activity:

Refer to "Learning Centers" and have your students do assignment 4.

Surveys

Materials:

clipboards for each student
paper
pencils
survey worksheet
dictionary

Identification Card

Name _____

Address _____

Town _____

Telephone _____

Amount _____

My Picture

#1 ←Fold→

#2 Staple

#3 ←Fold→

© 1985 by Natalie Madorsky Elman

Preparation:

1. Copy the "Survey Worksheet" (see page 332) for each student.
2. Write CENSUS on the chalkboard.

Directions:

1. Ask if anyone knows what the United States Census is.

2. Ask someone to look the term up in the dictionary. ("An official enumeration of the population of a country")

3. Explain that a Census is taken in the United States every 10 years. Survey people go from house to house and talk to people to find out information about the occupants. Some people answer questionnaires in the mail. Surveys are designed to find out specific information about people. Questions are asked like: How many people live in a household? What are their ages? etc.

4. Ask, "What kind of other surveys are taken?" (advertising)

5. Ask, "What kind of survey could we take in this school?"

6. List the students' suggestions on the chalkboard. Start with:

> How many boys? How many girls?
>
> What ages are they?
>
> What are their favorite TV programs?
>
> What are their favorite foods?
>
> What are their favorite colors?
>
> What are their favorite subjects?

Assign one task to each group member to use in the survey.

7. Explain that each student in the group will be taking a survey in the classroom.

8. Distribute the survey worksheets and explain how they will be filled in.

9. List these rules on the chalkboard.

Ask permission of the classroom teacher.

Politely and quietly ask each student if you can ask him or her a question for a survey.

Use your clipboard to write on.

Record the answers accurately and move on to the next person.

Thank the classroom teacher when you have finished.

Put the survey worksheet in a safe place until you need it again.

10. Explain to the students that they will learn how to graph their results at another lesson.

Reinforcement Activity:

Refer to "Learning Centers" and have your students do assignment 5.

Investigator _____

SURVEY WORKSHEET

TASK _____

Names

_____

_____

_____

_____

_____

_____

_____

_____

_____

_____

_____

_____

_____

RESULTS

_____

_____

_____

_____

_____

_____

_____

_____

_____

_____

_____

_____

_____

TALLY RESULTS

_____

_____

_____

_____

TOTAL NUMBER _____

Bar Graphing

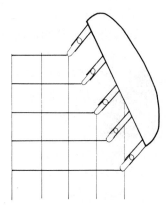

Materials:

survey results from previous lesson
graph paper
pencils
simple graphs to display
5-prong chalkboard line drawer and chalk

Preparation:

1. Locate simple graphs in math books to use as examples.

2. Draw a large graph on the chalkboard by drawing lines vertically all the way down the board and then horizontally over the vertical lines. (See the illustration.)

Directions:

1. Point to the graph on the board. Explain to the students that they will graph their results on graph paper that is a smaller version of the board graph.

2. Take a quiet survey of the group. Ask, "How many of you like pickles?" (Write down the number under Likes Pickle.) "How many don't like pickles?" (Write down the number under Dislikes Pickle.)

3. Demonstrate how this will be reflected on the graph. "First, the graph must have a title. Any suggestions?"
Example: "Pickle Popularity"

4. "Second, we must set up the measurement. Number by 5's down the side."

5. "Let's fill in our results. Show how you locate the number by counting by 5's." (See the illustration.)

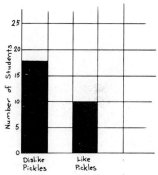

6. "Label each bar."

7. "Looking at the board graph, draw as many conclusions as you can from the results." For example:

> a. Most kids dislike pickles.
>
> b. Lots of kids do like pickles.
>
> c. More kids don't like them than do like them.
>
> d. The ratio is 17–10 against.

8. Explain to the students that they will graph their results from their own homeroom survey on graph paper at the learning center.

NOTE: The completed graphs (once corrected) can be copied for each group member and put in booklet form for a "mini-census report."

Reinforcement Activity:

Refer to "Learning Centers" and have your students do assignment 6.

LEARNING CENTERS

The following learning centers are designed to reinforce the lessons in the teaching unit on math skills. Of course, they may be used independently as well. The suggestions given with the Happy C Day bulletin board on page 320 can also be used as learning center activities. The important thing is that you emphasize all the math activities for this month as being fun as well as being educational.

(1) HIDDEN SHAPES
(PRIMARY-INTERMEDIATE)

Materials:

shapes worksheet
index card
marker
pencils
crayons
3-D shapes (plastic, wood, foam or paper)

Preparation:

1. Copy the shapes worksheet (see page 335) for each student.
2. Write the directions on an index card.
3. Place shapes on a backdrop or in a wicker basket at the learning center.

Directions Card:

SHAPES
1. Look carefully at the picture.
2. Find all the shapes.
3. Circle them with a pencil.
4. Color the picture.

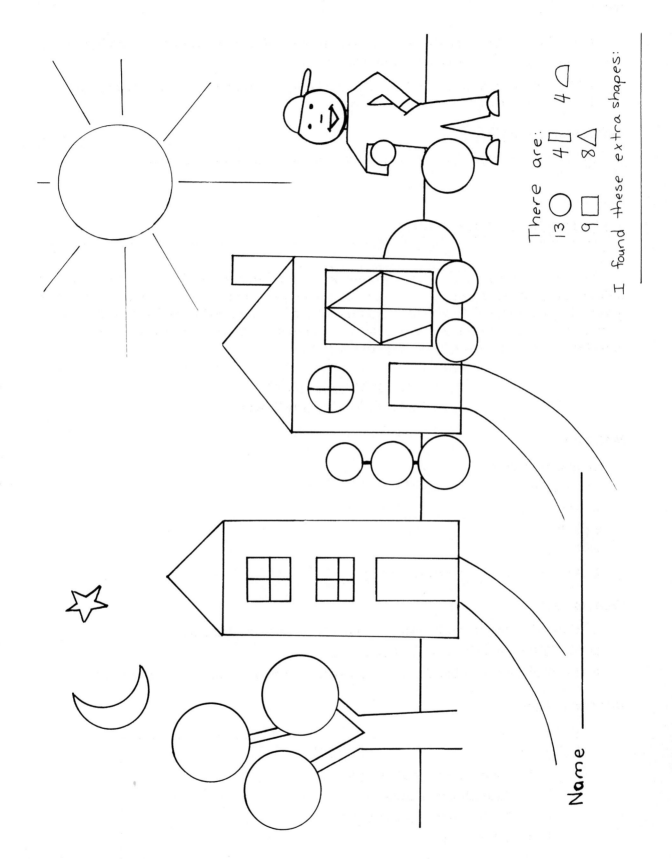

There are:
13 ◯ 4▢ 4◠
9▢ 8△

I found these extra shapes: _____

Name _____

(2) SETS
(INTERMEDIATE)

Materials:

two sets worksheets   pencils
index card   bundles of sticks in sets of 10 tied
marker

Preparation:

1. Copy the two sets worksheets on pages 337 and 338 for each student.
2. Write the directions on an index card.
3. Place the set bundles in a basket or box at the learning center.

Directions Card:

> SETS
> 1. Read the problems carefully.
> 2. Complete both worksheets.
> 3. You may use the set bundles to help you.
> 4. Have your work checked by the teacher.

(3) TREASURES TO MEASURE
(INTERMEDIATE-ADVANCED)

Materials:

tape measure, rulers, paper clips, crayons
ten 8½" × 11" pieces of oaktag
ten Treasure Chest illustrations
ten Treasure Chest worksheets
markers
toy shovel
planting soil or aquarium rocks for treasure base
clear Con-Tact
glue
large fish aquarium or box decorated to look like a buried treasure chest

Preparation:

1. Make ten copies of the task card illustration.
2. Glue each copy onto a piece of oaktag.

Name _____

SETS

Add up the sets. Write the
answer next to them.

$(\bigcirc \bigcirc \bigcirc) + (\text{🦷🦷}) = \square$

$3 + \underline{} = \square$

$(\text{🐦🐦🐦}) + (\text{🐦🐦🐦}) = \square$

$6 + \underline{} = \square$

$(\text{🍦🍦}) + (\text{☀️☀️☀️☀️}) + (\text{☂️☂️}) = \square$

$\underline{} + 4 + \underline{} = \square$

$(\text{🐕🐕🐕🐕🐕}) + (\text{🐕🐕🐕}) = \square$

$\underline{} + \underline{} = \square$

SETS

Name _____

Fill in the missing sets.

Fill in the missing numbers.

$5 + 5 =$ ___

$\}=$ ___

$12 - 6 =$ ___

$\}=$ ___

$7 + 8 =$ ___

$\}=$ ___

$10 - 6 =$ ___

$\}=$ ___

$\{ \ \} + \{ \ \}$

$\{ \ \} - \{ \ \}$

$\{ \ \} + \{ \ \}$

$\{ \ \} - \{ \ \}$

© 1985 by Natalie Madorsky Elman

3. Cover each task card with clear Con-Tact.

4. Write one measuring task on the front of each task card.

- Find something that is 100″ long.
- String together 100 paper clips and measure.
- Place 100 crayons on the floor and measure.
- Measure all the sides of the books in your desk.
- Measure your waist and ankles and wrists. Add them together.
- Measure how tall you are. Find out how tall you were at birth.
- Measure the tallest person in the room. How tall? Who is it?
- Measure the shortest person in the room. How tall? Who?
- Measure the length of both of your feet.
- Measure the distance around the room.

5. Place soil or rocks on the base of the aquarium. Place each treasure with the measuring task into the surface of the dirt or rocks. NOTE: If a box is used, it can be decorated to look like a treasure chest. Commercial corrugated boxes are available which look like chests. Magazine pictures of jewelry, coins, and other valuables can be cut out and glued to the sides of the aquarium or chest. Costume jewelry, plastic dinnerware, seashells, and other treasures can be used in place of or in addition to the oaktag task cards.

6. Copy the "Measure the Treasure" worksheet for each student.

7. Prepare the directions card.

Directions Card:

DIG FOR THE TREASURE

1. Place the shovel in the treasure chest. Dig out a treasure task card.

2. Read the task on the card.

3. Do the task.

4. Write your answer on the worksheet.

5. Have your work checked by the teacher.

---

(4) COUNT YOUR CHANGE, PLEASE
(INTERMEDIATE-ADVANCED)

Materials:

play money	index card
menu	1 sheet large construction paper
"Count Your Change" worksheet	marker

Your task is: _____

_____

_____

_____

_____

_____

_____

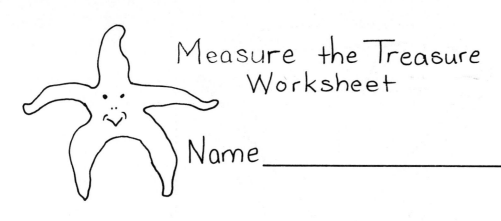

Measure the Treasure
Worksheet

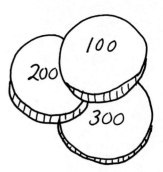

Name_____

Task_____

_____

_____

My Answer_____

_____

_____

_____

Preparation:

1. Copy the menu found on page 343.
2. Fold the construction paper in half and make a cover for the menu.
3. Write MENU on the cover with a marker.
4. Copy the worksheet (see page 344) for each student.
5. Write the directions on an index card.

Directions Card:

COUNT YOUR CHANGE CAFÉ

1. Look over the menu.
2. Use your worksheet and add up your meal. Figure out the change.
3. You may use the play money to help you.
4. Have your work checked by the teacher.

---

(5) JELLY BEAN SURVEY
(PRIMARY-ADVANCED)

Materials:

large glass jar (mason jar, etc.)   clipboard
jelly beans (enough to fill jar)   oaktag
worksheet   marker

Preparation:

1. Make a sign out of oaktag that says: GUESS HOW MANY?
2. Place the jelly beans in the jar, cover, and seal. (Be sure you have counted the jelly beans before sealing the jar!)
3. Place the jelly bean jar in a prominent place with the sign.
4. Write the directions on an index card.

Directions Card:

JELLY BEAN SURVEY

1. Take the survey worksheet and ask five students for their guesses.
2. Remember the rules of taking a survey.
3. Place answers on the worksheet.
4. Have your work checked by the teacher.

Count Your Change Café

Menu

Drinks

Cola	.50
Coffee	.50
Milk Shake	1.00
Juice	.80

Sandwiches

Ham	2.00
Egg Salad	1.75
Peanut Butter	1.50
Hot Dog	1.00
Hamburger	2.25
Tuna Salad	2.00

Salads

Tossed Salad	.50
Spinach Salad	.75
Cole Slaw	.50

Desserts

Pie	1.50
Cake	2.00
Rice Pudding	1.00

25¢ 25¢ Twenty Five cents Twenty Five cents

25¢ 25¢ Twenty Five cents Twenty Five cents

COUNT YOUR CHANGE WORKSHEET

Name _____

My order is: Cost

_____   _____

_____   _____

_____   _____

_____   _____

                                    TOTAL   _____

I paid with the following money: This should be my change:

_____ $1   _____

_____ $5

_____ $10

_____ $20

_____ 25¢

_____ 50¢

_____ 5¢

_____ 10¢

_____ 1¢

Name _____

JELLY BEAN SURVEY

Directions: Ask 5 people to guess the number
of jelly beans in the jar.

Name   Guess

_____   _____

_____   _____

_____   _____

_____   _____

_____   _____

Count the jelly beans. Tell the person

who guessed the closest number that they

are the winner.

(6) GRAPHING
(ADVANCED)

Materials:

worksheet
index card
marker

Preparation:

1. Copy the worksheet on page 347 for each student.
2. Write the directions on an index card.

Directions Card:

```
                        GRAPHING
1. Using the information on the worksheet, complete the
graph.
2. Have your work checked by the teacher.
```

MATERIALS OF THE MONTH

For those times when it becomes necessary to purchase items in local retail stores, don't forget to ask for a discount. Most merchants (stationery stores, department stores, toy stores, supermarkets, art supply stores, etc.) are very willing to give a percentage off if they know the merchandise is for the public school.

It is a good idea if you are ordering something special made (like a cake) to tell the business in advance that the purchase is for the school and ask about a discount when you place the order. You usually get the discount anyway, but it really is more considerate to ask first.

FREE FOR THE ASKING

Let's Talk About Money

This booklet explains a step-by-step approach to money management. It has handy worksheets geared more for the advanced student. It is an excellent resource for a money learning center activity. Write to:

Institute of Life Insurance
Dept W 277 Park Avenue
New York, NY 10017

Computer Town News Bulletin

This is a 12-page periodical that will tell you all you need to know about Computer Town. It gives news about various Computer Town activities all over the country. Com-

Name _____

GRAPH

Directions: Read the following information and
fill in the graph below.

Mrs. Fisher's class has 30 pupils.

Ms. Gordon's class has 35 pupils.

Mr. Mundy's class has 22 pupils.

Mrs. Benary's class has 25 pupils.

Mr. Walsh's class has 18 pupils.

Ms. Covey's class has 29 pupils.

40						
35						
30						
25						
20						
15						
10						
5						
1						

Number of Pupils

Classes _____   _____   _____   _____   _____   _____

1. Who has the largest class? _____

2. Who has the smallest class? _____

3. What is the total number of pupils in the school? _____

puter Town is a place where people of all ages have access to computers, with the goal of letting all who are interested learn more about them. If one exists near your area, it could make an excellent field trip. To get a free bulletin and learn the details, send a self-addressed, stamped envelope to:

> Computer-Town News Bulletin Sample
> Fritzi Loreau Memberships
> c/o Computer-Town
> P.O. Box E
> Menlo Park, CA 94025

Metric Practice Guide and Style Manual

This manual offers guidelines to instruct teachers and students in the correct usage of the SI Metric system. One copy is available free to professional staff members. Making your request on school stationery, write to:

> Polymetric Services, Inc.
> AMJ Publishing Co.
> P.O. Box 847
> Tarzana, CA 91356

Million Dollar Dream

This is a story that shows how everyone having a million dollars could be an economic nightmare! It is excellent to teach economy and money concepts. Single copies are available free to schools and libraries by writing to Foundation of Economic Education Inc.

Keeping Our Money Healthy

This free 16-page illustrated booklet discusses the role of the Federal Reserve System. Classroom quantities are available. Write to:

> Foundation of Economic Education Inc.
> 30 South Broadway
> New York, NY 10533

Key to Gold Vault

This free booklet unlocks some of the mysteries of gold. It explains the everyday operations of the New York Federal's gold vault. Classroom quantities are available. Write to:

> Federal Reserve Bank of New York
> Public Information Department
> 33 Liberty Street
> New York, NY 10045

GOOD BUYS

The following materials are suggested as good buys and can be used to supplement the math activities in the April section.

Math on the Job

Combining career awareness with basic math skills, these three books and spirit master are for skill levels grades 4–6. Fractions, perimeter, area, graphs, grids, decimals, and money are discussed. The cost is under $10 per book of 24 lessons. Contact:

Opportunities for Learning
8950 Lurline
Chatsworth, CA 91311

Preparing Young Children for Math: A Book of Games

Although this book is designed for parents who want to help their children, it gives excellent ideas for small group math activities. It utilizes everyday materials (like egg cartons) in very clever and fun-like ways. The book sells for under $15 and is an excellent math activity resource. Write to:

Schocken Books
200 Madison Avenue
New York, NY 10016

Abacus

This comes in two sizes—large and small. They both have 100 beads in color sets of 10. The small one fits in a student's desk. The large demonstration size sells for under $30, while the student size is under $12. They are available from DLM.

Logiblock Attribute Pieces

The plastic 3-D pieces contain circle, square, rectangle and triangle shapes. The shapes come in 3 sizes and colors. The set sells for under $30 and is available from DLM.

Coins and Bills

Excellent cardboard and paper coin and bill facsimiles to supplement the lessons on money transactions, the set is large enough for group activity. Selling for under $10, the set is available from DLM.

Money Wheel

This self-correcting money wheel provides practice in matching picture, numeral and word representations of money amounts from one cent to five dollars. It sells for under $10 and is available from DLM.

Shopping Lists Games I and II

Each game contains four 5″ × 7″ shopping lists, eight smaller lists, 90 small pictures of merchandise, and an assortment of coins and bills. Each game sells for under $15 and is available from DLM.

Clear Stencils

These large plastic stencils include the diamond, rectangle, square, circle and triangle. They measure 8½" × 8½" and can be taped onto the chalkboard. The set sells for under $15. Write to:

> Developmental Learning Materials
> P.O. Box 4000
> One DLM Park
> Allen, TX 75002

PhotoMath

This is a survival math program that focuses on student proficiency in comprehension of word problems. There are approximately 20 units, each containing four 10" × 14" color-coded flash cards. Functional vocabulary is used. Selling for under $75, PhotoMath is excellent for teaching survival skills to older students. Contact:

> Educational Activities Inc.
> P.O. Box 392
> Freeport, NY 11520

Menu Math for Beginners

For early grades, these colorful tear-out menus can become part of many problem-solving activities. The kit sells for under $10. Write to:

> Remedia Publications
> P.O. Box 1174
> Scottsdale, AZ 85252

I Can Solve Story Problems

This is a series of reproducible math books. Each offers controlled reading and sequenced skill development in real-life problem solving. A 40-page book is available for addition, subtraction, multiplication, division, and mixed operations. For grades 3–7, each book sells for under $10. Write to:

> Amidon Publications
> 1966 Benson Avenue
> St. Paul, MN 55116

All Star Math

These word problems for teenagers are organized in an excellent game format to increase the interest of sports-minded students. Available in levels 4.1–6.2, each kit sells for under $10. Write to:

> Thurman Publishing Co.
> 1428 Harvard Avenue
> Room 112
> Seattle, WA 98122

PROFESSIONAL RESPONSIBILITIES

PUBLICITY FOR YOUR PROGRAM

The existence of special education programs in the public schools is a well-known fact to most taxpayers. In many communities, the knowledge of the tax costs of special programming is well known, but the good that the programming accomplishes is often a well-kept secret. Since most districts do not employ a public relations person, it is the local school administrator or the teachers who must pursue positive publicity for the schools. Special education programs are good places to draw positive attention when something special is going on.

Educators have historically not been great publicity people. The reasons for this are sound ones. We have been busy educating children. However, with feelings about public education at an all time low, we can no longer afford to ignore public relations. Special education legislation of all types has a much better chance of being passed if the public looks favorably upon what is being done. We must educate the public at every opportunity.

Special events like a parents' tea, a Young Author's Book Fair, Happy C Day (especially if you send 100 balloons soaring into the sky), a presentation by a community resource person, etc., are excellent reasons to call the local paper and request coverage. If it is a small local paper, it may request that you take the picture and send it in with the article already written. This is certainly worth doing. Everytime a picture or an article appears in the paper about an exciting happening in the local schools, it is an excellent reminder of what is being done there.

Every opportunity to gain positive publicity should be used. Local radio stations are usually willing to publicize a coming event or even devote a program to something out of the ordinary going on in the community. Don't be afraid to get in touch with the local TV stations as well. They are constantly in pursuit of news and may welcome the opportunity to feature a special event going on in the public schools. A positive attitude and a little nerve can go a long way in gaining positive publicity for your special program.

Call the local station and ask to talk to the producer of the radio or TV show in which you are interested. Explain who you are and why you are calling. Write out the details (like the date, time, details of the event, what makes it special) in advance of the call. The producer will tell you what to do next. If there is no interest, he or she will tell you that, too. If so, all you have lost are a few minutes of your time. Call again the next time; you never can tell what might strike the producer's fancy. Aside from the great publicity a TV or radio spot gives, it is wonderful experience for the special students to get.

Don't forget the PTA or PTO newsletter. The parents' organization welcomes school news and will be happy to print your article about a special event. This informs the parents who don't have children attending special programs about what is going on.

Publicity for special education programs does take extra time and effort on your and/or the administrator's part. The outcome, however, is essential to promoting future funding and support of special programming.

PROFESSIONAL RESOURCE BOOKS

Dumas, Enoch. *Math Activities for Child Involvement.* (Boston: Allyn and Bacon, 1971)

Henderson, George. *Let's Play Games in Metrics.* (Skokie, IL: National Textbook Co., 1974)

Horwitz, Abraham, Arthur Goddard, and David Epstein. *Number Games to Improve Your Child's Arithmetic.* (New York: Funk and Wagnalls, 1975)

Kennedy, Leonard, and Ruth Michon. *Games for Individualized Math Learning.* (Columbus, OH: Charles E. Merrill Publishing Co., 1973)

Peterson, John, and Joseph Hashisaki. *Theory of Arithmetic.* (New York: John Wiley and Sons, Inc., 1967)

Platts, Mary E. *Plus: A Handbook for Teachers of Elementary Arithmetic.* (Stevensville, MI: Educational Service, Inc., 1976)

Scydam, Marilyn, and Donald Dessart. *Classroom Ideas from Research on Computational Skills.* (National Council of Teachers of Mathematics, 1976)

Westcott, Alvin, and James Smith. *Creative Teaching of Math in the Elementary School.* (Boston: Allyn and Bacon, 1967)

NOTE: Further information on several of the above books can be found in *The Elementary School Library Collection*, published annually by The Bro-Dart Foundation.

MODES FOR MAINSTREAMING

STAFF PREPARATION FOR I.E.P.'S

Procedures for setting up Individual Educational Plans (I.E.P.) for special education students vary from state to state and district to district. One thing is the same everywhere, however; I.E.P.'s must be developed annually for each classified student. This is generally done with school professionals, parents and sometimes the students planning together at a special meeting.

When regular classroom teachers are included in this process (and they should be for all mainstreamed students), they must be prepared in advance. Expecting a teacher (or anyone else) to participate productively in a meeting without preparation can cause the teacher much unnecessary anxiety and sometimes anger toward the program. This can easily be avoided.

A letter sent out well in advance of the meeting giving the name of the student, the date and time of the meeting and general guidelines is most helpful. A sample letter is shown on page 353.

In addition to an information letter, a meeting specifically to discuss the teacher's role at the I.E.P. meeting is very beneficial. Sometimes, time does not permit this. For those teachers who request it, however, a special time to answer questions should be found.

A knowledgeable and prepared staff makes the development of the student's I.E.P. more productive and presents a more professional and competent educational picture to the parents.

Dear Mrs. Kramer,

On May 6 from 9:00 a.m. until 10:00 a.m., an I.E.P. meeting for Roberta Smith will be held. A substitute will be provided for your class at this time so you will be able to attend.

The following items will be covered:

1. Current test scores compared to last year.

	19XX	19XX
Stanford Diagnostic		
reading comprehension	2.0	2.8
phonetic analysis	1.9	2.2
Batell Reading Inventory	3.2	4.0
Kottmeyer Spelling Inventory	2.0	3.0

2. Goals and objectives for next year:

Probably will concentrate on reading comprehension and phonetic analysis.

3. Recommendations for next year's program:

I think regular class placement with resource room back up, don't you?

Any additional input you may have will be most helpful. The student's parents have been invited, also.

If you have any questions, please contact me.

Sincerely,

Sue McDonald
Resource Room Teacher

TIP OF THE MONTH

INDEX CARDS

Even a person with excellent recall forgets some details from time to time. For those of us who don't have great memory skills, other devices must be found to help us record needed facts. With a busy program to contend with, interruptions, administrative duties, etc., it is imperative that a system be found to record those little things about a student which could be helpful to future planning and evaluating of goals and objectives.

Storing large index cards (usually 5″ × 7″) in an alphabetical file box for each student in the room is a quick and handy way to record incidences or observations. These cards can be invaluable aids at I.E.P. meeting times, parent conferences, student conferences, or classroom teacher conferences.

Keeping the file box very close at hand to be used when an incident takes place or a successful teaching approach is discovered makes the index cards very useful. Many times something happens that a teacher plans on remembering about a child but can't remember later. Having a method to immediately record those things makes reporting time that much more productive.

Keep track of things like:

"Has difficulty with near point copying, but far point seems fine."

"Wrote a story about a boy who no one likes. Could it be him?"

"Doesn't know all of her cursive letters! Confuses b and f. Work on this."

Another benefit is to be able to look over the remarks made at the beginning of the year and note whether progress has been made.

A FINAL WORD

TEST RESULTS

Once the end-of-the-year posttests are given and the scores are recorded, an evaluation of the student's progress is in order. Sometimes the test results really buoy a teacher's spirits. All the hard work and individual planning really seem worth the effort. It worked— the student made good progress—hurray!

Sometimes, however, a teacher puts in tremendous effort and planning and the results, if visible at all, are at least not visible through test scores. It is easy at these times to feel a great sense of frustration. We have all been trained in our society to believe that if one works hard—one succeeds! This, of course, is not always the case.

Learning disabled students by definition are inconsistent in their academic performance. Furthermore, many students, learning disabled or not, are just poor test takers. To base a total evaluation of a learning disabled student's progress or a teacher's effectiveness on test scores alone is not the most accurate or productive approach.

Certainly, test scores should be considered along with other criteria. Does the student exhibit better skills in the classroom? Does the student exhibit better skills in group work in the resource room? Has he or she progressed in the reading group or math group? What does the classroom teacher see? How does the student evaluate his or her progress? All of these things must be taken into consideration.

If, after evaluating many different criteria, it seems apparent that the student is not progressing at a satisfactory rate for his or her ability, then new approaches must be considered. If all approaches have been exhausted, perhaps more time is needed. The important thing is not to give up. This is certainly a goal for which to strive. Teaching students with special needs doesn't always offer immediate rewards for the teacher, but does offer a tremendous opportunity to affect the total direction of a student's life over time.

Many students have appeared not able to learn at a certain point in their education only to rally at a later time when they are seemingly more ready. Strong evidence for this can be seen in the lives of the Spotlight personalities each month.

APRIL REFERENCES

Bartlett, John. *Bartlett's Familiar Quotations.* (Boston: Little Brown and Co., 1955)

Britannica Junior Encyclopedia (Book D–E). (Chicago: Encyclopedia Britannica Inc., 1971)

The Elementary School Library Collection: A Guide to Books and Other Media. (Newark, NJ: Bro-Dart Foundation, 1977)

Goertzel, Victor and Mildred. *Cradles of Eminence.* (Boston: Little Brown and Co., 1955)

Hedges, William. "The Labeling Game." *Instructor*, February 1980, 176.

Thompson, Lloyd J. "Language Disabilities in Men of Eminence," *Journal of Learning Disabilities*, January 1971

World Book Encyclopedia (Book E). (Chicago: World Book Inc., 1980)

May

1 Mary "Mother Jones" Harris (1830) Mother Jones banged pots and pans/Walking streets with kids so small./She showed these kids to city folk/To save them, one and all./She told those folks of factories/Where kids so young were killed./She showed how some lost arms or legs/At work where cloth is milled. Read "Mom's" story. Write your own verse 2!

2 Theodore Hertzl (1860) and Bing Crosby (1904) Two dreams came true. Crosby sang a song of a "Christmas, just like the one (he) used to know" in his homeland, America. Hertzl's dream told that Jews who lost their homes in the war might come to a new "homeland" called Israel. A blue-and-white flag would fly on May 10, 1948. Are the dreams different?

3 Jacob Riis (1849) and Golda Meir (1898) A housewife in Wisconsin, a poultry farmer on a kibbutz in Israel, a member of the Parliament and finally, Golda was Israel's Prime Minister! Like her, Jacob Riis cared most about jobs and homes for families. And he cared about fun! He opened parks so kids on crowded New York streets could safely play!

4 Frederic Church (1826) What painting was worth the wait? 100,000 people waited patiently to see Church's *Niagara Falls*! They saw each drop of mist dancing in the sunlight. It was easy to hear the thunder of falling water. City people in crowded tenements felt the peace of the wilderness they might never see for themselves!

5 Elizabeth "Nellie Bly" Cochran (1867) Newspaper reporters need to know the news; Nellie Bly found out the hard way. She threw herself into a river to write about the rescue. She went to jail to tell of its tortures. To beat the 80-day record by Verne's Phineas Fogg, Bly was the first woman to go alone around the world. Leaving on 10/14/1889, she returned 1/25/1890. Who finished first?

6 Sigmund Freud (1856) What do dreams mean? Freud had good ideas about dreams. A PSYCHIATRIST, Freud talked to troubled children about their dreams and memories of the past. Because of his special training, he learned what the trouble was and what caused it. "Mental Health Month" honors Freud, the founder of DREAM ANALYSIS.

7 Edwin Land (1909) 1826 — A photograph of Joseph Niepce's French farmhouse took only 8 hours to develop! 1947 — An idea of how a photo may be seen in about 8 minutes began to develop in Land's mind! Does someone have an instant camera? You might take a picture of your class and see yourself develop a beautiful image!

8 Henry William Vanderbilt (1821) If you land on the B&O, buy it! Charles Darwin's game made owning a railroad MONOPOLY easy. But Henry Vanderbilt knew it took work and real $ to buy real railroads. Read the Vanderbilt family story to track these railroad men of America as they rode their way from "rags to riches" on wheels of fortune.

9 Howard Carter (1874) Carter had 2 months to find the tomb. For 10 years he dug in the blazing sun and choking sand storms to find the burial home of Tutankhamun, the king of Egypt 3,200 years before. The tomb had to be found before December, or he would never get another chance to try. November 4, stairs found. November 26 . . . ?

10 Sir Thomas Lipton (1850) Oh, dear me, all the cats had come to tea! Polly, put the kettle on — camomille for Peter! And that fellow with the large hat — looks quite mad. It IS tea time! Oh, may I bring a friend? [Can you find those 5 storybook tea parties? I know Mr. Lipton would be delighted to bring the tea!]

11 Irving Berlin (1888) He was first a singing waiter. Then America couldn't wait to sing his songs. Easter Parade and There's No Business Like Show Business and White Christmas and Alexander's Ragtime Band and . . . a song you may sing when you stand to pledge allegiance to our flag. Together, begin: "God bless . . ."

12 Lawrence "Yogi" Berra (1925) "Lawdi" became "Yogi" when his friend said that the short, stocky baseball player sat like a Yogi in meditation. But Yogi didn't sit still for long! In 1947, Yogi cracked the first pinch-hit homer in World Series history! After 3 MVP awards and 14 World Series games, Yogi managed to be a manager for what team?

13 Joe Louis (1914) and Stevie Wonder (1950) How are Joe and Stevie alike? Two wonderful people from Detroit, they both played music! Louis left violin lessons to become boxing's heavyweight champion at 23! Stevie was 12 when Motown Records named *Fingertips* a smash record! Louis knocked out his opponents. Stevie's knockout songs are wonders!

14 Gabriel Fahrenheit (1686) Can you tell whether the weather is warming up? Take its temperature! In 1714, Fahrenheit invented a thermometer. To measure warmth, mercury rose and fell inside a glass tube as temperature changed around it. Warm? Mercury went to HIGHER °. Cooler? Mercury went to LOWER °. Keep a weather watch, by °s!

15 Ilya Ilich Metchnikoff (1845) The aging Pasteur welcomed young Metchnikoff to his laboratory. Like Pasteur, Metchnikoff had original ideas. "I will prove that white blood cells EAT enemy germs," he roared. After injecting guinea pigs with bacteria, he proudly showed the white cells filled with enemy germs. Metchnikoff wasn't lyin'!

16 William Seward (1801) Seward lay moaning, his face badly slashed. Lincoln's killer wished him dead. But Seward lived. Secretary of State in 1867, he arranged the purchase of Alaska. The price? $17,000,000. Americans gave Seward a cold shoulder, saying frozen wasteland was wasteful of money. Was 2¢ an acre too much to pay?

Good health and good sense are two of life's blessings.

Pubilius Syrus

****

17   Edward Jenner (1749)   All the world feared that disease./It horrified every nation./Till Jenner stopped its deadly spread/With a simple vaccination./Smallpox disappeared that day./Jenner's name was hailed world 'round./Though no one at first believed that/A cure, at last, was found.

18   Thomas Midgley (1889)   Did you hear a knock? Tom did and he found a way to stop fuel from knocking, too! And he had another cool idea. He found FREON, a gas not poisonous or explosive, to keep the new home "FRIDGES" cold! Midgley inhaled FREON and exhaled it at a candle. Got a knock-knock joke for Midgley's knockout ideas?

19   Carl Akeley (1864)   For a fitting compliment to Carl and Mary Akeley, photograph a favorite animal. While drums rumbled in the distance, they filmed animals which would soon become extinct. They faced the dangers of African jungles to care for endangered animals in sanctuaries far from poachers who carelessly killed.

20   Emile Berliner (1851)   Caruso, McCartney, Crosby, Cole, etc., can appreciate the "platter" phonograph records invented by Emile Berliner. The idea was "tuned off" until the turning point came in the 1920s when Edison's phonograph turned millions of records and millions of ears to the sounds of music!

21   Mary Anning (1799) and Frances Densmore (1867)   "The beauty of the past must never be forgotten!" English Mary Anning chiseled the ancient Plesiosaur skeletons from the rocks, far above the angry ocean. Frances Densmore carried heavy equipment to distant Indian villages to record old tribal melodies. Their lives gave us eyes and ears to the beauties of the past.

22   Sir Arthur Conan Doyle (1859)   No details were missed by keen-eyed Holmes. He and Watson solved every case correctly. But their author, eye doctor Conan Doyle, didn't see HIS errors! Real people make mistakes while the super-people of stories are perfect! Be keen-eyed. Watch every detail when you write a scary tale today!

23   Margaret Fuller (1810)   Don't judge a book by its cover! Well, how then? By reading the newspaper, of course. Margaret Fuller wrote the first book "reports" for *The New York Times*. Don't let your class judge books by their covers! Publish a "You will (not) like this book because . . ." book report! Let your class "read all about it!"

24   William Gilbert (1540 or -44)   A POLE(ISH) LIMERICK . . . William Gilbert's compass, everywhere he'd go/Pointed N or S, that never changed. "I know,"/Said he, "the earth that's twirling 'round/Is a magnet, orbit bound./I'll call POLES, N tip above, S tip below."/. . . Those poles were cold, subzero caps of snow,/Nobody's been there, put up flags or said "hello,"/Said Perry, I'll be north POLE bound,/Amundsen that south POLE found,/Now flags flew, N tip above, S tip below.

25   Igor Sikorsky (1889)   He dreamed of super airlines but no one yet had flown! Encouraged by a Wright Brothers' flight, he tried, with homemade tools and makeshift parts, to build his own. Though his experiment crashed, his spirits climbed. The multi-engine bombers and helicopters he had built were young dreams come true.

26   John Wayne (1907) and James Arness (1923)   John Wayne turned down the role but James Arness took it! Arness (Matt Dillon) revived booming Dodge City, Kansas, a cattle town where thirsty cowboys rustled to the roaring Long Branch Saloon. Wayne galloped through 10 years of western films to round up an Oscar for *True Grit* as the gentlest cowboy of all!

27   Rachel Carson (1907)   The DDT killed the insects so the plants could grow healthy and tall. But the water which fed the plants carried DDT to rivers and the fish, and the birds which ate them, died. Carson warned that our beautiful world would soon be unbeautiful. Laws were passed to stop the use of DDT as she began the battle for beauty!

28   Louis Agassiz (1807)   Would you list animals by their color or plants by where they live? Two great NATURALISTS listed living things by FAMILIES. Carl Linnaeus classified animals and Asa Gray listed plants. Louis Agassiz collected SPECIMENS of these FAMILIES for his museum so students and their families could study them for real!

29   Bob Hope (1903) and John F. Kennedy (1917)   His nickname was Hopeless, but Bob gave hope to all! Always on the road to entertain U.S. troops, GIs said THANKS FOR THE MEMORIES of back home. We say thanks, too, for the memory of sailor Jack Kennedy who walked up the road to the White House, hoping to make everyone's hope for peace come true.

30   Mel Blanc (1908) and Aleksei Leonov (1934)   What's up, Doc? Aleksei Leonov, that for sure! The first man to leave his spaceship (1965) was the Soviet astronaut of the VOSHOD spaceflight! But that's not all folks! Mel Blanc, as Bugs Bunny or Porky Pig or Daffy Duck, could send even Leonov's spirits reeling in cartoon after cartoon after cartoon . . .

31   Ronald Laird (1938)   Why walk? It's good for you, for one thing. The more you walk, the less beats your heart beats to keep you walking! And the easier it is to beat other walkers! This 4-time Olympian won more titles (69) than any other walker! A walking wonder, Laird would wish you would walk to wish him birthday wishes!

These birthographies were prepared by Davida Shipkowitz of Northridge, California.

SPOTLIGHT ON

BRUCE JENNER (1949–   )

Bruce Jenner won the Olympic Gold Medal in July 1976. He scored a record 8,618 points in the decathlon, the ten running, throwing and jumping events that constitute the most grueling and comprehensive test of strength, skill, and endurance that exists in athletic competition.

Shortly after his Olympic victories, Jenner signed a contract with a major broadcasting company to be a commentator. He also does commercials and lectures regularly on college campuses and at business conventions. He aspires to become a movie actor and has written a book called *Decathlon Challenge*.

Born in Mount Kisco, New York, Jenner was raised in comfortable middle class surroundings. In high school, he was a letterman in football, basketball and track. He learned to water-ski at his lakefront home and won the East Coast overall water-skiing championship three times.

The young man who always emerged triumphant in sporting events was not so successful academically. According to Bruce himself on a national TV program (1971), he was a slow reader and felt "dumb." He was held back in the second grade to help correct his reading problems, but it didn't help. He struggled through academics until high school when he was told he had "dyslexia." According to Jenner,

"They just said, 'you're dyslexic.' See you later. That was about it."

When asked if his reading problem affected his self-confidence as an adult, Bruce Jenner replied,

"Because of the reading and of getting started (slow) in school, and always being in the slower reading classes . . . (I was) in the slower classes. (I didn't have the) confidence that you (need to) go into a situation. I would just stay quiet and wouldn't say much at all, and let everybody else sort of make decisions for me."

In order to compensate for poor reading ability, Bruce Jenner reported that he memorized what he needed to know. Whether it was giving a sportscast on a TV show or learning a movie script, he never used cue cards because they were difficult to read.

Jenner does attribute his strong motivation to achieving in sports as a compensation for failure in school.

"I think every young person needs a pat on the back. They need to hear by their peers that you did a good job. Well, I'd never get that in school. I was always hiding that."

In junior high school, Jenner discovered that he could do well in and receive recognition in sports. Because of that positive reinforcement, Bruce continued to excel in sports. In his early twenties after a history of sports excellence, Bruce Jenner decided that he wanted to run the decathlon. The rest is history.

Bruce Jenner's biography shows a bright, strong-willed, and motivated youngster who failed in school because of an inability to read. Needing recognition for himself as a worthy person, Bruce Jenner found that he had abilities in sports. He cultivated that ability with an almost neurotic need to win and became a champion. As Bruce Jenner said on national TV:

"If I would have gone through school and just breezed right through and done a good job, and had no problem, I don't think that I would have been as motivated in sports. I think as time went on and I got more heavily into it, . . . I really grasped it. That was one thing I could do and I could do it well, and it was all up to me."

SPOTLIGHT BULLETIN BOARD

The paper used for the personality and figures each month can be removed and replaced while the basic bulletin board remains. NOTE: If large sheets of construction paper are used for bulletin boards, they can be removed and stored for future use. Make a large envelope out of two large sheets of oaktag and staple them together. Slip in the construction paper and label. These can be stored flat against a closet wall or on a closet floor.

Materials:

white background paper

red or orange marker for figures and cast light

copy of the bulletin board illustration

black marker for outline of can lights

overhead projector or opaque projector (NOTE: If an opaque projector is used the transparency can be replaced by a paper copy of the bulletin board)

acetate transparency

transparency marker

Preparation:

1. Cover the bulletin board with the white background paper.

2. Trace the "Spotlight" bulletin board (see page 360) onto clear acetate using a transparency marker.

3. Project the transparency onto the backed bulletin board.

4. Trace the outlines and color in with markers.

BULLETIN BOARD IDEAS

WHEN BUTTERFLIES ARE READY, THEY FLY!

The message of this bulletin board deals with the development of spring as well as the development of learning. Butterflies emerge in the spring when they are able to sprout their wings and fly. Children, too, must be at the point of readiness to be able to "sprout their wings and fly." Although this concept is reinforced in many ways throughout the year, perhaps the nearing end of the school year is an appropriate time to be reminded again.

Spotlight on......

USA

Bruce Jenner

© 1985 by Natalie Madorsky Elman

Materials:

light blue shiny background paper

yellow construction paper for butterfly

dark blue felt-tip marker for lettering

water-soluble printer's ink (any bright color)

sponges, apples, or potatoes to make print of the butterfly shadows

stapler	copy of the bulletin board
scissors	pencil
scrap paper	shallow dish
opaque projector	

Directions:

1. Cover the bulletin board with the shiny light blue background paper.

2. Project the bulletin board picture (see page 362) onto the backed bulletin board.

3. Place the yellow paper for the butterfly in front of the projected design. Draw the design lightly in pencil.

4. Cut out the butterfly design. Affix the butterfly to the board with staples.

5. Write in the title with a dark blue felt-tip marker.

6. Have the students make the butterfly shadows by dipping the sponge, apple or potato cutout. Follow these directions:

    a. Cut out the sponge, potato or apple in the shape of a butterfly. (See the bulletin board.)

    b. Place the printer's ink in a shallow dish about ¼ inch deep.

    c. Press the cutout stencil into the ink, blot on scrap paper, and print onto the bulletin board.

HOW DO CHILDREN GROW?

The combination of flowers and good health are highlighted in the bulletin board. The bright flowers and sunshine certainly reflect the time of the year, while the concepts of safety and good health are reinforced by the written verse on the board. This is an excellent introduction to the health and safety unit presented later in "Teaching Units."

Materials:

blue gingham print wrapping paper or fabric for background (NOTE: If fabric backing is used, print the lettering on strips of white paper and staple onto the board.)

white construction paper for the watering can and picket fence

green construction paper for the leaves

bright pink construction paper for the flower petals

bright yellow construction paper for the flower centers

dark blue marker for face outlines and lettering

opaque projector	stapler
scissors	pencil

When Butterflies are Ready...... ...they fly!

Directions:

1. Cover the bulletin board with the gingham wrapping paper or fabric. Attach with staples.

2. Project the bulletin board illustration (see page 363) onto the board with the opaque projector.

3. Place the appropriate color construction paper in front of each design and copy with a pencil.

4. Remove the designs and cut out with scissors.

5. Draw in lettering, faces, etc., with a felt-tip marker.

6. Affix the designs to the board with staples.

7. Write in the headings and the verse with felt-tip marker directly onto the board. (See the note above if fabric is used.)

TEACHING UNIT

HEALTH AND SAFETY

When students come to your special program, they are usually missing an academic subject in the classroom. Math, reading, and writing are basic to a student's ability to progress in school. Consequently, subjects like science, social studies, and health are often the ones chosen to be "missed" if the student is able to participate in the other subjects in the classroom. It is generally felt that once a child has the basic skills to read, write and understand, he or she can make up what was lost in the other subjects later on in his or her schooling. Although this theory certainly has merit, science, health, and social studies are important and appealing subjects to most students. They offer exciting and important survival information and, often, an opportunity to work with other students in small groups.

Seldom does a special student come for remediation in science or health alone, except on a junior high or high school level. It is possible, however, that many basic skills in reading, writing and math can be taught using health and science as an occasional vehicle. This adds variety and dimension to the program and assures that the student is learning vital information for his or her future well being.

The following teaching unit represents a sampling of possible health and science lessons that can supplement individual grade level curriculum guides. (It is a good idea, if possible, to try to highlight the individual grade level science and health lessons being presented in the students' classrooms.)

Objectives:

At the conclusion of this lesson, students will:

• Realize how a person is like a machine.
• Know the basic components for good health.
• Be familiar with the do's and don'ts of good health.
• Know the components of a balanced diet.
• Become aware of safety rules in the home.
• Become familiar with safety rules outside of the home.

How a Person Is Like a Machine

Materials:

opaque projector

toy car

a tinkertoy machine with joints or a doll

"Meet A. Person" worksheet for each student

"Meet A. Person" poster

Preparation:

1. Put together the simple tinkertoy machine.
2. Project the "Meet A. Person" poster (see page 366) onto the screen or board.
3. Copy the "Meet A. Person" worksheet (see page 367) for each student.

Directions:

1. Hold up the toy car and discuss how it runs.
2. List all the parts of a car on the chalkboard.
3. Discuss what would happen if one of those parts broke down. (Either get it repaired or replaced.)
4. Ask the students, "Could a car repair itself?"
5. Repeat Steps 1–4 using the tinkertoy machine or doll.
6. Using the poster of a person, describe what is necessary to make a person "run." (NOTE: Explain that only the skeleton of a real person is shown.)
7. Discuss what would happen if one of the human parts broke down. Bring out the fact that sometimes humans need to be repaired (broken arms and legs) and/or have parts replaced (transplants). Sometimes, humans are self-healing, whereas machines are not.
8. Instruct the students to think about what is needed to keep a human body in good working condition.
9. Distribute the "Meet A. Person" worksheet to the students.

Reinforcement Activity:

Refer to "Learning Centers" and have your students do assignment 1.

Let's Stay in Good Condition

Materials:

toy car

worksheet for each student

magazine pictures of good food

magazine pictures of "junk" food

magazine pictures of good health habits

magazine pictures of poor health habits

scissors

Meet A. Person

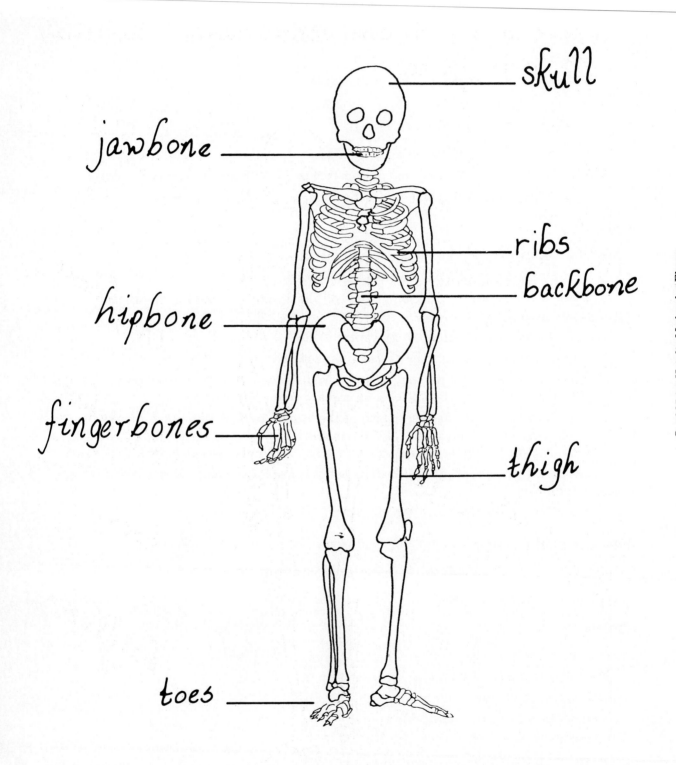

skull

jawbone _____

ribs

backbone

hipbone _____

fingerbones _____

thigh

toes _____

Meet A. Person

Name _____

Draw a line from each name to the correct bone.

hipbone

jawbone

ribs

fingerbones

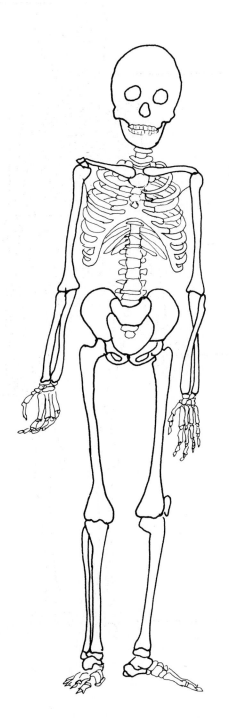

skull

thighbone

anklebone

toes

backbone

Preparation:

    1. Copy the "Good Shape for Good Health" worksheet (see page 369) for each student.

    2. Cut out the magazine pictures of a variety of healthy and unhealthy habits.

Directions:

    1. Explain that, like a car or any other machine, a person's body must be well cared for.

    2. Ask students for suggestions on how this might be done. Write them on the board.

    3. Hold up the magazine pictures one at a time. Ask the students to explain what kind of health habit each one depicts.

    4. During the discussion about the pictures, it will become apparent as to their attitudes about health. This is an excellent time to talk about:

> washing hands before meals and after toileting
> proper rest with good ventilation in the room
> good nutrition (well balanced)
> regular exercise
> regular bathing
> regular check-ups (medical and dental)
> eye and hearing check-ups when needed
> proper fitting shoes and clothes
> balanced activities: not too much TV, etc.
> etc.

    5. Distribute the "Good Shape for Good Health" worksheet to the students.

Reinforcement Activity:

Refer to "Learning Centers" and have your students do assignment 2.

Do's and Don'ts

Materials:

opaque projector
"Sick Cat" worksheet for each student
crayons
"Cool Cat" poster

Preparation:

    1. Project the "Cool Cat" poster (see page 371) onto a screen or board.

    2. Copy the "Sick Cat" worksheet (see page 372) for each student.

Directions:

    1. Using the poster as the focal point, ask students to point out the things that Cool Cat does to keep healthy.

Good Shape for Good Health

Name _____

Color only those things needed for Good Health.

Pizza

Ice Cream

Candy Bar

Daily Bath

TV

Doctor

SODA

Sunglasses

Vegetables

Bedtime

Fruit

Suntan Lotion

Milk

Hamburger

Jogging

Toothpaste

Toothbrush

Vision Check

Hairbrush

2. List the students' suggestions on the board. For example:

> exercises
>
> eats healthy food
>
> has regular check-ups
>
> etc.

3. Distribute the "Sick Cat" worksheet (see page 372) to the students. Ask the students to name the things on the picture that are not conducive to good health. List these on the board. For example:

> smokes cigarettes
>
> eats junk food
>
> watches too much TV
>
> does not exercise
>
> etc.

4. Discuss with the group the general guidelines of a balanced and healthy life. Encourage each student to talk about how he or she can improve his or her own health.

5. Have the students complete the "Sick Cat" worksheet.

6. They may color the picture when they are finished.

Reinforcement Activity:

Refer to "Learning Centers" and have your students do assignment 3.

What Foods Does Our Body Need for Good Health?

Materials:

"The Basic Five" worksheet for each student

chart of food groups

food pictures (See "Materials of the Month." NOTE: Food pictures representing all four groups can be cut from magazines and laminated.)

double-faced tape

Preparation:

1. Copy "The Basic Five" worksheet (see page 374) for each student.

2. Collect pictures from the different food groups. (Refer to the chart on page 375.)

Cool Cat

Good Things To Do
for
GOOD HEALTH

Get good rest
Eat a balanced diet
Get plenty of exercise
Get plenty of fresh air
Have good grooming habits
Have safety sense
Get regular checkups

Sick Cat

List all the things Sick Cat
can do to become healthy.

Name _____

_____

_____

_____

_____

_____

_____

_____

_____

_____

_____

CANDY

SODA

Candy

Pizza

Directions:

1. Write the five headings on the board, leaving about 6″ between each.

<u>Meat</u>   <u>Dairy</u>   <u>Bread</u>   <u>Fruit</u>   <u>Vegetables</u>

2. Hold up a picture from one of the food groups.

3. Ask a student to guess where it belongs.

4. With the double-faced tape, place the picture under the proper heading on the board. NOTE: Flannelboards are also excellent for this purpose.

5. Repeat the above procedure until each heading has several pictures under it.

6. Ask the students if they can think of any more items to place under each heading. Display the food chart.

7. Discuss the reasons for a balanced diet. For example:

a. Our body needs certain vitamins and minerals from these foods in order to function.

b. The body needs them to grow and repair, and for heat, energy, and regulation.

8. Ask the students what happens to a body that does not get the proper balance of food (obesity, malnutrition, anemia, hair falls out, tooth decay, skin is affected, etc.)

9. Distribute "The Basic Five" worksheet. NOTE: Depending on the level of the students, the pictures may be left on the board for them to copy onto the worksheet or removed to test memory skills.

Reinforcement Activity:

Refer to "Learning Centers" and have your students do assignment 4.

Safety Rules for Home

Materials:

large bottle marked: CAUTION—POISON
frying pan with handle
dirty rags
small stepladder
empty spray cleaners, medicine bottle, etc.

NOTE: Pictures of the above items may be substituted.

worksheet for each student
badge for each student
crayons
scissors

Preparation:

1. Copy the inspection worksheet and the badge (see pages 377–378) for each student.

2. Collect the items (or pictures) listed under the materials.

Name _____

THE BASIC FIVE

Meat	Milk

Breads & Cereals  Vegetables + Fruits

FOOD CHART

MEAT

beef
chicken
beans, nuts
eggs
fish
peanut butter
pork
shell fish
soybeans
turkey

BREAD & CEREALS

breakfast cereals
biscuits
crackers
flour
rye bread
white bread

MILK & DAIRY PRODUCTS

cheese
cream
dried milk
whole milk
ice cream
skim milk
butter
margarine

VEGETABLES

asparagus
beans (green, string and wax)
broccoli
carrots
peas
pumpkins
rutabagas
squash
sweet potatoes
kale
lettuce
tomatoes
potatoes
onions

FRUITS

berries
apples
peaches
limes
bananas
pears
lemons
figs
pineapples
plums
oranges
grapes
prunes

Directions:

    1. Ask the students if they can think of ways children have been hurt around the house.

    2. List the students' ideas on the board. For example:

> burns
>
> falls
>
> fire
>
> being poisoned

    3. Hold up each example of a possible hazard. Have students explain how each one can be dangerous. For example, if you hold up a medicine bottle, a student might say that a child who takes it unprescribed can be poisoned. Household cleaners can be poisonous. A small ladder can cause a fall. Dirty rags, when left unattended, can cause a fire. If a frying pan handle is pointed outwards, it can be pulled over onto a person to cause a terrible burn.

    4. Explain that these are but a few of the possible household hazards.

    5. Distribute the inspection worksheet. Explain to the students that they are going to be safety inspectors in their own houses. They will take the worksheet home and fill it out.

    6. Give each child a Safety Inspector's card to color, cut out and display. (Don't forget, you sign it as the Chief Safety Inspector!)

Reinforcement Activity:

    Refer to "Learning Centers" and have your students do assignment 5.

Safety Rules Outside of Home

Materials:

    oaktag for poster
    index cards for group tasks
    paper bag puppets (see learning center 6)
    markers

Preparation:

    1. Write safety rules (see below) onto oaktag
    2. Write one safety rule on each index card.
    3. Prepare learning center 6.

Directions:

    1. Using the poster, discuss the following rules:

> Always swim with a buddy
>
> Look both ways before crossing the street
>
> Never talk to strangers

SAFETY INSPECTION CHECKLIST

Inspector's name _____

Directions: Check each room in your house. Look for the following items:

☐ Detergents out of reach _____

☐ Poisons clearly marked and out of reach _____

☐ Cleaning materials stored away from small children _____

☐ Dirty rags in plastic container _____

☐ Old papers not stored in the house _____

☐ Objects picked up from the floor _____

☐ Boiling water carefully attended _____

☐ Pot handles turned inward on the stove _____

☐ Railings available on stairs _____

☐ Smoke detector system installed _____

☐ Fire exit plan in effect _____

☐ Iron turned off and unplugged unless in use by adult _____

This is to certify
That

_____

is an Official

Home Safety Inspector

_____
chief safety inspector

signed :

safety seal of approval

Never stand under a tree during a storm

Wear a life jacket while boating

Carry identification with you at all times

Avoid unknown animals

Never use electric appliances near water

Never play with an automobile

NOTE: More can be added to list.

2. Encourage students to talk about what could happen if a rule is not followed.

3. Ask for personal experiences with safety rules.

4. Divide the students into small groups of 2–3 students.

5. Give each group a task card with a safety rule.

6. Explain that the group is to make up a play about the rule on the card.

7. When the play is written, have the group make a paper bag puppet at the learning center.

8. The refrigerator box puppet theater can be used to present the puppet plays.

Reinforcement Activity:

Refer to "Learning Centers" and have your students do assignment 6.

LEARNING CENTERS

The following learning centers have been designed to supplement the lessons in the teaching unit. They may also be used independently to reinforce health and safety.

It is hoped that the lessons on health and safety will trigger an awareness of those things that protect human welfare as well as a reinforcement of the importance of human life.

(1) MR. MACHINE
(PRIMARY)

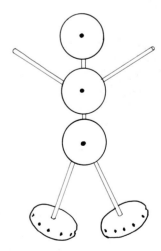

Materials:

tinkertoys or other manipulative building toys

sample of a toy person

index card

marker

Preparation:

1. Write the directions on an index card.

2. Make a person out of tinkertoys or other building toys.

Directions Card:

```
                        MR. MACHINE
1.  Using the building toys, design a person.
2.  Be sure to put in parts to make the arms and legs move.
3.  Have your person checked by the teacher.
```

(2) R$_X$ FOR GOOD HEALTH

Materials:

"My Plan for Good Health" worksheet for each student
index card
felt-tip marker

Preparation:

1. Write the directions on an index card.
2. Copy the worksheet (see page 381) for each student.

Directions Card:

```
                     R$_X$ FOR GOOD HEALTH
1.  Read over the plan for your good health.
2.  Answer each question thoughtfully.
3.  Keep your plan to refer to throughout the year.
```

(3) RHYMING YOUR WAY TO GOOD HEALTH

Materials:

"Rhyming to Good Health" worksheet for each student
index card
marker
"Cool Cat" postcard

Preparation:

1. Copy the worksheet (see page 383) for each student.
2. Write the directions on an index card.
3. Copy the "Cool Cat" poster from the Teaching Unit.
4. Place the poster at the learning center.

Name _____

MY PLAN FOR GOOD HEALTH

1. This is how I plan to change my diet. _____

_____

2. This is how I plan to organize regular exercise for myself.

_____

_____

3. My regular medical checkup showed I was . . . _____

_____

4. My regular dental checkup showed I had . . . _____

_____

5. My home safety inspection showed _____

_____

6. My eye examination showed _____

_____

7. My bathing habits are: _____

_____

8. My teeth are brushed _____ times a day.

9. Generally, I would rate my health habits as

☐ Fair   ☐ Average
☐ Good   ☐ Excellent

10. I plan to change the following areas: _____

_____

_____

_____

_____

Signed _____

Directions Card:

RHYME YOUR WAY

1. Fill in the missing words to complete the health rhymes.
2. Make up your own rhyme about good health.
3. Draw a picture to illustrate your rhyme.

---

(4) MURAL OF GOOD HEALTH

Materials:

long strip of mural (kraft) paper   index card
tape   marker
magazines   food chart
scissors   oaktag

Preparation:

1. Locate magazines appropriate for cutting out pictures of foods.
2. Tape the long mural paper on a flat, unused wall.
3. Write the directions on an index card.
4. Copy the food chart from the Teaching Unit onto oaktag.
5. Use the chart as a backdrop for the learning center.

Directions Card:

MURAL

1. Look at the chart of the food groups.
2. Cut out food pictures from the magazines.
3. Tape the pictures under the proper headings on the mural.

Name _____

RHYMING TO GOOD HEALTH

Complete the following rhymes about good health.

Early to bed, early to rise
Makes a man healthy, wealthy and _____

An apple a day
Keeps the doctor _____

First wash your hands and next your face
Then bend over and tie your _____

Run and jump and move around
Then dress yourself up and go to _____

First I eat fruit
Then I eat bread
Don't forget milk
Before going to _____

A balanced diet is what I need
Exercise, fresh air, and rest indeed
If I try real hard you'll surely see
All put together makes a healthy _____

Make a healthy rhyme of your own

_____

_____

_____

_____

_____

_____

_____

_____

Draw a picture of good health on the back of this sheet.

(5) COOKBOOK

Materials:

five food worksheets for each student
several easy-to-read cookbooks (see "Materials of the Month")
index card
felt-tip marker

Preparation:

1. Copy the five worksheets (see pages 385–389) for each student.
2. Locate easy-to-read cookbooks in the library and place them at the learning center.
3. Write the directions on an index card.

Directions Card:

```
                          COOKBOOK
1.  Look through the cookbooks.
2.  Find a recipe for each food group and write it on the
worksheet.
3.  Many recipes will be for more than one group.
4.  Have your cookbook checked by the teacher.
```

(6) PAPER BAG PUPPETRY

Materials:

brown lunch bags
construction paper
buttons
pipe cleaners
crayons
markers
scissors
glue
yarn
index cards

Preparation:

1. Prepare a paper bag puppet in advance.
2. Write the directions on an index card.

Fruit

Recipe: _____

Cook: _____

Ingredients: _____
_____
_____
_____
_____
_____

Directions: _____
_____
_____
_____
_____
_____

Vegetables

Recipe:_____

Cook:_____

Ingredients:_____

_____

_____

_____

Directions:_____

_____

_____

_____

_____

_____

_____

_____

Meat

Recipe:_____

Cook:_____

Ingredients:_____
_____
_____
_____
_____

Directions:_____
_____
_____
_____
_____
_____

Dairy

Recipe:_____

Cook: _____

Ingredients:_____
_____
_____
_____
_____

Directions:_____
_____
_____
_____
_____
_____
_____

Bread

Recipe: _____

Cook: _____

Ingredients: _____
_____
_____
_____
_____
_____
_____

Directions: _____
_____
_____
_____
_____
_____

Directions Card:

```
┌─────────────────────────────────────────────────────────┐
│                    PAPER BAG PUPPETS                      │
│  1.  Look at the sample puppet.                          │
│  2.  Use as many materials as you can to make a puppet.  │
│  3.  Keep your safety rule in mind as you design your    │
│  character.                                               │
│  4.  Practice with your puppet at the Puppet Theater.    │
└─────────────────────────────────────────────────────────┘
```

MATERIALS OF THE MONTH

Don't throw away those old magazines, catalogs, phone books, train schedules, newspapers, comic strips, etc.! They are goldmines of useful materials.

Phone books, and especially the Yellow Pages, make excellent resource books for learning centers on survival skills. Most middle grade (and younger) students need to know how to use phone books and Yellow Pages in everyday living. Giving them instruction and reinforcement in this skill is most important.

Train schedules need special instruction. Most adults have difficulty deciphering the crowded print and complicated format. Enlarge one page of a train schedule on a copy machine. Teaching how to read a schedule can serve a useful and valuable purpose in a youngster's life.

Magazines are great sources of pictures and titles to cut out. Many activities, especially for non-readers, include finding pictures in magazines.

Newspapers are excellent for finding out about current events as well as reading for comprehension. The print can be enlarged with a copy machine.

Comic strips make excellent backdrops for bulletin boards, wrapping paper, and for sequencing reinforcement activities.

Word finds or easy crossword puzzles, sports pages, etc., are all excellent resources for teaching materials. There are as many uses for a newspaper as your imagination can find.

FREE FOR THE ASKING

An All American Nuts Recipe Book

This 16-page booklet gives nut recipes for hors d'oeuvres, vegetables, salads, main dishes, and desserts. Nuts are excellent sources of protein and can supplement the meat group of foods. Information about the history and nutrition of peanuts is included. Write to:

All American Nut Co.
16901 Valley View
Cerritas, CA 90701

Free Recipe Folders

Best Foods offers a number of recipe folders. Write to the following address for a free list of available materials:

Best Foods
Dept. LL-1001
Box 307
Coventry, CT 06238

No Smoking Coloring Book

This is a 4-page coloring book for preschoolers with an anti-smoking message. It is available to schools and libraries free from the American Lung Association.

No Smoking Lungs at Work

This is a picture book for children stressing the ill effects of smoking. It presents a strong message that smoking is not worth the harm it causes our bodies. It is available to schools and libraries free from the American Lung Association.

Marijuana Smoking — A National Epidemic

This is a discussion of scientific evidence that marijuana is harmful to lungs. Six pages long, it is available to schools and libraries free. Write to:

American Lung Association
1740 Broadway
New York, NY 10019

Signs of Possible Eye Trouble in Children — No. G102

This is a fact sheet designed to help detect eye problems in children by observing behavior, appearance and complaints. It is for use in grades 1–8. Write to:

National Society to Prevent Blindness
79 Madison Avenue
New York, NY 10016

You and Your Health

This free booklet features 12 articles on health topics by prominent health experts that originally appeared as a newspaper series. An emergency reference chart is included. Write to:

Council on Family Health
633 Third Avenue
New York, NY 10017

Free Safety Manual

This is a booklet that tells how to make a home virtually fireproof. It also discusses home fire detection methods and inexpensive alarms. Write to:

Dynamics
2015 Ivy Road
Charlottesville, VA 22903

Silent Menace In and Around Your Home

This free booklet alerts the students on how to avoid explosions, toxic plants, toxic gases, poisons and burns from common substances in the home. Write to:

Communications and Public Affairs, Dept. D-1
Kemper Insurance Companies
Long Grove, IL 60049

GOOD BUYS

The following commercial materials are suggested to supplement the health and safety lessons for May.

Inside Me

This consists of six full-color 8½" × 11" action picture cards. Six blackline masters reproduce the x-ray views of the six systems found on the backs of cards. A teacher's manual is included. Selling for under $10, the set is available from DLM.

Body Parts Dice Game

Students learn to name 21 body parts with this game. Plastic chips are placed on depicted parts of the body. Selling for under $10, it is available from DLM.

All Purpose Photo Library

This is an excellent collection of 272 full-color photos in 12 categories, including animals, food, colors and shapes, and household items. An excellent resource to supplement many lessons with visual reinforcement, it sells for under $10 and is available from DLM.

Hound Dog and Turtle Puppets

These soft, cuddly, washable hand puppets measure 13" × 6" and 11¾" × 6" respectively. They are adorable and versatile supplements to many lessons. Selling for under $20 each, they are available from:

Developmental Learning Materials
P.O. Box 4000
One DLM Park
Allen, TX 75002

Safety and You

Four full color filmstrips, four cassettes and a guide make the student aware of the hazards of his or her environment. Selling for under $80, the set is available from Educational Activities, Inc.

Nutrition for Little Children

A full-color filmstrip and cassette (record available), the kit is directed toward developing positive attitude toward food and good health in grades K–3. The kit, with a guide included, sells for under $25. Write to:

Educational Activities, Inc.
P.O. Box 392
Freeport, NY 11520

Dudley

This is a functioning torso with a guide. It is excellent for lessons on body systems and functioning. The 3-foot high functioning torso model shows the interrelationship of its five body systems. The torso and guide, selling for about $250, are an excellent investment. Write to:

> Hubbard Science Materials
> P.O. Box 104
> Northbrook, IL 60062

PROFESSIONAL RESPONSIBILITIES

MONTHLY REPORTS

Some districts automatically require monthly reports from teachers for purposes of future planning as well as for keeping the administrators up to date on what is happening in the classrooms.

Whether monthly reports are a school requirement or not, submitting a report is a great way to let the administration know what you are doing.

An excellent technique for remembering what took place in order to write your report is to jot down notes in your plan book or on your calendar in another color (like red or green). Then at the end of the month it is easy to see exactly what should be included in the report.

If a set format is already required, copy several of these blank forms for extras. Keep your notes right on the form, which can be kept in your plan book or on your desk—wherever it is most convenient to use. At the end of the month, it is then easy to recopy your notes.

Such "happenings" as new projects, a new teaching approach, how effective new materials are, problems with scheduling, and parental involvement are all good inclusions. Sometimes presenting a problem or an issue that needs to be discussed first in writing is a good approach. It gives the administrator time to think about it and read it over if necessary. This prevents catching the administrator "off guard" and possibly causing a negative response.

For those months when something extra special takes place (like C Day or the Young Author's Book Fair), it might be a good idea to also send a copy of your report to the superintendent of schools or the board of education president. They appreciate knowing what is going on in the school and often can include the information in their own reports.

Finally, keep copies of your monthly reports for your own perusal. These make excellent records for your evaluations, future employment, and/or personal satisfaction. Reading over the year's reports is an excellent review for any teacher and can be very self-rewarding.

PROFESSIONAL RESOURCE BOOKS

Benziger, Barbara. *Controlling Your Weight.* (New York: Franklin Watts, Inc., 1973)

Deiner, Penny. *Resources for Teaching Young Children with Special Needs.* (New York: Harcourt Brace Jovanovich, 1983)

Fantini, Mario D. *Public Schools of Choice.* (New York: Simon and Schuster, 1973)

Leaf, Munro. *Health Can Be Fun.* (Philadelphia: J.B. Lippincott Co., 1943)

Miel, Alice, and Edwin Diester, Jr. *The Shortchanged Children of Suburbia.* (Institute of Human Relations, 1967)

Nourse, Alan E. *The Body.* (New York: Time, Inc., 1964)

Radabaugh, Martha, and Joseph F. Yukish. *Curriculum and Methods for the Mildly Handicapped.* (Boston: Allyn and Bacon, Inc., 1982)

Silverstein, Alvin. *The Skeletal Systems: Frameworks for Life.* (Englewood Cliffs, NJ: Prentice-Hall, Inc., 1972)

Smith, Sally. *No Easy Answers: The Learning Disabled Child.* (U.S. Department of Health, Education and Welfare, Public Health Service, Alcohol, Drug Abuse and Mental Health Administration, 1978)

Turner, Eloise, and Carol Fenton. *Inside You and Me: A Child's Introduction to the Human Body.* (New York: The John Day Co., 1961)

Walsh, John. *The First Book of Physical Fitness.* (New York: Franklin Watts, Inc., 1973)

Zim, Herbert S. *What's Inside of Me.* (New York: Morrow Junior Books, 1952)

MODES FOR MAINSTREAMING

SAYING THANKS

The month of May not only announces the coming of summer, it also heralds the nearing end of the school year.

Planning meetings for next year are either still in progress or close to being finished. The hustle and bustle of closing programs, finishing report cards, and planning end-of-the-year picnics are all part of the month. This is an excellent time to let the classroom teachers know that their efforts in cooperating with your program throughout the school year were appreciated. (For those teachers who were not the most cooperative, thank them in advance for next year!)

You can send thank-you notes to each teacher with personal comments about the school year. For instance:

```
Dear Joyce,

Your help throughout the school year really helped to
make this year one of progress for Larry and Mitchell.

Your good ideas and willingness to do whatever was
necessary to get the job done did not go unnoticed. I per-
sonally enjoyed working with you and look forward to
next year.

                              Sincerely,

                              Freda
```

Delivering a small plant with a note is usually very well received and a reminder to teachers throughout the summer of your appreciation. Plants can either be planted in advance by the students in small containers or purchased inexpensively at a supermarket or road side stand. Placing a colorful bow on a coffee stirrer and placing it into the plant adds a festive note.

If time permits, and the staff dynamics are conducive to permit socializing, a small gathering with refreshments can be another way of saying thank you. Placing a large banner that says "thank you" at the front of the room adds to setting the theme. A single carnation with a pretty bow for each teacher is always well received and can be taken home with them to further enjoy. Coffee, tea and cake or cookies are always appreciated.

Holding the party after school or during lunch time are two possibilities. This must be determined by how the staff meeting times have been set in the past. Certainly a party is meant to please the guests, not antagonize them by being held at a time that is inconvenient.

Be sure to invite the school administrator and the special services department administrator (often not in the same building). Do not forget to thank the custodial staff and the secretaries as well.

The important thing is to be warm and gracious at the party and generous with praise and thanks. Some special education teachers prefer giving a short speech to everyone at the same time, while others feel that a personal thank you to each teacher individually is better. This is really a matter of personal choice. Keep in mind that the success of your program depends upon the support of the staff. Don't be afraid to let each and everyone know just that.

NOTE: Similar procedures should be followed for thanking parent volunteers and aides.

TIP OF THE MONTH

HOME, JAMES!

Samples of work kept in the resource room should be sent home before the last day of school. At the end of the school year, classroom work is usually sent home. If resource room work goes home at the same time, it often gets lost in the shuffle.

Have each student make a folder cover out of construction paper. Each student should organize his or her papers according to date (beginning in September). As they go through their papers for the year, have them pick out the "worst" paper and their "best" paper. Have these papers placed in a prominent spot in their folders for their parents to see the improvement during the year.

In order to emphasize the importance of parent perusal of these papers, send home a receipt that the parents must sign and return with their son or daughter. For instance:

May 28, 19xx

Dear Mrs. Elman:

I have looked over _____ resource
                              (student's name)
room papers for the year.
I have the following comments: _____
_____
_____
_____

                              Signed _____
                                          (Parent's Signature)

A FINAL WORD

BURNOUT

Something all of us have heard a lot about is teacher burnout. The symptoms are varied and alarming depending on who is talking about them. The one thing on burnout about which everyone agrees is the damage it does to teacher effectiveness.

For those teachers who work very hard but the rewards are not obvious ones (like more money or frequent pats on the back), burnout is a danger. In a situation like a special classroom where tremendous energy is expended both in dealing with students and staff, teachers must take care to make rewards for themselves.

All too frequently, teachers are in situations where positive feedback is not forthcoming from administrators. Students are seldom able to "stroke" teachers directly, parents aren't around that often, and fellow teachers, if willing, are often too busy. Therefore, there is one source of positive stroking left: you! Although sometimes difficult, it is important to be good to yourself in order to sustain your teaching energy! There are several ways to do this both in and out of school. For instance:

1. *Ask for help when you need it.* Use resource people like volunteer aides, librarians, and paid school aides. If there is an administrative problem, refer it to the proper administrator. Don't take on everyone's job including your own.

2. *Be willing to say "uncle."* Not all problems are solvable. When faced with an impossible task, give it up! Don't overburden yourself with problems that have no solution. Better to concentrate your energies on something more productive; it's much less frustrating.

3. *Say "no" and mean it.* All of us like to be liked. Saying "yes" to another responsibility when you are already overburdened really does no one a favor. A burned-out employee isn't an asset to anyone. Take on those responsibilities that you can handle and enjoy, but turn down those that will overtax you. Someone else who has more time will agree to do the job.

4. *Review student's progress to see the results of your work.* The academic gains of special students can seem very small. Working on skills at a slow pace can be unrewarding. Teachers need to look at the progress being made over time by comparing where a child was academically to where he or she is now. This can be a big boost. Share this knowledge with the classroom teacher, who can also use the boost. Sharing the information can be reinforcing to you as well.

5. *Remind yourself about why you went into teaching.* All of us at sometime or other aspired to be teachers for very idealistic reasons. We saw a need and wanted to fill the void. In the daily grind of running a special program, these reasons can be forgotten. It is helpful to try and remember them again. Your job is still important, necessary, and all of those other altruistic reasons that motivated you to go into the field in the first place. Focus on those reasons occasionally. They help to make the job more meaningful.

6. *Take time off to grow.* Take advantage of professional workshops and meetings. Most districts provide substitutes for an occasional professional day for its teachers. Be sure to use yours. Watch for ACLD Conventions, CEC Conferences, etc. These meetings not only disseminate the latest professional information, but the opportunity is there to meet with other special educators and share ideas. It's truly an uplifting experience.

7. *Relax at home.* Don't forget to have fun and take time to nurture yourself. Listen to your favorite music, pick up your hobby, go for a long ride in the country, or any other thing that makes you feel special. Giving to children all day is taxing work. Find ways to give something back to yourself. It really is self preserving.

8. *Other Outlets.* Having other outlets like sports activities, enrichment classes, charitable organizations, book groups, etc., can be a great diversion. Even though it sounds like "more to do," it can be very enriching and exhilarating. Outside interests really help us to be better and more relaxed teachers in school. After all, TEACHERS ARE PEOPLE, TOO!

MAY REFERENCES

Bartlett, John. *Bartlett's Familiar Quotations.* (Boston: Little Brown and Co., 1955)

Current Biography. "Jenner, Bruce." (Bronx, NY: H.W. Wilson, 1977)

Donahue Transcript #08171. "The Phil Donahue Show." August 1, 1971.

Education for Survival: Ecology in Science and Social Studies. (Morristown, NJ: North Jersey Conservation Foundation, 1972)

Jenner, Bruce. *Decathlon Challenge.* (Englewood Cliffs, NJ: Prentice-Hall, Inc., 1977)

Nelson, Leslie, and George C. Lorbeer. *Science Activities for Elementary Children.* (Dubuque, IA: William C. Brown Publishers, 1967)

Probe: A Handbook of Ideas to Motivate the Teaching of Elementary Science. (Stevensville, MI: Educational Service, Inc., 1972)

Sports Illustrated. "Heading for the Eleventh Event." August 18, 1975, Issue 24.

June

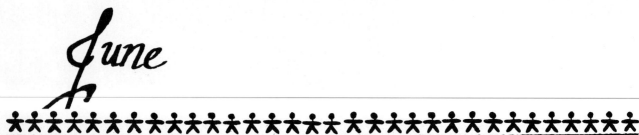

Happy birthday to . . .

1 Edward Angle (1855) IF your front teeth seem to stick straight out,/Or there are gaps where bottom cusps should be,/ Or two molars jam together and/Your bite's not right, you see!/ THEN hire a band or send a wire/And thank first orthodontist Angle./He found ways to align those teeth/Which grew in all a'tangle!

2 Johnny Weismuller (1903) Too weak to play? Swimming may help, the doctor said. Johnny Weismuller dog-paddled in the muddy Chicago River. He watched the other kids swim and learned so well he earned 67 records, won 52 titles and 5 Olympic gold medals. Weak in his old age, he taught handicapped kids to swim. TARZAN, YOU'RE TERRIFIC!

3 Charles Drew (1904) Did you know that blood, given to PRESERVE a life, is hard to PRESERVE? Drew discovered a way to PRESERVE it and send it to countries to save lives of all wounded people. Asked to keep blood from negro and white donors apart, he refused. He knew all blood saved all lives, even perhaps, your own.

4 King George III (1738) Sing the following verse to "My Country 'Tis of Thee": John signed it* first in line,/Told you in script, so fine,/GEORGE, you're not our king!/Your laws you would not bend,/On YOU we shant depend,/Our rights we did defend!/Let freedom ring! . . . *What did John sign?

5 Socrates (469? B.C.) He was a teacher, a Greek who taught that wisdom and honesty were more important than riches or fame. Socrates met people he thought were very wise. But they could not answer his questions. He knew they were only pretending to be WISE. Don't pretend! Be able to write 20 questions about Greece, wisely!

6 Bjorn Borg (1956) Tennis was, perhaps, first called TAMIS. The first tennis racket was a tamis—a French glove with strings stretched across it. Major Wingate published (1874) rules for lawn tennis, the game so well played by Sweden's Bjorn Borg! Winning ___ Wimbledon and ___ French Open games, he is an ace, in love with the sport!

7 Susan Blow (1843) and Virginia Apgar (1909) Kids took tests for Virginia Apgar and Susan Blow. What did their tests tell about kids? Passing Susan's test meant counting from 1 to 5 in the first U.S. kindergarten! But Dr. Apgar's kids couldn't count yet. They were newborn babies tested for physical fitness. Brag to a doctor about Dr. Apgar's test!

8 Charles Beck (1910) Captain Marvel, the world's mightiest mortal, was drawn marvelously by Beck! And from the wizard came his magic word, SHAZAM. That is an ACRONYM for names of 6 mighty immortals: Solomon, Hercules, Atlas, Zeus, Achilles, and Mercury! Beck's drawings were Bold, Easy to read, Creative, and Keen!

9 Charles Bonaparte (1851) What is the branch of the U.S. Government that solves crimes? The FBI! The initials FBI stand for Federal Bureau of Investigation, created by Bonaparte in 1908. J. Edgar Hoover's idea of FBI and CIA fingerprint files made an ID for a P.D. A.S.A.P. On a BD card for C.J.B., F.P. your P.S. classmates and SWAK.

10 Judy Garland (1922) Somewhere, over the rainbow, is Oz, where a Kansas schoolgirl, blown by a tornado, meets the Tin Man who has no heart, the Lion who has no courage, and the Scarecrow who has no brains—or at least they think so! The schoolgirl is Judy and Oz won her an Academy Award. Sing *Somewhere* over a rainbow cake.

11 Jeanette Rankin (1880) Should the U.S. fight WWI and II? Jeanette Rankin, first woman elected to Congress, was the only representative to say "nay." Young Jeanette was shy and disliked school, and thought she was a poor student. But the people of Montana knew she was smart and elected Rankin, a lady who always said "NAY" to war!

12 John A. Roebling (1806) 100 years ago from Brooklyn,/To Manhattan, arch to arch,/Spanned a bridge of steel suspenders,/ Where iron horse and cart did march./John A. Roebling did design it/But was killed—and thus his son/Though ill, spied it from his window/And directed till 'twas done.

13 Harold "Red" Grange (1903) You might know of a galloping ghost, a headless horseman who chased the easily terrified Ichabod Crane! But you may not know of Illinois' "Red" Grange who dazzled the not-easily-terrified Michigan team with 4 touchdowns in 12 minutes! Use ghostly words in the news story, GALLOPING GHOST GETS 4 TDS IN 12!

14 Karl Landsteiner (1868) Today is also Flag Day, so give 2 cheers for the white and blue: white for peace and blue for bravery. But no cheers for *red* blood spilled on the battlefields. Landsteiner's discovery saved millions of wounded soldiers. He discovered blood types (A, AB, B and O) and made transfusions safe! Salute Landsteiner! Do you know your blood type?

15 Josiah Henson (1789) Lincoln once asked if Stowe was the little woman whose book caused a great civil war. Stowe's book, UNCLE TOM'S CABIN, was based on Henson's life, a Maryland slave who had escaped to Canada and had already published his biography. He brought many slaves to freedom while the book brought many to think about the cause of slavery.

> The truth is found when . . . (people) . . . are free to pursue it.
>
> Franklin Delano Roosevelt

★★★★★★★★★★★★★★★★★★★★★★★★★★★★★★★★

16 Jennie Grossinger (1892) Even with no heat, plumbing or light, good food brought summer boarders to the Grossinger's little farmhouse. Now, year-round boarders go to Grossinger's Hotel in New York, where Jennie had become the best-known hotel keeper in the world. Sing Happy Birthday!

17 John Gregg (1867) It was never simple enough! Because John Gregg wrote and rewrote his shorthand so it would be the very easiest and fastest way to take dictation, it is now taught in schools around the world. Ready? In long hand: HAPPY BIRTHDAY, or, in Gregg shorthand: ✍ Which is simpler?

18 Paul McCartney (1942) He was born left-handed. He played his guitar upside down, but his music and the talents of John, George and Ringo came out right-side-up in worldwide concert tours. Beatlemania brought #1 songs, new sounds, new haircuts, and screaming fans. Millions of songs rocked from millions of records. Play one!

19 Henry "Lou" Gehrig (1903) He was the "Iron Horse." Playing ___ straight games proved Gehrig's enduring record. But then, disease struck him out of baseball. With "Lou Gehrig's" paralysis, Lou was no longer able to play. He never missed a day from June 2, 1925 until April 30, 1939. How many days did the Iron Horse "play ball"?

20 Helen Shepard (1868) Could you be in the Hall of Fame for Great Americans? Any U.S. citizen may nominate anyone else who did something extraordinary. A committee of 100 (some from each state) votes once every few years to elect GREAT Americans. Thanks, Helen Shepard, for this famous idea.

21 Arnold Gessell (1880) A birthday party should be special. But every year of childhood, SPECIAL means something different. Dr. Gessell taught parents about what kids CAN and LIKE to do best at every age. He suggested that special party games be chosen because they're AGE — O.K.! Ask guests to an AGE — O.K. party for Gessell!

22 Michael Todd (1909) Have you been to a fuzzy movie that you "defuzzed" with 2-colored eyeglasses? Todd invented that kind of 3D movies! In those films, things were seen in 3 ways: short or tall, wide or narrow, and near and far! Todd's eyeglasses made things look CLOSE AND DISTANT! Mention Todd's 3-Dimension movies today!

23 Wilma Rudolph (1940) Three yards ahead of the next runner, Wilma Rudolph crossed the finish line and won her first of 3 gold Olympic medals. Affectionately called "Black Gazelle," her speed was a victory over illness, also. Unable to walk for 4 years didn't "make her cross." It did help make her determined to outrun the rest in Rome!

24 Ernst H. Weber (1795) You have 1 pound of candy in your right hand and 1½ pounds in your left. Can you tell (eyes shut!) which you'd rather keep? Can you tell the difference between heavy and light, soft and loud, near and far, or hot and hotter? Weber found a way to tell HOW WE TELL HOW DIFFERENT DIFFERENCES ARE!

25 Jesse Strauss (1872) It was the world's largest department store! It all began with Jesse's grandpa's small New York crockery shop (1865). Jesse's dad expanded that to middle-size Macy's. When Jesse took over, Macy's grew into the world's largest department store. Have you ever made a purchase at monumental Macy's?

26 Jesse Field Shambaugh (1881) It takes math to manage a farm. Shambaugh wrote a fine text so Iowa kids could solve farming problems. And kids everywhere love her "a bushel and a peck" for founding farming clubs where kids, in friendly competition, could work with the H___, H___, H___, and H___. The 4-H Clubs of America keep multiplying!

27 Bob Keeshan (1927) A kangaroo has one pocket but the gentle, white mustached Captain had two, filled with surprises. Once the Howdy Doody clown, Bob Keeshan, with the able assistance of Mr. Green Jeans, Mr. Moose, Miss Frog, Bunny Rabbit and Tom, taught terrific TV lessons to trillions of kids. Good morning, Captain!

28 Alexis Carrel (1873) It is not unusual to know that some people have kidney, heart or liver transplants! Doctors have replaced one of their diseased organs with a healthy organ from another person. Dr. Carrel invented a way to JOIN veins and arteries so transplanted organs could keep on working to keep people alive!

29 George Hale (1868) Be a stellar speller! The word? SPECTROHELIOGRAPH. That's a camera astronomers use to take pictures of the sun. Hail Hale, its inventor, with a sunny singing of Happy Birthday and get a star for spelling SPECTROHELIOGRAPH . . . a 17-letter word that means a way to see the sunshiniest suntan of all.

30 Lydia Lane Roberts (1879) Especially during war, hunger happened! By boiling pots of water, neighbors never knew there wasn't soup to eat with bread, the only food many had. Lydia Roberts found a way to put extra vitamins and minerals into each loaf to make sure it was as nourishing as the soup they didn't have to eat with it!

These birthographies were prepared by Davida Shipkowitz of Northridge, California.

SPOTLIGHT ON

JULIETTE LOW (1860–1927)

Founder of the American Girl Scout movement in 1912, Juliette Low wanted young women to think for themselves. "She brought girls of all backgrounds into the out-of-doors, giving them opportunity to learn about nature and develop self-reliance and resourcefulness" (Media Services 1982).

In 1911 Juliette, a world traveler, met Sir Robert Baden Powell in England. Sir Baden Powell was the founder of Boy Scouts and Girl Guides in England. Discussions with him led to the idea of starting the Girl Scouts of America. When Juliette returned to Savannah, Georgia, she reportedly gave this historic message to her cousin over the phone: "I've got something for the girls of Savannah, and all America, and all the world, and we're going to start it tonight!"

The activities of this new young woman's movement was considered radical in 1912. Juliette Low was one of the forerunners of groups interested in developing human potential in all women. In those Victorian days it was considered daring for this new young group of girls to wear bloomers, go on two-week camping trips, and be concerned about ecology and natural foods.

It is important to note that this dynamic, perservering woman had a severe handicap. Treated for an earache with silver nitrate (a "new treatment"), she was left partially deaf in one ear. At her wedding a few years later a grain of rice lodged in her other ear. After its removal she was left completely deaf in that ear. With a fraction of her normal hearing left, Juliette Low carried on with the same zeal for life as ever.

With a severe hearing loss, she single-handedly started an organization which has grown to include 3,000,000 young women. It is the world's largest voluntary organization for girls and has influenced the lives of more than 46 million girls and adult women who have belonged to Girl Scouts. Her dream of bringing together women from every walk of life to help each other grow into responsible womanhood was fulfilled.

After her death in 1927 her friends honored her by establishing the Juliette Low World Friendship Fund which finances international projects among Girl Scouts throughout the world.

On July 3, 1948, President Truman authorized a bill to commemorate Juliette Low on a three-cent stamp, one of the few stamps ever to be dedicated to a woman. During World War II a liberty ship was named in her honor. Savannah, Georgia honored Juliette by naming a school after her. She is also a member of the Woman's Hall of Fame in Seneca Falls, New York.

In spite of many odds, of both societal attitudes and her personal handicap, Juliette Low achieved her goal. Her following wish came true:

"We shall make scouting so much a part of our life that people will recognize the spirit and say, 'why of course. She is a Girl Scout.'"

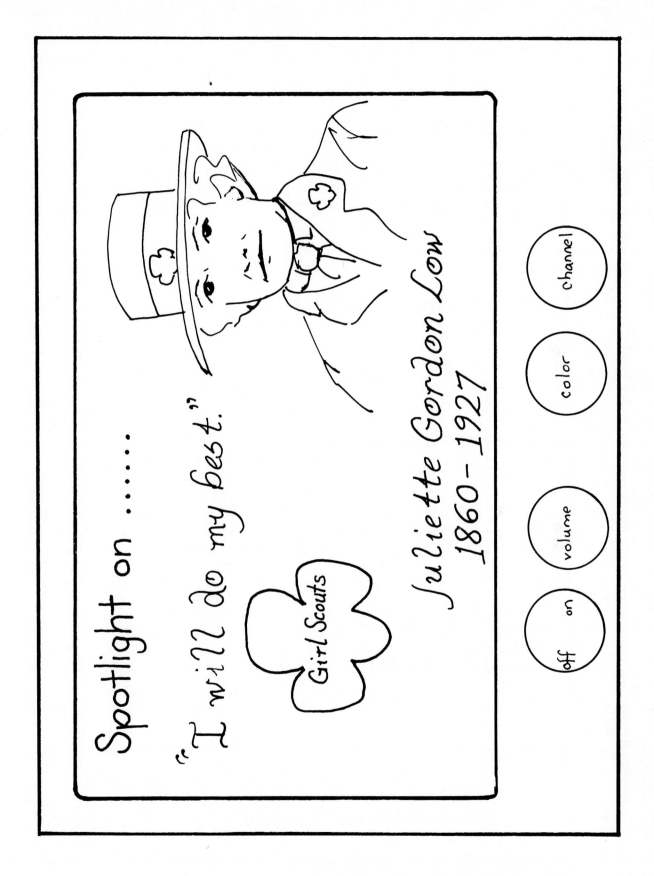

SPOTLIGHT BULLETIN BOARD

Materials:

white background paper

green marker for figures

copy of the bulletin board illustration

black marker for outline of TV, knobs, and lettering

overhead projector or opaque projector (NOTE: If an opaque projector is used, the transparency can be replaced by a paper copy of the bulletin board)

acetate transparency

transparency marker

Preparation:

1. Cover the bulletin board with the white background paper.
2. Trace the "Spotlight" bulletin board (see page 401) onto clear acetate using a transparency marker.
3. Project the transparency onto the backed bulletin board.
4. Trace the outlines and color in with the markers.

BULLETIN BOARD IDEAS

SUMMER WAVES

The simplicity of the waving hands (which the students have made) prepares the students for the summer farewell. It is suggested that each student make a hand (see directions) to add to the bulletin board so that they can all be represented in the good-bye sentiment.

Materials:

white background paper	pencil
black construction paper for hands	scissors
broad black felt-tip marker	tape
pipe cleaners or small pieces of sponge to give 3-D look	stapler or glue

Directions:

1. Cover the bulletin board with the white background paper.
2. Write the title across the center of the board with a broad black marker.
3. Have each student make his or her own hand imprint:
   a. Place hand on piece of black construction paper.
   b. Outline hand with a pencil.
   c. With scissors, cut out the traced hand.

    d. Either glue or staple a coiled pipe cleaner or small piece of sponge onto the back of the hand.

    e. Affix the hand to the bulletin board by taping the other end of the pipe cleaner or sponge. (The hand should hang in a suspended fashion to give the effect of waving.)

    4. A sample of the bulletin board is found on page 404.

DIVE INTO SUMMER FUN

This board is most effective if warm summer colors are used. It is a good way to reinforce the warm seasonal weather of summer and a time for more leisure activities. The carryover skills emphasized this month follow through with this theme.

Materials:

copy of bulletin board on page 405

opaque projector

orange background paper

yellow construction paper for sun

red and yellow construction paper for alternating sun rays

broad red felt-tip marker for bulletin board title and diver

Directions:

    1. Cover the bulletin board with the orange background paper.

    2. Cut out a large circle from the yellow construction paper.

    3. Alternate large and small triangles of red and yellow construction paper around the sun. (Cut square pieces of paper on the diagonal.)

    4. Staple the sun and rays onto the backed bulletin board.

    5. Project the bulletin board design onto the sun already attached to the board. Outline the swimmer after the image has been projected diagonally across the sun. Fill in with a red marker.

    6. Write the title across the bottom of the board with a red marker.

TEACHING UNITS

CARRYOVER ACTIVITIES

The lessons in this unit reinforce survival skills. Since summer is a time when students have more opportunity to use these skills, now is the time to reinforce them.

Objective:

At the conclusion of this unit, students will:

- Be able to read a train or bus schedule.
- Be able to use the card catalog in the library to find books.

Summer Waves

Dive Into Summer!

- Be able to establish the difference between fact and fiction in advertisements.
- Be exposed to the need for banking and the use of deposit slips, withdrawal slips, checks, and loan applications.
- Be able to read a simple map for his or her own use.
- Be able to read a movie or TV schedule for a purpose.

Reading Train Schedules (Advanced)

Materials:

copies of the two train schedules

"Their Schedule" worksheet for each student

opaque projector

Preparation:

1. Copy the train schedules on pages 407–408 to use with the opaque projector.
2. Make a copy of the worksheet (see page 409) for each student.
3. Set up the opaque projector near an appropriate wall or screen.

Directions:

1. Introduce the lesson by asking how many students have gone on a train or bus.
2. Ask how they knew when to catch the train or bus. (Usually, their parents told them.)
3. Explain that they are going to learn how to read a schedule so they can find out for themselves when and where trains and buses run.
4. Project the schedules onto the wall or screen.
5. Distribute the worksheets.
6. Read the first question on the worksheet. Use the schedule to show the students how you found the answer.
7. Be sure the students are able to answer the questions on their own.
8. Let the students finish the worksheet independently.

Reinforcement Activity:

Refer to "Learning Centers" and have your students do assignment 1.

How to Use the Card Catalog
at the Library (Intermediate-Advanced)

Materials:

the Bookworm poster of catalog cards

worksheet for each student

large sheet of posterboard

broad felt-tip markers

LITTLE ENGINE TRAIN SCHEDULE

Westbound–From Merryville

Merryville	Happytown	Glad City	Toyland	Candy Hill	Balloon Heights
12 30	12 43	1 10	---	---	---
5 55	6 08	6 34	---	---	---
6 30	6 44	7 12	---	---	---
7 02	7 14	7 46	7 49	7 52	7 59
7 25	7 38	8 00	---	---	---
7 30	7 44	8 15	---	---	---
7 45	7 58	8 20	---	---	---
8 00	8 14	8 44	---	---	---
8 17	8 31	9 05	9 09	9 17	9 22
8 35	8 48	9 15	---	---	---
9 00	9 13	9 40	---	---	---
9 30	9 43	10 13	10 16	10 19	10 23
10 00	10 13	10 39	---	---	---
10 30	10 43	11 13	11 16	11 19	11 23
11 00	11 13	11 39	---	---	---
11 30	11 43	12 13	12 16	12 19	12 23
12 00	12 13	12 39	---	---	---
12 30	12 43	1 13	1 16	1 19	1 23
1 00	1 13	1 39	---	---	---
1 30	1 43	2 13	2 16	2 19	2 23
2 00	2 13	2 39	---	---	---
2 30	2 43	3 13	3 16	3 19	3 23
3 00	3 13	3 40	---	---	---
3 30	3 43	4 10	4 14	4 19	4 23
3 45	3 58	4 14	---	---	---
4 00	4 13	4 35	---	---	---
4 10	4 23	4 53	---	---	---
4 26	4 39	4 58	---	5 07	5 11
4 29	4 42	5 05	---	---	---
4 40	4 53	5 12	---	---	---
4 46	5 00	5 21	5 24	5 28	5 32
4 50	5 03	5 24	---	---	---
4 52	5 05	5 27	---	---	---
5 00	5 13	5 35	5 38	5 42	5 46
5 10	5 23	5 52	---	---	---
5 15	5 28	5 48	---	---	---
5 22	5 36	5 55	6 00	6 04	6 08
5 25	5 38	6 04	---	---	---
5 35	---	---	6 12	6 15	6 19
5 41	5 54	6 14	---	---	---

LITTLE ENGINE TRAIN SCHEDULE

Eastbound–To Merryville

DAILY EXCEPT SAT., SUN., & MAJOR HOLIDAYS

Balloon Heights	Candy Hill	Toyland	Glad City	Happytown	Merryville
---	---	---	5 39	6 08	6 21
---	---	---	6 14	6 41	6 54
6 32	6 36	6 40	6 44	7 01	7 13
---	---	---	6 50	7 05	7 18
---	---	---	6 55	7 23	7 36
7 05	7 09	7 13	---	7 30	7 43
---	---	---	7 10	7 32	7 45
7 11	7 15	7 19	---	7 38	7 52
---	---	---	7 26	7 43	7 56
---	---	---	7 34	7 56	8 10
7 28	7 32	7 36	---	7 58	8 12
---	---	---	7 44	8 05	8 18
---	---	---	7 50	8 16	8 29
---	---	---	7 52	---	8 22
---	---	---	8 07	8 28	8 40
7 59	8 03	8 07	8 12	8 30	8 42
---	---	---	8 14	8 42	8 56
---	---	---	8 18	8 38	8 52
---	---	---	8 24	8 48	9 01
8 25	---	---	---	8 50	9 02
---	---	---	8 37	---	9 05
---	---	---	8 50	9 14	9 27
---	---	---	9 09	9 37	9 50
9 13	9 17	9 20	9 25	9 40	9 53
---	---	---	9 30	9 58	10 13
---	---	---	9 35	9 52	10 05
---	---	---	9 58	10 26	10 39
---	---	---	10 28	10 56	11 09
10 45	10 49	10 52	10 58	11 26	11 39
---	---	---	11 30	11 56	12 09
11 45	11 49	11 52	11 58	12 26	12 39
---	---	---	12 28	12 54	1 07
12 45	12 49	12 52	12 58	1 26	1 39
---	---	---	1 28	1 54	2 07
1 45	1 49	1 52	1 58	2 26	2 39
---	---	---	2 28	2 56	3 09
2 45	2 49	2 52	2 58	3 26	3 39
---	---	---	3 28	3 56	4 09
---	---	---	3 58	4 26	4 39
---	---	---	4 29	4 44	4 58
4 15	4 19	4 22	4 30	4 58	5 11
---	---	---	5 01	5 17	5 31
---	---	---	5 10	5 38	5 52
5 03	5 09	5 12	5 15	5 40	5 54

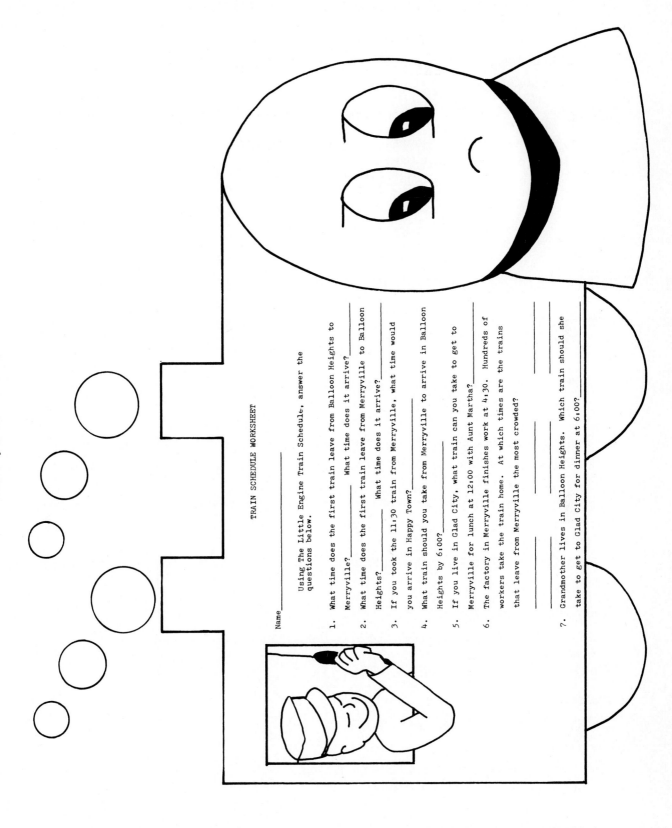

TRAIN SCHEDULE WORKSHEET

Name _____

Using The Little Engine Train Schedule, answer the
questions below.

1. What time does the first train leave from Balloon Heights to
    Merryville? _____ What time does it arrive? _____

2. What time does the first train leave from Merryville to Balloon
    Heights? _____ What time does it arrive? _____

3. If you took the 11:30 train from Merryville, what time would
    you arrive in Happy Town? _____

4. What train should you take from Merryville to arrive in Balloon
    Heights by 6:00? _____

5. If you live in Glad City, what train can you take to get to
    Merryville for lunch at 12:00 with Aunt Martha? _____

6. The factory in Merryville finishes work at 4:30. Hundreds of
    workers take the train home. At which times are the trains
    that leave from Merryville the most crowded?
    _____ _____

7. Grandmother lives in Balloon Heights. Which train should she
    take to get to Glad City for dinner at 6:00? _____

Preparation:

   1. Copy the Bookworm poster on page 411 onto the posterboard.

   2. Make a copy of the worksheet (see page 412) for each student.

   3. Arrange for a visit to the school library during the lesson.

Directions:

   1. Discuss with the students about the availability of the public library for getting books to read during the summer.

   2. List on the board the following kinds of books.

mystery	joke books
fiction	picture books
adventure	science books
science fiction	art books
biographies	textbooks
	reference books

   3. Ask the students how they would find a particular kind of book in the library.

   4. Call their attention to the poster of the catalog cards.

   5. Explain that a book can be found in 3 different ways: by looking up (1) the author, (2) the title of the book, or (3) the subject, depending upon what information is known.

   6. Discuss with the students when they would use each type of card.

   7. Point out where the title, author, publisher, and subject matter are found on each card.

   8. Take the group to the school library to see an actual card catalog and its cards.

   9. Distribute the worksheets. Allow the students to complete the worksheets independently.

   10. Encourage each student to find a book by looking for it in the school library card catalog.

Reinforcement Activity:

   Refer to "Learning Centers" and have your students do assignment 2.

Advertising: Fact or Opinion

Materials:

   newspaper advertisements
   Yellow Pages directory
   "Crazy Claims" worksheet for each student
   black marker
   clear Con-Tact paper
   tape

BOOKWORM STORES AWAY BOOKS

SUBJECT

TRAINS

JE Potter, Marian
THE LITTLE RED CABOOSE.
Racine, Wisconsin, Weston Publishing
Co, Inc. (1953.)

TITLE

THE LITTLE RED CABOOSE

JE Potter, Marian
THE LITTLE RED CABOOSE.
Racine, Wisconsin, Weston
Publishing Co, Inc. (1953.)

AUTHOR

JE Potter, Marian
THE LITTLE RED CABOOSE.
Racine, Wisconsin, Weston Publishing
Co., In. (1953.)

LIBRARY CARD CATALOG WORKSHEET

Name _____

```
        Trains
  J E   Potter, Marian
        The Little Red Caboose. Racine,
        Wisconsin, Weston Publishing Co.,
        Inc. (1953)
```

Directions: Use the above information to answer the following questions:

1. What is the title of the book? _____

_____

2. Who is the author? _____

_____

3. What is the subject of the book? _____

_____

4. Who is the publisher of the book? _____

_____

5. Which letter drawer would you look in if you were finding the author card? _____

6. Which letter drawer would you look in if you were looking for the book title? _____

7. Which letter drawer would you look in if you were looking for the subject? _____

8. Name the title and the author of the book you are going to look for in the library. _____

_____

_____

_____

_____

_____

_____

Preparation:

1. Find newspaper and directory advertisements that have obvious exaggerations.
2. Cover the advertisements with clear Con-Tact paper.
3. Copy the worksheet (see page 414) for each student.

Directions:

1. Temporarily tape the ads onto the table or chalkboard, wherever they are most easily seen by the students.
2. Talk about "fact" and "opinion." Give examples of each one, such as:

"Today is Tuesday. Is that a fact or an opinion?"

"Today is the most beautiful day of the year. Is that a fact or an opinion?

3. Read one of the ads (alternate between the newspaper and Yellow Pages) and decide whether each statement is a fact or an opinion.
4. Write each opinion statement on the board. Next to it, write the same sentence in a factual way.
5. Have each student take a turn deciding between fact and opinion.
6. Distribute the worksheets. Explain to the students that they will independently be able to re-write advertising to make it more factual.

Reinforcement Activity:

Refer to "Learning Centers" and have your students do assignment 3.

Banking Skills

Materials:

deposit slips from the bank
withdrawal slips from the bank
blank check from the bank
worksheets for each student
scissors

Preparation:

1. If possible, try to arrange a field trip visit to a bank.
2. Borrow enough withdrawal and deposit slips from the bank so each student has one to see.
3. Copy the worksheet on page 415 for each student.

Directions:

1. After the visit to the bank, discuss all the services a bank can offer a person:

checking accounts
savings accounts
loans for houses, cars, etc.

2. Distribute a banking worksheet to each student. Show actual samples of the various banking slips and a blank check.

CRAZY CLAIMS

Name _____

Read the ads. List the claims in each ad that are not true.

The Best Talking Fish in the Whole World!
Holds the records for talking the most.
Will announce when it is time for school.
Why not buy one yesterday.

_____
_____
_____
_____
_____
_____
_____

The World's Greatest Singing Dog!
Sings for his supper.
Will sing for your supper too!
Supplies limited.

_____
_____
_____
_____
_____
_____

The World's fastest Swimming Cat!
Stays dry in water.
Will help you become the fastest swimmer in the world.
One to a customer.

_____
_____
_____
_____
_____
_____

The Resource Room Bank

Number_____

DATE_____ 19___

PAY TO THE ORDER OF_____

For *Play Only*_____

DEPOSITS

DATE_____ 19___

Deposited in

The Resource Room Bank

	DOLLARS	CENTS
CASH		
List CHECKS Here		
TOTAL		

SAVINGS WITHDRAWAL

DATE:_____

_____ DOLLARS

ACCOUNT NUMBER

The Resource Room Bank

SIGNATURE_____

ADDRESS_____

The Resource Room Bank

Number_____

DATE_____ 19___

PAY TO THE ORDER OF_____

For *Play Only*_____

DEPOSITS

DATE_____ 19___

Deposited in

The Resource Room Bank

	DOLLARS	CENTS
CASH		
List CHECKS Here		
TOTAL		

SAVINGS WITHDRAWAL

DATE:_____

_____ DOLLARS

ACCOUNT NUMBER

The Resource Room Bank

SIGNATURE_____

ADDRESS_____

3. Ask if anyone knows what it is and why it would be used.

4. Once the reasons for making a deposit and withdrawal are ascertained, take each line of the deposit slip on the worksheet step by step and have the students fill them out.

5. Let students practice doing this a few times.

6. The concept must be explained to the students that a withdrawal can only be made if they have previously put money in the bank. The only way they can take money out of a bank, if they haven't first put it in, is if they get a loan. (Loan applications will be filled out at Learning Center 4.)

NOTE: A good reinforcement to this lesson is to have a classroom bank where the students earn play money for work done or for good behavior. This money can be deposited in the classroom bank and kept track of in a mock bank book for each child.

7. Allow students to take turns being bank tellers and customers when they have filled out the appropriate slips. Play money can be used as well.

Reinforcement Activity:

Refer to "Learning Centers" and have your students do assignment 4.

Map Reading

Materials:

copies of the 3 worksheets for each student
"Amusement Park" map
large school or local map
crayons
opaque projector
glue

Preparation:

1. Copy page 418 for each student.
2. Prepare a large school or local map for display.
3. Project the large "Amusement Park" map (see page 421) onto a wall or screen.

Directions:

1. Discuss the reasons why a person needs to be able to read a map. Suggestions are:

> To find a store in a shopping center.
> To find your way in an amusement park.
> To locate animals in a zoo.
> To find a specific street in town.

2. Project the "Amusement Park" map using an opaque projector.
3. Ask the students to identify the kind of map shown. (Amusement Park)
4. Call upon students to mention the different kinds of places shown on the map. Have them guess what kinds of rides and amusements these might be.

5. Distribute the "Amusement Park Worksheet." Beginning with the first question on the worksheet, show the students how to find the individual places on the map. For instance:

   a. In which direction would you go to get to Eerie Mountain from the entrance? (North)

   b. From Eerie Mountain, in which direction do you go to get to The Haunted House? (Northeast)

   c. How many gates do you pass to get to E.T.'s house from The Haunted House? (4)

   d. What is the quickest way to get to Dunk the Clown from E.T.'s house? (Row across the lake)

   e. How much time do you need at the Amusement Park to see everything if each ride has a line that lasts about 5 minutes before getting on the ride? Be sure to add time for refreshments and boating. (More than 2 hours)

   f. What is your favorite ride?

Reinforcement Activity:

Refer to "Learning Centers" and have your students do assignment 5.

Movie Guide

Materials:

index card for each student

"Movie Guide Worksheet" for each student

movie guide from a local newspaper

scissors

clear Con-Tact paper

Preparation:

1. Copy the "Movie Guide Worksheet" (see page 423) and the local movie guide for each student.

2. Write the rating codes for movies on the chalkboard:

G	= general rating
PG (also PG-13)	= parental guidance needed
R	= restricted audience (no children)
X	= out of bounds for children and some adults

3. Cut out the local movie guide and cover it with clear Con-Tact paper. Display it in a prominent place.

Directions:

1. Ask, "How many of you go to the movies?"

2. Ask, "How do you find out what is playing on a particular day?"

AMUSEMENT PARK WORKSHEET

Name _____

Fill in the answers to the questions about the Amusement Park
Map.

1. In which direction would you go to get to Eerie Mountain from the entrance? _____

_____

2. From Eerie Mountain, in which direction do you go to get to The Haunted House?

_____

3. How many gates do you pass to get to E.T.'s house from The Haunted House? ____

4. What is the quickest way to get to Dunk the Clown from E.T.'s House? _____

_____

5. How much time do you need at the Amusement Park to see everything if each ride
takes about 5 minutes, and each ride has a line that lasts about 5 minutes before getting on the ride? Be sure to add time for refreshments and boating.

_____

6. What is your favorite ride? _____

Directions: Cut out each sticker. Glue it onto a logical spot on the map. Don't forget to name your park.

Design-A-Park

Name

THE

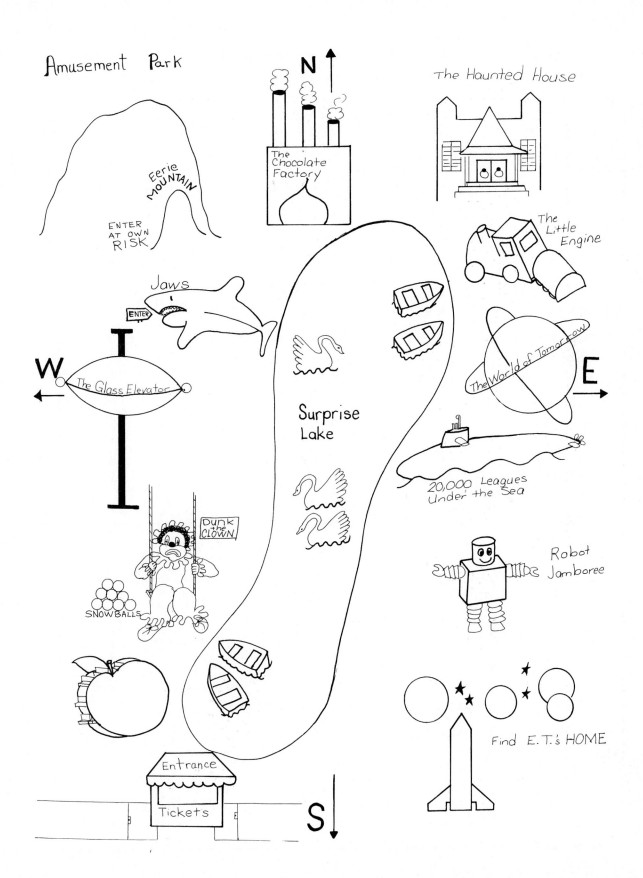

Amusement Park

N

The Chocolate Factory

The Haunted House

Eerie MOUNTAIN

ENTER AT OWN RISK

The Little Engine

Jaws

ENTER

The World of Tomorrow

W

E

The Glass Elevator

Surprise Lake

20,000 Leagues Under the Sea

Dunk the CLOWN

SNOWBALLS

Robot Jamboree

Find E.T.'s HOME

Entrance

Tickets

S

3. Ask, "How do you find out the correct time to go?"

4. Direct the students' attention to the movie guide section of the newspaper.

5. Show them where the ratings, the times, and the days are placed.

6. Ask if anyone knows what movie ratings are. Show them the ratings on the "Movie Guide Worksheet." For each rating, discuss for whom the movies would be appropriate. For instance, the G-rated movies, which admit all ages, would be *Mary Poppins* and *Charlie and the Chocolate Factory.* Follow the same procedure for the remaining codes.

7. Distribute the "Movie Guide Worksheet" and an index card to each student.

8. Using the index cards as markers, discuss each listing, noting the times the movie is playing and the rating. (See the illustration.)

9. Discuss for whom the different ratings might be appropriate.

10. Allow the students to complete the worksheet independently.

Reinforcement Activity:

Refer to "Learning Centers" and have your students do assignment 6.

LEARNING CENTERS

Carryover skills are reinforced in this month's learning center activities. The use of following directions, reading comprehension, and reasoning skills are all applied in the survival skills activities.

Summer vacation brings with it more free time to put into practical use many of the skills learned in school. This month's activities give the students practice in using survival skills in probable situations.

(1) ALL ABOARD!
(INTERMEDIATE-ADVANCED)

Materials:

"Little Engine" train schedules (see the "Teaching Unit")

large index cards

felt-tip marker

"All Aboard" worksheet for each student

large train schedule or several small ones for the center's backdrop

Preparation:

1. Write a task on each index card. (See the samples.)

MOVIE GUIDE WORKSHEET

Name _____

Directions: Give a rating to the following films. Read the descriptions
carefully and choose one of the standard ratings.

G   = General audience (children admitted).

PG (also PG-13) = All ages admitted. Parental guidance needed.

R   = Under 18 requires accompanying parent.

X   = No one under 18 admitted.

THE MONSTER FROM THE DEEP – A film of scary cartoon characters with a happy ending.

Rating: _____

THE HAPPY CLOWN – A happy film about a circus. Lots of singing and dancing.

Rating: _____

THE FORBIDDEN – An adult movie with violence and serious situations.

Rating: _____

MURDER AT MIDNIGHT – A funny mystery with James Bond. Small children may be scared.

Rating: _____

FAMILY FUN – A family movie about fun on vacation. Rating: _____

DISNEY'S DANCING DWARF – A Walt Disney cartoon about a dancing dwarf and his forest

family. Rating: _____

DISASTER IN DENMARK – A disaster movie about dangerous mountain climbing. Gory

and scary. Rating: _____

SPACE SHUTTLE ADVENTURE – An adventure movie with tense situations.

Rating: _____

ROCK AND ROLL – A loud and lively musical. Parents needed for small children.

Rating: _____

SEA ADVENTURES – A documentary film about the world beneath the sea.

Rating: _____

```
ALL ABOARD!

Task 1

You have an appointment in Happytown at 9:00 a.m. You live in Candy
Hill. What train should you take? _____

In order to get to Happytown by 8:30 a.m. to make a bank deposit, which
train would you take? _____
```

```
ALL ABOARD!

Task 2

Gordon lives in Merryville. He travels to Toyland everyday, where he
works at the Spinning Top Factory. The factory whistle blows at 8:00
a.m. Which train must he take if it is a 10-minute walk to the factory
from the train station? _____
```

```
ALL ABOARD!

Task 3

Miss Solomon's third grade class is going to the circus in Balloon Heights.
The first act begins at 2:45 p.m. Which train must the class take from
Glad City? _____

How much time will they have to get settled before the circus begins?
_____
```

```
ALL ABOARD!

Task 4

Looking at the train schedules, which train do you think is usually the
most crowded? _____

Which train do you think is usually the least crowded? _____
```

2. Copy a worksheet (see page 425) for each student.

3. Copy the "Little Engine" train schedules for each student or use the two schedules as one large poster.

4. Use the preprinted schedule(s) as the backdrop of the center.

5. Write the directions on an index card.

Name _____

ALL ABOARD!

Write your answers to the task card questions
on the lines provided.

TASK 1

_____

_____

_____

TASK 2

_____

_____

_____

TASK 3

_____

_____

_____

TASK 4

_____

_____

_____

Directions Card:

```
┌─────────────────────────────────────────────────┐
│               ALL ABOARD!                        │
│   1.  Read one task card at a time.              │
│   2.  Think about the solutions carefully.       │
│   3.  Write your answers on the worksheet.       │
│   4.  Have your work checked by the teacher.     │
│                                                  │
└─────────────────────────────────────────────────┘
```

(2) CARD CATALOG
(INTERMEDIATE-ADVANCED)

Materials:

small box or basket

felt-tip marker

catalog card poster (see "Teaching Unit") for center backdrop and as a sample

3" × 5" index cards

"Card Catalog" worksheet for each student

Preparation:

1. Have the card catalog poster on display as both the backdrop and for reference.
2. Write the directions on an index card.
3. Copy the worksheet (see page 427) for each student.
4. Place the index cards in a small box or basket.

Directions Card:

```
┌─────────────────────────────────────────────────┐
│             LIBRARIAN FOR A DAY                  │
│   1.  You will make 3 catalog cards:             │
│                 One Author Card                  │
│                 One Title Card                   │
│                 One Subject Card                 │
│   2.  Use the information given on the worksheet. │
│   3.  Follow the form on the poster.             │
│   4.  Have your cards checked by the teacher.    │
│                                                  │
└─────────────────────────────────────────────────┘
```

CARD CATALOG WORKSHEET

Name _____

Directions: Complete each card below using the
following information.

Book Name: Where the Sidewalk Ends
Author: Shel Silverstein
Publisher: Harper and Row
Subject: A book of silly poems for children.
Number of pages: 164
Date of publication: 1974

```
Title
```

```
Author
```

```
Subject
```

(3) AD MAN
(PRIMARY-ADVANCED)

Materials:

"Design an Ad" worksheet for each student

newspaper ads as backdrop

Yellow Pages directory

variety of felt-tip markers

index card

pencils

can or jar

Preparation:

1. Affix colorful advertisements as the backdrop.
2. Copy the worksheet (see page 429) for each student.
3. Write the directions on an index card.
4. Place the felt-tip markers in a can or jar holder.

Directions Card:

> DESIGN AN AD
> 1. Read the facts on the worksheet carefully.
> 2. Using the facts, make up your own appealing ad.
> 3. You may exaggerate for purposes of selling your product.
> 4. Use as many colors as needed.
> 5. Have your work checked by the teacher.

(4) FEDERAL RESOURCE BANK
(INTERMEDIATE-ADVANCED)

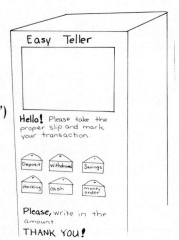

Materials:

refrigerator box for bank

loan application worksheet for each student

copy of withdrawal and deposit worksheets (see "Teaching Unit")

envelopes to hold deposit slips, etc.

index card

sharp cutting edge

felt-tip markers (narrow and broad)

authentic bank slips to use as a backdrop

stapler

DESIGN AN AD

Name _____

Directions: Using the following information, design an appealing advertisement. Choose only one item to advertise.

FACTS: House for Sale. 100 years old, bad repair, leaky roof, broken furnace, broken windows, old kitchen, big lot (2 acres), 12 rooms. Near schools and railroad. Across the street from a piano factory. $1,000,000.

FACTS: Car for Sale. 1 year old. 20,000 miles. Has air conditioning, electric windows, automatic transmission, leather seats. Has new motor, new paint job. Color: Red. $10,000.

FACTS: Dress for Sale. Designer dress, off the shoulder design, wool material. Colors: Black, white or red. Sizes: 2–12.

Preparation:

1. Following the illustration, create a bank counter from a refrigerator box. (NOTE: Broad felt-tip markers and a sharp cutting edge work best.)

2. Write the directions on an index card.

3. Copy the worksheet (see page 431) for each student, place them in an envelope, and staple onto the refrigerator box.

4. Place withdrawal and deposit slips in separate envelopes and staple onto the refrigerator box. (NOTE: Shallow boxes can be used on a tabletop if preferred.)

Directions Card:

FEDERAL RESOURCE BANK

1. Fill out a loan application worksheet as if you were an adult.

2. Choose one other bank transaction to write out.

3. Have your work checked by the teacher.

---

(5) MAP DESIGNING
(PRIMARY-ADVANCED)

Materials:

amusement park worksheets for each student (see "Teaching Unit")
crayons
glue
index card
marker

Preparation:

1. Copy the worksheets for each student.

2. Write the directions on an index card.

Directions Card:

MAP DESIGN

1. You are going to design your own amusement park.

2. Cut out the circles on the first worksheet.

3. Decide where you think each place should go.

4. Glue it on that spot on the second worksheet.

5. You may color your park when finished.

FEDERAL RESOURCE BANK
LOAN APPLICATION

Name _____

Address _____

_____

Age _____

Place of birth _____

Are you a U.S. citizen? _____

If not, of what country are you a citizen? _____

Do you own your home? _____

How long have you lived at your current address? _____

Are you employed? _____

Where? _____

How long have you worked there? _____

What is your salary? _____

What are you requesting a loan for? _____

_____

How much money are you requesting? _____

How long will you need to pay it back? _____

Will someone co-sign with you? _____

If so, who? _____

_____

I swear that the above information is true to the best of my knowledge.

Signed _____

(6) ENTERTAINMENT GUIDE

Materials:

copy of a TV programming guide
TV advertisements to use as the backdrop
"TV Programs" worksheet for each student
index cards
marker
holder

Preparation:

1. Conduct a lesson on reading a TV programming guide.
2. Copy the worksheet (see page 433) for each student.
3. Write the directions on an index card.
4. Place index cards in a holder to use as markers.

Directions Card:

```
┌────────────────────────────────────────────────────┐
│                    TV PROGRAMS                       │
│  1. Using the TV program schedule, answer the        │
│  questions on the worksheet.                         │
│  2. Use an index card as a marker.                   │
│  3. Have your work checked by the teacher.           │
└────────────────────────────────────────────────────┘
```

MATERIALS OF THE MONTH

Materials that are seen as a great help during the school year suddenly become a huge problem when they have to be packed up and put away for the summer. The space available for storage seems minute in comparison to the volume of goods that needs to be put away before the room can be closed.

There is the temptation, in the haste of getting ready for summer vacation, to throw things haphazardly into drawers, onto shelves, into boxes . . . anywhere to get them put away. But when the start of the new school year rolls around, there will be a price to be paid for this haste. Things will not be easily located and setting up the room will be that much more difficult.

Use folders to store and label ditto masters for forms and other important papers. A file cabinet is an invaluable aid to being organized. In it can be kept leftover worksheets, test booklets, and folders about the students. All those odds and ends that shouldn't be thrown out, but you don't know where to put can often be placed in a folder.

Corrugated boxes either designed purposely for classroom use or found in supermarkets make excellent storage containers. Use broad felt-tip markers to label, and list as

Name _____

TV PROGRAMS

MORNING

5:00 (4) Marsha Moore's Talk Show	8:30 (2) Which Way to Go?
5:05 (9) News	(4) Music Encore
5:30 (4) To Be Announced	(7) Discover Your World
(6) Movie Closeup	9:00 (2) Good Morning!
6:00 (4) Lucille's Roundup	(4) For Teens Only
(8) Eye on Your State	(5) Wondering
(9) News	(6) Animal Adventures
6:20 (5) News	(8) Movie of the Morning
6:30 (2) Children's World	9:30 (4) Celebrity Showing
(4) Bobby's Show	(5) Movie
(5) Timeout for Fun	(7) African Safari
(7) News	10:00 (4) Cartoons
7:00 (2) Captain's Cartoons	(7) Cartoons
(4) Adventure Journey	10:20 (9) For Kids Only
(7) This Morning's Faith	10:30 (2) Today's Courts
7:30 (4) Lucille's Roundup	(4) Movie
(7) Here's to Life	11:00 (2) Makers of News
(9) To Be Announced	(7) Today's Government
8:00 (2) Signs of the Times	11:30 (5) Movie
(4) Bobby's Show	(9) The World's Zoos
(7) Movie Closeup	

DIRECTIONS: Answer the following questions using the above TV programming guide.

1. Will you be awake in time to watch Marsha Moore's Talk Show? _____

2. For what part of the day is this guide used? _____

3. What are the first and last times listed in this guide? _____

4. What program begins at 6:20 _____

5. What time is Timeout for Fun on? _____ Which channel? _____

6. When can you watch Adventure Journey? _____

7. How long does Adventure Journey last? _____

8. How many times is Bobby's Show shown _____

9. What time should you get up to watch Captain's Cartoons? _____

10. What time is For Kids Only on? _____ Which channel? _____

many items on the side as you will need to know in September. If necessary, add additional sheets of paper and tape or staple on the side.

For those rooms where learning centers are utilized, place the materials used at individual centers in one box. It is helpful if the boxes can be on hand to pack throughout the year. In that way, when the learning center materials are changed, the old ones can be stored in the boxes for the next year. By the end of the year, they are ready to be closed, labeled and stored. Examples of how the boxes might be labeled are:

SOCIAL STUDIES: map skills, history, geography

HANDWRITING: gross motor, visual discrimination dittos, printing upper and lower case, script letters—individual

COMPREHENSION: paperback books with dittos, cassette tapes and worksheets, play scripts, fast steps for backdrop

AUDITORY: musical tapes, DLM tapes, buzzer board, dittos

READING: Palo Alto series plus workbooks, 3-D letters, Peabody Language Kit I

Heavy duty plastic bags with ziplock tops are excellent storage units for cassettes and small books. By attaching a metal clip or clothespin, they can be stored on a clothesline in the closet. They are easy to label and find when you need them.

Shoeboxes are also excellent storage containers for small items. They store easily and can be labeled. They are excellent to use for blocks, loose crayons, small toys, chalk, and puzzle pieces.

REMEMBER: Store everything with the thought in mind of how retrievable it will be in the fall. This makes the job of running a program much easier and less time consuming if the materials are at your fingertips.

FREE FOR THE ASKING

Rainbow Toy Katcher

Made of colorful netting with a sewn-on rick-rack hanger, these bags are safe for children to use. You get a free sample ($1.00 for postage and handling which is refundable with the first order) plus a descriptive materials order form with color samples. Send $1 to:

Rainbow Toy Katcher
Dept. FB, P.O. Box 54
Vandalia, OH 45377

Otto Otter for Safe Water

This 16-page coloring book features Otto the Otter, who tells how to enjoy water safety in rhyme. *Otto in Espanol* is also available. Published by the Department of the Interior and the Bureau of Reclamation, teachers can order up to 50 copies. Send a postcard to:

Otto for Water Safety
Bureau of Reclamation
Attn.: D-922
P.O. Box 25007
Denver, CO 80225-0007

Basketball Freebies

Freebies magazine researched the National Basketball Association to find out what each team is offering to its fans free for the asking. The following is taken from their October 1982 issue. Please caution the students to be clear about what they are requesting. Send postcards to the following:

Team/Address	*Items Available*
Atlanta Hawks 100 Techwood Dr., N.W. Atlanta, GA 30303	Schedule Bumper Sticker Novelty List
Denver Nuggets Box 4286 Denver, CO 80204	Schedule Decals Photos (sometimes)
Detroit Pistons Pontiac Silverdome Pontiac, MI 48057	Schedule Souvenir List
Golden State Warriors Oakland Coliseum Arena Oakland, CA 94621	Team Photos Schedule Order Form
Houston Rockets The Summit 10 Greenway Plaza East Houston, TX 77046	Bumper Sticker Schedule
Indiana Pacers Public Relations Dept. 920 Circle Tower Indianapolis, IN 46204	Roster Schedule Souvenir Price List
Kansas City Kings 1800 Genesee, Suite 101 Kansas City, MO 64102	Send SASE Postcard (price list) Schedule Picture Postcard
Los Angeles Lakers Mail Order Concessionaire The Forum Box 10 Inglewood, CA 90306	Price List Schedule
Milwaukee Bucks 901 N. 4th Street Milwaukee, WI 53203	Send SASE Specify individual items: Decal Schedule Price list of novelty items

Team/Address	Items Available
New Jersey Nets Byrne Arena 185 E. Union East Rutherford, NJ 07073	Souvenir Catalog Stickers Schedule Autograph Page Souvenir List
New York Knickerbockers Public Relations Dept. Madison Square Garden 4 Pennsylvania Plaza New York, NY 10001	Send SASE Bumper Sticker Team Photos (as available) Decal Schedule
Phoenix Suns Box 1369 Phoenix, AZ 85001	Souvenir List Schedule
Portland Trail Blazers 700 N.E. Multnomah Street Lloyd Building Portland, OR 97232	OREGON OR SW WASHINGTON RESIDENTS ONLY Sticker Schedule
San Antonio Spurs Hemisfair Arena Box 530 San Antonio, TX 78292	Bumper Sticker Schedule
Washington Bullets Capital Centre Landover, MD 20786	Schedule

GOOD BUYS

The following materials are recommended to supplement the lessons on carryover skills presented this month.

Survival Skills

This consists of 6 cassettes, 6 filmstrips, and accompanying worksheets. Presented are varied experiences with a shopping center map, program guide, clothing label information, want ads, etc. Good for grades 4–6. Contact:

> Pied Piper Productions
> P.O. Box 320
> Verdugo City, CA 91046

Counting Money

The kit includes five workbooks on counting money. Each book offers 76 reproducible worksheets. Each book sells for under $5. Write to:

> Dormac Inc.
> P.O. Box 1699
> Beaverton, OR 97075

Forms

This work-a-text contains 13 current real job-related, bank-related and consumer related forms presented in increasing order of difficulty. The reading level is 4.0. The text is 80 pages and sells for under $5. It is available from Fearon.

Finding a Job

This work-a-text with 30 student activity sheets gives direct experience in job finding, from job search to interview. Telephone book reading and newspaper want ads are included. The reading level is 3.0 Consisting of 80 pages, it sells for under $5. It is available through Fearon.

Keeping a Job

This work-a-text has topics including developing a positive self image, discovering and carrying out job duties, and getting along with others. With a 3.0 reading level, this 80-page text sells for under $5. It is available through Fearon.

Checking Account

This work-a-text offers practice in opening and maintaining a checking account. Walk-through examples and activity sheets with simulated bank forms, signature cards, deposit slips, etc., are included. With a 4.0 reading level, it is an excellent companion for the banking learning center. 80 pages long, it sells for under $15. Write to:

> Fearon Education–Pitman Learning
> 6 Davis Drive
> Belmont, CA 94002

Badge-a-Minit

This small hand press badge maker personalizes badges that can be used for rewards and skill reinforcements. The starter kit sells for under $30. Contact:

> Badge-a-Minit Ltd.
> Dept. E832
> Box 618
> Civic Industrial Park
> LaSalle, IL 61301

PROFESSIONAL RESPONSIBILITIES

CLASS REUNION

"I wonder what ever happened to . . ." conversations are heard from time to time whenever teachers gather. All teachers have experienced thinking and wondering about past students. Since so much emotional and physical energy goes into teaching youngsters, it is often a very rewarding experience to be able to keep track of how past students are doing. Having a class reunion from time to time provides this opportunity.

DATE: _____

PLACE: _____

TIME: _____

Fold 1

Fold 2

Come to a
Reunion

Keep a log of names and current addresses. A special book (like a bound guest book) set aside exclusively for graduating students to sign their names and addresses is a good way to do this. The students also feel very special when they are allowed to sign it. It is an additional graduating honor! Of course, the list will need to be updated so keep your ears open for news of moving families, etc.

Place: Having the reunion in the classroom allows the students to see their "old stomping ground." If your room is in a new location, don't fret because the material and room design are probably very similar.

Time: After school hours on a school day like 4–6 p.m. usually yields the largest turnout. An early evening time, like 7–9 p.m., is also good if arrangements can be made to have the building open in the evening. (Many schools have adult classes or community sporting events in the evenings. Check on which nights the building is already open before choosing a date.)

Invitations: Invite as many past students as there is space. Not all students will attend. Generally, as the students get older, their attendance drops. Therefore, a large number of invitations can be safely sent. Many students who won't attend the reunion will at least drop a note (a chance to see their handwriting!) or call. Be sure to put R.S.V.P. on the invitation. (See the invitation on page 438.)

All teachers, administrators, secretaries, and other staff members in the school should be included on the guest list if possible. Most have had contact with your students and will add to the enjoyment of the reunion. Besides, being able to discuss how well the individual students are doing since they left your school is much more fun if everyone is there. The students will be thrilled to see old friends, teachers, and other school-related personnel.

Refreshments: Simple refreshments, like cookies and lemonade or brownies and tea, are always well received. Cookies or cakes that are prepared by current students make a big hit. A card left by the dish of goodies which says "Have a Happy Reunion" and signed by each of the students who helped to make the refreshments and/or decorations adds to the festivities.

PROFESSIONAL RESOURCE BOOKS

Burback, Harold. *Mainstreaming: A Book of Readings and Resources for the Classroom Teacher.* (Dubuque, IA: Kendall/Hunt, 1980)

Clure, Beth. *Why Didn't I Think of That?* (Glendale, CA: Bowmar, 1971)

Faas, Larry A. *Children with Learning Problems: A Handbook for Teachers.* (Boston: Houghton Mifflin, 1980)

Hammill, Donald, and Nettie Bartel. *Teaching Children with Learning and Behavior Problems.* (Boston: Allyn and Bacon, Inc., 1978)

Krulik, Stephen, and Jesse A. Rudnick. *Problem Solving: A Handbook for Teachers.* (Boston: Allyn and Bacon, Inc., 1980)

Longhurst, Thomas M. *Functional Language Intervention.* (Edison, NJ: MSS Information Corp., 1974)

Schlassberg, Edwin, and John Brockman. *The Pocket Calculator Game, Book #2.* (New York: William Morrow and Co., 1977)

TIP OF THE MONTH

SAYING GOODBYE

The end of the school year is a time of much added responsibility and plain hard labor. Final reports, room inventories, end-of-the-year report cards, meeting new parents for next year, final disposition meetings on this year's students, and packing up what seems like two tons of books and materials to fit into a very small space of closet(s), are all part of the last few weeks of school. Add to this burden, a regular schedule of teaching as well as the end-of-the-year parties and PTA teas and you often have a frazzled teacher.

With all the responsibilities mentioned above, it is very easy not to respond to feelings of separation by the students as well as by yourself. Each year a number of students will be going into another school, either junior high or high school. Often, these students have been receiving special services for several years. Naturally, and hopefully, a relationship has developed between teacher and student. Leaving is both happy and sad. The leave-taking represents the student's progress, which has been the mutual goal of the student and the teacher. At the same time, it will probably be the last time you will see the graduating students. Even (and sometimes especially) those difficult students who posed the most troublesome challenges are difficult to say goodbye to.

The important thing is to recognize that separation is difficult for everyone. Even though the surface reactions are those of joy at leaving, the exiting students are usually scared and ambivalent about leaving. These feelings should be acknowledged and discussed.

An open discussion about the fears the students have about their new school is usually quite productive. Most children have a great need to share in the bravado of their peers at this time. The relief of being able to sit down with a small group of students and talk about their real feelings and dispel unfounded fears is most helpful.

You can easily initiate the discussion by openly saying, "Many students who are going to the middle school next year have expressed concern about it. How do you people feel?" If the students are reluctant to express their concerns, try to start them off. Try comments like, "The school seems so large that I'll bet some students are afraid of finding their classes on the first day." Eventually, the students will begin to open up and their concerns can be handled with reassurance, honesty, and a sense of humor. Those same anxious youngsters will leave this discussion much more relaxed. Just having the opportunity to say that they are frightened and to know that they are not alone in their feelings is tremendously helpful.

Having a little celebration on the students' last day of school when everyone has the opportunity to say goodbye is very important. If at all possible, invite them to come visit next year. Let them know that you will be happy to see them and that this is not a complete severing of the relationship. (Some teachers have class reunions each year for past students. See "Professional Responsibilities.") This is an excellent way to let students know that you are providing an opportunity to see them again.

For those returning students, wish them a good summer and assure them that you will spend the summer months thinking of new and wonderful ideas for next year. (Students' groans are the usual response to this idea!)

MODES FOR MAINSTREAMING

PREPARING PACKETS FOR SUMMER

Many parents and teachers are concerned about resource room students losing the momentum of their studies during the summer months. Some districts offer summer programs. Some parents seek out private tutors to work with their children throughout the summer.

Whether or not the above alternatives are available, sending home study packets is a useful activity. Students like the idea of having their own work to do at their leisure, parents are pleased that the student will continue to work on academics, and tutors can see the type of work that the student has been doing in your program.

The best place to get the material for these packets is from extra worksheets and dittos that have been saved throughout the year. Every teacher has a supply of "extras" which were not used over the year.

You can do this in several ways. Go through the file of extra worksheets and hand pick the appropriate worksheets for each student. A folded cover of construction paper can be used to house them with the appropriate student's name on the front.

Another approach is to have a "pick your packet day." Piles of worksheets can be placed on tables, hung from clip-on clothespins on a line across the room, or displayed in any number of other ways. Have each student make a folder for his or her papers. Then one by one the students can choose the worksheets they would like to have. A way to control the difficulty of worksheets being taken is to number them one, two or three. Primary-level students may only take number ones, intermediate-level students can take ones or twos, and advanced students can take only three. In this way, students will not end up taking worksheets that are too frustrating for them.

Further categorizing can be done by skills and similarly coded. Allowing students to take worksheets for a variety of skills that they may or may not need help with has educational merit. Also, the act of *their* choosing their own work can be more motivating for them.

It is generally a good idea to have a system for these packets to be returned to school for checking. This can be done through the mail or returned in total at the beginning of the next school year. In addition, an award of some kind should be given for returned work.

A FINAL WORD

In your enthusiasm to achieve the individual academic goals for each student, it is sometimes easy to forget the overall picture—the reason for education.

Certainly, you want to teach the student all the academics you can in the best possible ways for him or her to learn. This *Almanac* is filled with ideas to do just that. There are some unspoken goals, however, which are necessary to keep in mind.

Society needs caring, competent, and capable citizens who are able to make sound judgments for themselves and others. Yes, it is important to know how to read and write and add and subtract. These are essential. But equally, if not more important, is the need to develop the student's abilities in making decisions, being compassionate, becoming aware of the world around him or her, and in understanding himself or herself.

You, as a teacher, are helping to develop human potential. You can do this by helping the students to understand that they are unique with individual strengths, interests, and talents. You are setting the stage for their futures. It is essential that they not only understand their uniqueness but *appreciate* it. This involves a positive self image which must be enhanced right in the classroom on a day-to-day basis. This is done by showing the student what he or she can do just as often as concentrating on improving what he or she cannot do well. Education must include much more than academics, especially for the student with learning problems.

In short, don't neglect to see the forest for the trees. Keep in mind that you are preparing future citizens and people. The person all of you would like to see as a product of our schools is well rounded, open minded, and secure.

You need to work toward that aim. Henry Brooks Adams said it this way many years ago:

"A teacher affects eternity; he (or she) can never tell where his (or her) influence stops."

You can structure that influence to assure the development of the total person. That's really what education is all about.

JUNE REFERENCES

Bartlett, John. *Bartlett's Familiar Quotations.* (Boston: Little Brown and Co., 1955)

"Biographical Sketch: Juliette Gordon Low, Founder, Girl Scouts of the U.S.A." (New York: Media Services, Girl Scouts of the U.S.A., December 1982)

Choate, Anne, and Helen Ferris (eds.). *Juliette Low and the Girl Scouts.* (New York: Girl Scouts of the U.S.A., 1928)

The Elementary School Library Collection: A Guide to Books and Other Media. (Newark, NJ: The Bro-Dart Foundation, 1977)

Elman, Natalie M. *The Resource Room Primer.* (Englewood Cliffs, NJ: Prentice-Hall, 1981)

Lyon, Nancy. "Juliette Low: The Eccentric Who Founded the Girl Scouts." *Ms. Magazine,* November 1981.

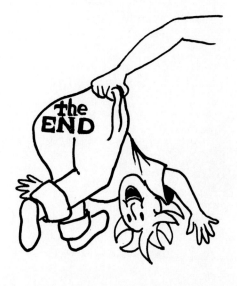